Preface to Theology:

CHRISTOLOGY AND THEOLOGICAL METHOD

Preface to Theology:

CHRISTOLOGY AND THEOLOGICAL METHOD

John Howard Yoder

Introduction by Stanley Hauerwas
and Alex Sider

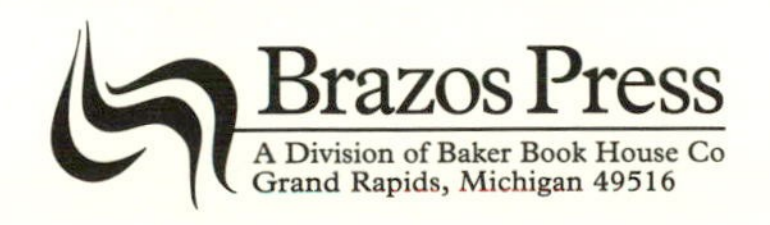

Brazos Press
A Division of Baker Book House Co
Grand Rapids, Michigan 49516

Published by Brazos Press
a division of Baker Book House Company
P.O. Box 6287, Grand Rapids, MI 49516-6287

Printed in the United States of America

Library of Congress Cataloging-in-Publication Data

Yoder, John Howard.
Preface to theology : Christology and theological method / John Howard Yoder.
p. cm.
Includes bibliographical references.
ISBN 1-58743-020-7
1. Theology, Doctrinal. I. Title.
BT75.3 .Y63 2002
230′.01—dc21 2001043788

For current information about all releases from Brazos Press, visit our web site:
http://www.brazospress.com

Contents

Prayers of the Theologian, Set for Antiphonal Reading

Prophezei

Almighty, eternal and most merciful God,
  Whose word is a lantern to our feet and a light to our path,
Open and enlighten our hearts
  That we may understand your holy Word in its purity and holiness
And do those things that we have rightly understood
  So that we may in no way offend your Majesty,
Through Jesus Christ our Lord
  AMEN[1]

Baruch Attah

Blessed are you, O Lord our God	King of the universe,
Who sanctified us with your commandments	and commanded us to study Torah.
May the words of your Torah,	O Lord our God,
May we, and our children,	and all the children of the house of Israel
know you,	and study your Torah with devotion.
Blessed are you, O Lord,	who teaches Torah to his people Israel.
Praised are you, O Lord,	King of the universe,
who has chosen us from all peoples	by giving us his Torah.
Blessed are you, O Lord,	Giver of the Torah.[2]

1. Huldrych Zwingli, June 9, 1525, reported this as his prayer at the opening of the Zürich Bible study lecture series, called "Prophezei," which ultimately grew into the University of Zürich.

2. *Weekday Prayer Book,* Rabbinical Assembly of the USA, 1966.

Acknowledgments

The publication of *Preface to Theology: Christology and Theological Method* has been made possible by Anne Marie Yoder's commitment to make John Howard Yoder's work available to a wide readership. Anne is so committed not only because of her loyalty to her husband, but because of her steadfast conviction, which she shares with John, that nonviolence is at the heart of the gospel. We are extremely grateful to Anne for her permission to prepare this book for publication.

We are also in Anne Meyer Byler's debt for doing the hard work necessary to put John's text onto computer file. Without her work, the further editing of the text by Alex Sider would have been impossible. Alex was aided in that task by Peter Dula. Roger Owens undertook the painstaking task of preparing an index for the text. Along the way, Mark Nation was an invaluable resource in answering questions about the text.

Rodney Clapp and Rebecca Cooper of Brazos Press have obviously made this project viable, but the obvious can hide both the risk Rodney takes as editor at Brazos in publishing this book and the work Rebecca has done to ensure that the final form of the book might have satisfied even John.

Finally, of course, we must thank John Howard Yoder for his extraordinary work, not only in this book, but in everything he did. We believe it will take many years for his work to be properly appreciated and understood. It has been an honor to make *Preface to Theology* available as part of that process.

Stanley Hauerwas and Alex Sider
Duke University

Introduction

Stanley Hauerwas
and Alex Sider

1. On the Importance of Preface to Theology: Christology and Theological Method

Preface to Theology: Christology and Theological Method has never been published, but the mimeographed lectures have been available since 1968. That "book" could be bought from the Co-Op Bookstore at the Associated Mennonite Biblical Seminaries in Elkhart, Indiana. In that form these lectures have had a limited but substantive impact on people outside both Elkhart and the Mennonite world. We are convinced, however, that these lectures need to be published as a book so that they will be available to those readers who know little of either the Mennonite world or John Howard Yoder. Yoder, however, might have doubted that non-Mennonites would be interested in these lectures. Everything he wrote was for a specific audience and particular purpose, and these lectures were for Mennonites studying for the ministry. He was often puzzled that anyone not part of the original audience would think what he had written important. He was, however, pleased when I (Hauerwas) wanted to use the book in one of my courses at Duke, which resulted in Cokesbury bookstore at Duke becoming the place the mimeographed lectures could be purchased.

In some of our more perverse moments we like to think of Yoder as a revolutionary pamphleteer. Revolutionaries often began the attempt to form a cadre of sympathizers by creating a literature that is both hard to find and risky—at least if you are caught reading it. The pamphlet (or recording) may be part of the technology associated with the regime they are trying to overthrow, but the means of communication is transformed by the conditions necessary for its production and con-sumption. Yoder, whose position is even more radical than most revolutionaries can imagine, sometimes appeared to go out of his way to make it hard to acquire his work. His essays seem to exist, like the revolutionary pamphlet, in pirated versions that make anyone who reads or listens an enemy of the state. Did he think the retraining his work requires begins with the difficulty in getting hold of what he wrote? We doubt even Yoder was that clever, but the hard-to-get character of his work can have a Khomeni-like result.

We hope Yoder would have approved making *Preface to Theology: Christology and Theological Method* into a book. We believe John Howard Yoder is one of the most important theologians of the last century. We are even more convinced that his work provides some of the crucial hints to help the church negotiate current and future challenges facing Christians. Accordingly, we think the publication of this book is important not only because it makes available previously unpublished work that helps us understand Yoder, but because, dated as some of the material in this book is, we believe this book is not simply part of our theological "past," but rather is our future.

Toward the end of *Preface to Theology* Yoder observes that theology has two primary functions: (1) the catechetical task of teaching new believers what Christians know and (2) testing the tradition that is passed on for coherence. Theology is therefore a process the church cannot live without, if for no other reason than that one of the primary functions of theology is to be suspicious of theology. For example, Yoder notes that some think of the theological process as boxes along a chain. There is the Old Testament box, which must be expanded because the canonical deposit gets bigger. Then you get the right theology in the first century, followed by the right theology of the second century, and so on. The theological task is to bring the boxes to the present with minimum change.

In contrast, Yoder asks us to think of theology not as a series of boxes on a chain, but as a historical stream constituted by communicators—e.g., a prophet, an Old Testament historian, or even Jesus himself. These theological commentators look back on the source of the stream as well as the channels of the present. The commentator then makes a statement, the ripple effects of which reshape the stream. For example, the coming of Christ determinatively reshapes the stream by making a difference between the two ages. The boxes appear to offer safety, but Yoder knows that what we believe as Christians means any presumption that we are safe cannot help but betray the gospel.

Yoder would not claim nor would we claim on his behalf that his understanding of theology is unique. He understands his task as but an instance of what Christian theologians in the past have done, yet few recent theologians have stood in the stream in which Yoder stood. He represents that form of Christianity called Anabaptist or Mennonite, yet he refused to let the mainstream make him an "exception," even if the exception was praised. Rather, he sought to do nothing less than help catholic Christianity rediscover itself in the water that flows from the left wing of the Reformation. In like manner Yoder was intent on helping Anabaptists discover that their "uniqueness" could not be bought at the expense of the unity of the church. His recovery of what might be called the "great tradition" is not only important for Mennonites but also for catholic Christians, because Yoder's retrieval of the Christian tradition can help all Christians to see the tradition through fresh eyes.

2. The Mennonite Context

We suggested above that Yoder was never comfortable when he was forced to speak without a clear sense of the task given to him. He almost always began his lectures or his essays naming what he took to be "his assignment." He did so because he distrusted "thought" in the abstract. One of the reasons so much of his work remains unpublished is he assumed what he had said in this place or time would not be "useful" to others in other places and times. His distrust of any theology not consciously located in the history of a people or circumstance is correlative to his ecclesiology. Yoder's church cannot be "invisible," which means it is as real as the students who heard and read these lectures at AMBS in Elkhart from the early 1960's through the spring of 1981.

It is therefore important for those who might be tempted—an understandable temptation given our general reading habits—to read this book as but another book about Christian theology to have some sense of Yoder's context. We can too readily assume that the course Yoder taught at AMBS was just another course that appears in any seminary's curriculum. *Preface to Theology,* however, grew out of Yoder's fundamental conviction that Christian discipleship requires an open, respectful, repentant and doxological awareness of "particular historical identity."[1] Yoder's teacher and mentor, Harold S. Bender, was the fount of that conviction.[2]

In mid-twentieth century Mennonite life, Bender was a larger-than-life figure who seemed to be everywhere at once. He not only served as both dean of Goshen College and founding dean of the biblical seminary, but he also represented the reclaiming of Anabaptist origins as an imaginative resource for Mennonites in the United States. Bender was

1. See John Howard Yoder, *The Priestly Kingdom: Social Ethics as Gospel* (Notre Dame: University of Notre Dame Press, 1984), 3.

2. For our account of Bender and is significance, we are indebted to Albert N. Keim's biography *Harold S. Bender, 1897–1962* (Scottdale, Pennsylvania: Herald Press, 1998).

at once a conserver of tradition and a modernizer. Trained as a church historian at Tübingen, Bender both helped Goshen College skirt the fundamentalist-modernist controversy and worked to reform Goshen into a version of the Protestant liberal arts college.

In 1945, Yoder entered the Bender-led Goshen College.[3] In 1946, when the seminary curriculum was being reformed, Bender told the Mennonite board of education that the curriculum, though divided into the four conventional parts of Bible, church history, systematic theology, and practical theology, would have a "Bible emphasis" and a "Mennonite emphasis." Bender explained, "the Mennonite church expects its ministers to know the Bible and use it effectively." This meant that two-thirds of the required 90 hours was in Bible, and that in place of most of the systematics requirement Bender inserted two year-long courses in church history. He justified this concentration by noting that Mennonites do not emphasize creeds and theology.[4]

Bender also authored a famous pamphlet entitled "The Anabaptist Vision," which was originally written as his presidential address for the American Society of Church History and was subsequently published in the 1944 *The Mennonite Quarterly Review*.[5] For many Mennonites, Bender's identification of the defining marks of the Anabaptist church—discipleship, voluntary church membership, and nonviolence—named the "essence" of what it meant to be a Mennonite. For many, Bender's "Anabaptist Vision" was the document that distinguished Mennonites from other forms of Protestantism. But in the process of distinguishing itself by specific marks, the Mennonite church became but another form of Protestantism.

At least John Howard Yoder and the other young Mennonite theologians who banded together in the Concern Group thought that the result of Bender's work.[6] Bender, they argued, provided the resources and ideology that turned the Mennonite church into an American denomination. Bender had created the world and fostered the historical sensi-

3. Mark Thiessen Nation reports that Yoder, whose extraordinary intellectual gifts had been noticed early, did not want to attend a Mennonite school. Instead he wanted to go to a university with a "great books" curriculum. However, out of respect for his mother he went to Goshen, resolved to spend no more than two years there. He graduated in 1947 with a B.A. in Bible. See Mark Thiessen Nation, "John H. Yoder, Ecumenical Neo-Anabaptist: A Biographical Sketch," in *The Wisdom of the Cross: Essays in Honor of John Howard Yoder*, edited by Stanley Hauerwas, Chris K. Huebner, Harry J. Huebner, Mark Thiessen Nation. (Grand Rapids: Eerdmans, 1999), 11.

4. Keim, 341.

5. Bender also founded the *MQR*.

6. The members of the Concern Group were young Mennonites who were working or studying in Europe. Their first meeting was in Amsterdam. Besides Yoder the group included Irvin Horst, Orley Swartzentruber, John W. Miller, Paul Peachey, David Shenk, and Calvin W. Redekop.

tivity that made these young theologians possible, but through the very life he had discovered they found his vision of Anabaptism lacking. In a paper the young Yoder wrote at the end of the Concern Group's first meeting in 1952, wonderfully titled, "Reflections on the Irrelevance of Certain Slogans to the Historical Movements They Represent, Or, the Cooking of the Anabaptist Goose, Or, Ye Garnish the Sepulchres of the Righteous," Yoder claimed that the Anabaptist vision was not to "regain original anabaptism, but rather, with the use of anabaptism as a motto, to make possible a surprising degree of assimilation to the surrounding culture."[7]

In his defense, Bender denied that the Mennonite church equaled the Anabaptist vision, but Yoder responded that Bender's denial was too easy, just to the extent that he and his colleagues had reached that conclusion. With his usual bluntness Yoder explained:

> What has happened to me is that in the process of growing up, I have put together an interest in anabaptism, which you gave me, an MCC experience to which you were instrumental in assigning me, and theological study to which you directed me, to come out with what is a more logical fruition of your own convictions than you yourself realize.[8]

It was, as Keim notes, "a biting assessment."[9]

Yoder had been sent to Europe to help the French Mennonites, who had been devastated by World War II, recover their Mennonite heritage. During his stay he began studies in Basel where he wrote his dissertation in Anabaptist history. He also attended Karl Barth's lectures and seminars. In response to a letter from Bender that expressed concern about Yoder's failure to study theology, Yoder pointed out that "apart from Jaspers on History of Christian Philosophy" all his other work was in theology. However, Yoder also observed, "from an Anabaptist point of view, I'm not sure theology is worth that much . . . and three more years, even though enjoyable, would hardly be justifiable if I don't plan to be a theologian, which I don't."[10]

Bender did not let Yoder's disavowal of theology dissuade him, noting that though Yoder might not plan to be a theologian,

> the trouble is that you are one anyway. You always have been one and you always will be. The only question is what kind of a theologian you want to be. You do not have to be a theologian of the type of any particular school of thought, but among the very few men who have endowments and atti-

7. Quoted in Keim, 453.
8. Quoted in Keim, 456.
9. Ibid.
10. Quoted in Keim, 460.

> tudes which enable them to be the real theologians we need, you are one.[11]

The judgment was not only true, but also testifies to Bender's extraordinary commitment to the Mennonite church. He was not about to let Yoder's criticisms of him determine the service Yoder could render the church.

Yoder, however, never understood himself to be a theologian. He often said if he had any scholarly home, it was as a historian of the left wing of the Reformation. When he returned from Europe he did not assume an academic position, but for the first year worked at "J. S. Yoder and Son" greenhouses in Wooster, Ohio.[12] From 1959–1965 Yoder was primarily employed as an administrative assistant for overseas missions at the Mennonite Board of Missions, yet during that time he often taught at the Seminary. Indeed, he filled in as a sabbatical replacement for J. C. Wenger in 1958–1959. He began by teaching New Testament Greek and contemporary theology. In 1965 he began to teach in the Seminary on a full time basis.

Those outside the Mennonite world might be tempted to think that Mennonite life and thought is relatively homogeneous. After all, if the Mennonites do not have a clear self-identity, who does? Hopefully, however, the account of the circumstances surrounding Yoder's training and early work should put to rest any assumption that the Mennonite world was "set." If anything, Yoder was the beneficiary of and a participant in a Mennonite *ressourcement* movement similar to the developments in Catholicism associated with Yves Congar, Henri de Lubac, and Hans Urs von Balthasar. Under Bender's direction, Yoder and other members of the Concern Group returned to Mennonite sources and found that those very sources made it impossible to ignore the entirety of the Christian tradition. *Preface to Theology: Christology and Theological Method* represents Yoder's attempt to help Mennonites locate their lives within the ongoing stream of Christian theology. To the extent that Yoder successfully performs that task, he also helps non-Mennonite Christians discover themselves in Anabaptism.

Yoder being Yoder would find these claims on behalf of his book both ambitious and immodest. Just as he always maintained that *The Politics of Jesus* was no more than a report on scholarship, he would no doubt claim that *Preface to Theology* is no more than an attempt to acquaint Mennonite seminarians with the theological developments required by the Gospel. Accordingly we have left in the text Yoder's assignments and bibliographies to make clear *Preface to Theology* was

11. Ibid.
12. Nation, 17.

and is a book meant to instruct. Yet Bender was right, John Howard Yoder was always a theologian with extraordinary analytic and constructive gifts that are on display in these lectures.

3. *Preface to Theology* in the Context of Yoder's Work

Yoder would regard much of *Preface to Theology* as "reporting" on the work of others. Yet even when he was "reporting" he could not hide his constructive theological passion. There are a number of ways to suggest the significance of the way Yoder works in *Preface to Theology*, but everything he does in this book, as the title clearly suggest, is determined by his Christological focus. Of course everything Yoder ever wrote, as might be expected from one shaped by Barth, is determined by his Christological focus. That Yoder's work was so determinatively Christological, however, is not very informative. Much more important is the way Yoder refused to separate Christology from discipleship.

Yoder understood that in the deepest sense Jesus Christ *is* salvation. This led him in *Preface to Theology* to relativize accounts of Christ's person and work that separate belief from practice, as well as juridical and forensic accounts of the atonement, but the way he relativized those accounts was quite subtle. Salvation, Yoder thought, had to be taught in terms that emphasized the historical nature of Christ's obedience to the One who sent him. Otherwise, it would be merely a function of arbitrary *fiat*, not at all a reflection of the God who has dealt patiently with Israel through thousands of years.

During the time Yoder taught *Preface to Theology*, he wrote and published his most famous book, *The Politics of Jesus*. Some may wonder how one person could have taught *Preface to Theology* and at the same time written *The Politics of Jesus*. Even though *Preface to Theology* begins with Scripture, the close exegetical style of *The Politics of Jesus* is not as prominent in *Preface to Theology*. Nor is *Preface to Theology* as concentrated on "ethics" as is *The Politics of Jesus*. For example, the emphasis on nonviolence in *The Politics of Jesus* is not nearly so conspicuous in *Preface to Theology*. Yet we think *Preface to Theology* and *The Politics of Jesus* to be of a piece with each other. Indeed reading them together adds strength to both books.

In *The Politics of Jesus* Yoder explicitly refers to the work he continued to do in *Preface to Theology*. He observes that "the radical rabbi Jesus" was far more of a political figure than the Ebionitic view was usually ready to concede. Yoder may have thought some would interpret his own position in Ebionitic terms, and therefore thought it important to show how that position might be both right and wrong. The Ebionites were wrong, Yoder thought, in that they failed to appreciate that the apostolic church made Jesus' political humanity normative for their lives. Yoder then observes that if he were to follow the developments Christian doctrine underwent, he could show how those developments were logical outcomes of "the politics of Jesus." He then briefly summarizes the main story line of *Preface to Theology*:

> When the later, more "theological" New Testament writings formulated the claim to preexistence and cosmic preeminence for the divine Son or Word (John 1:1–4; Col. 1:15ff.; Heb. 1:2ff.) the intent of this language was not to consecrate beside Jesus some other way of perceiving the eternal Word, through reason or history or nature, but rather to affirm the exclusivity of the revelation claim they were making for Jesus. The same must be said for later development of the classic ideas of the Trinity and the Incarnation. "Incarnation" does not originally mean (as it tends to today in some theologies of history, and in some kinds of Anglican theology) that God took all of human nature as it was, put his seal of approval on it, and thereby ratified nature as revelation. The point is just the opposite; that God broke through the borders of our standard definition of what is human, and gave a new definition in Jesus. "Trinity" did not originally mean, as it does for some later, that there are three kinds of revelation, the Father speaking through creation and the Spirit through experience, by which the words and example of the Son must be corrected; it meant rather that language must be found and definitions created so that Christians, who believe in only one God, can affirm that that God is most adequately and bindingly known in Jesus.[13]

It is extremely important to understand what Yoder is and is not saying in this remarkable paragraph. He is *not* saying that Mennonites are as orthodox as those churches that call themselves Catholic when it comes to the creeds. Yoder had no reason to distance himself from being identified as orthodox—at least not if orthodoxy is associated with the creeds. It is more important for him that we understand the work the creeds should do. Christians do not become "creedal" because we need to get our theology straight as an end in and of itself. Rather, in *Preface to Theology* Yoder helps us see that Christians become creedal because of the kind of life they must lead to be faithful disciples of Jesus. The early "Christologies" developed in the New Testament were expressions required when followers of Jesus confronted the challenge of making their way of life, a way of life shaped by following Jesus' teachings, intelligible in contexts that had no way of imagining how God could be found in this Galilean.

Yoder is about the difficult task of resisting the attempt to make the dogmatic tradition the dogmatic tradition. When Nicea and Chalcedon are turned into thought, and direct attention to themselves rather to the One who made the creeds' affirmations necessary, then the church risks

13. John Howard Yoder, *The Politics of Jesus: Vicit Angus Noster*, 2d ed. (Grand Rapids: Eerdmans, 1994), 99. *The Politics of Jesus* was orginally published in 1972.

separating the inseparable, that is, belief from discipleship. We are not only asked to believe in Jesus but also to follow him, and it is a mistake to think that belief is intelligible apart from a faithfully lived life. That is why in *The Politics of Jesus* Yoder claims that the view of Jesus he develops through his exegesis of Luke is more radically Nicene and Chalcedonian than other views. He does not advocate some modern understanding of Jesus, but rather asks "that the implications of what the church has always said about Jesus as Word of the Father, as true God and true Human, be taken more seriously, as relevant to our social problems, than ever before."[14]

In 1990 Yoder delivered a lecture on the occasion of Jim McClendon's retirement from the Church Divinity School of the Pacific entitled, "Catholicity in Search of Location." In the process of trying to reconfigure how the Catholic character of the church can be conceived as a ongoing conversation, Yoder asks whether Catholicity so understood must include the wording of Nicea, episcopal succession, some special understanding of the Eucharist or predestination, or the Methodist Quadrilateral. Answering his own question he says, "We'll have to see."[15] Some might think Yoder's answer suggests that he really has no stake in Nicea, but is only concerned that Jesus' ethic be realized, but to so read Yoder is to impose a dualism that his reclaiming of the dogmatic tradition as an appropriate development of Christian discipleship has made unintelligible.[16]

14. Yoder, *The Politics of Jesus*, 102. Craig A. Carter maintains the heart of his book on Yoder is to show that "Yoder's work shows us how the trinitarian and christological orthodoxy of the fourth and fifth centuries contains the key to the survival and flourishing of the church's witness to Jesus in the post-Christendom era that is now dawning." See *The Politics of the Cross: The Theology and Social Ethics of John Howard Yoder* (Grand Rapid: Brazos Press, 2001), 23. This quote can give the misleading impression that Yoder had some stake in throwing us back into the orthodoxy of the fourth and fifth century in order to promote the survival and flourishing of the church. Not only did Yoder not think we could take up the orthodoxies of the past in any simple or transparent way, but "survival" and "flourishing" are not themes that particularly resonated with him. Faithfulness is what interests Christians. So, even as sympathetic an interpreter of Yoder as Carter can reproduce the habits of speech Yoder challenges. Another example is in Carter's chapter on Yoder's Christology, one of the subsections of which is quite innocently entitled, "The Implications of Yoder's Christology for Discipleship" (106). Yoder, as Carter otherwise shows quite well, taught us that a mistake has been made when we try to do "Christology" in a manner that requires us subsequently to ask what its implications might be for our understanding of discipleship.

15. John Howard Yoder, "Catholicity in Search of Location," in *The Royal Priesthood: Essays Ecclesiological and Ecumenical*, ed. Michael Cartwright. (Grand Rapids: Eerdmans, 1994), 319.

16. In *The Politics of Jesus* Yoder names five dualisms he thinks must be called into question if Jesus is to be acknowledged as Lord. They are (1) the choice between the Jesus of history and the Jesus of dogma, (2) the choice between prophet and institution, (3) the choice between the Kingdom of God as external and catastrophic or subjective

Nowhere does Yoder make this clearer than in his unpublished paper, "That Household We Are," written for the Bluffton Conference in 1980 to address the question "Is There a Believers' Church Christology?" This paper reprises many of *Preface to Theology*'s themes, suggesting that in John, Hebrews, Colossians, and the Apocalypse apostolic writers respond to the challenge of a previously formed cosmic vision by: (l) refusing to fit Jesus into the slots of a cosmic vision, but rather placing Jesus above the cosmos; (2) concentrating on the rejection and suffering of the human form as accrediting the Lordship of Christ; (3) making clear that behind the cosmic victory is the preexistence, coessentiality with the Father, and the participation of the Son in creation and providence; and (4) insisting that the writers and readers of these writings already participate through faith in the victory of Christ.[17]

Those who suggest that "Trinity" or "two natures" are unbibical, that such categories are the result the Hellenistic mind's imposing the alien categories of Greek ontology upon a message from another world, or who argue that the need for an empire-wide agreed formula would not have been possible without Constantine have some historical basis for their arguments. But they are wrong if they infer from such observations that Nicea or Chalcedon are not the natural result of the church's missionary invasion of the world beyond Palestine.[18] Nicaea and Chalcedon are but particular outcomes of developments begun in Scripture and, in particular, in the hymn of Philippians 2. As Yoder puts it:

> the development of the Christology of preexistence and *kenosis*, far from being the product of whimsical imagination, or of ahistorical and unjewish speculation, represents the product of an aggression by the bearers of

---

and inward, (4) the choice between the political and the sectarian, and (5) the choice between the individual and social. See 103–109. For a good discussion an analysis of the charge of reductionism in Yoder's work see Carter, *The Politics of the Cross*, 126–136.

17. We are indebted to Mark Thiessen Nation for making this paper available and to Professor Denny Weaver for giving us permission to quote it.

18. In *Preface to Theology* Yoder uses the language of fences to describe the creeds. He observes that the creeds are probably not something Anabaptists would think worth fighting over, but neither would they be willing to join with those who think it important to fight against the creeds. He observes, the creeds "are part of . . . the history to which God has chosen to lead his confused people toward perhaps at least a degree of understanding of certain dangers, certain things not to say if we are to remain faithful" (223). Because Christianity is historical, we have no history without the creeds to which we can appeal in our efforts to produce faithful readings of Scripture. In describing the creeds as fences, Yoder seems to be making the point that the proper use of the creeds sets parameters beyond which faithful readings of Scripture will be unlikely. Craig Carter suggests that Yoder's position is quite similar to Lindbeck's rule-theory of doctrine in *The Nature of Doctrine*. Of course that is to associate Yoder with one of the more controversial suggestions by Lindbeck, but I think Carter may be right, especially if one understands "doctrine" as a guideline for reading Scripture. See, *The Politics of the Cross*, 119–121 and 133.

> the story of the crucified man Jesus, in all his Jewish particularity, against the religious cosmovisions of the wider world, whose sages thought their systems could swallow anything that could come along. They proclaim Christ above Culture, but this is the opposite of what Niebuhr designated by that phrase. It is not the world, culture, civilization, which is the definitional category, which the church comes along to embellish with some corectives and complements. The Kingdom of God is the basic category. The rebellious but already in principle defeated cosmos is being invaded and brought to its knees by the Lamb. The development of a high Christology is the natural cultural ricochet of a missionary ecclesiology, when it collides as it must with whatever cosmology explains and governs the world it invades.[19]

Yoder has no stake in claiming such a Christology to be the peculiar possession of the Anabaptists. Indeed the opposite is the case. "A high Christology is a prerequisite for the renewal of a believers' church, whether this should come to pass through the tragic breakage of a radical reformation or through more organic patterns of revitalization." According to Yoder, to the degree that the Enlightenment made the rational ontology into which orthodoxy had bought no longer self-evident, the church will again be tempted to repeat the christological heresies in new forms. Any tradition that reclaims the "missionary arrogance (arrogance need not be a pejorative term) that dares to claim that Jesus, proclaimed as Messiah and *Kyrios*, transcends rather than [is] transcended by each new cosmos as well" will again be a believers' church Christology.[20] Yoder, therefore, would not be surprised to discover that Roman Catholicism may represent, at least in some of its forms, the believers' church.

We find it fascinating that when Yoder turns in the third part of the course to the Christology associated with systematic theology, he utilizes the Reformed notion of the *munus triplex*, Christ's threefold office of prophet, priest, and king. He makes it clear that he has no interest in claiming that the threefold office is the only or best way to develop christological themes in a systematic fashion. He finds the threefold office "helpful because it tells us not to take it seriously."[21] Rather it is simply one way of classifying material that may help us to discover what we may have missed, as well as to check for balance, completeness, or coherence.

Yoder's use of the threefold office, however, is quite interesting for no other reason than nowhere else in his work does he employ it as exten-

19. Yoder, "That Household We Are," 6. Cf. "'But We Do See Jesus: The Particularity of Incarnation and the Universality of Truth," in *The Priestly Kingdom: Social Ethics as Gospel* (Notre Dame: University of Notre Dame Press, 1984), 54.

20. Yoder, "That Household We Are," 7.

21. 238.

sively as he does in *Preface to Theology.* One of the reasons Yoder may have been drawn to the offices of the prophet, priest, and king is they not only keep him closer to the text of the Bible, but also suggest a strong linkage between the Old and New Testaments. Richard Hays, commenting on Yoder's exegetical work in *The Politics of Jesus,* notes that Yoder had an "almost prescient" grasp of important developments in the field of New Testament Studies. In particular, Hays commends Yoder for his attention to the social context and meaning of the texts, the placement of Jesus in the political matrix of first-century Palestine, the emphasis on the apocalyptic horizons of the "powers" language in Paul, his interpretation of Galatians as an argument about the social form of the church (rather than about individual guilt), and "his sympathetic understanding of the Torah as a vehicle of grace within the Jewish tradition."[22]

No doubt Yoder drew on some of the work in New Testament scholarship that was just beginning to emerge when he wrote *The Politics of Jesus,* but we suspect that what Hays calls "prescient" has more to do with how Yoder had learned to read the Bible by studying and imitating how the Anabaptist reformers read the Bible. According to Yoder, the Anabaptists of the sixteenth century were alone among the reformers in insisting that the New Testament be read as a continuation of and development from the Old. This meant that the Anabaptists alone understood that revelation is historical. Consequently, Yoder was particularly interested in rethinking the Jewish/Christian divide. He was so not only because of the murder of European Jewry, but because he was convinced that one of the reasons Christians had lost the ability to read the Scriptures was due to the attempt to make Christianity intelligible without Israel. That the creeds do not mention the promise to Israel may be one of the reasons Christians have developed a "forgetfulness" toward not only Jews but our own Scripture, that is, the Old Testament.

Yoder does not say in *Preface to Theology* why he does not follow the usual ordering of the *munus triplex* through prophet, priest, and king.[23]

22. Richard Hays, *The Moral Vision of the New Testament: A Contemporary Introduction to New Testament Ethics* (San Francisco: HarperCollins, 1994), 245.

23. In his recent book, *For Our Salvation: Two Approaches to the Work of Christ* (Grand Rapids: Eerdmans, 1997), Geoffrey Wainwright also finds the threefold office a useful and comprehensive way to reflect on the person and work of Christ. Wainwright's treatment of the offices differs perceptibly from Yoder's, however, in that it downplays the correlation of each office with a specific topos of theology in favor of highlighting the analogies with the life of the church that each office elicits. It would also be fascinating to know what Yoder would have made of Wolfhart Pannenberg's criticisms of the threefold office for Christology in his *Jesus—God and Man,* 2d ed., trans. Lewis Wilkins and Duane Priebe (Philadelphia: Westminster Press, 1977), 212–225. Pannenberg does note that "the doctrine of the offices had the particular merit that it expressed the relation of Jesus activity and fate to ancient Israel" (224).

It would be a mistake to make too much of the ordering of the offices or how Yoder correlates eschatology, atonement, and revelation with Christ as king, priest, and prophet. Yoder rightly maintained that the offices are interrelated just as eschatology, atonement, and revelation are not independent themes in theology. But if indeed he calculated that departure, he may have begun with Christ as king because he understood that the church's eschatology is inseparable from its Christology.

Jesus, the lamb that was slain, is the king who rules as a servant. If one claim can be taken as the heart of Yoder's theology, this is it. Jesus is no savior who saves us from time, but rather, Jesus is the savior who makes time possible. Accordingly Yoder distrusts any accounts of eternity that are nontemporal, or of salvation that seek to secure us from time. For Yoder the past is not "back there," irredeemable, but is part of God's time. Morevoer, we are made part of God's time through the ongoing work of the Holy Spirit. We live through memory.[24]

But time and history as such are not Yoder's prime concerns. A robustly Christian eschatology requires the patient labor of coming to terms with our rootedness in a particular history. This helps account for Yoder's worry about the creeds. To the extent the creeds invite Christians to think Christianity is a set of beliefs about ideas more real than the existence of the Jews and church, a mistake has been made. To the extent the creeds suggest that "theology" can be separated from a life of discipleship, a mistake has been made. To the extent the creeds tempt Christians to believe they represent a universal set of truths accessible to anyone without membership in the concrete and visible church, a mistake has been made. These concerns animate Yoder's account of Christ as king, priest, and prophet.

Moreover, we can now see why discipleship is constitutive of the very way Yoder thinks about Christology. "Atonement" is not about accepting that Christ died because we sinned. Rather, it is a faith-union, or participation, in Christ's victory through his obedience. Because Yoder has no use for a strong distinction between justification and sanctification, his account of participation is ethical, or perhaps better, it is about our perfection. This distinguishes him from some contemporary retrievals of participation language, which stress training ourselves to attend to Christ in a neoplatonic mode. For Yoder, salvation is the obedient life of the disciple of Jesus. Clearly an Anselmian account of the atonement, especially as construed in Protestant scholasticism, will be

24. Robert Jenson's account of time in his *Systematic Theology: The Triune God*, vol. 1 (New York: Oxford, 1997), 215–217, makes for useful comparison with Yoder, though it is fair to say that Jenson's modified Augustinianism and his extended conversation with Pannenberg renders talk about time more theoretical than Yoder would probably think necessary.

deeply challenged.[25] But we also see that interpreting Yoder's account of the atonement in Abelardian terms of moral influence or in straightforwardly *Christus Victor* terms bespeaks a failure to see how Yoder has forced us to abandon a distinction between objective and subjective accounts of Christ's work. We quite literally become through the work of the Holy Spirit participants in Christ's reconciliation of the world.

It may seem odd that we have said so little to this point about Yoder's understanding and use of Scripture. *Preface to Theology* clearly begins with Scripture, but just as importantly it ends with Yoder's understanding of revelation. All theology, for Yoder, is to be tested by its faithfulness to faithful readings of Scripture. Yoder thought Bender's comment that Mennonites expect their ministers to know the Bible was not only descriptively correct, but was an important normative claim. Yoder knew his Bible, but he also knew that to "know" the God to which the Bible is a witness requires a storied community. The Bible is a narrative and can be recognized as such only through the work of the Spirit creating and sustaining a community that seeks no greater certainty than that narrative can give.

4. Dating *Preface to Theology*

"The synthesis represented here is based upon the state of scholarly opinion in 1960. There has been no effort to update it thoroughly." John Howard Yoder cared about many things, but one of the things that can be overlooked is how deeply he cared about scholarship. Yoder had been educated in Europe and he continued the habits of European scholarship. He often described himself as an amateur when asked about a book like *The Politics of Jesus*. He really believed that book was but a report on the scholarly concensus in New Testament studies. That is why he thought "updating" it a good idea even though I (Hauerwas) argued that would give readers the false impression that the book had no constructive focus. So he meant it when he said that the scholarship in *Preface to Theology* only reflected the state of the field up to 1960.

That is one of the reasons Yoder would have hesitated to have the book published in its current state. In it he clearly accepted some scholarly conventions that have now been called into question or at least require modification. We need to attend to these "mistakes" with care if we are to read this book with the historical consciousness Yoder instilled in his students, but we do not think they undercut his primary narrative or argument. Given Yoder's intellectual power he might well

25. But see, for a subtle and compelling account of Anselmian theology that challenges textbook versions of Anselm in a way with which we think Yoder might have been sympathetic, D. B. Hart, "A Gift Exceeding Every Debt: An Eastern Orthodox Appreciation of Anselm's *Cur Deus Homo*," in *Pro Ecclesia* 7 (Summer 1998): 333–349.

have found ways to defend what we think are mistakes. However, it must be said that he was always ready to be shown where he might be wrong, or at least how what he tried to do could be done better.

For example Yoder's use of the contrast between Hebrew and Greek modes of thought in *Preface to Theology* clearly needs to be more nuanced. He suggests that it is more Hebraic to talk about God as light than to use Greek philosophical concepts such as omnipotence, omniscience, and omnipresence. Yet it is by no means clear that the latter are in fact "Greek," or that they lack Scriptural warrant. Moreover, to speak of God as light is entirely compatible with the eminently Greek philosophical notion of *energeia*, used by the Stoics and later by the church fathers. Additionally, some of the contrasts Yoder draws between Hellenist and Jewish influences in the New Testament do not do justice to the extent that the Judaism of first-century Palestine had already been shaped by Hellenism. His suggestion that the fathers attempted to solve with the doctrine of the Trinity a problem created by the encounter between the gospel-bearing culture and the Greek philosophical tradition fails sufficiently to credit those Greek fathers' struggle with Scripture itself. After all, trinitarianism was not foremost an attempt to resolve a metaphysical problem, but was rather the attempt to produce a faithful and coherent reading of Scripture.

To be fair, Yoder simply drew on scholarly consensus and in particular on Thorlief Bowman's famous book, *Hebrew Thought Compared with Greek*. Perhaps more problematic than his assumption that Bowan's contrast between Hebrews and Greeks could be justified is the understanding of language correlative to that position. In *Preface to Theology*, Yoder seems to imply that each language "contains" a logic, such that the Hebrew mind focuses on the particular and the Greek mind concentrates on the general. Yoder rightly concludes from this that no language is correct or better than any other. They are just different. The problem, however, is twofold: not only is the contrast between the Hebrew and Greek languages far too monolithic, but the assumption that "a logic" is somehow present in a language also is philosophically suspect.

In an essay written in 1964, called "The Message of the Bible on Its Own Terms," Yoder makes exactly this criticism of Bowman. This only makes us wonder why he did not qualify his use of Bowman in *Preface to Theology*. He observed that Bowman's argument is helpful, but confusing:

> It is helpful in that it seeks to identify the specificity of the biblical thought mode in terms that can be objectively ("scientifically") described by people studying literature and language. Biblical faith is more than a system of ideas; it is a specific culture and worldview. Yet it is ultimately misleading to count on linguistics as the proof of the proof. Hebraic (or "Semitic") language can be used for quite ungodly messages. Nor does

> the shape of language (especially when its peculiarities are multiplied and distorted by the difficulties of a foreigner learning it) predetermine the thoughts one can use it for.[26]

Another lingering dualism that we think on Yoder's terms would best have been left behind is the contrast he draws between priests and prophets. For example, he suggests that priests interpret nature, that is, the priest offers interpretations of the heavens and crops. The priest specializes in what happens day in and day out with regularity. The prophet on the other hand is said to interpret events as part of an ongoing history. Yoder does not, as do many who use this conventional characterization of difference, privilege the prophet against the priest, nor does he hang much theological weight on the distinction. However, this contrast between the prophet and the priest has increasingly been called into question as failing to do justice to both the prophetic literature and the theological context of the wisdom literature.

Again we do not think Yoder's acceptance of these conventions renders the story of *Preface to Theology* invalid. Some may think Yoder's presentation of the development of Christology in the New Testament is a more difficult problem. His distinction between the more "primitive" forms of the gospel and those developed by "theologians" such as Paul, John, and the writer of Hebrews may suggest that the closer the sources were to Jesus the more likely they were to have gotten it right. We are not calling into question Yoder's account of the necessity of the church always testing itself by "looping back" to Jesus. Indeed, if all existing churches are not merely in theory fallible, but in fact peccable, and if the church must therefore cultivate a readiness for radical reformation and the renewal of the original revolution in a new missionary context, it will always have to be humbly, repentantly and doxologically aware of its own dependence on those who went before.[27] "Looping back" is essential to the faithfulness of the church. Rather, we worry that when Yoder writes about the "core message" to which we loop back, he can invite the assumption that the core of the message itself was not already embedded in a rich theological matrix.

Some of Yoder's expressions suggest he regarded historians' ability to get the facts straight more highly than do we. Of course careful reading and testing of hypotheses are important, but as Yoder's practice clearly witnesses, it is theology all the way down. Whatever the "wider body of primitive traditions such as we have in the Gospels" (279–80) may be, they will be as laden as Paul or John with theological claims. What is interesting is that Yoder's own understanding of "Bibical realism," which simply names his refusal to get "behind" the text, is suffi-

26. *To Hear the Word* (Eugene, Oreg.: Wipf and Stock Publishers, 2001), 135.
27. See, e.g., Yoder, "The Authority of Tradition," in *The Priestly Kingdom*, 69–70.

cient to make one worry about the very distinction between the primitive "kernel" and the theologians' subsequent development of it.[28]

Though we obviously think Yoder's use of the distinction between the *kerygma* and the theologians ill advised, we also do not think much should be made of it. It was obviously more a pedagogical device than a crucial move he used to try to get to the "real Jesus." For Yoder the real Jesus is Jesus who was born, lived, taught, ate with tax collectors and prostitutes, healed lepers, the lame and the blind, drove out demons, opposed the Jewish authorities, was crucified, died, was buried, was raised again on the third day, and ascended to the right hand of his Father in heaven. That is, the real Jesus is not a Jesus whom we find somewhere other than in the narratives of Scripture. So even though he employs a distinction that sounds like some who quest for the historical Jesus, Yoder's historical Jesus is the risen Christ.

A final aspect of *Preface to Theology* we think indicative of the age of the lecture might be best described as a lapse in the prescience to which Richard Hays referred when describing *The Politics of Jesus*. It is a lapse, however, for which Yoder can hardly be faulted. When these lectures were written and delivered, there was simply no way to anticipate the sea change in historical studies seen in the last two decades. The twentieth-century's debates about the relationship of theology, philosophy and history were often rather sterile. In part this was a function of the inherited oppositions between Hellenism and Hebraism, or assumptions about Christianity's transformation by "Greek" culture, to which we have already referred. At least in part it was also a function of the late nineteenth- and early twentieth-century presumptions about the character of revelation, which Yoder discusses at length in this text. And in part it was a function of the assumed adequacy of purely historical-critical criteria for scriptural interpretation.

The last fifteen or twenty years has seen these themes and assumptions come under increasing scrutiny, enabling renewed appreciation for the complex interaction between conceptual and scriptural reasoning in early Christianity. The increasing realization that the ante- and post-Nicene fathers not only considered scripture their primary imaginative resource, but were also theologically motivated in the first place to produce coherent readings *of Scripture*, as opposed to coherent and

28. Yoder seems to have given up on the description "Biblical Realism." In "The Message of the Bible on Its Own Terms," he describes "The Place of 'Biblical Realism' as a Failed School in the History of Recent Protestant Thought." He notes not only that he "retain[s] the term . . . because of its historical meaning, but . . . [does] not propose to advocate its use in the 1990s," but he also maintains, somewhat characteristically, that "it is not at all clear that to 'succeed' in becoming a 'school' is always a good thing spiritually or theologically, especially in a world as preoccupied with trends as is ours." See *To Hear the Word*, 125.

comprehensive worldviews, has begun to dismantle the prevailing mid twentieth-century prejudices against the "mythological" character of Nicene Christianity. It is clear that Yoder had deeply imbibed those prejudices, prompting him to adopt a certain level of dismissive ahistoricism in the patristics lectures of *Preface to Theology* that is inconsistent with his own considered judgments elsewhere, and even in this text. Given Yoder's concern for responsible historiography, had he been able to predict that change in patristic scholarship would outpace even change in biblical studies in the years after he delivered these lectures, the text would undoubtedly have looked quite different.

We said earlier that we do not think our reservations are telling against the text of *Preface to Theology.* This is the case for at least two interconnected reasons. In the first place, Yoder himself made no claim on these lectures in a way that makes them unrevisable. Indeed, the ongoing need for repentant, self-critical revision even—or perhaps especially—in scholarship is part and parcel of Yoder's views on and practice of teaching. Hence, he is unabashed in the first pages of *Preface to Theology* about telling his readers that "much of what you will read here is not fully true" (41); that if the reading "includes time wasted on unrewarding debates, it will also be good to know about that" (39); and that the primary concern of the course "lies not in any final accuracy in detail but rather in the inductive portrayal of how theological discourse proceeds within the life of the church" (33).

This last point touches already on the second reason we do not think our concerns about Yoder's text irreparably damage the argument or aim of the book. That is, Yoder conceived of the course that became *Preface to Theology* as a semester (or two) in which his students would be introduced into a process of self-conscious theological discourse. As he says, the reference to theological method in the subtitle of the text indicates "a somewhat simple concern for asking, as we go along, 'Why are we doing it this way?'" That question, while it admits of normative answers, can always be asked anew, and indeed always must be asked anew if our process of inquiry is to reflect the patience Yoder thought required of faithful Christian thought. This is not to suggest that we are utterly unimpressed when Yoder "gets it wrong" in the text. On Yoder's own terms history matters, precision matters, and care with words matters. It is simply to say that Yoder expected faithful theology to require revision, and included his own work in that expectation.

We also noted earlier Yoder's understanding of the Christian theological tradition as a stream. Streams, of course, can become floods, destroying anything in their paths. Our temptation is to try to protect ourselves with dikes and dams. Indeed, we even try to turn some of the residue of past floods into dams. For example, we may think the achievement of the canon or of Nicea means questions of biblical authority or the status of the Trinity are "solved." Yoder's reclamation of the tradition was not an attempt to create a dam, but rather it was a reminder that we can be no less courageous in facing our challenges that those Christians who changed the tradition by locating the canon or hammering out the doctrine of the Trinity.

Yoder had no desire to create disciples to his way of doing theology. Rather, he sought to help us—and himself—be more faithful disciples of Jesus. That is why we think it so important, and a pleasant duty, to make this book available to the wider Christian community.

5. Addendum: Textual Matters

Editing any author's work is a difficult process, but the difficulty is compounded in a case like *Preface to Theology*. In the first place, the editorial process was complicated by Professor Yoder's death. Thus, the natural court of appeal in adjudicating textual problems was ruled out. In the second place, the process was complicated by the nature of the material. *Preface to Theology* was both delivered as lectures and transcribed from lecture tapes with minimal editorial revision. Creating from that transcription a readable book was often quite difficult. Not only did the transcription retain traces of its oral presentation, especially as regards syntax and vocabulary, but at times entire paragraphs were composed of sentence fragments, the relationships among which were unclear. In addition, the age of the material complicated the editorial process, primarily through the need to adjust the text to reflect contemporary conventions regarding inclusive language. Together, those complications issued in a number of changes to the mimeographed lecture transcriptions:

We have inserted some breaks and section headings in the text that Yoder did not indicate, but which seem to us to be warranted by the logic of his lectures.

Large portions of the text have been entirely rewritten. The aim of rewriting Yoder's prose was to make it more readable, not to change the substance or even, in most instances, the vocabulary, of what he wrote. Those who want to make scholarly use of *Preface to Theology* are encouraged to check the mimeographed lectures against this revised edition.

Quotations of Scripture have been standardized. Yoder appears to have had no preferred version of Scripture, though he seems to have liked James Moffatt's translation of the New Testament.[29] Indeed, in giving these lectures, Yoder seems most often to have quoted Scripture

29. See Yoder's discussion of the Moffatt translation in "'There is a Whole New World': The Apostle's Apology Revisited," in *To Hear the Word*, 9–27.

from memory. While that attests to his copious knowledge of Scripture, it makes it difficult for students of the text to reference the Scriptures Yoder discusses.

When Yoder revised *The Politics of Jesus* for the second edition, he used gender- inclusive language. We have followed that lead in *Preface to Theology*. We wonder, however, whether the transition to inclusive language substantially alters Yoder's meaning in certain instances. Perhaps the most salient case is Yoder's repeated reference to how the "logic of solidarity" constitutes believers as "sons of God" just as Jesus was Son. He does not say "sons and daughters," nor does he say "children," except when the biblical text says children. Were it not for the *logic* of solidarity, we might have made the language inclusive without second thought. But Yoder appears to be making the Christological point that the "sonship" in which all believers participate depends for its intelligibility on the sonship of Christ. "Sonship," as it pertains to believers, indicates both that we participate in Jesus' relation to the one who sent him and that we do so not of our own accord but rather by virtue of Christ's solidarity with us. So, to render Yoder's language inclusive at just this point obscures the precise christological connection.

This is not to say that there is an unambiguous case for letting the gender-specific language stand, however, and this for two major reasons. In the first place, it is unclear that Yoder would have considered Jesus' relation to the Father who sent him a gendered relation. It is now common to observe that the Christian God is more than either male or female, those being categories of God's revelation's accommodation to finite human nature. In this sense, it seems that the language of begottenness, generation, and offspringhood—language that indicates the relation of the Son to the Father without using gendered terms—could have been used to make Yoder's Christological point. On the other side of that coin, however, is Yoder's consistent emphasis on the particularity of Jesus Christ. Yoder is clear that Christ's divinity is inseparable from his agency as a concrete, historical, human actor in God's economies. As such, the use of language that downplays the particularity of Jesus, and the particular contours of his humanity, tends in what Yoder would have considered either a Gnostic or rationalist direction. If Jesus is called "Son" in Scripture, it cannot be abstracted from the historical specificities of the incarnation.

In the second place, it was part and parcel of what might be called Yoder's anticlericalism to be consistently critical of nonegalitarian practices that fostered the restriction of certain ecclesial charisms to male believers. In terms of his texts, relevant passages include but are not limited to "Revolutionary Subordination" (chapter nine of *The Politics of Jesus*), "The Hermeneutics of Peoplehood," "Sacrament as Social Process: Christ the Transformer of Culture," and "A Free Church

Perspective of Baptism, Eucharist and Ministry."[30] Through all these texts the common thread is "the universality of giftedness" within the Christian community. Yoder insists that every member of the gathered community participates in the charism of the Holy Spirit, but, more than this, he insists that how any particular Christian exhibits giftedness cannot be specified in advance of a concrete community's process of discernment. By this logic, anyone, male or female, can exercise any role in the church and indeed will be expected to do so, though not on any a priori set of justifications, but rather as an outcome of the normal political processes of communal decision making. This antipatriarchal argument, we think, indicates that the normal contours of the Christian life require gender-inclusive habits of speech.

Finally, we have formatted the text of *Preface to Theology* to reflect Yoder's penchant for lists. Certain portions of the text, which were presented as block paragraphs in the mimeographed edition, have been broken up into logical divisions, indented and set off from the rest of the text by large dots. Not only do we think this makes the pages of text easier to read, but it makes a pedagogical point. Yoder's well known opposition to methodologism, and therefore to theological procedures that have a place for everything and put everything in its place, prompted him often to ring the changes on whatever theme he was discussing *ad infinitum*. There is always another, slightly different, example to which we can point. Lists were an important way of reminding his readers that theology is historical, that is, messy. But wonderful in the messiness.

30. See especially, "The Hermeneutics of Peoplehood," 22–26 in *The Priestly Kingdom*, and "Sacrament as Social Process," 370 and "A Free Church Perspective on Baptism, Eucharist and Ministry," 287 in *The Royal Priesthood*.

Introduction

The following material brings together the bulk of the instructional content of a semester course offered approximately every other year at Associated Mennonite Biblical Seminary (AMBS) from the early 1960s through the spring of 1981.[1]

At first this material constituted the first semester of the required two-semester offering in systematic theology offered on behalf of the Mennonite Biblical Seminary. When the offering in systematic theology was reviewed and coordinated on the AMBS level, this material was called "Preface to Theology." The remaining course contents that had been in the second semester were dropped, and further requirements in the theology field were to be absolved by courses in specific subtopics of the theological cycle of five courses then offered by Clarence Bauman. More recently the course was renamed, no change in content, with the more descriptive but also more ambitious title "Christology and Theological Method." For present purposes we shall refer to the title "Preface to Theology."

The material is being reproduced with a view to three possible kinds of use:

1. It may be used as background readings for a course in theology taught by any other instructor, who will then assign those segments considered useful with full freedom to be selective.
2. The material may be used for self-guided work by a student desirous of working independently. It is with a view to the latter kind of use that the "study guide" material used at AMBS has been retained.
3. It may be dipped into occasionally, with attention to one theme or another, to broaden one's general background without extensive study. With this usage in mind, the sectional/topical bibli-

1. Editorial note: John Yoder's Introduction was written in 1981. Material in other parts of the book may come from earlier time periods and will be noted as such when this is clearly the case.

ographies have been slightly expanded beyond what would be used in formal course work.

The bulk of the prose material is edited only minimally for clarity of language but retains the traces of the spoken form. It was initially transcribed from tapes made in October 1968. It has been used at AMBS in mimeographed form since 1973. The rewriting for print needed to be done rapidly in the late spring of 1981; apologies are hereby extended for gaps and duplication.

When the format of the seminary course was extensive discussion based on prior readings both in the written lectures and collateral texts, the entire course time was taken up with free discussion. The student working independently does not have that opportunity for reinforcement and clarification and will therefore need to make more regular and thorough use of the preparation material.

Although the particular construction of the course offerings at AMBS in the 1960s and 1970s was under constant change throughout that period and will no longer obtain at the time when this book is used, it may still be appropriate as part of the effort to locate our enterprise that it be compared and contrasted with other related offerings.

Clarence Bauman has regularly taught a course named *Discipleship*, which in a sense could be called *Applied Christology.* There is constant reference to New Testament material, but only marginal recourse to the language and the agenda of systematic theology. Clarence Bauman has also taught a course on *Jesus in Recent Thought*; the New Testament material we shall deal with was always in the picture but was not itself the subject matter. J. C. Wenger has taught courses with titles like *Introduction to Theology* aiming at a broad overview of all of the major systematic theological topics.

The first third of this course is based on the New Testament and overlaps with various New Testament offerings of AMBS in the areas of hermeneutics, Luke and Acts, and the thought of Paul. The middle section follows the thread of intellectual history and overlaps with courses in church history or the history of Christian thought in the patristic period. In none of these cases should the overlapping be so construed as to let the student think it would be appropriate after this study to skip taking full-fledged courses in those areas. What is offered here is not substitute for full-length treatment of those many fields. This rapid passage through those several areas has its own purpose, namely to observe inductively how theology operates by watching it work. This is quite different from offering a valid survey of the thought of any time or person or text.

The synthesis represented here is based upon the state of scholarly opinion in 1960. There has been no effort to update it thoroughly.

The usefulness of this material in its present form, according to those who have determined that it should be made available even with only minimal editorial reworking, lies not in any final accuracy of detail but rather in the inductive portrayal of how theological discourse proceeds within the life of the church. This consideration, however, must not hide the fact that in numerous areas the way the material is presented represents "the state of the art" two decades ago.

In some areas, especially part 3, little has changed since the 1950s to call for much rewriting. The New Testament themes on the other hand (part 1) have been the objects of very substantial additional scholarly research. To take account of all this, without upsetting the basic outlines, would call for much updating in detail. Especially does this caution apply to the student who might want to use the cited background readings as a guide for further research. The middle, patristic/creedal section (part 2) covers proportionately more ground in a far more schematic way; new research would change it less than part 1 but more than part 3.

Alternative Ways of Labeling and Understanding the Field of Study

The realm of systematic theology is a realm of great variety. Most of the sources you will be reading (especially in the older collateral readings) will be trying to come up with one solid statement of "the truth"; all the more so if they see themselves as working over against someone else's recent mistakes, or responding to challenges provoking defensiveness. A major part of Protestant identity since the sixteenth century is that it stands over against Catholicism. Such divisions creating new postures "over against" others have marked the beginnings of most additional Protestant communities, producing unbalanced reactions from both sides. Those issues are not unimportant. Here we decide intentionally not to begin with them, but simply to watch the process of theology growing in the experience of the earliest Christians. Perhaps this choice of method will be illuminated by identifying, and to some extent setting aside, some of the ordinary language in the field.

If you were studying in a European university a course working with this material would be called "dogmatics." This term points to the central place within the tradition of a few limited statements, which have been given a special solidity by the way in which those statements were drafted or came to be accepted as crucial. "Dogma" simply means a statement that has been set down firmly. The word "dogmatic" is pejorative only in a certain cultural context where one makes a virtue of flexibility and uncertainty. "Dogma" means the solid core of of necessary Christian convictions. Sometimes "dogmatic theology" is limited in the strict sense to the interpretation of the statements made by or implied in the classic Christian creeds. This is especially the case in some of the Catholic and Anglican textbooks.

"Apologetic theology" is another term needing to be preserved from the North American pejorative lay meaning. To do theology "apologetically" means to attempt to communicate to people with the awareness that they do not believe what one is trying to tell them. In a court of law the *apologia* is the defense. In the debate it is "the case for" something. The *apologia* grants that the person being addressed does not know and probably does not accept what one is trying to say. Statements are formulated with a view to bringing conviction. "Apologetic theology" is an older word for what now comes to be called philosophy of religion.

"Philosophical theology" is not the same thing: it deals with those aspects of the theological enterprise that focus especially on meanings of terms, the meaningfulness of language, and the cogency of demonstration. Such matters as the existence of God or human nature are analyzed, giving weight to the kinds of arguments with which the philosopher deals.

"Polemic theology" is a stronger form of the apologetic undertaking. It assumes not simply that the party being spoken to does not hold one's own position, but in fact that a wrong position is held and needs to be refuted. Professorships in systematic theology in European universities began after the Reformation with a primarily polemic assignment. It was the business of Protestant theology to show how Catholicism was wrong and vice versa. Soon it was also the business of Calvinist theology to show how Lutheranism was wrong and vice versa. Only with time did the agenda of the professional theologian evolve from controversy to system building and the concern for inner coherence.

Obviously "moral theology" overlaps with what we call ethics. "Ascetic theology" as a term is familiar only in Catholic traditions, but what it deals with is not avoidable in other traditions: it has to do with the disciplining and organizing of the Christian life on other levels than those of direct moral imperative.

"Historical theology" deals with the same material, with special attention to how it came into being, how people first came to speak in certain ways, and why that happened. Historical theology is what we should be doing most of the time in this course, but we shall be doing it with our faces turned toward the systematic agenda and not limiting ourselves to simple narration.

The term "constructive theology" is a more recently coined American term, asking the same questions as "systematic theology" does, but with more concern to start over from scratch and to build one's own system in a way that has its own contemporary conviction.

"Systematic theology" is the older word describing the older practice with that same concern, whereby "system" is taken to designate the concern for the consistency, coherence, and completeness. We shall be beginning in the historical mode and moving toward the systematic.

The phrase "biblical theology" has a number of different shadings of meaning. Sometimes it focuses especially on the concern that the language used and the concepts given prominence should be those of the Bible itself. Then one proceeds in a very systematic way to reorganize those concepts. In other times the effort is made to organize the material less systematically because the Bible itself is not systematic in literary or mental style. Then it can be claimed that to be "biblical" is not simply a different thought pattern but a more correct way to reason. We shall have occasion toward the end of the course to look again at this notion of a specifically biblical theology. Meanwhile our beginning with the biblical material can best be understood as historical.

Alternative Ways of Organizing the Study

How we should approach the discipline of theology is itself a subject of considerable debate. It often constitutes a first chapter of a theology text, if not the first of three volumes. The first pages in *this* collection of materials do not handle the problems that the student will find filling the first pages of most systematic theology texts. In most texts there is a section called "presuppositions" or "foundations" or *prolegomena* (Greek for "the things that need to be talked about first"), with each theologian making his or her own priority decisions about what belongs at that place. Sometimes it is the existence of God. Sometimes it is the meaningfulness of religious language. Sometimes it is revelation and scriptural authority. It belongs to our assignment to study all of those matters sometime in these pages, but for reasons that will become more visible later, they will be left for later attention. The procedure followed here, for the first portion of the course outline, is historically descriptive and therefore inductive. It is descriptive in that it simply recounts how theological discourse took place in the earliest Christian communities. It is inductive in the sense that out of that account the attempt will be made to draw some generalizations. If the student, for a particular reason, is especially concerned to look at matters of "foundational" nature, they may be pursued by reading out of order in the last chapters of this collection.[2]

A "logical" way to begin would be first to define one's terms and state one's assumptions. For instance one could begin with the Bible and explain why it has authority. Yet that explanation of why the Bible has authority would point to other assumptions that would need to be proven by appealing to still other arguments, and the very concept of revela-

2. Editorial note: See chapter 14, "Conclusions Concerning the Discipline of Theology."

tion would need explanation: How is revelation to be recognized if we really need it and how do we know our need for it? So some would begin by discussing the human condition as a way to explain why we need the revelation we then say we get from the Bible. But why do we trust ourselves to describe the human condition? Later in our outline, there will be a wider survey of the various ways to begin. We do not attempt *here* to prove that God exists, or to explain why the Bible should be believed, or to ask what the minimum truths are that we must believe or what the maximum body of truth is that we can know. All of this, for present purposes, will be left to develop inductively, out of the story, as we go on.

The Function of the Preparation Guides and Collateral Readings

The student is advised to read three major systematic theology texts, following in each text the same themes discussed in the written lectures. The preparatory material offered for each chapter sometimes instructs the student to prepare by studying biblical texts, but most of the time the preparation guides are aids in making the best use of the collateral texts.

The purpose of the collateral texts is to teach the students to compare and contrast different ways of dealing with the same question. The concern is more for how questions are dealt with than for coming up quick with answers deemed correct. The student should therefore choose texts differing in style and orientation. The bibliography provided below identifies these texts in categories of both denominational and cultural identity, and the student will do well to read contrasting texts, differing from one another and from the student's own background both in denomination and what is here being called "style."

First of all, it is recommended that the subject matter of a chapter be reviewed in a general way by reading one of the two available introductory Mennonite texts by J. C. Wenger and Ed G. Kaufman.[3] Next it is suggested that the student identify his or her own questions in the area, as clearly as those questions come to mind before having done the bulk of the reading.

Next the student will survey the questions in the preparation guide for that topic, and with those questions in mind will read the major collateral readings. If the student aims to do an amount of work comparable to a three-hour semester seminary course, there should be at least

3. J. C. Wenger, *Introduction to Theology: An Interpretation of the Doctrinal Content of Scripture, Written to Strengthen a Childlike Faith in Christ* (Scottdale, Pa.: Herald Press, 1954); Edmund G. Kaufman, *Basic Christian Convictions* (North Newton, Kans.: Bethel College, 1972).

two such readings. In the first reading note-taking will be sketchy, mostly taking note of where which things are found in the text and identifying points where one finds what is said to be especially questionable or especially helpful. Then the student might read the materials in the written lecture for that hour. That may well throw some light on the questions already identified and place them in a wider context. Then it would be fitting to review the questions the student identified initially, as well as those in the preparation guide, and return to sketch a fuller characterization of the specific dimensions of the positions of the collateral text that are still worthy of note, of challenge, or acceptance, when read in the light of the entire discussion.

The reason for comparing the treatment of different authors is not simply to make sure that we do not miss anything. It is to observe to what extent it is the case that every different theological position involves different ways of reasoning and different ways of organizing material, rather than simply different answers on certain subjects. It is desirable to know something of the spectrum of the available views on a subject, so that if this material were used in a class, then one would not only ask that each student deal with different types of sources. One would also seek a distribution, across the class, of most of the types and traditions, so that the class discussion can bring to bear the fruit of readings in all of those directions. We know that Catholics and Anabaptists differ about some specific points of controversy; but how do they reason? How does such and such a view fit especially well when we know that it is coming from such and such a spokesman? Is it possible that the same statement would have a different meaning when coming from a different pen? Does the same creed mean the same thing to a Roman Catholic, or to a Russian Orthodox, or to a Pentecostal?

In the course of preparation the student is advised especially to concentrate on clarity of understanding of what is going on rather than deciding step by step whether certain ideas are interesting or acceptable or not. The student should check out terms that seem to need more definition than is given. He or she should watch whether the assumptions behind the reasoning process are clear, whether they are stated, and how much is being taken for granted by each of the writers being read as well as by the written lecture material.

Other Prefatory Comments

What is the place of a preface in a book? The preface is not the same as the whole book. It is not a summary of the contents of the book. It is not even the table of contents. It is not a blurb, although it might be nearer to that. It is neither a *Reader's Digest* summary nor a capsule version of the book.

A preface gives the reader an impression of why the rest of the book might be found worthwhile or interesting, suggesting in what attitude it would be appropriate to read it and why it was written. A "preface" describes the objective of an effort rather than simply the terrain that it covers. Its intention is in no sense completeness. It rather suggests what the reader might expect and the mood with which one might approach the study.

In a similar way, the intention of this collection of materials is not to *survey* either sketchily or exhaustively the bulk of the content of a theological system. Rather, this collection indicates by means of sample specimens the kind of thing done in the discipline of systematic theology, and the kind of task that is incumbent upon the bearer of the vocation of theologian in the Christian community.

The other title that has served to describe the following material in the AMBS curriculum has been *Christology and Theological Method*. This does fairly describe the principles of selectivity, whereby it was decided which particular elements would be pulled out of the history of Christian thought for direct attention. This selection was done with a view to a search for representative samples and the learning values of those samples. It does not constitute a claim that these materials matter the most, or that it is theologically appropriate to ignore all the other topics that were not chosen for this purpose. The reference to "theological method" does not point to the degree of sophistication sometimes identified with that phrase in contemporary academic circles, nor should the reference to "method" be interpreted ambitiously or technically, as if there were such a thing as just one way to do theology, as there is one best way to type or to run a marathon.

"Theological method" points rather to a somewhat simple concern for asking, as we go along, Why are we doing it this way? Why does that thought follow from this one, and what would the alternatives be? We begin therefore with a minimum sampling out of the life of the early Christian communities, as testified to in a few sections of the New Testament. We shall then shift gears very consciously and deal with postbiblical material along a narrative historical outline in the second major section of the course, since that postbiblical history is indispensable to explain how many Christians have been reading the Bible. Then in a third and larger section we shall pursue three specimen topics that have taken on special importance in early modern times: the themes of eschatology, atonement, and revelation.

Along the way we shall ask not only how to think on the level of logic but also how that thinking goes on concretely in the Christian community with regard to institutions, offices, patterns of church life, and discipline.

We have chosen, from among the many topics of the theological program, to stay with Christology and with matters derived closely from Christology. This means setting aside the doctrine of God, the doctrine of humanity, or what could have been said about sin, salvation, creation, or the church. Preparation in all of these areas is not the intent of this course, although at the very end we shall give attention to how many other such areas there are. The choice of Christology, instead of spending the semester especially talking about God or about sin as a center, is not arbitrary. It was not pulled out of a hat. Part of the reason is that the earliest Christians themselves thought about Christology the most. By following that vein through history, we are never far from the issues that mattered then the most.

The student should expect to become acquainted with many kinds of things that one does when reading ancient texts; observing debates between competing positions, seeking to understand clearly the rise of tradition. So, the exercise centers around the awareness, which must be developed in the practice of reading attentively, that theology is a process more than it is a finished subject matter. Recent pop use of phrases like "doing theology" or "theologizing" have overdone the swing away from the search for a package of settled truths, but the corrective was needed.

It would be possible, either here at the beginning or at the end of the initial chapters' material, to set out the author's own understanding of the discipline of theology as it should properly be exercised. The choice has, however, been made not to do that directly, but rather to proceed inductively, descriptively, watching the theological activity of the early Christian church, drawing our conclusions about how we ought to do theology from watching how it has been done in the past.

Now we may very well decide that the way it was done in the past is not the right way for us to do it; but anyone drawing that conclusion should become acquainted with the experience of the church in the matter. Such a first acquaintance is the purpose of our "preface"; we are not describing how one particular theologian thinks theology ought to be done but rather how as a matter of experience it has been done. If that includes time wasted on unrewarding debates, it will also be good to know about that. If it includes developing consensus on things that will no longer need to be discussed at all because they are so sure, we should be grateful for that; but above all we need a general picture of what people have been doing in the field we are talking about. I said our method is "inductive"; that means that instead of registering right answers already distilled, we go through the process of distillation observing variety as well as similarity. As we walk through the history of a question we shall be paying special attention to how and why people reasoned as they did, to the place of a given question in the life of the church—asking how a question becomes important, how it is that we know a given answer fits a given question, whether all questions are equally important or equally in need of being answered, whether there is such a thing as a wrong question, and whether to every question there is only one right answer.

Physics as a subject matter is about one segment of the reality of nature (the Greek *physis* signifying nature). Especially within the nature of things physics studies how the forces work which make things appear and act the way they do. The atoms, forces, or velocities are things out there that one can watch and measure. Theology is about ideas about God. In a simple etymological sense, any talk about God is theology. But, to be an academic discipline, a ministry in the Christian community, or a subject of reading and writing articles and books, theology as an activity with ideas about God must be self-aware and organized.

One AMBS student returned from a clinical experience, reporting as its major learning, "I learned that criticism does not mean rejection." It may be important for some students to transfer that same learning into our field as over against the modern notion that everyone has a right to see things his or her own way. Our task is to be critical because not all ways of seeing things are equally sustainable. As over against specific orthodox traditions in which someone assumes that there is only one set of right answers because the particular sub-world in which she or he has been living supported that reading, we shall have to be critical because there are other worlds and other questions. But in neither direction does the criticism mean rejection of the person or even of the thought being criticized. To criticize a thought is to take it seriously, and ask what its claims are to be believed.

As a kind of slogan symbol of the discipline we are looking toward, let us note a striking juxtaposition of two phrases in the second letter of Paul to Timothy:

> Follow the pattern of the sound words
> which you have heard from me,
> in the faith and love which are in Christ Jesus;
> guard the truth that has been entrusted to you
> by the Holy Spirit who dwells within us (2 Tim. 1:13–14).

So there is a pattern to follow and the pattern is expressed in sound words. As we shall observe, some techniques of scholarship enable us to determine what might very well have been some of these "sound words" which were circulating independently before the apostle himself inherited the tradition.

For instance, such a "sound word" is probably meant by the "sure saying" which occurs a few verses later:

> If we have died with him,
> we shall also live with him;
> if we endure, we shall also reign with him;
> if we deny him,
> he will also deny us;
> if we are faithless
> he remains faithful. . . (2 Tim. 1:11b–13a).

After this recitation of a "sure saying," which is probably a quotation of an earlier tradition received from Paul's predecessors in the faith, he then goes on to another direct admonition to Timothy:

> Remind them of this,
> and charge them before the Lord
> to avoid disputing about words,
> which does no good,
> but only ruins the hearers. . . (2 Tim. 2:14).

How are we supposed to "guard the sound words" without "disputing about words"? That tension can be taken to represent the heart of the task of working with words in the light of faith, which is in the simplest sense the meaning of "theology."

In what order should the course material be offered? We could start with your own ideas as a student or with all of the ideas and questions brought to the course by all of the students taking it in a given semester. We could go on from there seeking to make sense of the questions raised or of the convictions thought most important. We could take the instructor's own convictions. We could take one particular authoritative person, as for centuries systematic theology in many Catholic institutions was taught simply by working through the writings of St. Thomas Aquinas. Our approach is to be inductive and historical. That is, we shall watch Christians at work doing theology and conclude from what we see what we can learn about what they were doing and why it was fitting that they should be doing it. If along the way we develop the conviction that they could have done it better, that conclusion would be justified only if we had been walking with considerable patience and empathy.

Much of what you will read here is not fully true. That will be especially the case in the New Testament section. The change in scholarly opinions and the progress and the clarification of scholarly consensus has brought about great fluctuation in the data in this field in the last quarter century; that being in any case a field in which the author is only an interested amateur. But in other areas as well, the presentation is over-simplified and without embarrassment is presented in the knowledge that it is out of date. It represents the scholarly consensus that was obtained in the late 1950s on a great number of different subject matters. Any student who goes on to careful scholarly work in any of the particular areas we cover will have occasion not only to clarify and analyze more closely but also to unlearn some of the generalizations offered here. Why then are they offered? Because the purpose of the course is to project a general acquaintance with an area and with a set of method questions, not to offer exactitude in substance or the latest assured results in matters of continuing scholarly debate.

Now to orient the further definition of our discipline and what you bring to it, fill out the following inventory:

Theological Background Inventory

1. How many hours of related courses in the following areas have you had in college?
   a. Bible
   b. Church
   c. Doctrine and philosophy of religion
2. Have you learned substantially in these areas by other means, such as the following?
   a. Independent study and reading
   b. Congregational educational program
   c. Other:
3. How has this background has prepared you, if you were now to stop school and enter non-church employment? Check the closest statement or write a more fitting one:
   — I am basically confident and competent to function as a Christian in the modern world though still needing to know and to grow.
   — I am able satisfactorily to hold my own faith, explain it to myself, function in home and congregation, but unsure about how to "witness" and to encounter hostile worldviews.
   — I am willing to identify myself as a Christian but unable or not inclined to explain or to express it outwardly.
   — I am unsure about the whole business.
   — I . . . .
4. Check those of the following names or concepts that you are *unable* to identify or to explain to your own satisfaction:

—rapture	—regeneration	—transubstantiation
—Chalcedon	—patristics	—justification
—charismatic	—Newbigin	—Bultmann
—tribulation	—Athanasian	—*communicatio idiomatum*
—kerygma	—hypostatic	—*homoiousios*
—existential	—Anselm	—*imago Dei*
—forensic	—limbo	—ontological
—kenosis	—amillennial	—imputation
—Sabellius	—entire sanctification	

5. What does "theology" in the course title represent to you?
   — Collecting and organizing biblical teachings in a manageable form
   — Answering questions about the reasonableness of faith
   — Pursuing philosophical questions for which the common man has no time
   — Stating one's own beliefs in an ordered whole
   — Stating what all Christians should believe
   — Practicing in the skill of thinking carefully about God
   — Learning what other Christian thinkers have said and why
   — Other:
6. Do you come to the course with one or two consciously focused but unresolved questions of a theological nature? If so, state the question(s) and why the answers hitherto given do not satisfy you.

Part of the purpose of the above inventory exercise is to permit the teacher, if this material is being used in a group setting, to have some notion of the level of preparation of his students. On the side, however, it points also to the question of an understanding of the nature of our discipline that underlies the particular way in which we have chosen to present the material.

It can be held concerning any field that the best way to study that field is to know all of the right answers as presented by the best specialists who know what there is to be known at a given time. Such a body of correct answers under the control of the specialist does not exist in the field of theology unless one limits oneself to a very small denominational world. There were times when people thought that was what they were doing and our exercise shall demonstrate how mistaken they were.

But neither is theology, on the other hand, a realm of free search where everyone is free to think whatever he or she wants and where the last resort is simply how one feels about something. The last twenty years of American intellectual life have given rather wide currency to the idea that anyone with a moderate degree of self-confidence is free to pass judgment on what makes sense in almost any area, including theology, without needing much homework. This understanding has been further fostered by such ideas as the priesthood of all believers, the ministry of the laity, and democracy. Without denying the element of truth to which each of those slogans points, it is our duty to come to terms with the existence of a solid and sizable body of tradition: a host of terms whose precise definition makes a difference, a wealth of experience with ideas whose validity is not strictly correlated with whether they happen to turn me on or not, and a story of both intellectual combat and consensus that challenges our capacity for insight and empathy in the most creative cross-cultural research.

One of the questions that should have surfaced in the "inventory" was your prior understanding of what theology is about. You must have thought about this when deciding to study at a seminary instead of a conservatory. You must have thought of it more precisely in taking a course from the department of history/theology/ethics, and specifically a course with this title.

For some, "theology" is the content: a body of correct answers that are under the control of a specialist and are most reliably dealt with when the specialist is the most thorough. For the people on the other hand, "theology" is simply a realm: a territory or a set of questions within which you may do your own thing, make your own choices, and pursue your own inclinations, with the basic criterion of truth being simply whether it sounds right to you. Our present undertaking would be pointless if either of those positions were correct. What we are to do is much more disciplined than the latter view but also much more descriptive and flexible than the former. For present purposes "theology" is the label for that realm of human endeavor where people are careful and accountable about the language they use about God. However that care about language expresses itself, that is the theme for which we are responsible.

Bibliographies

Texts in systematic theology are identified in most cases in two ways:

1. by denomination, and
2. by "style," with regard to their attitude to their received tradition.
   a. By "orthodox" (O) is meant a commitment to keep teaching what was always truly taught.
   b. "Contemporary" (C) describes the effort to reinterpret the heritage with relatively great confidence and respect, but with reformulation so that twentieth-century readers can *follow*.
   c. "Reconstruction" (R) is the strategy that—in order that the modern reader can *believe*—is ready for sweeping reformulations.

Systematic Texts Found Most Appropriate for Parallel Use

Aulén, Gustaf. *The Faith of the Christian Church*. 1960. Lutheran (C)

Berkhof, Hendrikus. *Christian Faith: An Introduction to the Study of the Faith*. 1986. Reformed (R)

Brunner, Emil. *Our Faith*. 1962. Reformed (C)

Burrows, Millar. *An Outline of Biblical Theology*. 1946. Biblical (C)

Hodge, Charles. *Systematic Theology*. 1871–1872. 3 vols. Reformed (O)

Kaufman, Gordon. *Systematic Theology: A Historicist Perspective*. 1968. Mennonite (R)

Kaufman, Gordon. *Systematic Theology: A Historicist Perspective.* 1978.	Mennonite	(R)
Pieper, Franz. *Christian Dogmatics.* 1950–57. 4 vols.	Lutheran	(O)
Strong, Augustus Hopkins. *Systematic Theology: A Compendium Designed for the Use of Theological Students.* 1907. 3 vols. in 1.	Baptist	(O)
Wiley, H. Orton. *Christian Theology.* 1969. 3 vols.	Nazarene (Arminian)	(O)

Others Found Helpful

Bancroft, Emery H. *Christian Theology, Systematic and Biblical.* 1976.	Conservative Baptist	(O)
Berkhof, Louis. *Reformed Dogmatics.* 1932. 3 vols.	Orthodox Reformed	(O)
Buswell, J. Oliver. *A Systematic Theology of the Christian Religion.* 1962. 2 vols.	Fundamentalist	(O)
Clarke, William Newton. *An Outline of Christian Theology.* 1914.	Baptist	(O)
DeWolf, L. Harold. *A Theology of the Living Church.* 1968.	Liberal	(C)
Hall, Francis J. *Theological Outlines.* 1961.	Anglican	(O)
Hunter, Sylvester Joseph. *Outlines of Dogmatic Theology.* 1895. 3 vols.	Roman Catholic	(O)
Lewis, Edwin. *A Manual of Christian Beliefs.* 1927.	Methodist	(C)
Macintosh, Douglas Clyde. *Theology as an Empirical Science.* 1919.	Evangelical Modernist	(C)
Moule, Handley C. G. *Outlines of Christian Doctrine.* 1899.	Anglican	(O)
Mullins, Edward Young. *The Christian Religion in Its Doctrinal Expression.* 1917.	Baptist	(C)
Pope, William Burt. *A Compendium of Christian Theology: Being Analytical Outlines of a Course of Theological Study, Biblical, Dogmatic, Historical.* 1881. 3 vols.	Methodist	(O)
Shedd, William G. T. *Dogmatic Theology.* 1891. 3 vols.	Reformed	(O)
Scheeben, Matthias Joseph. *The Mysteries of Christianity.* 1947.	Roman Catholic	(C)
Sheldon, Henry C. *System of Christian Doctrine.* 1903.	Methodist	(O)
Schmid, Heinrich. *The Doctrinal Theology of The Evangelical Lutheran Church.* 1899.	Lutheran	(O)
Thiessen, Henry Clarence. *Introductory Lectures in Systematic Theology.* 1949.	Fundamentalist	(O)

Thomas, W. H. Griffith. *The Principles of Theology: An Introduction to the Thirty-Nine Articles.* 1930.	Evangelical Anglican	(O)
van Oosterzee, J. J. *Christian Dogmatics: A Text-Book for Academical Instruction and Private Study.* 1874. 2 vols.	Nineteenth-Century Reformed	(O)

Compilations

Clarkson, John F. *The Church Teaches: Documents of the Church in English Translation.* 1973.	Roman Catholic
Wesley, John. *A Compend of Wesley's Theology.* Ed. Robert W. Burtner and Robert E. Chiles. 1954.	
Allis, Oswald T. et. al, *Basic Christian Doctrines.* Ed. Carl F. H. Henry. 1962.	Conservative Evangelical
Heppe, Heinrich. *Reformed Dogmatics Set Out and Illustrated from the Sources.* 1950.	
Campbell, Alexander. *A Compend of Alexander Campbell's Theology: With Commentary in the Form of Critical and Footnotes.* 1961.	
Niesel, Wilhelm. *The Theology of Calvin.* 1956.	
Luther, Martin. *A Compend of Luther's Theology.* 1966.	
Smith, George D., ed. *The Teaching of the Catholic Church: A Summary of Catholic Doctrine.* 2 vols. in 1.	

Recommended Subject to Some Interpretation

Barth, Karl. *Church Dogmatics.* Ed. G. W. Bromiley and T. F. Torrance. 1950–1961. 4 vols.	Contemporary Reformed; large, not easy to find relevant parts
Berkouwer, G. C. *Studies in Dogmatics* series. Titles include: *Holy Scripture, The Person of Christ, Divine Election, Modern Uncertainty and Christian Faith,* etc. 1952.	Contemporary Conservative Reformed
Chafer, Lewis Sperry. *Systematic Theology.* 1947. 8 vols.	Dispensationalist
Schleiermacher, Friedrich. *The Christian Faith.* 1928.	Nineteenth-Century Philosophical Theology
Tillich, Paul. *Systematic Theology.* 1951–63. 3 vols.	Twentieth-Century Philosophical Theology

The Development of New Testament Christology

Barclay, William. *Jesus As They Saw Him: New Testament Interpretations of Jesus.* 1962.

Bornkamm, Gunther. *Jesus of Nazareth.* 1960.

Cullmann, Oscar. *The Christology of the New Testament.* 1959.

Filson, Floyd. *Jesus Christ, the Risen Lord.* 1956.

Fuller, Reginald Horace. *The Foundations of New Testament Christology.* 1965.

Grillmeier, Alois. *From the Apostolic Age to Chalcedon (451).* 1965.

Hengel, Martin. *The Son of God: The Origin of Christology and the History of Jewish-Hellenistic Religion.* 1976.

Hunter, Archibald M. *Jesus: Lord and Savior.* 1976.

Knox, John. *Jesus, Lord and Christ: A Trilogy Comprising "The Man Christ Jesus, Christ the Lord, On the Meaning of Christ."* 1958.

Marshall, I. Howard. *The Origins of New Testament Christology.* 1976.

Marxsen, Willi. *The Beginnings of Christology: A Study in Its Problems.* 1969.

Moule, C. F. D. *The Origin of Christology.* 1977.

Sykes, S. W. and J. P. Clayton, ed. *Christ, Faith and History: Cambridge Studies in Christology.* 1972.

Taylor, Vincent. *The Names of Jesus.* 1953.

Taylor, Vincent. *The Person of Christ in New Testament Teaching.* 1958.

Vermès, Géza. *Jesus the Jew: A Historian's Reading of the Gospels.* 1973.

The Development of Theology from the Apostles to the Creeds

Bauer, Walter. *Orthodoxy and Heresy in Earliest Christianity.* 1971.

Crehan, Joseph. *Early Christian Baptism and the Creed: A Study in Ante-Nicene Theology.* 1950.

Grant, Robert M. *Augustus to Constantine: The Thrust of the Christian Movement into the Roman World.* 1970.

Hanson, R. P. C. *Tradition in the Early Church.* 1962.

Robinson, James M. and Helmut Koester. *Trajectories through Early Christianity.* 1971.

O'Neill, J. C. *The Theology of Acts in Its Historical Setting.* 1961.

Wilken, Robert L. *The Myth of Christian Beginnings: History's Impact on Belief.* 1971.

New Testament Theology: Its Mood and Structure

Cullmann, Oscar. *The Earliest Christian Confessions.* 1949.

Dodd, C. H. *The Apostolic Preaching and Its Developments: Three Lectures with an Appendix on Eschatology and History.* 1936.

Filson, Floyd V. *The New Testament Against Its Environment: The Gospel of Christ the Risen Lord.* 1950.

Minear, Paul Sevier. *Eyes of Faith: A Study in the Biblical Point of View.* 1946.

Wright, G. Ernest. *God Who Acts: Biblical Theology As Recital.* 1952.

New Testament Theology: Systematic Presentations

Adeney, Walter F. *The Theology of the New Testament*. 1906.

Bonsirven, Joseph. *Theology of the New Testament*. 1963.

Bruce, F. F. *The Message of the New Testament*. 1972.

Bultmann, Rudolf. *Theology of the New Testament*. 1951–55. 2 vols.

Conzelmann, Hans. *An Outline of the Theology of the New Testament*. 1969.

Grant, Frederick C. *An Introduction to New Testament Thought*. 1950.

__________. *A Historical Introduction to the New Testament*. 1963.

Hunter, Archibald M. *The Message of the New Testament*. 1944.

Kümmel, Werner Georg. *Introduction to the New Testament*. 1975.

Ladd, George Eldon. *A Theology of the New Testament*. 1974.

Richardson, Alan. *An Introduction to the Theology of the New Testament*. 1958.

Stauffer, Ethelbert. *New Testament Theology*. 1955.

Biblical Theologies

Burrows, Millar. *An Outline of Biblical Theology*. 1946.

Lehman, Chester K. *Biblical Theology*. 1971–1974. 2 vols. (Mennonite)

Oehler, Gustav Friedrich. *Theology of the Old Testament*. 1883.

Vos, Geerhardus. *Old and New Testament Biblical Theology*. 1947.

Theologies of the Old Testament

Eichrodt, Walther. *Theology of the Old Testament*. 1961–1967. 2 vols.

Jacob, Edmond. *Theology of the Old Testament*. 1958.

Payne, J. Barton. *The Theology of the Older Testament*. 1962.

Rad, Gerhard von. *Old Testament Theology*. 1962–65. 2 vols.

Contemporary Christology

Aldwinckle, R. F. *More Than Man: A Study in Christology*. 1976.

Baillie, D. M. *God Was in Christ: An Essay on Incarnation and Atonement*. 1948.

Boff, Leonardo. *Jesus Christ Liberator: A Critical Christology for Our Time*. 1978.

Brunner, Emil. *The Mediator: A Study of the Central Doctrine of the Christian Faith*. 1934.

Ferré, Nels F. S. *Christ and the Christian*. 1958.

Hodgson, Peter C. *Jesus—Word and Presence: An Essay in Christology*. 1971.

Kasper, Walter. *Jesus the Christ*. 1976.

Moltmann, Jürgen. *The Crucified God: The Cross of Christ As the Foundation and Criticism of Christian Theology*. 1974.

Pannenberg, Wolfhart. *Jesus: God and Man.* 1968.

Robinson, John A. T. *The Human Face of God.* 1973.

Routley, Erik. *The Man for Others: An Important Contribution to the Discussions Inspired by the Book Honest to God.* 1964.

Schoonenberg, Piet. *The Christ: A Study of the God-Man Relationship in the Whole of Creation and in Jesus Christ.* 1971.

Sobrino, Jon. *Christology at the Crossroads: A Latin American Approach.* 1978.

Sölle, Dorothee. *Christ the Representative: An Essay in Theology after the "Death of God."* 1967.

PART

1

New Testament Themes

I

The Apostles' Message

Preparation Guide

The theme is the Book of Acts, to be read with the question: "What do the apostles proclaim about Jesus?"

Read through once in one sitting; then return to the following passages; 2:14–39, 3:13–26, 4:10–12, 5:30–32, 10:36–43, and 13:17–41, asking:

1. What basic affirmations (apart from Old Testament quotations) occur in more than one of these texts?
2. Do any occur in nearly all of them?
3. Is any one of these affirmations logically or literally central, around which the others cluster?
4. Is it possible to conflate these essential statements to produce one consistent, continuous narrative? If so, what would it say?

Supplementary Readings for Possible Further Reference:

Barclay, William. *Jesus as They Saw Him: New Testament Interpretations of Jesus*. 1962.

Beskow, Per. *Rex Gloriae: The Kingship of Christ in the Early Church.* 1962.

Cullmann, Oscar. *The Christology of the New Testament.* 1959.

Dodd, C. H. *The Apostolic Preaching and Its Developments: Three Lectures with an Appendix on Eschatology and History.* 1936.

Grillmeier, Alois. *Christ in Christian Tradition.* 1965.

Marxsen, Willi. *The Beginnings of Christology: A Study in Its Problems.* 1969.

Minear, Paul Sevier. *Eyes of Faith: A Study in the Biblical Point of View.* 1946.

Taylor, Vincent. *The Names of Jesus.* 1953.

Wright, G. Ernest. *God Who Acts: Biblical Theology as Recital.* 1952.

Apologies are extended at this point to the student working independently. The next exercise is most appropriate to working through the materials together in a classroom with an overhead projector. The grid that follows is set up in such a way that each item, each "information bit" that one finds affirmed with some clarity in the early apostolic sermons is first listed in a word or two in the left column. Then a checkmark or a chapter-and-verse reference is included in the second column. This enables the class together to develop, as one reads from one passage to the next, a picture of which affirmations are made most frequently and which occur in only one text or two.

When this is being done in the classroom, the instructor can suggest on which line to place each of the major affirmations when it first arises so that as the total picture develops the various items of testimony can form a meaningful sequence. The independently operating student who works through this material in the same way cannot know ahead of time on which lines to put which topics. It is therefore suggested that the student work simply from the top, paying no attention to whether the items entered as significant affirmations come in a logical sequence. Then after having done this work inductively the student can move on and compare with the completed list of major affirmations, as that list has been developed and adapted over the years in the experience of the course. For the present exercise only the sermons from Acts listed at the top of the second column are to be used. At later points in the course work, the student will return to check comparable material in the other columns, as it is found in other parts of the New Testament.

Induction Grid

	Acts 2:14–40 3:12–26 4:8–12 5:29–32 10:34–43 13:16–41	1 Corinthians 15:1–11	Acts 14:15–17 17:22–31	Romans 1:1–4; 2:16 8:34; 10:9 Galatians 1:4; 3:1; 4:6 1 Corinthians 15 1 Thessalonians 1:10 1 Timothy 3:16
1.				
2.				
3.				
4. etc.				

The following are the topics that seem to be the most basic affirmations made in the sermons in Acts. The student should test whether one or a few more important statements should be added to the list and at what point:

1. God led our fathers.
2. This is the promised age; Scripture is fulfilled.

3. We talk about Jesus.
4. Jesus was of Nazareth.
5. Jesus was the Servant.
6. Jesus was promised and welcomed by John the Baptist.
7. Jesus was accredited by signs and mighty deeds.
8. Jesus met the fate for which he was destined.
9. You killed Jesus, or Jesus died.
10. Jesus was buried.
11. God raised Jesus from the dead (on the third day).
12. Jesus was seen.
13. We are witnesses.
14. The signs you see are witnesses.
15. Jesus is exalted/ascended.
16. Jesus has been given the title Lord/Exalted.
17. Jesus has been given the title of Christ/Anointed.
18. The Spirit is promised.
19. The Spirit has been given, attests to the above.
20. You should repent.
21. You should be baptized.
22. The promise is to you.
23. You will be forgiven.
24. You will receive the Holy Spirit.
25. Continuing miracles attest to this.
26. Christ will return.
27. Christ will judge.

Looking back on this list, after the student has checked the frequencies of the various statements, it becomes clear that lines 9 and 11, "You killed Jesus" or "Jesus died," and "God raised Jesus from the dead" are far more frequently represented than any of the other statements. On a second level of frequency we can place, as roughly similar in weight, line 2, "This is the promised age," line 13 "We are witnesses," as well as the call to repent (line 20) and be forgiven (line 23).

The British New Testament scholar C. H. Dodd interpreted this minimal outline inductively in his book *The Apostolic Preaching and Its Developments*. Some have come to use the phrase "primitive Christian *kerygma*" for just these five or six points. This is a contemporary slogan that you may find at some places in the following texts, but we should be careful not to overvalue such code language. Dodd does describe from within the New Testament two kinds of literature. He calls *kerygma* the narrative proclamation addressed to outsiders, and *didache* the instructive kind of information brought to members of the Christian community. What Dodd says descriptively is quite right. There are different audiences to whom the apostles speak in different ways. When they speak to members of the believing community they say one kind of thing; when they speak to outsiders the message is first of all about the crucified and risen Lord. A later debate has arisen about the use of the terms *kerygma* and *didache* in which some have attempted to make more of the distinction than others think can be made. That debate does not belong at this point. Archibald M. Hunter already uses the phrase "primitive *kerygma*" as an established scholarly convention, and so may we. This is not to deprecate the importance of other kinds of communication in the early church or today.

Before going on let us make some evident formal observations about this outline.

- The sermons we see here are just as important for what they do not say as for what they say. They are altogether about the impact of Christ, what we call Christology. There is no discussion of the internal experiences of believers, of our need, and how our need is met. There is nothing about God as such; whether God exists, whether God is one, whether God is all powerful. These are the two routes most often taken today when beginning to preach. You have to begin by knowing whom the God is you are talking about, or you have to begin by knowing about the experience of the person to whom you are talking. These preachers do neither of those things. God is involved, as the one who raised Jesus from the dead and exalted him and gave him a title, but God's existence and power and holiness are taken for granted rather than needing to be talked about. The addressees of the sermon also matter; they know they are guilty for having a share in the execution of Jesus, and they are invited to trust the name of this Jesus and repent.
- Another formal observation: the material is all narrative. It is rooted in the Old Testament story, with the claim that that story fulfills the expectations raised by the prophets. It is about a specific event in the work of Jesus, namely his resurrection, which is more important than his life and teaching, although the life and teaching are referred to, without which it would not be clear who is resurrected or what the resurrection means.
- The narrative includes the speaker. The speaker claims to be a witness to those events. Witness does not mean, as in modern evangelical English, somebody who tells you about his or her own experiences, as if you were interested in those experiences. A witness is in a courtroom someone who tells you what happened, who points to events outside himself or herself and puts his or her own integrity on the line by claiming, "it is truly the fact that I saw that happen." We are observing this strong courtroom meaning of the "witness" here: people who in a situation of decisiveness and

stress are willing to take sides with the claim that events were as they say they were.

- The event quality of this preaching also includes the listener. There are no anonymous hearers in an undefined audience. There are no spectators who can decide at their leisure whether or not to be a part of the communication event. The listeners have already committed themselves to the communication process by wondering what was going on. Now they are grasped by the preacher who tells them they are participants in the guilt of the rejection of the anointed one and that they may be beneficiaries of the promised redemption if they believe.
- The last of the observations of a formal kind for us to note right now is that all of this has happened "according to the Scriptures." Peter quotes extensively from Joel as well as from the Psalms. Genesis 12:3 and Deuteronomy 18:15 are both cited in Acts 3. Psalm 110 is appealed to as the prediction that is fulfilled in the exaltation of Christ.[1]

Now if the student has not already done so, the additional affirmations from sermons in the first column of the "grid" may be filled out and any further conclusions drawn from that. Especially note whether the preaching of Peter to a non-Jew in chapter 10 or the sermon of Paul to Jews in Antioch of Pisidia in chapter 13 are any different in what they contain, and, if so, whether you can explain this difference on the basis of a different audience or a different situation. Collect all of your thoughts on these matters before moving on to the next portion of the analysis.

The next portion of the analysis is in column four on the grid, the two sermons Paul is reported as addressing to Gentile audiences, Acts 14 and 17. Do that analysis before moving on.

What is different in these addresses? Notice especially items that do not fit with the original list at all. Instead of entering them on the grid, just make a separate list.

In the first place, Paul's beginning with a general understanding of God in these addresses is unprecedented. One text deals with creation as placing the peoples on the map in an orderly way; the other with providence as administering time and events in an orderly way. Both presuppose a single, personal, benevolent, powerful deity.

1. It seems that Psalm 110: "The Lord says to my lord: 'Sit at my right hand, till I make your enemies your footstool'" is the one single Old Testament text that is most often quoted in the New. The exaltation of Christ, his proclamation as Lord, is a fulfillment of that promise. Probably the original meaning of that Hebrew psalm had to do with the coronation of a king in Jerusalem. Now it means the kingly honor of the risen one; but we are ahead of ourselves explaining what words mean.

Second, this God is clearly projected as an alternative to the view of the world that the people already had: God is one over against their polytheism; God wants to be served in spirit rather than being an idol.

These two items, present in the message of Paul now, but not appearing before in the messages addressed to Jews or to the God-fearing Cornelius, are simply the Jewish belief about God that separated Jews from Gentiles. Since there were Jews of this conviction in all of the major cities of the Mediterranean world, this picture of God was not new to those audiences. Paul was simply checking in as a Jew before giving them his message about Jesus. So we have taken one step toward talking about theology as such. Now there are statements to be made about the nature and purpose of God as such, rather than simply a message about Jesus. Yet the centrality of Jesus remains. The discourse was proceeding toward him, even though we are not given the report of it successfully getting there. God's providential history is now coming to a time of judgment. That judgment is related to a man. That man is accredited by his being raised from the dead.[2]

Before we go on to watch later developments, let us attempt to peg down our sense of the distinctiveness of what we have here observed by going through the exercise of contrasting this message with earlier experiences you have had of Christian preaching. What was the central content of the sermons you remember having heard in your past that were addressed to people not assumed to be believers? Were they centered on the resurrection?

What picture of Jesus do you remember from your youth and the preaching you heard in the past? What picture of the center of the Christian message prevails in the minds of those who consider themselves to be doubters or unbelievers?

It seems to be firm in this original testimony that the apostles were concerned to communicate a story and not a metaphysic. They were not argumentative about the ultimate nature of reality or about what set of words fit best to explain everything important. They were reporting something that had happened, something whose very quality as event had bowled them over and changed their lives, had surprised them. They were throwing themselves completely into the meaning of that event as its witnesses, and they were inviting their hearers to join as participants in the same story.

The report on the resurrection must be protected against later debates as well. We see here no discussion of whether resurrection is pos-

2. In Athens people actually thought that "Resurrection" *(Anastasis)* was the name of a second deity besides Jesus. The term must have appeared so often as Paul spoke and been so unfamiliar that the uninitiated Greek audience thought it was a proper name: "He seems to be advocating strange gods; since he preached to them Jesus and Resurrection" (Acts 17:18).

sible in the face of a worldview that would have known ahead of time that it could not happen. We see no discussion of whether miracle is possible or whether specific miracles have really happened. Some of those things may need to come later. Some of them may not need to come later; in any case their absence here is significant.

2

The Gospels

Preparation Guide on Matthew or Luke

1. Does the author indicate explicitly, or by the way the story is told, what his special concern and emphasis is in retelling the Gospel story? If so, what is it? Compare his account to that of Mark. How is it different? Is some editorial purpose or organizing principle visible?
2. What names and titles for Jesus are used by
   a. the author in the narrative?
   b. the other personages in the narrative, in different relationship to Jesus?
   c. angels or voices from heaven?
   d. evil spirits?
   e. Jesus himself?
3. What is the purpose and significance of Jesus' work?
   Is it stated
   a. in the author's words?
   b. in Old Testament words?
   c. in Jesus' words?
   d. by implication as the story unfolds?
   e. by implication through the use of symbol?

As we move on from the analysis of the preaching of the apostles, our purpose is to observe how the thinking of writers in the rest of the New Testament reflected and developed this simple first message.

We can, for our purposes, divide the New Testament into two types of literature. We are not speaking now of literary form—whether stories or letters or visions—but rather of two kinds of relationships in which different texts stand to this story about Jesus.

One might call "primitive" or "uncritical" a certain portion of New Testament writing. By this it is meant that this literature arises out of the life of the church in a way that does not involve self-criticism, analysis, self-consciousness. It is gathered together by writers but it doesn't matter much who the writers were. The report, the material, is not greatly affected by the individual mind of the particular reporter. On this level, we could point to three different kinds of thought, or three strata within this uncritical level, which we could try to distinguish if we were working very technically and carefully.

- First of all, there must have been what we could call "the Christology of Jesus," what Jesus thought about himself. We have no writings from Jesus, so this would need to be lifted from those elements of the Gospel accounts where Jesus talks about himself, explains himself, reflects what he thinks about himself, about his office, about his assignment, about his function in God's purposes. In gathering such statements we must be aware that they all have been first transmitted orally and that everyone who passed them on did so in the light of his or her own understanding.
- Second, there would be the level of what we might call "the Christology of the Gospels," meaning the thought of the Gospel writers. These writers do not simply report what Jesus says and does. They also show by the way they report it what they think it means. Every writer selects the materials he or she uses, puts them in a framework, and analyzes the total body of reports and memories that he or she recounts with some point of view in mind. So we could try to ask Matthew, Mark, and Luke what was their understanding of Jesus, to the extent to which we could distinguish it from what we have in the words of Jesus himself.
- Still more general, but still on this uncritical level, are those parts of the rest of the New Testament that are sometimes spoken of as "primitive Christianity." The term is borrowed from Vincent Taylor, a British New Testament scholar, and it is a purely descriptive term. For some people, the primitive is bad: not developed, not mature, not complete, not enough. This is not what I mean here by the use of this term. For some other people, the primitive is good: it is the original, the best, the genuine, that to which you ought to go back. Our use of the term does not point to that either. We are making the simply descriptive observation that there is one such level of the life of the churches in the New Testament that is reflected in certain writings, especially the so-called general epistles—Peter, James, Jude. Perhaps we should also include on this level the book of Revelation and probably also the non-

canonical book, the *Didache,* which is very early and also reflects the life of that kind of church.

In this material we don't see the mind of the author selecting and sifting his or her material very consciously, he or she simply reflects the faith of the church in which he or she lives. This is *not* to say that *no* sifting or interpreting is going on.[1]

We are talking on the "uncritical" level. We are using the Gospels and Peter, James, and Jude as the sources for asking what the earliest early church—before the impact of the "theologians"—thought about Jesus. For our purposes, we will not try to segregate these three levels. It is significant to segregate them for scholarly purposes and to recognize that within those three levels as well there can be difference of shading and development. But for our purposes, we need not be so precise. We have to use basically the same sources for all of those levels, and once we get them separated, as scholars do with careful dissection, we find that what they say is pretty similar. It is similar because there is not here an analytical mind at work. There is not an editor trying to penetrate his or her material with a particular point of view.

It takes some remembering to be aware that the great thinkers of the New Testament, like Paul or the author of the Epistle to the Hebrews, are not at the center of the life of the church. They are at the center of our canon. And because they help us the most to understand the Gospel, we tend to assume that they must have had the same centrality in the life of the church itself. But this was not the case. We shall see in greater length later how and why it was not the case. The common fund of faith—memories of Jesus, stories about him, words of his remembered, Old Testament passages interpreted in the light of this faith—was far more important in determining what the church was and how people prayed and believed than the things that we read in our canon in the writings of Paul or John or the Epistle to the Hebrews.

Because the outline we worked up out of the documents of Acts in the last lecture is a narrative, here we shall try to take a quite different approach to asking, "What is the Christology of primitive Christianity?" Before someone tried to analyze thought and to think regularly and systematically, what was the early church saying about Jesus? Since we took a narrative line, or since we found a narrative in the documents the last time, let us now turn in a different direction and just look at words, at vocabulary, namely at names, the names and titles with

1. The second level, beyond the threefold "uncritical" stage, we may call the "theologians," the great minds of the New Testament. We think in principal of three writers in this connection, as you may see in our reading guide for the next few chapters. That will be the next step.

which the early Christians spoke about Jesus. We shall try to see through these titles what they were affirming. We could choose these names in any order; there is not any special logic to the order that we happen to follow in these notes.[2]

Son of Man

When Jesus talks about himself in the Gospel reports, he very seldom says "I," apart from the book of John. Very often he speaks in the third person, of a personage not quite the same as "I," yet making it clear that he associates himself with this person so much that he is really talking about himself. This term most often is "son of man," a term or title that has numerous levels of meaning which we shall try to untangle one by one. In Hebrew or Aramaic, "son of" is a way of pointing to the nature of a person. "I am the son of my father," is not a genealogical statement but rather a statement of character. Jesus calls Judas the "son of perdition." This does not mean his father's name was Perdition. It means he was that kind of person whose character was marked by his lostness. Well, then what does "son of man" mean? It means a being whose nature is that of being human. So initially the title is a roundabout Hebraic way of saying "a human being." This meaning is very clear in some of the earlier usage. See Psalm 8:4: "What is man that thou art mindful of him, and the son of man that thou dost care for him? "Son of man," and "man," both simply mean the human being in its place in creation. In Psalm 80:17 we have "Let thy hand be upon the man of thy right hand, the son of man whom thou hast made strong for thyself." The reference is either to "man" in general or to the king, but even if it refers to the king, it still just means a human being. We could follow with a concordance through the rest of the Old Testament and find numerous such cases where "the son of man" simply means one who has the character of being human.

In the book of Ezekiel we have another usage, eighty-nine times. Ezekiel is usually addressed by the angel who is guiding him as "son of man." That again simply means a form of address, just as in modern English, especially in the recent modern American use of the term "man" to address a person. It is simply one formal way to say that you are taking a person seriously and calling upon him or her as a person to listen. For example, "Son of man, I send you to the people of Israel . . .'" (Ezekiel 2:3)—this kind of statement speaks of Ezekiel as an ordinary human, but one called upon to accept a mission.

2. The older works, cited in the bibliographies, which support most directly this way of analyzing, are those of Vincent Taylor, *The Names of Jesus* (New York: St. Martin's, 1953) and Oscar Cullmann, *The Christology of the New Testament* (Philadelphia: Westminster Press, 1959).

It might even be that some of the New Testament usage has this general meaning of "man" as human being and not a particular title. In Mark 2 we have it in a very familiar passage, a debate about the disciples plucking grain. Jesus' conclusion to the controversy is, "The sabbath was made for man, not man for the sabbath; so *the Son of man* is lord even of the sabbath" (Mark 2:27). Now we tend to assume that here Jesus is talking about himself in a unique way, but the rest of the passage does not make that clear. He might just mean that "man" in general, humanity, is more important than regulations like the Sabbath. That is a meaningful, possible interpretation.

Earlier in the same passage, Mark 2:1–12, is the story of the paralytic. People question whether Jesus should be able to tell this man, a sick man, that he is forgiven. There follows a parenthetical turn to the critics: "that you may know that the Son of man has authority on earth to forgive sins," then he turns to the man and says, "Get up." "Son of man" here can mean his own office, but again there are some interpreters who suspect that, in view of the fact that later in the New Testament all Christians are supposed to forgive sins, Jesus in this passage was not necessarily making the point of his unique authority.

But we find a quite different set of meanings that came into the same phrase in the inter-testamental period, though resting on the same foundation—that is, still presupposing that the original meaning was that of a human personage. We have in the vision of Daniel, chapter 7, an apparently different meaning for the same words: "I saw in the night visions, and behold, with the clouds of heaven there came one like a son of man, and he came to the Ancient of Days and was presented before him. And to him was given dominion . . ." (Daniel 7:13–14).

This is a human-like figure, but not just an ordinary human being. It has two kinds of meaning. It may have some kind of corporate or symbolic significance. This figure may stand for the human race. Maybe "man properly so-called" or maybe "Adam: man as symbolizing the meaning of humanity," or "the head of humanity." But then, more precisely, in this text it is a heavenly human figure, one that is to come. This picture of a heavenly human figure coming in the clouds to take over the reign was apparently picked up in the later literature between the testaments, not in the canonical Old Testament but in other texts of the time just before Jesus. And thus it came to be just another word for what we often call Messiah—the one who is going to be King: the one who is coming in divine authority to take over the rule. So when Jesus started calling himself "son of man," this usage was ringing in people's ears. It was first of all a phrase that meant simply a human being, but it was also this unique heavenly, human figure who, at the end, according to the vision of Daniel, was going to come and take over dominion of the world.

Now what does Jesus say about himself when he uses this term of himself? Sometimes he seems to be describing a third person, a party not necessarily identical with his own activity. "The days are coming when you will desire to see one of the days of the Son of Man and you will not see it. . . . As the lightning flashes and lights up the sky from one side to the other, so will the Son of Man be in his day" (Luke 17:22–24). It seems almost as though Jesus were talking about somebody else. He might later equate himself with that somebody else, but literally he neither equates himself with that personage nor names himself in the passage. At other times, he seems to use it very clearly about himself, but then it does not seem to be a special title bearing this particular reference to the one who is going to come to judge. There are still other times, and these seem to be the most representative, when it is clear, at the same time, that Jesus is using the phrase about himself and that he is using it as a unique title. In these passages we find a remarkable falling together of certain elements. There seems almost always to be reference to suffering. The son of man must suffer. He suffered in the present, he must suffer in the near future, and then there will be triumph; then there will come that victory which would be like the vision of Daniel. Thus, although the word in its original linguistic form means a human being, its more important usage is not simply a human being but rather what we would call technically a "messianic" title, a label for "the-one-who-is-to-come-to-suffer-and-then-to-reign."

When you translate this term—which makes perfectly good sense in Hebrew or Aramaic—into Greek, you get "the son of the man," which doesn't mean anything in Greek. This way of describing a character or "nature" with "son of" does not have the same meaning in Greek, so it is understandable that in the Greek usage the term should have withered away, not being used much. Consequently, we have it almost uniquely in Jesus' own usage, on his own lips. Very seldom do we find it used as a description of him or a pointer to him from the pen of the writers of the Gospels. This fact is taken, by some at least, as a proof that "son of man" was the title that Jesus preferred, because it withered away when other people used a title that was meaningful to them.

The preceding interpretation with reference to the use of the term "the son of man" represented the simplest statement of a relative scholarly consensus as formulated twenty years ago by Oscar Cullmann. Since the phrase is reported only from the lips of Jesus and makes no sense in Greek, it is probable that the term is his own rather than being put in his mouth by the later church. The term seems to point to a "title" in the strong sense: that is, a role label that says something unique about the person of whom it is predicated, so that the role can be spoken about without knowing the identity of the person to whom it is then to be applied. This "title" quality seems to be indicated by the fact that Jesus uses the term in the third person and not always in such a way that one could tell from the passage that he is talking about himself. Its "title" quality also seems to be indicated by the fact that it was translated literally into Greek by people who apparently wanted to retain something of a distinctive meaning.

If there is such a use as a title, then the only place in Scripture that such usage seemed to apply is in Daniel 7:13, which could be taken, especially as embroidered later, to be some kind of heavenly savior figure.

But all of this construction is challengeable. If "son of man" is a major title of majesty, it would hardly be easy to imagine Jesus using it in the midst of his earthly ministry; or if he did use it, that he would use it of himself, rather than of someone yet to come. Therefore some scholars keep the notion of the "son of man" as a title, but deny that Jesus used it, or that he used it of himself. This is done with special thoroughness and conviction by Tödt and Hahn, and represents a high point of deconstructive New Testament criticism.[3]

The other way to reason is to say that "son of man" was not a title after all. The passage in Daniel taken alone is not clear in reference to any kind of office or special function: it may only say that there was a human-like figure in a vision. There are no other references to that title or just that image anywhere else in biblical literature. It is especially hard to think of it as indicating a title when at the same time its ordinary meaning is simply "a human being." So professor Ragnar Leivestad, among others, has argued that the term is not a title at all in the strict semantic sense.[4] But then there is no reason for denying that Jesus probably did use it, and we still have to ask what he meant in choosing such a term.

Why would Jesus use this term to describe himself directly? Might he be simply putting himself in the succession of the prophet Ezekiel, who was referred to as "son of man" (that is, human being) by the messages addressed to him by God or the angels? Might it be to dramatize his full humanity, thus anticipating the usage made of the phrase by modern Western liberal Protestant thought? Or might he specifically have desired to maintain an element of puzzlement by using a code term without an immediate definition because he desired to postpone full realization and explanation for his hearers during his prepassion ministry?

Secondly, what would he mean to say by the use of this term? Interpreters have sorted out the "son of man" sayings and observe that they have three distinct foci. Some of them talk about earthly servanthood, some talk about a fate of suffering, and some talk about the "son of

3. See, e.g., H. E. Tödt, *The Son of Man in the Synoptic Tradition* (Philadelphia: Westminster, 1965) and Ferdinand Hahn, *The Titles of Jesus in Christology: Their History in Early Christianity* (New York: World Pub., 1969).

4. In *Christ, the Conqueror: Ideas of Conflict and Victory in the New Testament* (New York: MacMillan, 1954).

man" coming as a judge. Obviously, with the former of these, Jesus' identification with "the son of man" would be the easiest. Scholars have attempted to argue that one of these sets of passages is more authentic than the others as a word of Jesus himself.[5]

It is in the immediately preceding pages that the material presented in this study outline is the most subject to scholarly challenge. In contrast to the later portions of the course, even the later portions of the New Testament section, the above materials are those most subject to change in the light of continuing scholarly work. They are as well the ones concerning which the breadth of contrasting scholarly opinions is the greatest, as the pace of change in such opinions is the greatest. All of the following works, published since the above outline was first projected, will generally tend to support the description of the New Testament data that has been offered above, but will also demonstrate that the way it attempted to summarize them in the mid-1960s was incomplete. It is useful today (1981) as a specimen of how theological discourse operates, not necessarily as a set of acceptable conclusions to be believed and taught in the churches.[6]

Servant

By beginning with the term that was the most peculiar to Jesus, we left aside the term that occurred first in the sermons of the Acts of the Apostles. The term *servant* is the closest thing to an established new title that we find in the first sermon of Peter, in Acts 2. It has been suggested, for instance by A. E. J. Rawlinson in *The New Testament Doctrine of Christ,* that we have here the trace of a very early indication of the interpretation of the cross in terms of the suffering servant of Isaiah 53.[7] The interpretation of *servant* as a functional title in this sense is also present in the very early hymn in Philippians 2, as we shall soon

5. Howard Marshall, who is the most affirmative about wanting to believe that these passages all go back to Jesus, is still respectful of the scattering of scholarly opinion to such a degree that he does not help us much to know what Jesus would have meant by the choice of the term.

6. Norman Perrin, "Son of Man" in *The Interpreter's Dictionary of the Bible: An Illustrated Encyclopedia Identifying and Explaining All Proper Names and Significant Terms and Subjects in the Holy Scriptures, Including the Apocrypha, with Attention to Archaeological Discoveries and Researches into the Life and Faith of Ancient Times: Supplementary Volume,* ed. Keith Crim (Nashville: Abingdon, 1976), 833–836; H. E. Tödt, *The Son of Man in the Synoptic Tradition;* and Géza Vermès, "The Use of Bar Nash in Jewish Aramaic," Appendix E to *An Aramaic Approach to the Gospels; with an appendix on The Son of Man by Geza Vermes,* 3d ed., by Matthew Black (Oxford: Clarendon, 1967), 310–330. See also the other texts listed under "The Development of New Testament Christology."

7. A. E. J. Rawlinson, *The New Testament Doctrine of the Christ: The Bampton Lectures for 1926* (London: Longmans, Green and Co., 1926), 241.

see. Like some of the other terms we shall use, this one is multileveled: it is on the one hand a simple social function and on the other a messianic term describing a personage specially called by God to a saving ministry through his suffering. We now move to a few other titles that are much less frequent but necessary to fill out the picture.

Teacher

Jesus was a teacher in the simple, descriptive, social sense. He had learners and he taught them. So it was appropriate that we should find the terms, rabbi, rabboni, master, and teacher in the Gospels. We do not find them often but when we find them they are used naturally and they fit. In Luke the disciples use it; in Matthew mostly outsiders and Judas use it. So Jesus as the teacher is certainly one of the appropriate phrases. People from the Jewish "establishment" call him that. But, understandably, it is not one that was developed and given wide meaning later. It was true, really, only of his social relationships to his disciples. He was not the teacher of later believers in the same way.

Prophet

The next term is prophet. Everyone knows what a prophet is. It had been an office, a function in the Old Testament writings and in Old Testament society, and the Jewish people knew what that was. So when they talked about him as a prophet this was a term that had a self-evident definition. You do not have to ask what this word means, the way you do about some others.

Jesus fit the pattern of a prophet. He had ecstatic experiences, although they are not reported in great detail. We have Luke 10:21: "In that same hour he rejoiced in the Holy Spirit and said. . . ." This was an ecstatic conversation between him and his Father, after the mode of the prophets, rather than what ordinary people usually call prayer. In Luke 7:16 he is called "prophet" after a miracle. He set himself in parallel with the prophets, saying it was fitting that he should have the fate of the prophets. That kind of statement we find in various forms: "A prophet is not without honor except in his own country . . ." (Matthew 13:57) or ". . . it cannot be that a prophet should perish away from Jerusalem" (Luke 13:33b). He said these things about the prophets and the prophet's role, and thereby about himself.

A special question arises in John's Gospel when people came to ask whether Jesus was *the prophet* or whether John the Baptist was *the prophet*. John the Baptist has the question addressed to him in John 1:21. This shows that the expectation was alive that in the end time there would be someone called Prophet: The Prophet. Acts 3:22 cites Deuteronomy 18:15 as fulfilled in Jesus. He would be not just another prophet, but *the Prophet*—properly called. We might look later at the nature of that expectation, what it meant, and what it means that sometimes Jesus fulfills it and sometimes John the Baptist fulfills it.

Jesus

We should not forget, along with these other names, that Jesus had the ordinary, human, social name of Jesus. In the language of the times it was something like Yeshua, or Yehoshua, the same name as Joshua, meaning "YHWH is my salvation" or "YHWH is salvation" or "YHWH saves." It was usually the case then—as is not the case in our language—that every name had a meaning, and that that meaning was understandable in the usage of the name. The giving of a name was meaningful—we have that in the birth story. Carrying about this name meant something to the person of Jesus. We see that kind of significance also in other names like Peter.

These names—teacher, prophet, and even Jesus—gradually dropped from use. These are the most humanly and socially direct and correct terms. They are the terms that would fit the best for someone telling the story of Jesus during his life. But that made them less apt as terms to use to describe what was special or unique about Jesus. In addition to "son of man," the obvious other unique terms are the ones to which we can turn now.

Messiah/Christ

There is the name, Messiah—in the Greek, *Christ*—that corresponds to "anointed" in Hebrew. It is a simple adjective, a participle. In the Old Testament it does not appear with a clear technical meaning. When we talk about "the Messianic expectation," that is, when scholars ask whether Jesus was aware of being the Messiah, we bring this meaning to the question from New Testament studies or from the period between the Testaments. In the Old Testament, the label "Messiah" is not an important term. Only between the Testaments and in the New Testament does the question, "Are you the Messiah?" or "Are you the Christ?" become significant. In the Old Testament, a prophet could be anointed, a priest could be anointed, and a king could be anointed. Even a pagan king could be spoken of as anointed. But by the time of the New Testament, it means anointing as designation of the one who is to be king, not at the point in time when he is crowned, but before that. By the time we come to the confession of Peter—"Thou are the Christ"—this meant the one designated uniquely to be king. This term is thus parallel to the other terms that Jesus accepts for himself: son of man, and son of David. All of these mean "the-one-who-is-to-be-king." They refer to him, therefore, as one who is going to be exercising sovereignty or reign.

In the Gospels, we do not find Jesus using this name for himself. We do find him quoting texts in which it is used. We find it in Peter's confession and negatively, critically from Caiaphas. We find it indirectly once in John 4:26, where Jesus says to the woman at the well, "I am he." Still it is not a frequent term and not an obvious title that Jesus uses of himself currently. He much prefers "son of man." And when "Messiah" or "Christ" is used, it always designates an office: the anointed one. It is not a personal name at all. It is a title, a function.

To jump ahead—and this is the reason it is worth noticing what we just said—for the later writers of the New Testament, especially Paul, Christ becomes a personal name. Paul will use the name "Christos" without thinking at all about anointing or about a king. It has become the name for the person of Christ, and so it is of course also in modern usage. In Greek, the adjectival meaning bore no evident sense. The word was known. It was an understandable adjective in Greek just as in Hebrew, but it had no settled meaning. It had no poetic ring to it, nor any history. Even the verb "anoint" is an old-fashioned word for us; we do not use it much. "Greased" or "salved" would be our ordinary language. So *Christos* came to be a proper name—the common, proper name for reference to the man Jesus—by the time we get into Paul's usage.

Son of God

One of the more frequent titles we have not yet touched is "Son of God." This is, like "son of man," is a term that has an ancient career. Linguistically it has the same tone. A "son of God" is a being whose character is defined in relationship to God. It does not mean a little God. The oldest usage might be what we find in the book of Job where *the angels* are "sons of God." Some of the "sons of God" rejoiced that Job was such a successful product of God's creativity. But one of the sons of God, namely the devil (who is thus also a son of God), said, "He is only living this way because it pays." Thus there is a kind of angelic being that is called "son of God."

But the "son of God" in the Psalms can also be the righteous person, the representative righteous human. Sometimes (for instance, in Psalm 2:7) it is the king who is spoken of as the "son of God." These meanings both continue to function in the New Testament. On the one hand is the human under God, the righteous person, the one who is in fellowship with God, who is subject to God. 1 John 3:2 says that we are now the "sons of God."[8] On the other hand is the king. Jesus is tempted at the beginning of his career, in Matthew 4 and John 1:34, in connection with

8. Editorial note: Here Yoder has misquoted the New Testament. In 1 John 3:2, the manuscript tradition is unanimous in reading "νῦν τέκνα θεοῦ ἐσμεν," "now we are God's children."

this status of being "son of God." This is not a discussion of his divine nature; it is a discussion of whether he has a particular status under God—that of king.

In the Gospels we find this name used for Jesus by demons, by Caiaphas, and by the centurion at the cross. We find Jesus using it indirectly of himself, again in the third person, in Matthew 11:27, "No one knows the Son except the Father; and no one knows the Father except the Son and any one to whom the Son chooses to reveal him." Again as with "son of man," Jesus is clearly speaking of himself but in the third person. What it means is not deity in the sense of metaphysically sharing in the nature of God (the kind of thing we will be discussing later in the doctrine of the Trinity). It means closeness to, or subordination to, God. We have it in John 3:16, of course. Later this will come to be a part of the Christian creed—that he is the Son of God, and very soon when we deal with the Pauline writings we shall find that the phrase "son of God" has become a part of the core *kerygma,* as in Romans 1:4 and 2 Corinthians 1:19. Gradually, moving on from the Gospel usage that we are now talking about, where it just means "a man who is a man of God," or "the king as a man of God," it will come to mean something different.

We shall come back to the meaning "Son of God" as a unique, divine status. But even then, when "Son of God" comes to a more developed meaning, the uniqueness of the Son of God is still a human uniqueness, still something that he has in common with us. Romans 8 leads up to a majestic ending in verse 29, "For those whom he foreknew he also predestined to be conformed to the image of his Son, in order that he might be the first-born among many brethren."[9] Jesus is Son of God in a sense not completely distinct from our being sons and daughters of God. So even when it comes to have that strong meaning in the writings of Paul, it is not a philosophical or metaphysical term; it is not a statement in the strict sense of deity.[10]

Lord

We move to a term that was probably more important than all of the others in the early church, one whose meaning we flatten by making it current and therefore forget that it was a strong term—probably stronger than any of those of which we have been speaking. That is the term "Lord," *Kyrios,* which we find in the confession in Philippians 2, a term with which we will have to spend more time.

9. See also Hebrews 2:10ff.

10. Another synonym for "king" is "son of David," especially used by people asking Jesus for help.

This is also a word that has a simple, human, social meaning. It is the same word that we have in many other forms in many other languages: "sir," "master." You use it ("mister") when you are speaking respectfully to a male stranger you meet on the street. Sometimes it means you are calling upon him because you recognize him as your superior. Sometimes it is just a form of politeness. When Mary in the garden saw this figure whom she did not recognize, she said: "Tell me, *sir,* where they have put him." It does not mean, "Tell me, Lord," because she did not know it was *the* Lord. She probably was thinking it was the gardener and was using ordinary polite language to refer to this person. We find this also used of Jesus in this sense, especially in the preresurrection narratives.

But it means far more than this in the overtones of the word, in both the Greek and the Hebrew heritages. In Greek, it happens that "Lord" was the term that was used in the worship of Caesar. "Caesar is Lord" was the confession of faith of the official Roman state worship. It was to be called out or to be sworn as a sign of one's loyalty as a Roman citizen or subject. This term, therefore, even before it was applied to Jesus, had far more than just a minimal meaning. It was a religious term. It was a statement that just this Caesar is of divine character and therefore entitled to reign and exercise lordship over his empire. It is far more than merely a statement that he is boss, that he is in charge, that he rules: He is confessed to be worthy of ruling because of his unique character.

We have something almost equivalent in Hebrew, for a somewhat peculiar reason. The Old Testament text, as you probably have read elsewhere, was written only in consonants. The name of God himself, "Yahweh," was written only in four consonants, YHWH. This name was so holy that when a Jewish reader came to that place in the text of the Old Testament he would not say "Yahweh." In fact, they even forgot what the vowels were. We do not even know today for sure whether the vowels that belong there are really *a* and *e* so that it comes out "Yahweh." They instead put in another word, which we translate "Lord," the ordinary Hebrew word for Lord—*Adonai*—for the one who exercises rule over people. When in reading they would come in the Hebrew text to the consonants YHWH, they would say instead *Adonai.* Then later, when the scribes tried to make it easier to read the text by putting vowels below the line, they put there the vowels of *Adonai.* When you add the vowels of *Adonai* to the consonants of YHWH you come out with Jehovah. That is just to show how current was the word "Lord" when the reader came to the name for God. So that in ordinary Hebrew usage "Lord" rings with a tone of deity. To sum up: in both the Greco-Roman and the Hebrew worlds, when the first Christians said of Christ that he is Lord, this was using the language of deity about him, more than would have been understood with either "son of man" or "son of God." Yet behind this all there is still the ordinary civil meaning of "sir," "boss," "teacher."

In Philippians 2 (we reach ahead from the Gospel in order to clarify) we are told that following the self-humiliation of Jesus, his emptying and suffering, being found in human form obedient unto death, God "exalted him" and "gave him the name above every name." Now what is that name? There is a Gospel song that says the name that is above every name is Jesus. That seems at first glance to be what it says. The text goes on to say "at the name of Jesus." But that is only the beginning of the sentence. The title that is above every other name is the title "Lord": at the name of Jesus every knee will bow and every tongue will confess, "Jesus Christ *is Lord.*" So the title of Lord is the center of the early Christian confession of faith. This was the strongest thing that the early church could say about Jesus.

The text says this position comes as a result of what he did. He humbled himself. He gave himself. *Therefore* God has *given him* the title of Lord. This we can observe elsewhere as well—the concept that his being Lord is the result of a series of events. It is in the sermon in Acts 2 we read before. At the very end of Peter's sermon, before the crowd interrupts, he says, "Let all the house of Israel therefore know assuredly that God *has made him both Lord and Christ,* this Jesus whom you crucified" (Acts 2:36). Thus, lordship is a position or an honor to which Jesus has come by virtue of what happened in the death and resurrection. This takes us beyond the usage of the Gospel story itself. Therefore we shall have to set the title aside and come back to it in a later section.

Now let us leap from simply looking at the text to a more systematic question that has often been asked, especially in recent critical scholarship (recent meaning the last 60–80 years as over against the earlier centuries). The debate has been about whether Jesus had a "messianic consciousness."

Did Jesus think of himself as Messiah? As we have already pointed out, in the Old Testament the word Messiah does not have a highly focused meaning. Yet by the time of Peter's confession, recorded in Matthew 16:16, it meant something to ask, "Are you the Christ?"

- The most extreme answer is the idea we find in some of the noncanonical Gospels, some of the Gnostic or heretical Christian legends, in which the baby Jesus or the young child Jesus already knew "who he was" with great clarity.
- There are others for whom the story of Jesus in the temple at the age of twelve is the point at which it is clear that he thinks of himself now as *Messiah.*

- There are others who believe it was at his baptism. The words that came from the clouds, "Thou art my Son, I have chosen Thee" (see Mark 1:11 and parallels), were the point at which Jesus became clear about his mission.
- There are still others who say Jesus never made such a claim: it only came to be made on his behalf by later Christians, who then read it back into the Gospel stories. This last position has been argued quite strongly by scholars in the first half of our century.

This variety of answers can be complicated by more careful definition of the questions. There is the "secrecy" theme, according to which some people argue that Jesus considered himself the Messiah but did not want people to know it. That makes it even more complex to read the record. Others believe he thought himself to have a unique ministry but did not think "Messiah" was the word for it. Thus there are many ways of putting this question, and there would be a variety of levels of answers. For our purposes we will simply try to take the Gospel report in its own terms, since it is the theology of the Gospel writers we want to study, and ask, "What did Jesus think about his status?" without asking whether "Messiah" is the right word for it or how or whether Jesus' awareness of his mission evolved.

Take now the mature, active Jesus in his public ministry, as reported. What does he say about himself? We saw that he lays claim to the title "son of man" in the meaning that it has as an eschatological figure, that mainline personage coming in divine authority to take over dominion. He accepts this. He lays claim to it for himself even in times when it is dangerous to do so, for example at the trial before the high priest, in Mark 14:61–62. The high priest asks, "Are you the Messiah, the Son of the Blessed One [Son of God]?" And Jesus said, "I am"—which is an affirmation, although scholars warn us not to take it too crudely. He continues, "And you will see the Son of Man seated at the right hand of Power, and coming with the clouds of heaven." So he accepts the other labels indirectly but he does not repeat them; he repeats, instead, the label "son of man" and uses the traditional apocalyptic picture. Seldom, then, he does lay claim to his eschatological title—this picture of the one who was to come. Again, seldom and cautiously, he does accept *Christ* as a title but he wants to keep it quiet; then he reinterprets it. Mark 12:35, for example, says: "How can the scribes say that the Christ is the Son of David?" The way Jesus puts this question to the scribes in the temple makes it clear that he is talking about himself, but he does not quite say it about himself. Thus frequently when the term is used, he tells people in effect, "That's right but do not say it," or "That's right but it doesn't mean what you think." When Peter uses the term in Matthew 16:16, he accepts it but then says, "Remember, he's going to have to suffer." Peter wasn't ready to accept that, because he didn't have the picture of a suffering Messiah.

Luke speaks of Jesus' ministry as involving in a unique way the victory of God over evil. In Luke 11:20 (as part of a controversy with his critics about whether he is doing the work of Beelzebub when he casts out demons): "If it is by the finger of God that I cast out demons, then the kingdom of God has come upon you." This claim, "the kingdom is coming in me, God is acting in me," quite apart from any title (here he uses no title), is certainly a claim to unique authority. This claim is prominent all the way back to the struggle in the desert and through to the temptation in the garden. The entire way through Jesus' ministry he sees himself wrestling with evil, in the process taking the victory over the forces of evil through a clash of wills and through his suffering.

Another dimension of Jesus' own claim to a special calling is his claim to unique authority to interpret traditions. In Matthew 5, he goes up a mountain just as Moses had been on a mountain, and gives his law, the "Sermon on the Mount." He uses dramatic formulae: "It was said, but I say." He does not place himself in contradiction to the Old Testament, but he does place himself in the position of the authoritative interpreter of what the Old Testament meant, as over against the misinterpretation of "those other people who told you other things." In Matthew 19 he does the same kind of thing with regard to the issue of divorce. "Moses made a concession, but I say unto you . . . from the beginning this is the way it was." In Mark 7:19 he wipes away the food regulations, claiming that he knows better what it is that makes impure.

Then, of course, there are Jesus' "signs," his actions that are interpreted as pointing to his unique status. The classical understanding of miracles and prophecies was that they proved his deity. We see a man who can do things nobody else can do; that proves he must be God. Or there were prophecies in the Old Testament, and he fulfilled them; that proves he must be God. This is too simple. It is not a biblical way of arguing. Devils can do miracles too, or at least in the biblical picture they can. We just noted a text that talked about casting out demons by the power of Satan. The arguments from fulfilled prophecies are very often not logically convincing. If you hadn't accepted the fulfillment you wouldn't have recognized that the text was fulfilled there. But still there is this concept of the *sign,* not a proof but a pointer, which we see in many of Jesus actions. Miracle in that sense is a great deed making people marvel. It is certainly a part of Jesus' unique claim.

He is also unique in his possession of the Spirit. Matthew 12:28, "But if it is by the Spirit of God that I cast out demons . . . ," is the parallel to the Luke 11 passage we just read.

He claims a unique relationship to his Father. He does not use frequently the titles "Son of God" or "son of man" to claim a unique relationship to the Father, but it is said in his baptism; he is called "Son" by the heavenly voice. Other times he speaks of "the Father" in such a way it's clear he's not simply saying "our Father." In fact, Jesus does not use the term "our Father." He either says "my Father" or "your Father." The one place where we find "*our* Father" is when he is teaching *us* how to pray. He speaks of God as his Father, and as our Father, but not in the same breath, and not in quite the same meaning (compare Mark 13:32 and Luke 10:22).

The new element of Jesus' claim for himself is that his suffering is going to be for humanity (Mark 10:45, 14:24). This wasn't in the old picture of the son of man, but it is quite clear in his new statement of the son of man. His calling is to be an innocent one suffering, suffering for others, that is, vicariously, suffering at the hands of the authorities. This is the real meaning of his calling. We could pursue this at greater length.

Jesus, in sum, does not appeal to any special status by virtue of his peculiar kind of birth, a sacrament that initiated him into unique status, or because of his having the only right teaching. And yet, he moves with authority. He simply assumes authority. And his authority is verified by the listener who is impressed. It is verified by the fact that a community springs up composed of people who accept his authority. There is no fixed answer in the Gospel to the question of who he is. He dodges most labels and uses one that he obliges us to redefine, for his first concern is the "kingdom" he is talking about. The unique claims he makes are the claims to be representing that kingdom.[11]

Jesus presupposes a special authority more than he argues it; he lets it be operative without explaining it. He does not ground it in his birth, or in any training, ordination, or event of vocation. The authority with which he moves is verified by the listeners who are moved to trust him, by his destiny of suffering, which is the fate of the prophets, and by the fact that a community remembering him survives. There is no fixed statement of who he said he was that can serve as a touchstone or key. The center of his claim is the kingdom he represents, not any statement about himself that could be separated from that proclamation.

11. It might be said that where "son of man" meanings are expanded (suffering before victory) so as to be offensive, as in Matthew 16:21ff., the additional elements are from those of the Servant tradition. The greater originality correlates with citations from Isaiah 39 through 53:

- his baptism, Mark 1:11 (cf. Isaiah 42:1)
- death as ransom, Matthew 20:28 (cf. Isaiah 53)
- counting as transgressor, Luke 22:37; perhaps it is also the reference in 24:26 (cf. Isaiah 53:12)
- the sermons in Acts 3:13, 4:27 (cf. Isaiah 52:13)

Let us be modest about how much we know. We have been looking at the text because that is all we have, but let us remember that the early Christians lived without the texts in the New Testament. The average New Testament Christian was illiterate. The average literate Christian had no manuscripts. Even the average congregation did not have in its possession, in manuscript form, many of the books that now form the New Testament canon.

What did the average Christian know, then? They had things they had learned by rote, what was called "tradition." We will soon analyze the rhyme about the resurrection that Paul quotes in 1 Corinthians 15. They had fragments of the Old Testament and traditions as to how to interpret them, and they had warnings about heresies. They had some simple creed to which we shall return, but all of this we can only find indirectly.

The early church lived without the New Testament. We have to understand what its life was like by imagining how they could have lived, praised, shared, and worshiped without this text. The efforts we make have to get back through the text, behind the text, to the nature of their early life, rather than to assume that they were living around the New Testament the way we try to do. We especially need to guard against the assumption that all of the early churches were the same in thought or practice, laying back upon them the picture of consistency we have created by harmonizing all the witnesses of the New Testament. The New Testament is more diverse, when each text is read for itself, than most of us assume; the same was true to a still far greater degree of the total Christian movement.

If we were pretending to offer coverage rather than a sampling, we should treat next the christological statements and assumptions of the general epistles (what Vincent Taylor calls "primitive"). According to Taylor, these sources see the event of the resurrection as confirming the Lordship of Jesus but not as thrusting into prominence the problem of his deity. In him they see the Old Testament fulfilled in such a fundamental way that the primary exercise of the community's thought is tracing those elements of fulfillment, like the believers in Beroea (Acts 17:10–11) or as exemplified in the fulfillment texts of Matthew. They look forward to a coming judgment rather than having seen the resurrection as judgment. They call for a life of sobriety, morality, and suffering. They face no need to elaborate, evolve, adapt, or update their understandings, since the world in which they go on living and believing is the same one in which they met Jesus. This is the level of theological articulation of most of the Christians for the first two centuries.

There would also be the Christology of the book of Revelation, so distinctive that it could have been added to the "three theologians" to whom we give more attention. There would be the specific thought of each Gospel writer seen also as, in his editorial way, a theologian. A few of these issues will be noted briefly later in flashback form; most must be left to the student's own further work. As a stimulus to such further work, the following preparation guide is supplied. The data arising from that review will not be discussed further in our text.

We go on now to ask about the "theologians," who, because of their place in the canonical literature, have become for us the dominant expression. Yet we shall need to be reminded more than once that it is only after the first two centuries that the theological synthesis that said "theologians" represent came to centrality in the life of ordinary churches.

Preparation Guide on the General Epistles

Read *Peter* or *James* (or, if studying alone, both in comparison/contrast).

1. Which elements of the "apostolic message" are present? Which are not? Can you explain the selection?
2. What does the writer say about the person of Jesus?
   a. How much discussion of Jesus is there in proportion?
   b. What terms and titles are used?
   c. Is there reference to his earthly ministry?
   d. What of the epistle's teaching is dependent on Jesus for its validity?
3. How does the author relate to Old Testament and Jewish tradition? To Jewish people?
   Are there
   a. explicit quotations?
   b. pictures and allusions?
   c. any negative references (contrast)?
4. What are the dangers warned against?
   a. Wrong teaching in the church?
   b. Wrong behavior in the church?
   c. Wrong relationship to the world outside the church?

3

The Tradition Paul Received

Preparation Guide

Study the following texts:

1. The Hymn of the Servant Lord (Philippians 2:5–11).
2. The following creedal material embedded in Pauline letters (a formal sign of the possibility that a given fragment of text may be "older" than the text in which we find it is the presence of a logical rhythm or parallelism):
   Romans 1:3–5; 4:25; 8:3; 10:9; 14:6ff.
   2 Corinthians 5:14–21; 8:9
   Galatians 3:13; 4:5
   1 Thessalonians 4:13ff.
   2 Timothy 2:8
   Titus 2:13
   Hebrews 2:14ff.

Compare these to the several levels of christological statement already studied. What is added to the outline from column 1 of the grid from chapter 1? What is dropped?

Sources to Pursue Further:

Hunter, Archibald M. *Paul and His Predecessors.* 1961.
Stauffer, Ethelbert. "Appendices III and V" in *New Testament Theology.* 1955.

The Hymn of the Servant Lord: Philippians 2:5-11[1]

5 (Be so minded among yourselves		
as [befits those you are] in Christ Jesus:)		
6 Who existing in God's Image	Gen. 1:26	*(morphe)*
Did not think being like God	Gen. 3:5	
A thing to be seized		
7 Nay he poured himself out	Isa. 53:12	
taking a slave's image		*(morphe)*
Becoming in human likeness		
And being found in human form		*(schema)*
8 He humbled himself	Isa. 53:7	
Becoming obedient unto death (—even death on a cross—)		
9 Wherefore God has exalted him	Isa. 52:13	
And granted him the title		
The one above every name		
10 That at the name of Jesus		
Every knee might bow	Isa. 45:23	
Of heavenly and earthly and underworldly [beings]		
11 And every tongue confess:		
"JESUS CHRIST IS LORD!"	Isa. 45:23	
To the Glory of God the Father		

We dealt in the last lecture with the theological concepts of the earliest Christian church. In order to get at those concepts in their simplest forms, we talked about words and titles. One of the places to find the earliest Christian thought is where we found it—in the general epistles and in the Gospels. But there is another way to find what the church was thinking in those earliest periods. That is to take the later literature, such as the writings of Paul, and read it critically, in order to find where

1. Editorial note: Consistent with his deep love of hymnody and poetic interpretation of Scripture, Yoder indicated in his text of Philippians 2:5–11 (1) phrases added to complete the sense of a clause in brackets [ ], (2) phrases that may have been added to the pre-Pauline hymn by Paul himself in parentheses ( ), and (3) rhythmic stresses with underlining. Old Testament allusions and the Greek words translated "image" and "form" are noted in columns to the right of the text. Yoder cites his sources for this configuration of the hymn as: Archibald M. Hunter, *Paul and His Predecessors* (Philadelphia: Westminster, 1961), 24–28; Ernst Lohmeyer, *Die Briefe an die Philipper* (Göttingen: Vandenhoeck & Ruprecht, 1929), *Kyrios Jesus; eine Untersuchung zur Phil. 2, 5–11.* (Heidelberg: C. Winter, Universitätsverlag, 1961); and R. P. Martin, *Carmen Christi: Philippians ii. 5–11 in Recent Interpretation and in the Setting of Early Christian Worship* (Carmen Christi: Cambridge, 1967).

the writer seems to quote or allude to something that he did not make up but had instead learned. We shall return to one striking example of this in 1 Corinthians 15. There Paul reports at length that he is quoting something he "received." There are other cases. The more carefully one reads, the more one finds snatches of quotations. The way of writing in the first century did not provide for quotation marks in anything like the modern sense, therefore we must find out where quotation is taking place by the use of more intuitive and more literary surmises. Scholars have been able to do this with at least a relative degree of agreement.

Philippians 2

We turn to the theology of the church before Paul as we see it reflected by Paul, by means of the critical reading of his writings to find where it seems that he is quoting. We shall turn first, and at greatest length, to the hymn of Philippians in chapter 2 as a document of the confession of the Lordship of Christ. This hymn is now widely accepted as a quotation; that is, it is pre-Pauline. In order to make a point to the church at Philippi, Paul quotes a text he knows will be known to his readers because it is part of the common treasury of the church's thought. It is probably a quotation from a hymn—a text that had a certain rhythmic form and was probably singable. Since it preserves a sizeable sample of the pre-Pauline tradition that we are trying to find, it will reward our analysis more than some of the smaller sections to which we will later turn.

Paul calls upon the Christians in Philippi to be united. In order to be united, they need to be more humble. In order to call them to humility, he says they should be "minded" as it "befits" those who are in Christ Jesus. It probably is not appropriate to translate this in the modern form—simply "have the mind of Christ"—as this has been done, as if Christ's inner attitude could automatically be ours. It is a more complex thing. "Have the disposition that befits one, or which is appropriate for one, who is in Christ." To be "in Christ" is, for Paul, as we will see later, also a description of being in the church or in the stance of faith.

The rest of the hymn is a description of what Jesus Christ did. Perhaps the song did not begin here. The quotation does. There might have been part of the song that went before. The segment we have says that he was in the image of God, or in the likeness of God, and did not think equality with God "a thing to be grasped" (the Authorized Version reads, "thought it not robbery to be equal with God").[2]

2. Editorial note: The Greek noun *harpagmos,* found in the accusative case in Philippians 2:6, is quite rare in secular Greek. Typically, it designates the act of robbery in the abstract, but in Christian literature it came to take on the concrete sense of the more common noun, *harpagma.* Thus, where the Authorized Version retains the abstract

The first question for interpretation is, What is meant by being in the image of God or the form of God? And what is that equality with God that he did not consider robbing, did not seek to grab? There are two obvious interpretations. Both would seem to be possible for the meaning of these two concepts—likeness of God, equality with God.

- We can assume the two terms are identical or parallel; that is, they mean the same thing. This reality was already in his possession and then he, in humiliating himself—in emptying himself—let go; he gave up this possession, the possession of being equal with God and in the image of God. In that case, "being in the form of God" would mean about what the Greek word *doxa* means, namely *glory,* parallel to the Old Testament *kabod,* which is also translated *glory* but can mean "weightiness," the presence of God.

  The presence of God or the glory of God is thought of very concretely in Hebrew thought, especially in poetic thought. How? What is the form of God? What shape does God take when people see God? Of course, the normal emphasis is that people don't see God, but if you talk about the *form* of God then what might that mean? It has to mean light. And we have statements, phrases, and allusions that permit us to think of God particularly as light. Take for instance 2 Corinthians 4:6, "For it is the God who said, 'Let light shine out of darkness,' who has shone in our hearts to give the light of the knowledge of the glory of God in the face of Christ." In Revelation 21:23, of course, God is spoken of as the light, or the lamb is spoken of as the light. In Luke 2, God is present as light. The presence of the angels blinds the shepherds. There is an ancient tradition that we could follow through the Old Testament as well: God is made known by the presence of brilliance, or of glow. When Moses had met God, his face shone (Exodus 34:29ff.). In Exodus 24:10 the word is "clearness," in 24:17 "like a fire," and in Revelation 4:3 like brilliant jewels.

  Now if we are going to talk about what makes God God, it is more Hebraic to talk about God as light than to use the Greek philosophical concepts of omnipotence, omniscience, and omnipresence. It is more in the spirit of the biblical view of things, but we have not determined yet whether this is the right meaning, so let us not argue it at length.

---

sense, the RSV and others take the word to mean "a thing or prize to be grasped eagerly." See Walter Bauer, F. W. Gingrich, and Frederick Danker, *A Greek-English Lexicon of the New Testament and Other Early Christian Literature,* rev. 2 ed. (Chicago: University of Chicago Press, 1979), 108–109, as well as Gerhard Kittel, ed., *Theological Dictionary of the New Testament,* vol 1., trans. Geoffrey W. Bromiley (Grand Rapids: Eerdmans, 1964), 472–474.

If possessing equality with God was something already in the hands of this figure in the hymn (of course, he isn't called Christ Jesus in the hymn; we shall see later whether there is another label which might be more appropriate, like *Word* in the Gospel of John), then to say it was "not robbery" means, not quite literally, it was not something to which he had to hold on. Equality with God was not a thing to be seized or not a thing to be held on to. He was willing to give it up.

The word *kenosis* means emptying and comes from the verb *kenoso,* "I empty." He "emptied himself," he "poured himself out." This term has come to be a technical term for the idea of God's—or the Son of God's—condescension, giving up certain qualities, certain power, certain attributes in order to become a man. Some say that Jesus incarnate had all the attributes of God. He was really omniscient but he chose not to use his omniscience. He was really omnipotent, he could have made anything happen just like the creator God, but he chose not to use that power, and so on. Consequently, one finds in theology textbooks a discussion of the way Jesus chose not to be divine in his behavior in order to accept the limits of humanity.[3]

For others, becoming human is the condescension because God is, by definition, not human. Taking on human form itself constitutes the emptying. For still others, *kenosis* (as in the "Death of God theology," and especially Thomas J. J. Altizer), simply becomes a label for the idea of giving up any supernatural dimension.

- But there is another possible way to understand the whole set of concepts. The form of God is conceived not as something Christ possessed. Rather, equality with God is something that was still ahead of him, to be seized in the literal sense of something he doesn't have but could seize—could rob. This makes him parallel to Adam. Adam was "in the image of God." This is language we have very clearly in the creation account in Genesis 1. And yet, Adam was tempted. Eve and then Adam were tempted by the servant with the promise, "You will become as God."(Genesis 3:5b). They fell for that temptation to grasp equality with God; they accepted that (deceptive) promise. The result of their disobedience was a kind of answer to that promise, that is, some kind of insight or knowledge—knowledge of their guilt and their nakedness in the Genesis story.

In this view the self-emptying, the *kenosis,* or the humiliation consists not in divesting oneself of absolute attributes of divinity

3. This is the first time the student would do well to check out a topic in the collateral readings. What do they say of *kenosis?*

in order to become a man, but rather, after the model of what Adam should have done, refusing to seize that which was not yet his; refusing to disobey. So the humiliation is not a metaphysical humiliation, ceasing to be absolute and becoming finite—but a moral humility of staying in one's place, of doing what Adam didn't do—accepting the position of creatureliness. The parallel with Adam, the place of the word "image" or "form of God" in the Genesis story, and the more concrete meaning of *hapargmon,* a thing to be seized, seem to argue for this second meaning.

You see the difference. One concept entails an eternal being who gives up his eternal attributes in order to become a man. The other would be a man in the image of God who does not choose to try to rise to deity under his own power, by his own authority, but accepts the humiliation of his human form. The difference is not enormous, but it will have implications as we go on into further development of Christology.

In either case, we can make two affirmations:

- The first affirmation is renunciation, or acceptance of humiliation, or obedience. There was condescension involved in the work of Christ. This is the literal sense of the first third of the poem at least.
- The second clear affirmation is the genuine humanity of this person. There is no idea of just playing at being a man, but a total humanity even to the point of death. Here is the language of servanthood. He took the form of a slave. It has been suggested that here in Philippians 2, as in Acts 3, there is a parallel to the servant of Isaiah 53. This term is not used very often in the New Testament church as a description of Jesus, but it is there in Peter's first sermon.[4] It may reflect the place of Isaiah 53, the Song of the Sufferings of the Servant, as one of the elements of Jesus' own understanding of his suffering. So his is genuine humanity, and not simply in a metaphysical sense. He had the attributes, the character, the definition of being a man. He had the destiny of a man. He met the fate of a man. He went all the way to death.

  This death was not simply a normal, natural death of old age or sickness. It was specifically death *on a cross.* Some scholars who try to analyze this text rhythmically suggest—we don't know enough

4. Editorial note: Peter's first sermon in Acts 2:14–36 does not mention Jesus' role as a servant. In Acts 3:12–26, his second sermon, Peter refers to Jesus as τὸν παῖδα αὐτοῦ (i.e., τοῦ θεοῦ), the "child of God," in verse 13. The RSV translates *ton paida* as "servant," which is an acceptable sense of the word, but is lexically dissimilar to *"morphēn doulou labōn,"* taking the form of a slave/servant in Philippians 2:7.

> about ancient Greek poetry to be sure about these things—that "death on a cross" was probably a parenthesis. It may very well not have been part of the original poem, but an aside that Paul himself inserted into the middle of the quotation for special emphasis.
>
> The reference is then not simply to death, any old death, the way all people die, as a proof that Jesus was really a man, but to "death on the cross" as an especially humiliating way to end one's life. To the Roman Empire's citizens, "death on the cross" was a reference, not primarily to the exceptional physical pain or to the aspects of that torture we would think of when we try to imagine ourselves being crucified; it was rather a reference to his criminal status. Death on a cross was the punishment meted out to serious criminals. It was an indignity; it was a special sign of rejection by society. Other people could be executed in other ways, but the worst criminals, the rebels, were crucified. Thus this insert points to the depths of Christ's association with human destiny. It is not a discussion of how the death on the cross contributes to the forgiveness of sins—what we call *atonement*. We'll come to that later. It describes the acceptance of the position of those who are rejected by humanity as the extreme point of the acceptance of the position of a man.

We have seen the first affirmation, namely *renunciation*. The second is genuine *humanity*. But the conclusion is what really matters in the text: *exaltation*. "He is given the title of Lord." At least the way the song is phrased, this is *granting* a title, something that happened at a given time. He is *now* given this title because of what went before. "Therefore God has exalted him and granted him the title." We saw that in the Greek usage of the title, Lordship was ascribable to Caesar. In Hebrew usage, *Lord* was the name used to replace the name of God. Thus this is the highest title that could conceivably be given a person in either of those language realms.

This ultimate fulfillment is that *"every* knee will bow." The beings who will confess will be *all* beings: heavenly beings, earthly beings, underworldly beings. This is not a statement about the church. It does not say that we Christians call him Lord, although that is the case, of course. This is a statement that God's exaltation of Jesus will bring it about that all creation, the whole universe, will be subject to him. This is future, but it's sure. And it is the meaning of the exaltation that has already begun. He *is now* Lord. The time will come when every knee will bow and every tongue will *confess him* as Lord.

We must repeat here what we observed in the vocabulary section when we asked about the meaning of the title "Lord." It is a common line of admonition within the traditions of pietism and revival to distinguish between accepting Christ as "Savior," which means letting his suffering be the basis of our reconciliation of God and the answer to our guilt, and accepting Christ as "Lord," which means consecration to do his will. This distinction has become so deeply rooted that it sometimes stands in the way of understanding our present text. Here the title Lord has to do with his relation—as exalted at the right hand of the Father—with the universe, not only with the individual or the church. The church is the people who call him Lord, but his being Lord is not dependent upon their calling him that. They rather can call him that only because he is that. This distinction matters when we ask whether the Lordship of Christ applies in any way to the rest of the world.

Another example of this debate arises when we are conversing not about revivalism but with social conservatives who say we should not proclaim Christian morality as relevant to the wider society because those who do not believe cannot be expected to obey. How can Christ be Lord over those who do not obey him? That Ronald Reagan is president of the United States in 1981 does not depend on whether you voted for him or whether you like him or even on whether you plan to obey him. His status as president is objective, determined by considerations independent of your will. In the same sense the dignity of Christ as cosmic Lord is independent of whether his creatures like it or whether any particular one of his creatures confesses it. They all will in the end. When we call him Lord, the difference between us and the rest of his creatures is that we know it and commit ourselves to obey him, whereas they may not know of or may reject his lordship.

Is this exaltation the reward, the results, and the recompense for his humiliation and his death? Or is it simply the unveiling of what was always the case? Many would tend to think the latter. He obviously was already Lord. God does not change. The Son of God does not change. He went through his human career and its results and then returned to where he was before, restored to the status he had given up. He is now unveiled and will in the future be more widely unveiled as the one who always was Lord.

If we came to this text with a full concept of the prior exalted status which he forsook, then we would tend toward this idea of emptying out, being restored, and then simply made manifest or unveiled, as what he had always been. Then, when Paul quotes the hymn, saying, "he is given the title of Lord," it would be just a poetic way, a time-bound way, of saying that God revealed what always was the case. He always was Lord.

If, however, we were to take the other line of interpretation, we would see Jesus as tempted, in the line of Adam, to add to "being in the divine image" a further God-likeness that he would have grasped. Yet he didn't grasp it. He let it slip away. He didn't seek to avoid the limits of humanity. *Then* it would also make sense to take literally the concept that his Lordship is the result of his work. He was not Lord before in the same sense that he is now Lord, because something really happened at the cross, and something really happened in the resurrection. They were not simply an unfolding of what always was. This is the more literal, the more historical, and therefore, on general grounds, the more likely reading. It is of course what we shall have to test through the course. It might be that the hymn first had the simpler second meaning and then took on the former.

Conclusions

Now let us look back over what we have said about this text and draw some conclusions on how the church that used this hymn thought, comparing it to the earlier core message that we worked up out of the apostolic sermons.

The apostolic sermon, you remember, concentrated on death and resurrection. Everything else was built around this, the claim that this death and resurrection were the fulfillment of expectation or promise or prophecy, and the call to the listener to respond in faith. Those same elements, humiliation and exaltation, are here, yet the humiliation does not concentrate in the death; in fact, just the opposite is the case. It concentrates on accepting humanity, the form of a slave, human likeness, human form. Death is simply the culminating point of his humble identification with humanity. In the early apostolic preaching it was probably the other way around—it was the death itself that was first affirmed. In fact the very earliest texts we saw didn't even say, "He died." They said, "You killed him."

The other extreme is not resurrection. That concept doesn't appear here. It looks beyond resurrection to exaltation to what the church has talked about under the heading of ascension. Resurrection is not affirmed. We might say it is assumed, but perhaps it need not be. The view of the hymn's singers is already wider. They are not simply saying that Christ came out of the tomb or was seen again. They are rather saying that he is *exalted*. He is already given the title of Lord and we look forward to that title being confessed by all creatures. So the core shape is the same (his humiliation and his exaltation), but the content is different. It is no longer just death and resurrection, but a *pattern* of humiliation that culminates in death, a *pattern* of exaltation that takes off from resurrection.

Another observation of note is that there is in this text no special reference to atonement—that is, the specific study of how Jesus' death relates to our forgiveness. That will be discussed later but it isn't here. In fact, the point of the quotation is to make a different connection between the Christian and Christ—not that he died so that we don't have to die, or that he died so that we might be forgiven but rather that because he was humiliated we should accept humiliation. This underlies and enables the call to the unity of the church that is the reason Paul introduced the quotation in the first place. Paul pleads with the Philippians to be more united. In order to be more united you have to respect the other person. The reason you should be able to respect the other person is that Christ humiliated himself. The example of Christ is a norm for you Christians in Philippi. Although the pattern of humiliation *unto death* is unique (none of us have yet died), and although the exaltation and title of Lord is unique (none of us have yet ascended), this pattern is still a norm for us. We are still called to share in that humiliation, in that servanthood. Specifically, in this case, we are called to share in it in a way that permits us to serve the unity of the church.

Let us look back at the wording of the plea that led up to the quote: "If there is any encouragement in Christ, any incentive of love, any participation in the Spirit, any affection and sympathy, complete my joy by being of the same mind, having the same love, being in full accord and of one mind. Do nothing from selfishness or conceit, but in humility count others better than yourself. Let each of you look not only to his own interests but also to the interests of others. Have this mind . . ." (Phil. 2:1–5). That is a very long, urging windup that Paul finally concludes with reference to the example of Christ.

Other Pre-Pauline Traditions

The other bits that we can find of the thought that went before Paul very often have about them this same two-phase structure. We saw in the earliest preaching, "You killed him but God raised him." Now in Philippians we see, "He accepted humiliation and renunciation but God exalted him." That kind of double movement of thought seems to have been congenial to the mind of the early church. Many phrasings that stick out of the text as possible quotations have this character about them, with rhythmic phrasings that refer to descent and ascent.

- Ephesians 4 begins with a quotation from Psalm 68:18 that Paul works into a New Testament confession: "'When he ascended on high he led a host of captives and he gave gifts to men.' (In saying, 'He ascended,' what does it mean but that he had also descended into the lower parts of the earth? He who descended is he who also ascended far above all the heavens, that he might fill all things.)" (Ephesians 4:8–10). Here is a picture of the work of Christ—he went down, he went up, and then he fills all things. If we compared this to Philippians 2, "filling all things" would mean Christ's ultimate lordship and being recognized by all creation. But in Ephesians 4, Paul makes another point. He is talking about the gifts of the Spirit. "Filling all things" in this context therefore means giving to the whole church the gifts of the Spirit—some to be prophets, some apostles, and so on. So we see the flexibility with which this picture of the two-fold work of Christ—descending and ascending, humiliation and exaltation—is flexed, bent, and reformulated to fit the particular topic Paul has in mind.

- In Romans 10:6–8 we read, "The righteousness which is based on faith says, Do not say in your heart, 'Who will ascend into heaven?' (that is, to bring Christ down) or 'Who will descend into the abyss?' (that is, to bring Christ up from the dead). But what does it say? The word is near you, on your lips and in your heart (that is, the word of faith which we preach) . . . ." All of this wording—"the word of faith which we preach"—is probably Paul's equivalent of a quotation mark, identifying a pre-Pauline phrasing that immediately follows: "Because if you confess with your lips that Jesus is Lord and believe in your heart that God raised him from the dead, you will be saved" (Rom. 10:9). Again, bringing Christ down, raising Christ. This language is reflected in the lowest strata of the confessions of the early church and shows protruding in various forms.
- Another way this duality appears, however, no longer refers to "down" and "up" (the spatial image). Some texts talk about two different qualities of being, such as "flesh" and "spirit." Romans 1:3–5, the beginning of the epistle, is one of the texts listed on the "induction grid" because of its descriptions of Jesus: "descended from David according to the flesh and designated Son of God in power according to the Spirit of holiness by his resurrection from the dead." There is the level of "flesh" and then another level of reality, in this case, "resurrection."

  This text may throw light on the question we asked before. Was the Lordship something eternal that was unveiled, something that always was, or was it the result of Christ's work? Paul seems to say Christ was "appointed Son of God" by virtue of the resurrection. He seems say that the status of divine Sonship is Christ's as a part of his work in history rather than something that was eternally a part of his nature.
- Second Timothy 2:8 is a later writing, but again it has the form of a remembrance, of a creed: "Remember Jesus Christ, risen from the dead, descended from David." The same two statements we had in Romans 1 are here, but in reverse order. These are not only two natures, but also a way of describing what Christ does for us or what was done for him.
- First Peter 3:18 reads, "For Christ also died . . . being put to death in the flesh, but made alive in the Spirit." Here it is no longer just resurrection, but Spirit. In Romans 1 the alternatives were "flesh" and "resurrection." Now the opposite of "flesh" is "Spirit." We are reading now less about events and a little more about entities.

- In 1 Timothy 3:16: "Manifest in the flesh, justified in the Spirit" (AV). The concept of justification will grow in the early church. In it we observe the beginning of the concept of atonement, that is, what is done with our sins.
- In Romans 4:25: He "was put to death for our trespasses and raised for our justification." The notion that trespasses are the grounds for death and the concept of justification, or being made righteous through his work, are probably both borrowed from Isaiah 53, a passage we already saw reflected in Philippians 2.

Thus we observe, with considerable variety but also considerable faithfulness, a recurrent pattern of seeing the work of Christ as two-fold, with both its element of humiliation, condescension, becoming flesh, and its element of resurrection, Spirit. It seems that this was an easy way for the early church to preach, remember, or praise. Therefore, we can find traces of this two-fold pattern running all the way up and down the epistles, if we have the techniques of seeing them under the surface of the text.

Because we centered on the tradition Paul received about Jesus, we paid less attention to words *of* Jesus that Paul knew because they also had been passed on to him. Paul seems, without saying so, to cite Jesus in the following ethical and parabolic materials:

Romans 8:15 (Gal. 4:6) We pray to "abba."
  12:14 Bless those who persecute you.
  13:8 Owe nothing but love; love fulfils the law.
  16:19 Be wise about goodness and innocent of evil.
1 Corinthians 6:7 Why not rather suffer evil?
  13:2 Faith can move a mountain.
2 Corinthians 1:17–20 Do not be yes and no together.
Galatians 5:9 Leaven penetrates the entire lump.[5]

5. See C. H. Dodd, "Matthew and Paul." *The Expository Times* 58, (1946–47): 293; Lucien Cerfaux, *Christ in the Theology of St. Paul* (New York: Herder and Herder, 1959), 189; Alfred Resch, *Der Paulinismus und die Logia Jesu in ihrem gegenseitigen Verhältnis* (Leipzig: J. C. Hinrichs, 1904), 110, 523; and Archibald M. Hunter, *Paul and His Predecessors* (Philadelphia: Westminster, 1961), 24–28. Paul's express references to "traditions from the Lord" are 1 Corinthians 7:6–10, 9:14, 11:23 and 1 Thessalonians 4:2. The Paul of Acts quotes Jesus at Ephesus in 20:35. In all these cases, can you locate in the Gospels the word of Jesus that Paul is citing?

4

The Theologians: Paul

Preparation Guide (for Chapters 4 and 5)

1. Read carefully one of the following (all of them if working alone):
   a. Colossians and Ephesians,
   b. Hebrews, or
   c. John (with attention to the discourses more than to narrative) and 1 John.
2. Compare what is emphasized here to the apostolic *(kerygma)* outline.
   a. Are themes added?
   b. Are themes omitted?
   c. What is the relative emphasis of various themes?
3. What is the attitude toward:
   a. The text of the Old Testament? (Is it cited? How?) Does the New Testament writer's meaning coincide with the original contextual Old Testament meaning?
   b. The Old Testament heritage of law, etc.?
   c. The Jewish people?
4. Is there specific reference to Gentiles?
5. What are the names and titles used for Jesus? Compare to Paul's.
6. What dangers or adversaries does the author warn against? Is this explicit?
7. How does the writer deal with the following themes? How often? How explicitly?
   a. Virgin Birth
   b. Status of divine Sonship
   c. Humanity of Jesus
   d. Resurrection
   e. Future return

8. Are any themes important to one of the authors which are not yet named above? Can you characterize the differences in mental and literary style which distinguish these authors from one another?

Our next step takes us to the "theologians" of the New Testament. First, a few remarks about the whole category. What do we mean by "theologians"? We are moving to writings that differ from what we called "the primitive consensus" of the church in several ways:

- They differ in volume. We have, especially for Paul but also for the others to whom we shall turn later, a body of literature that is sufficient to give us some confidence that we know the mind of the individual writer. Instead of a brief collection of exhortations that almost anyone could be saying, we have sustained argument or sustained narrative.
- They differ also in depth, in the extent to which the writer pursues an idea, develops its implications and assumptions, and unfolds its facets. This happens when one mind is working in a sustained way at one problem.
- These writers differ, as well, in their originality. Not only do we observe one mind working at length and at depth at a problem, we see the writer come up with something. He finds ways of saying things that have not been said before. He adds something to the deposit by way of interpretation. There is no question about whether these theologians stand on the base of "primitive theology." They never suggest that they do anything else. They never suggest that they add to the deposit in the sense of changing its character, or finding revelations that were not present before. The closer we look at these texts, the more we find how solidly they stand on the base of what went before. Thus a New Testament scholar can write a whole book on "the predecessors of Paul," tracing, as we were doing, the early church's thought as it was taken up into the fabric of Paul's own writing.[1]

What is it that leads them to their greater originality? We can summarize three tests they try to meet, or three challenges to which they respond:

- First, the test of *coherence*. They try to make the faith stick together. They test an expression of one thought by whether it fits

1. Editorial note: The reference is to Archibald M. Hunter, *Paul and His Predecessors* (Philadephia: Westminster, 1961).

with another statement. They argue by consistency. We see Paul insist, "If you affirm this then you cannot deny that." They bring logic to bear, or they rise to a higher level of generalization in the affirmations they make.

- Secondly, they meet the test of *communication*. They have in mind a given readership or audience. They try to say things in a way that will be understood by that particular population. They do not simply repeat the words of the earlier proclamation. They do not simply go through the liturgy or the catechism again. They make statements about how these things are to be understood in a new context, by a new audience, as answering some new question.
- There is a third test after coherence and communication. We could call it the test of conviction. The "theologians" try to prove something. They argue points. We do not find this kind of argument in Peter or James. We find urging and exhortation there, but here there is actual arguing going on, a process of trying to make a point by reasoning and proof.

We have to be careful not to assume that these "theologians" were normative or representative in the apostolic church. When we look back on the New Testament, these are the writings that dominate. They make the most sense. They have volume. They have logic, sequence, and argument to them. So for our impression of the New Testaments, we are most illuminated by the thought of these writers. We must recognize that most early Christians did not read them. The faith of most Christians most of the time was on the more naive, less complicated, and less analytical level of the very brief confessions, the duality of humility and exaltation, the simple creeds, and the very simple liturgies with which the predominantly illiterate church had to live. The authority of these "theologians" grew with time. We shall see later how they came to be recognized in the development of the canon, but at the beginning their writings were not as well known as other writings. They had no unique authority. They were competing with many other kinds of writing. It was only with the passage of time that they came to be seen as central, the way we see them, as we look back on the whole story. It takes a little intellectual exercise and stretching of the mind to imagine a church where not everybody had read Paul, so as to grasp how their doctrinal stance was quite different from that of Protestant biblicism since the Reformation, when the reading of Paul became the center of New Testament interpretation

On your induction grid are references to some of Paul's preaching. We could fill out more of the points where he says, "This is my message." We shall not do that at length, but it could be profitably done. In Acts 13, Paul preaches to Jews at Antioch. In Acts 14, he preaches to

Gentiles at Lystra, and in Acts 17 at Athens. There are other little snippets in addition to these three extended discourses in Acts. At other times there are phrases and hints of a sermon or second-hand references to the fact that he said something. For instance, in Acts 16:17 the slave girl following Paul said, "These men are servants of the Most High God who proclaim to you the way of salvation." In the beginning of Acts 17, Paul was in the synagogue at Thessolonica arguing for three weeks from the Scriptures, explaining "that it was necessary for the Christ to suffer and to rise from the dead, and saying, 'This Jesus, whom I proclaim to you, is the Christ'" (vv. 1–3). Here is a case, of course, where "Christ" (Messiah) is still a substantial affirmation and not just a name.

In Acts 19:26, Paul is said to have "persuaded and turned away a considerable company of people, saying that gods made with hands are not Gods." He launches an attack on idolatry. Paul, in Luke's narrative, is reported as preaching. When talking to Gentiles there is an element that was absent in the other apostles' preaching addressed to Jews. There is the reference to the God of creation and providence, *and* there is a critique of idolatry. This is the same as what the Jews were saying at these points. The Jews affirmed a Creator God, one God, a unique God in the face of whom idolatry and polytheism are wrong. So Paul adds, as it were, to his proclamation of Jesus that was addressed to the Jews, a proclamation of the uniqueness of the one true God, Father of Jesus, which was the same as the Jewish message to the Gentiles.

This is a normal addition. If you are preaching to Jews, you presuppose one God. You presuppose creation, providence, and the divine governance of history. You presuppose the rejection of idolatry and of polytheism. But if you are talking to Gentiles, you have to say those things too. Does one say them immediately or later? This will depend. At least they have to be added to the message. It is evidently added to the message when Paul preaches to the Gentiles.

1 Corinthians 15

We are interested in Paul theologizing in his own writings. We go back to the text that was listed before as pre-Pauline, 1 Corinthians 15. Remember that he begins this passage with an appeal to tradition: "I would remind you on what terms I preached to you the Gospel, which you received, in which you stand, by which you are saved, if you hold it fast—unless you believed in vain. For I delivered to you as of first importance what I also received" (1 Cor. 15:1–3a).

The tradition's essential content is a set of rhythmic phrases, a kind of rhyme, as far as the structure of the text is concerned, which is directly equivalent to the apostolic preaching:

Christ died
  for our sins
    according to the scriptures.
He was buried.
He was raised
  on the third day
    according to the scriptures.
  He was seen . . . (1 Cor. 15:3b–5a).

In a new form we have our old outline:

a. The central duality of death/resurrection.
b. The fulfillment of the promise of the (unspecified) Scriptures.
c. The witnesses (with the chain extended vv. 5–8 all the way to Paul himself).

It is of special importance to Paul to make clear that his message is not his invention; he received it, he passed it on, and if the Corinthians are believers it is because they received it as well. Our interest now is in understanding the context in which he does this, in which he makes this appeal. "This is what you believed; this is what I preached. But I did not make it up. I also had to receive it." So he gives us a picture of a chain of transmission—"from before me, through me, to you. You accepted it. You believed it. If you are believers it is because you believed that. Now I appeal to what you already accepted. This chain of transmission is what defines our relationship. I can appeal to you because you accepted from me what I accepted from the others."

The picture is of the church as an organism carrying on a message, and the appeal is to the reader to accept being in that chain of tradition. Paul's own authority is a part of that picture because he extends the tradition he received, "Christ died for our sins according to the Scriptures, was buried, raised on the third day in accordance with the Scriptures, appeared." The original report probably ended with "appeared to Cephas and the twelve." Then it was extended to "more than five hundred brethren at one time. . . .Then he appeared to James, then to all the apostles"—perhaps the original text went that far. But Paul adds, "Last of all, he appeared to me." (See 1 Cor. 15:5b–8). Paul gets his own authority from the fact that he is one of these witnesses.

There is a very popular contemporary way of interpreting the early church that makes a strong polarization between Jesus and Paul. On the one hand is the faith of Jesus that was a God-centered faith, and then, on the other hand, is the religion that Paul developed—a religion about Christ. If we compare this to views that fail to recognize that there was movement in the early church—that faith did develop—then there is a point to the argument. We do have to see the faith developing, but this is one of the clear places where we see that the growth is not a split. Paul associates himself with the other apostles. He claims that he teaches precisely what he received from those who went before. He denies originality at the point of the central message.

Why does Paul appeal to this tradition? What moves him? We see this when he moves to the question, "Now if Christ is preached as raised from the dead, how can some of you say that there is no resurrection from the dead?" (1 Cor. 15:12). Some people were denying the resurrection. What resurrection? They weren't denying Christ's resurrection; Paul just said they affirmed that. But they are denying that there is a resurrection for all humanity. The logic of Paul's answer is: You cannot affirm that Christ is risen and deny the general resurrection. If there is no general resurrection, that is, one for all humanity, then there can't be the resurrection of Christ either. "If there is no resurrection of the dead, then Christ has not been raised; if Christ has not been raised, then our preaching is in vain" (1 Cor. 15:13–14). Christ cannot be divided from humanity. If he rose, we shall rise. If people deny that we can rise, then he must not be risen.

Watch what happens here logically. Paul is not simply saying, "There is a message of resurrection that we have proclaimed. Jesus is risen." He has inserted another assumption. If we try to diagram his logic according to mathematical criteria of coherence, we shall have to say, "This doesn't hold, Paul; this doesn't follow. Unless you have made some assumptions about the relation of Christ to all humanity, you cannot say, 'If there is not a general resurrection of the dead, then Christ has not been raised.'" Paul assumes that the solidarity of Christ with all humankind is such that one cannot deny the resurrection of all without denying the resurrection of Christ. He does not explain that assumption. He does not even state it. He does not affirm it. He just takes it for granted and reasons from there.

Let us identify this assumption; we shall have occasion to come back to it. We might call it "the logic of solidarity." With this label we identify the assumption about the relationship between Christ and all humanity, according to which one cannot deny that all will be raised without denying that Christ is risen. We call it "solidarity" or "participation." Christ is so linked with humanity that you cannot say something about humanity that does not apply to him. Nor can you deny something about humanity without denying it to him.[2]

This was not a stated part of the primitive faith. It was not in the simple faith of the church before Paul. This is an element of logic, an as-

2. In this effort to play back the challenge at Corinth, we have an example of the risks of error one must run. The most credible reconstruction, which we have followed, is that the Corinthians doubted the general resurrection. Another possibility is, however, that they affirmed that the resurrection had already happened. This idea is present in 2

sumption, a way of thinking, a way of *proving*. Paul has brought it to the primitive tradition. It permits him to argue from that tradition in a way that answered the question of his readers, and in a way that the early church obviously had not done before.

What else can we observe about Paul's theological message from this viewpoint? When we went through the texts on the induction grid we noted that Christ's death *for our sins* was not stated very often. It is stated here. Here again it applies in the logic, "If the dead are not raised then Christ is not raised. If Christ had not been raised, your faith is futile and you are still in your sins." So we see here the development of a doctrine of the atonement in rudimentary, simple form. Paul begins to relate the death of Christ to the sins of humanity in a way that the earlier texts had not.

Let us move to another question about theological method. What use does Paul make of the Old Testament? In this passage there is no direct quotation of the Old Testament until the very end of the chapter in verse 55: "Death, where is thy victory?" But there is reference to Old Testament thought at one very significant place in the passage. Verse 21 reads, "As by a man came death, by a man has come also the resurrection of the dead. For as in Adam all die, so also in Christ shall all be made alive." Again in verse 45: "Thus it is written, 'The first man Adam became a living being'; the last Adam became a life-giving Spirit." The Old Testament story is in the back of Paul's mind, in the figure of Adam who is representative of human solidarity. In Adam all die. In Christ, all rise. So the concept of solidarity applies to human mortality as well as to the resurrection.

Another observation we can make about how Paul's reasoning proceeds is the way an issue the Corinthians probably thought not very important becomes central. The Corinthians were orthodox Christians. They believed all that they knew they had to believe about the resurrection. They simply did not affirm the promised resurrection of all humanity. They had never seen that stated so clearly before or taken so seriously. They could think it must not have been very important; it must not have been crucial. It was something that Christians could differ on. We do not see any debate about the question anywhere else in the New Testament except perhaps once in Timothy. But Paul makes this a big issue. Paul makes this *one* issue the center of the faith. If you deny this, you are denying everything. If you deny that all will be raised, then you

---

Timothy 2:18. Someone must have claimed that this is already the age of fulfillment. Then the center of Paul's argument would be verse 6b ("some are dead") and his point would be the incompleteness of salvation in the present eon, and the need for a still unrealized hope. Should this alternative view of the Corinthian challenge be correct, it would make no change in our reading of what the resurrection tradition was, but it would change the weight of the solidarity argument.

deny Christ's rising, and therefore your faith is vain and you are still in your sins. Any little issue may become a test for the whole thing. We shall see this way of reasoning at work in other places as well. At any one point—a minor point in terms of logical priority, perhaps, an insignificant point in the minds of the person Paul argues with—the whole faith is at stake. If you deny this, then (at least by implication) you are denying everything.[3]

So Paul catches the Corinthians at the point where some of them were denying something. He makes an issue of it because it reflects the linkage of our thought with the tradition, and specifically with the reference of resurrection to us, the centrality of the resurrection as the point from which we must reason. We reason from this point especially because Christ is representative of us, because in this solidarity Christ takes us with him. If he rises, we shall rise. If he conquers death, we shall conquer death. If he did not rise, we cannot conquer death either. This reasoning by solidarity that Paul brought to the early tradition is now a new part of the tradition.

Summary

We began our introduction to the way Paul theologizes by looking at 1 Corinthians 15 and observing the interrelation of tradition and innovation. Paul makes very clear that he is appealing to what he had preached before. His fresh and contemporary argument concerning the problems the Corinthians put before him is derived from the tradition. He cites the tradition in such a faithful form that we can sometimes discern the literary form it had when he learned it. Yet, at the same time, he makes an application that is new to his readers. That is why he had to give it to them. It was not self-evident to them, nor to the people against whom he argued, that the conclusion he drew would follow from the tradition. He built a bridge from the tradition to their question in a fresh way that involved original argument. This argument, we observed, makes one special assumption, what, for want of a better label, we can call "the logic of solidarity." Paul assumes that what we say about Christ must in some sense be true about us, in such a way that, if certain people at Corinth doubted the resurrection of all human-

3. A sample parallel to this would be the issue of baptism in the sixteenth century. Baptism is not crucially important if you look only at the question of this practice versus that practice and various meanings that can be given to it. But the people who let themselves be called "Anabaptists," and let themselves be put to death for the sake of baptism, saw that in their situation it was representative of a much bigger issue. It represented the whole issue of what it means to be Christian. It represented the whole question of the nature of the church, and so they let the renewal of the church and their own faithfulness come to bear on just one breaking point, namely whether you baptize babies.

ity, by that denial they doubted by implication the resurrection of Christ. This follows if and only if there is some kind of solidarity linking the risen Christ with our resurrection, or linking us with him. Fuller analysis might well identify other such assumptions.

We went on to observe some other things about the way Paul's argument proceeded. We noted his use of the Old Testament, not by quoting a proof text but by picking up the Old Testament the image of Adam. In this image there is already something of the same kind of solidarity. In some sense, the sin of Adam stands for the sin of all humans, and the death of Adam stands for the death of all humans. This is thus parallel to what Paul says about Christ in his solidarity with believers.

Another observation we made was that an issue that might not have seemed crucial for everyone, and perhaps did not seem important to believers at Corinth—they probably did not think their faith was vain—became very important for Paul. He said, "On this one issue the whole meaning of your faith hinges. If you don't take Christ seriously for this issue, then the whole thing collapses."

1 Corinthians 12

Now we turn to another place in the same letter where Paul speaks, this time not to substance but to form. Here he does not write about a particular doctrine but rather gives instructions about how the church ought to operate, how to think together, what the church does about issues, and how the church proceeds in dealing with challenges. First Corinthians 12 has many other things to say, but we shall look especially at its first verses for what they say about theologizing (1 Corinthians 12:2ff.):

> "You know that when you were heathen, you were led astray to dumb idols, however you may have been moved." ["Any old way," we'd say in American English.] "Therefore, I want you to understand that no one speaking by the spirit of God ever says 'Jesus be cursed!' and no one can say 'Jesus is Lord' except by the Holy Spirit."

The key to Paul's argument lies in the contrast implicit in the statement of the second verse. Such a thing as *spirit* works among the heathen. There is ecstasy in which people are the mouthpiece of a divine oracle, of a god, or a spirit, or a demon. The oracles in Hellenistic temple worship are a reality in which, through the priest or some other technique, people believe a god has spoken to them and revealed his or her will. When you were heathen, Paul says, there was this kind of spirit-leading, but it was erratic. It was irregular. It was not rational. It went any which way. The idols themselves were dumb. There was no clear meaning or clear coherence, and it arbitrarily led you. It went in any direction, "however you may have been moved." That irresponsible, incalculable, unmeasurable, arbitrary character of pagan spiritualism is set up in contrast with verse 3: "no one speaking by the Spirit of God ever says 'Jesus be cursed' and no one can say 'Jesus is Lord' except by the Holy Spirit." There is a criterion for observing the working of the specific Spirit by whom the Christians are to be moved. This is the contrast: pagans are moved any old way by spirits, but Christians are moved in certain ways by the Holy Spirit. There must be a set of guidelines. Spirit-working is not arbitrary as it is in paganism. It is not self-authenticating. It has a standard. It has a particular character. That character has criteria by which we can measure it.

Let us stop to notice something that Paul did not need to say, but nevertheless needs to be said now. Paul expects the Corinthians to expect workings of the Holy Spirit in their community. He does not assume they have a closed canon, that they have all the Scripture and all the truth they need, that all they have to do is to spell it out to deduce from it. No, they expect revelation. Paul reckons with the possibility that the Spirit will speak, lead, reveal. But let it be consistent. Let it be subject to standards.

At the other end of the passage—basically a three-chapter unit from 12 through 14—is another statement that has the same kind of implications. We read in 14:29: "Let two or three prophets speak and let the others weigh what is said." There is a weighing process, an evaluation process, when the Spirit speaks through the prophets. What is the center of this weighing process? It is the confession that Jesus is Lord. If the Spirit makes somebody say something compatible with "Jesus is Lord," then it is the Holy Spirit. And if it is to the contrary, then this is not the Spirit of God.

We may conjecture about the actual social context of this passage. The Christians to whom Paul wrote were not yet subject to the most severe persecution about which we can read later, toward the end of Paul's ministry, but it is likely that there was some kind of local persecution. Persons coming under testing, whether from the government or from some other source, were asked to disavow their faith. Of course, the natural way to do this would have been simply to ask them to counteract the Christian confession by saying something like this formula, "Jesus is cursed." This would prove to the police that they were not Christian. Now, Jesus had told the disciples—we have the report in Matthew 10:19–20—that they should not do any advance thinking about how they would face persecution. When they were hauled before the courts, the Spirit would tell them what to say. It is not certain, but it is a likely conjecture, that there were people who let themselves be pushed away by the persecution. Then they would come back to the church. The church would ask, "Why did you do that?" They said, "The

Spirit told me. Jesus promised that we would have the Spirit; here I was in a tight spot and this is what it came to me to say." Paul responds "If that is what you said, it wasn't that Spirit. There is, after all, a set of standards by which you can tell whether it is the Spirit of God or some other. The Spirit of God does not lead one to deny the faith."

How then can we imagine the process of testing going on as Paul asks for it in Corinthians? Especially in Corinth there must have been a great degree of freedom for many ways of speaking, many patterns of formulation, many kinds of language, many forms of expression—some rational, some more irrational, some prose and some poetic. But there was constant vigilance over this process to determine whether it fit with the affirmation that Christ is Lord. That means there is already functioning here something like a creed. A very brief creed, but a very clear one. So we have learned something about the theological process, not about truth versus falsehood but about how the church is supposed to think. We are supposed to think in the expectation that the Spirit will speak, in the confidence that the Spirit will speak freely and relevantly to a situation. But the Spirit will not say anything that does not fit with Jesus. Now, this may seem self-evident, or perhaps it seems merely semantic, but we shall see as we continue through the field of theology how often people had a very different notion of what it means to be thinking straight. Often people did not assume, for instance, that the Spirit would use new formulations. They did not assume that the Spirit was still active. Or, on the other hand, many assumed that the Spirit speaks, but not that such revelatory experience is subject to any kind of judgment. So the combination of expecting Spirit-speaking *and* a clear standard of judgment is not so self-evident a thing as one might think at first, when we see it so simply said.[4]

Galatians

Now we move to another place where Paul is at work. The letter to the Galatians responds to certain things Paul heard had been happening in a set of churches, but there is not nearly the variety of topics as in 1 Corinthians. The topics in Galatians are not immediately as practical. Here it is more a matter of the theological or doctrinal understanding of the church, especially the understanding of the place of good works and the place of the Old Testament law in salvation.

Again this is a problem that *comes* to Paul. Paul does not tell these people their problem. It comes to him out of their situation. He responds to an issue brought to him. Because of the knowledge he has of

4. That prophetic utterance needs testing was also said in the Old Testament in Deuteronomy 13, 18:15–22, and Jeremiah 26–29.

the problem they have, he can provide the background he does for answering it.

Traditionally we approach the letters of Paul with the idea that each has a doctrinal part and a practical part. The doctrinal part is the first chapters and the practical part is the last chapters. In Romans, the division comes at chapter 12. In Ephesians it comes at chapter 4 or 5. First Paul talks about God and important things, then he gets around to practical details. This division does not belong if we want properly to understand any of these letters; the beginning is always the preparation for what follows. The particular beginning is a preparation for a particular issue that will follow. What he says about the nature of faith in the beginning of Galatians is the background for speaking to how the Christians in Galatia should deal with ethical problems, with community problems, with Jew-Gentile problems in their community.

Once again, this letter works with the appeal to "what you heard before":

> I am astonished that you are so quickly deserting him who called you in the grace of Christ and turning to a different Gospel—not that there is another Gospel, but there are some who trouble you and want to pervert the Gospel. . . . But even if we, or an angel from heaven, should preach to you a Gospel contrary to that which we preached to you, let him be accursed. . . . If anyone is preaching to you a Gospel contrary to that which you received, let him be accursed (Gal. 1:6–9).

As in Corinthians, Paul makes a very "conservative" appeal to tradition. "You received something. You received it from me. All I am doing is calling you to be faithful to what you received." Again in 3:1 is the appeal to what went before, with a closer pointer to the alternative, to the question: "Who has bewitched you, before whose eyes Jesus Christ was publicly portrayed as crucified?" What does it mean to say that before their eyes Christ was publicly portrayed as crucified? It probably means Paul's preaching. He is saying: "I made it dramatic before you. I painted for you a verbal picture." (Maybe he even had a chalkboard or flannelgraph.) "I made dramatically visible to you what the crucifixion of Christ meant, and now you are being led astray; you are being bewitched."

Paul follows in 3:2, "Did you receive the Spirit by works of the law, or by hearing with faith? Having begun with the Spirit, are you now ending with the flesh?" In these next verses the appeal is not only to the tradition of which he had talked but to the fact that they had received it. They accepted the tradition. They received the message. They received the Spirit. Paul calls them back to faithfulness to their own beginning.

Any issue can become a test for the whole faith. Whatever the issue is, it is their problem that matters most. Paul deals with the present issue as though they were in danger of losing the whole faith. He does not tell them that they are all right in general but have one problem. No, he warns them that they are near to making a shipwreck of their faith. They may be believing something that is not the gospel at all.

In this particular case other teachers were on the other side of the issue. Thus, Paul makes an issue of his status as a teacher. He does this especially in the last half of the first chapter and in the second chapter when he tells the story of his own call in order to accredit himself. "The gospel which was preached by me is not man's gospel. For I did not receive it from man, nor was I taught it, but it came through a revelation of Jesus Christ" (Gal. 1:11b–12). All through the book we find other places where he makes the point that the message is *his own*. We read of "the gospel that was preached by me," or of "the gospel to the uncircumcised," as if it were a specific aspect of the message that was his personal business to take to the Gentiles. Yet all the way through this he still claims that it is the same faith as that of the other apostles, that the other apostles recognized him, accepted him, and gave one another the hand of fellowship. Although he received the directive from Christ, it is the same message as that of "two who were before me."[5]

As before, this argument finds its rootage in history. This is especially clear in chapter 3 with its extensive reference to Abraham, beginning with verse 6: "Abraham 'believed God and it was reckoned him as righteousness.'" This quotation is from the story of Abraham's acceptance of the covenant. Abraham was, of course, before Moses. Therefore the promise of grace is prior to and independent of the law. Now we begin to see the problem. The Galatians are working at the problem of the Jewish heritage and its laws and whether these laws are binding on all Christians, including the Gentiles. They make their case by claiming that because Jesus was the fulfiller of the law, therefore all Christians should fulfill the law. Paul reaches back into that same heritage, but reaches back further, to see something about Abraham that moves beyond the authority of the law. Abraham was acceptable before God because he believed when there was not yet the Mosaic law. Thus, believing is prior to law, independent of it in its validity.

We see another aspect of the way Paul works in his constant reference to the Jesus story—especially clear in Galatians 4:4–7:

> When the time had fully come [here is our *kerygma* theme again: fullness of time; this is the accepted age], God sent forth his Son, born of

5. Editorial note: "The two who were before me" is not a direct citation. Yoder's apparent reference is Galatians 1:17–18, where Paul insists that he did not "go up to Jerusalem to those who were apostles before me, but . . . went away into Arabia; and again . . . returned to Damascus. Then after three years I went up to Jerusalem to visit Cephas. . . . But I saw none of the other apostles except James the Lord's brother."

> woman, born under the law [strong emphasis on his humanity again], to redeem those who were under the law, so that we might receive adoption as sons. And because you are sons, God has sent the Spirit of his Son into our hearts, crying, "Abba! Father!" So through God you are no longer a slave but a son, and if a son then an heir.

Sonship is the gift that was brought to us by the Son. Here the identity of Jesus with humanity is centered in his birth. "God sent forth his Son, born of a woman, born under the law." This was not in 1 Corinthians 15. There the identity of Jesus with humanity was simply affirmed or presupposed. Paul reasoned with the logic of "solidarity"; it was the unspoken assumption that worked in his argument. Here, on the other hand, it is formally affirmed. The birth of this man—born of woman, born under the law, born within the conditions of human existence, is what qualified him to do this for us, who are under the law. Solidarity is not just an assumption; it is an affirmation, an argument. It is the theme being demonstrated. It is something Jesus did. It is (we might paraphrase) the positive meaning of *kenosis*.

There is a parallel here to one of the passages on which we worked before. Philippians 2 described the condescension of Christ as his willingness to be servant: his taking on himself the form of a servant, his obedience, his not grasping at independence or equality with God. Here again the place that the Son takes when he identifies with humanity, when he is born of woman, is a place under the law, a place of subjection. Thus we see in Paul's reasoning process similarities and differences with the earliest traditions, similarities in going back to the Jesus story, differences in what about the Jesus story applies. Here there is actually no reference to either the death or the resurrection, only the birth. But the effect of the birth was to free those who were under the law, to create identification with us and then take us in that identification with him in his freedom. So that we are now adopted, we are made sons as he was Son.

In chapter 6 of the Galatians there is still another kind of argument. Paul still works against the same adversary but he uses a different way of making the point:

> It is those who want to make a good showing in the flesh that would compel you to be circumcised, and only in order that they may not be persecuted for the cross of Christ. For even those who receive circumcision do not themselves keep the law, but they desire to have you circumcised that they may glory in your flesh. But far be it from me to glory except in the cross of our Lord Jesus Christ, by which the world has been crucified to me, and I to the world (Gal. 6:12–14).

That is not quite the end of the argument, but it is enough to identify the way Paul argues. Again it is different. Here there is no reference to the birth, or to the resurrection, but there is reference to the cross. The cross is spoken of, not as simply an event in the biography of Jesus or the prerequisite for a resurrection: the cross in itself is of significance. This is the first time we have found that in the passages with which we have been dealing. But what is the significance of the cross? It is not said here that he died "for our sins." "The cross" rather denotes a stance in the world, in line with "subjection" in Philippians 2, or "being under the law" in Galatians 4. The cross is the way the world and I have become dead to each other. The death of Christ is the model for something that has happened to me. "In the cross of our Lord Jesus Christ . . . the world has been crucified to me, and I to the world." It is a new kind of solidarity, not simply that we can talk about the resurrection of Christ as somehow drawing us along in a promised (future) resurrection. Here the death of Christ makes me in some sense already dead because I share in it. It somehow breaks the linkage of commitment between "the world" (whatever that is—of course, that would call for an extended definition) and me. The cross is now. It is not just an event in the past, but it is the model for the stance of the Christian in the world. It is therefore quite significant that in verse 12 the cross had another aspect of meaning—persecution. Those who want to compel you to be circumcised want to do so in order not to be persecuted for the cross of Christ. How how could that be? How could circumcision involve persecution?

This is very early. This is a time when there is not yet a great amount of governmental persecution. But there is persecution of the church, as mixed Gentile-and-Jewish, by the most severe Jews. Of course, that is the only kind of persecution circumcision would help anybody avoid, by living up to the Jewish rules so that the other Jews would not be offended by a church that is partly Jewish but also partly Gentile. The people who thus insist on living up to those Jewish rules are the ones who are not willing to accept the reproach of other Jews for the sake of their fellowship with Gentiles. The cross of Christ is the reason for their fellowship with Gentiles.

We are very far from the cross of Christ just being an event of the past, or the prerequisite of resurrection, or Jesus' answer to the question of his mission. The cross is now our whole attitude in the world. It is the fact that Jew and Gentile relate as sisters and brothers; that is what they would have been persecuted for. It is the fact that I have given up boasting. I have nothing to glory about. So again, it is the concept of solidarity. But here it is the individual's solidarity. In chapter 4 it was humanity's solidarity. Christ became a man under the law by being born of a woman in order to take the Christians all along with him into Sonship. Here it is the other way around. I share in his crucifixion. In chapter 4, the solidarity was that he took the initiative. In chapter 6, the solidarity is my response—I accept for me the meaning of the cross, and that does something to that about which I boast. That does something about persecution.

Summary

We can observe from these passages from the major epistles Paul's enormous liberty in finding many ways to make the connection between Jesus and me, or Jesus and us as a people. To every question, somehow, a line can be drawn from Jesus. It is drawn especially from his cross and his resurrection, although if we went through the whole body of New Testament literature, we would of course find lines that are drawn to his earthly career as well. This is very far from a rigid doctrinal approach, having only one right way to deal with every question, only one right answer, and having them all fit together in the system. But it is an attitude, a "feel," as to how you work when you are in the church. Whatever your question is, you can somehow draw a line from Jesus to there, and thereby throw light on your question. It may well be done in different ways with different kinds of reasoning, but always something of this being involved in the person of Jesus—something of the solidarity of Christ with all people.

1 Timothy

Now we move to the other end of the Pauline literature and to 1 Timothy. Many critical scholars think 1 Timothy to be so late that Paul could not have written it. It is not our concern to speak to that kind of question. Clearly, this text is different in literary style as well as in the kind of themes with which it deals. Again, we shall watch the thought process going on here. At the end of 1 Timothy 3, there is another quotation of some kind of poem or hymn. In the Revised Standard Version it is actually set in verse form, though there are other translations that do not consider it verse; at least it is visible that it is a somewhat different literary form.

Verse 16 begins: "Great indeed, we confess, is the mystery of our religion." This phrase is already a strong windup, a visible flag. With it, Paul tells us, "There's a quotation coming; this is going to be a summary statement." "The mystery of our religion" is a title, perhaps, for this hymn, or at least it is a warning that a statement in a nutshell is coming. Here a central theme is going to be affirmed. Then we have this statement of six lines:

> He was manifested in the flesh,
> vindicated in the Spirit,
>   seen by angels,

preached among the nations,
believed on in the world,
  taken up in glory (1 Tim. 3:16b).

In one sense, this is two groups of three lines. In another sense, it is three groups of two lines. Each group of two lines is a polarity, a duality of two realms. Flesh and spirit, angels and nations, world and glory. That duality, I think we would have to assume on literary grounds, is the same duality coming back in three shapes. We have on one side flesh, nations, world, and on the other side of the duality, Spirit, angels, and glory. This is a difference of lines and is supposed to represent two levels—the back and forth of these two—down-up, up-down, down-up. This duality is stated in the imagery not of time but of space.

Before, the confessions with which we dealt were narratives. They told us a story. They looked back to the ancient expectations and said that this is the awaited age. "This Jesus did mighty works, then you killed him, then God raised him, then he appeared, then he was exalted, and we look forward to his coming." That was a temporal line. The drama of salvation and the majesty of the confession was that this is the story through which we move. "Now we are in the age of the Spirit, when the Spirit has been poured out. You see these signs and the Spirit is a promise to you; we are witnesses, you repent, you will receive the Spirit, you will do mighty works, and then he will come." The message of the apostles in the earliest form placed the listener and the speaker in the contest of God working in time.

This hymn uses a different framework for making its confession—not time but space. Down and up. The "mystery of religion," the work of God, is the interrelation of these two realms. He was manifested in the flesh, that is, he broke into our realm. He was vindicated in the Spirit—that is the realm on which it has its validity. "He was seen by the angels and preached to the nations"—the element of appearance, or visibility, revelation, is on both levels. He was believed on in the world and taken up into glory.

This way of describing the work of Christ—that he relates to two realms, the transcendent and the imminent, the Spirit realm and the flesh realm, and takes us up into glory by manifesting in the flesh what is vindicated in the Spirit—reflects a particular view of the human situation different from that of the earliest preaching. It is different because the gospel is now working in the Hellenistic world. It is working among people who do not have, like the Jews, a strong sense of history. They do not look back, like the Jews, to what God did with our father Abraham, and what God did with our father Moses, and David, and what he promised to do with another David or with another "prophet." The Jews had that sense of God working through history, and the events of Jesus were the culmination of their history. But the Hellenistic religious-type person looked at the whole problem of the world differently. His or her concern was with the alienation of these two realms—the realm of spiritual reality "out there" somewhere and this fleshly existence in which we are stuck, the realm of ultimate reality, of the ideal, and this down-to-earth ordinary reality in which we are taken captive.

What is wrong with humanity is not so much sin that will be judged by God or captivity from which God will bring us back into our land. What is wrong with humanity is the alienation of these two levels, between what I really am and what I ought to be. The self that I find here, existing with all my problems, I know is not my real self, not my best self. The *word* self, of course, is modern language, but Hellenistic people sensed something of this kind of alienation between *realms*. On the one hand is the realm of the real, spiritual, and the ideal, while on the other hand is this ambiguous, shadowy, dirty, confused, unreliable, and changing world in which we live most of the time. Christ overcomes the alienation between those two realms; he manifests the reality of the Spirit and the angels in glory in the world of the nations and of the flesh.

And yet, in all of the variety of form, in the face of the fact that this language is very different from the language we had before—not only in the words but also in the framework of the language and the imagery behind it—it still has much in common with what went before. It is still all about Jesus. It is not a discussion of creation. It is not a discussion of the religious individual. It is not a discussion of the nature of the political structure. It is what happened in and to Jesus.

There is a second point in this passage. God did it. It is the deed of God. All the verbs are active. Manifested. Vindicated. Seen. Preached. Believed. Taken up. This is the working of God in this Jesus.

We are not trying to be thorough in this kind of treatment. It should suffice to pick up samples where we see thought processes operating. Now that we have observed this duality of realms or worlds operating, we can go back into the earlier writings and see it again perhaps more clearly.

2 Corinthians 5

Second Corinthians chapter 5 is a very well-known passage, speaking of God being in Christ, reconciling the world to himself, giving to us the message of reconciliation. Here the key thought is another way of unfolding the solidarity concept. Verse 15 is a very complex sentence but makes all the more clear the character of exchange: Christ in our place and we in his. "He died for all, that those who live might live no longer for themselves but for him who for their sake died and was raised." If you try to diagram that as a grammatical construction, you will go around in circles. But that is part of the point. The attention moves back and forth from him to us, to him from us, he for us, we for him. This is what it means. He died that we might share that death with him, and so live for him who shared our life and our death. There is a trading of place or identification between Christ and humankind, in both his life and his death. This is thus parallel to Galatians 6: in that Christ died, I am dead to the world. But Paul goes beyond Galatians and says also that in this life we live for Christ. We share in both his dying and his life. If you are on your toes, you, of course, have remembered that this is also in Romans 6 and Romans 8; we share in both his dying and his rising. It is also in Colossians 2 and 3. Death and rising is the standard pattern for the way a Christian has to understand herself or himself.

There has been a shift in the *meaning* of death and resurrection from Acts 2 to where we are now. When Peter preached, there was a clear antithesis between death and resurrection, but it was a narrative antithesis, two different actors. "You killed him and God raised him." That is a clear polarization. In both cases, Jesus is passive: *you* killed him, *God* raised him. The polarization between these two events is the center of the preaching.

Now Paul is no longer preaching to the Jews who killed him. He is no longer in that context of Jerusalem and the immediate generation of the people who were around at the time of Jesus' death and resurrection. Paul is not interested in the kind of "hold" Peter had on his listeners as the ones who were there when Jesus was crucified. He keeps, however, the duality of death and resurrection. He makes of it a pattern of life and death in which the Christian is already living. The Christian is someone who in some sense is dead with Christ, and in some sense is living again with Christ. The solidarity of Christ with humankind is a new pattern of total understanding of what it means to be human, what it means to be a person as a Christian. A Christian is someone who sees, cast over her or his life, the light of this two-step work of God. Jesus died. Jesus rose. We share in both of these. That is what it means to be *in Christ*. The concept of solidarity, which we first observed as a logical assumption, as a presupposition which was necessary to make the argument work in 1 Corinthians 15, now provides the whole pattern of Paul's thought about the way Christ is relevant to us.

This has been a very rapid sampling. We have not looked long at any passage. We have only looked for what we were looking for. We could have found other things if we would have looked longer, but we have been asking for a vision of the variety in the way Paul works, the way that he theologizes. What have we now observed?

- There is no one clear body of doctrine in the sense that people develop later. When we read the great systematic theologies of the Middle Ages, or of the eighteenth and nineteenth centuries, we shall see an overriding concern to use the same logic all the time, to use the same definition of terms all the time, and to have each statement fit in with every other statement. Integrity in a system of thought is determined by logical coherence and consistency. We do not find that in Paul. We find an enormous variety, a very creative flexibility. Whatever question comes to him from Corinth, from the Galatians, or from the situation of Timothy, he can speak to from Jesus. But every time it is different. Sometimes it is by telling the whole story. Sometimes it is by emphasis on the cross with no reference to the resurrection. Sometimes it is the other way around. Sometimes it is by talking about the relation of cross and resurrection. If we dug longer, we would see still other ways. There is always a reference to the story, but always differently. Romans 1 accentuates that he was the Son of God, as that fits with what comes next. Galatians 4 emphasizes that he was son of woman, that is, fully human, because that fits with what comes next.
- There are times when Paul quotes Jesus. We have not noticed much of that, but he makes the point in certain cases that "this is a word of the Lord." First Corinthians 7, for instance, is a passage that deals with several different issues of marriage and social status. In 7:10 we find, "To the married I give charge, not I but the Lord, that the wife should not separate from her husband." Verse 25 of the same chapter reads, "Now concerning the unmarried, I have no command of the Lord, but I give my opinion as one who by the Lord's mercy is trustworthy." Now what does it mean that "here I have a word of the Lord and there I do not"?

  Some have taken it as a measure of Paul's subjective certainty. At one point he is very sure of himself and at another he only thinks himself worthy of respect. It is not that! Some think it is a matter of whether he had had any visions on the subject, or whether he had heard a voice in the night, so that he was very sure on this one and not that one. That is not the point either.

  The point is much simpler: the church had gathered quotations from Jesus. When Paul knew of a quotation from Jesus he used it and said, "This is a quotation from Jesus. This is a word from the Lord." And in another place where he had no quotation, he said, "I do not have a quotation, but you will still have to listen to me because I am an apostle." He is not qualifying his authority, he is rather making the careful difference between the issues on which he has a quote from the lips of Jesus as the church had preserved those, and those on which he does not have quotations. That is one more of the ways to make the link with Jesus—to remember something he said. The church was careful about that. That is why we have so many Gospels.

- In Philippians 2 the way to make the link with Jesus was reference to the cross as an example of submission. That mattered especially because the people in Philippi ought to be more subject one to another in order to get along together better. In Galatians 6 it was the cross as death to pride. The Galatians ought to learn about that because they were proud about keeping the law. In 1 Corinthians 1, at which we have not looked, is reference to the cross as alternative to human wisdom and power. The cross is a stumbling block to the Jews but it is the power of God, foolish to the Gentiles but the wisdom of God. The cross is a standard of value counter to human standards. 1 Corinthians 15, where we started the story, details the pattern of resurrection as it speaks to our resurrection. Later in the same chapter, a passage about which we did not speak, it is the exaltation of Christ as he reigns until his enemies are all defeated. In 1 Thessalonians the reference is to the predicted return.

So in this process of linking the story, what some people call the *kerygma,* to the present question, there are many kinds of links—or we could call them types of logic, different ways of making the connection between the story and us.

- There is the logic of solidarity. We found it in many places, sometimes just as a logical assumption and sometimes as a statement. The the new Adam, the new man, living in me. Some texts step beyond that, exchanging solidarities—two Adams, old Adam and new Adam. He becomes sin for us and we become righteousness in him. He dies for us so that we live in him: Sonship and new life. His obedience and our obedience. The humanity of Jesus is, of course, essential, for that kind of taking each other's place to be meaningful.
- Another part of the logic is spelling out the first point of the *'kerygma':* fulfillment. "This is the awaited age," Peter said. How does Paul do this? By making all kinds of links between the Old Testament and the present—links that he makes in different ways, with different types of arguments. In 1 Corinthians 15 he did not quote the Old Testament, really, but he used the imagery of the Old Testament. There are other times that he makes very precise use of a particular text. In Galatians 3:16, for instance, he uses a proof text in the narrow sense: "The promises were made to Abraham and to his offspring. It does not say, 'And to offsprings,' refer-

ring to many; but, referring to one, 'And to your offspring,' which is Christ."[6]

Thus Paul makes a very careful proof text point on the basis of the fact that in Genesis 12:7 the promise was made to the seed of Abraham in the singular, so it must mean Christ instead of all the Jewish people. But back in Genesis 22:17 and 26:4 you find that the promise was that the seed is going to be "as numerous as the stars in the heavens," so the grammatical singular is not meant to be nonplural in the original. It is a singular that is collective; it talks about a multitude. Paul is not using the kind of exegetical method that one learns to use in seminary in which you check whether a word is in the singular or plural, not only grammatically but also in the context whether its meaning is singular or collective. Some other time we should ask how Paul could get away with that kind of exegesis if we cannot! But now we are just observing the freedom with which he picks up the Old Testament and says, "That is our book; it speaks to our point."

- There are still other ways to argue the fulfillment point. People of faith are the sons of Abraham in Galatians 3:6–9. This is especially significant because Paul probably didn't make it up. In Matthew 3:8, John the Baptist talks to the Jews who came to challenge his message. John says, "Who told you *you* are sons of Abraham? God can make sons of Abraham out of these stones." "Son of Abraham" is one who believes. In John 8:31ff., Jesus talks this way to the Jews who challenged his authority. Jesus tells them that they are not sons of Abraham but sons of the devil. Sons of Abraham are those who believe. So when Paul says the same thing here—sons of Abraham are the sons of faith—he picks up a tradition that has been there for some time. The church from the very beginning had the problem of dealing with the Jews who used the Old Testament to defend their non-Christian Jewishness. The Christians took the radical response of saying, "Truly to be the sons of Abraham is to have the kind of faith that Abraham had," and it is quite significant that John the Baptist, and then Jesus, and then Paul all use the same argument. So it must have been a patterned approach.
- We could look back from here to a strand of Matthew with which you are probably familiar. Very often we find: "This happened that it might be fulfilled which was said by the prophet . . ." Then is a reference to some prophetic text that corresponds to something Jesus

6. Editorial note: In Galatians 3:16 the RSV translates the Greek word *sperma,* or seed, as "offspring" in the singular and "offsprings" in the plural. The collective descendants, children, offspring, or posterity of an individual ancestor, usually Abraham, is the conventional, if figurative, use of the word *sperma* in the Septuagint.

had just done. Often, if you go back to the original, it does not look like what Jesus has just done, except in some superficial, verbal sense. It would be an excellent supplementary exercise to take all the "fulfillment" quotes of Matthew, and then review the original text in the original setting to ask what it must have meant then.

Again, we have the problem of the way the New Testament uses the Old Testament in this kind of allusion or citation. It is not a model as scientific, linguistic exegesis, but it is our model in the claim to continuity! Matthew implies, "That is our book so we can always use it to describe our story." Paul is saying this too, and it is the basic thing we must say with them. (Incidentally, this is also a warning against literalism in the interpretation of biblical texts.) The fulfillment of the promise with which the *kerygma* claim begins is so overwhelming that we can find that promise anywhere back there. The confession of faith about the history of the Jews is point one in the story. Sometimes we use Old Testament texts; sometimes we bend Old Testament texts. Sometimes you use Old Testament concepts or imagery, like Adam, but the church is always free to reach back into the Old Testament and say, "That is our story; that is the Jesus story getting ready back there," and this is part of the logic with which the church is always able to work.[7]

7. *Composite quotations.* It happens frequently, and at important places in the Gospel narrative, that a quotation or allusion from the Old Testament conflates two texts rather than quoting one literally. It *might* be that the patterns of oral/aural memory and recitation favored such telescoping, but it is also possible that the doubling up of quotations was intentional, following the "two witnesses" rule of Deuteronomy 19:15. We do know that "testimonies" was the term used then to express the New Testament claim to be fulfilling the promises of the Old Testament.

New Testament passage	Old Testament passages
1. The Mission of John. Mark 1:2–3	Exod. 23:20; Isa. 40:3–4
2. Birth in Bethlehem. Matt. 2:6	Mic. 5:2; 2 Sam. 5:2
3. Triumphal Entry. Matt. 21:5	Zech. 9:9; Isa. 42:11
4. Sonship at Baptism. Mark 1:11	Ps. 2:7; Isa. 42:1, 44:2; Gen. 22:2
5. Sonship at Transfiguration. Mk. 9:7, Matt. 17:5	Deut. 18:15; Ps. 2:7
6. Cleansing Temple. Mk. 11:17 and par.	Isa. 56:7; Jer. 7:11
7. Judas' Betrayal. Mk. 27:10	Zech. 11:12ff.; Jer. 27:7; Exod. 9:12 or 37:20
8. Promise of Parousia. Mk. 14:62 and par.	Ps. 110:1; Dan. 7:13
9. Signs of Parousia. Matt. 24:30b and Rev. 1:7	Zech. 12:10ff.; Dan. 7:13
10. Imminence of Parousia. Heb. 10:37ff.	Isa. 26:10; Hab. 2:3f.
11. Hardening of Israel. Rom. 11:8ff.	Deut. 29:4; Isa. 29:10; Ps. 69:22ff.
12. Resurrection Victory. 1 Cor. 15:54ff.	Isa. 25:8; Hos. 13:15

See Jindrik Manek, "Composite Quotations in the New Testament and Their Purpose," *Communio Viatorum* 12 (1970): 181–188.

5

The Other "Theologians": The Author of Hebrews, and John

The Letter to the Hebrews

There is a sense in which we could say that the Epistle to the Hebrews is the very first treatise on systematic theology. It seems not to have been written, as far as we can tell, to speak to one particular crisis or to answer a particular question. In most of Paul's writings we can figure out quite clearly just why it is that he wrote a particular text precisely to the Corinthians and why it is that he uses a particular argument in that particular letter. There is none of that in the letter to the Hebrews. We don't even know who "the Hebrews," the exact addressees, are, where they live, and what their problems are.

We are told that their faith is being tested by a degree of suffering, so that there is a danger that they might fall away, but we perceive less of the character of that suffering than in the epistles of James and Peter. The danger of denying the faith is a permanent aspect of the believers' condition, not a specific challenge that would help us date or place the letter, as being tied either to a given readership or to a given occasion for writing. This makes it more a treatise of systematic thought than an epistle, although in a strict literary sense it is put together like a letter, yet it tests for systematic logic, for being consistent, for applying the same line of thought farther down the road that applies at the beginning. These are systematic theological concerns.

How does Hebrews deal with Christology? We find that Christology is the immediate theme with which the book begins. To paraphrase the first verses: "God spoke before in words and now he has spoken in His Son." This is a way of stating, in a very different literary form, the same thing stated elsewhere in other ways. The reference to the past, in Hebrews 1:1 is immediate: "In many and various ways God spoke of old . . ." always in words to the prophets. So the theme of fulfillment, "this is the awaited age," is here again. And how has God now spoken? In the Son. As we continue we shall find strong emphasis on the humanity of Jesus, on his suffering and his obedience as a man.

The unfolding of the fulfillment concept has all the meanings it usually has had, but here it is more than one theme among others. It becomes the topic of the book. This is a book about the sense in which the gospel is fulfillment, about the relationship between the covenants or the Testaments.

First of all, Hebrews affirms the continuity of what God has done in Jesus with what God was doing before. The Old Testament text is taken for granted. The imagery from the Old Testament, especially the priesthood and the sacrificial system, are taken for granted and used as the framework within which Hebrews makes its point.

The readers of this book are sophisticated Hellenists. They are people who appreciate good Greek writing. With the exception of a few verses at the beginning of Luke, this is the most polished, most Greek piece of writing in the New Testament as far as literary quality and style are concerned. It was written for people who were not simply immersed in the Old Testament but who were cultivated, contemporary thinkers. It is thus all the more striking that for them the Old Testament text, its authority and imagery, can be taken for granted.

In fact, the exegeses of the Old Testament texts that are quoted are generally more faithful to the original literal meanings of those texts than is the case with either Paul or Matthew. If you take these quotations seriously and go back to the original context from which they come, you will find that the author to the Hebrews reads the Old Testament with genuine literary perspective. He or she (some think the author may have been Priscilla) senses the unity of a text with its context. She or he watches the movement of the thought within the quoted passage. The author bases his or her own argument on the quoted text in a way that strikes us as genuine, as having really understood the original. This is not always the case with Paul and Matthew. Too, the quotations are longer. The author of Hebrews quotes passages and not just phrases.

So the first characteristic of the whole book of Hebrews is a proclamation of continuity. God has been working. What God has done in Christ is a part of what God has always been doing. That is the message we saw before, but Hebrews says it a different way.

The second characteristic is the contrast between the new and the old. Fulfillment is at the same time novelty. What was promised, once it has come, is different from what had been expected. The new covenant is not just a new edition of the old one; there is something novel in its fulfillment.

The old covenant provided for sacrifices over and over. Every day, every year, there were various prescribed ceremonies, but now something has happened *once for all* and there is an end to the repetition. This difference is argued in chapter 10 with its specific reference to the priesthood:

> We have been sanctified through the offering of the body of Jesus Christ once for all. And every priest stands daily at his service, offering repeatedly the same sacrifices, which can never take away sins. But when Christ had offered for all time a single sacrifice for sins, he sat down at the right hand of God, then to wait until his enemies should be made a stool for his feet (Heb. 10:10b–13).

This puts an end to the daily repetition of sacrifice. The last sacrifice is the same as all the others in that it is a sacrifice. It is part of a series. But the series stops here, and that makes a difference, bringing continuity and change at the same time. In 13:8 we read the phrase that has become very familiar in our piety and hymns: "Jesus Christ is the same yesterday and today and forever," but that does not mean no change. It means the change that took place at the point of incarnation stops the series. From now Jesus Christ is always the same as what he is there, rather than going round and round and constantly beginning new editions.

This affirmation of fulfillment, the same as the old and yet the end of the old, is much like what Paul said about "the works of law" in Galatians and Romans, but here the theme is priesthood, not the law. Here the author has an expository intention. He or she is not arguing with anybody. Paul was. Paul argued with the so-called "Judaizers," with the people whose particular understanding of the Mosaic law was such that they could not let the Gentiles in as full citizens in the church. Paul was polemic. This author is simply expository, simply using the twoness as part of an outline that makes the systematic theme appear. He or she is neither against anybody nor trying to save the church at this point, but is simply teaching us about the way Christ is at the same time new and old. Paul's argument was occasional. We always know he's writing to the Galatians for this reason and to the Romans for that reason. Hebrews is an essay that is written in order to make sense to any reader who reads carefully. Still, the same type of relationship between the two covenants is being stated.

In chapters 1 and 2 especially the title "Son" comes to have a fuller meaning than it had had before. Remember that the words "son of God" in the Old Testament were applied to angels, even to rebellious angels like Satan, or to the king in the Psalms, or, in the New Testament, to the Messiah in the temptation of Jesus. All of these are figures within history, humans or angels, not identified with God by "nature," but God's "sons" in the sense of dependence upon or subjection to God. Then in Romans 1:1–4 we noted that the creed that Paul quoted calls him "Son by declaration." Moreover, it almost seemed, in Peter's sermon in Acts 2 that God had elevated him *because* of his obedience. Here in Hebrews we have a stronger statement. Here the meaning of "Son" must be more than that:

> In these last days he has spoken to us by a Son whom he appointed the heir of all things, through whom also he created the world. He reflects the glory of God and bears the very stamp of his nature, upholding the universe by his word of power. . . . To what angel did God ever say, "Thou art my son . . . ?" Or again, "I will be to him a father, and he shall be to me a son"? . . . Of the Son he says, "Thy throne, O God, is for ever and ever" (Heb. 1:2–8a).

Throughout the first two chapters of Hebrews, the author develops a much higher concept of divine Sonship than is the case elsewhere. Whereas in the book of Job the sons of God were angels, here the Son of God is *more* than the angels. He is contrasted with the angels in two directions. On the one hand is identity with the Father—the word "Father" isn't used, but it is obvious the entire pattern of thought would fail to make sense if the author were not presupposing what Jesus said about God as Father. But then the Son also differs in being *human*—in being identified with humankind, in a way the angels are not:

> But we see Jesus, who for a little while was made lower than the angels, crowned with glory and honor because of the suffering of death. . . . For it was fitting that he, for whom and by whom all things exist, . . . should make the author of their salvation perfect through suffering. . . . Since therefore the children share in flesh and blood, he himself likewise participates of the same nature, that through death he might destroy him who has the power of death (Heb. 2:9–14).

The Son is thus different from the angels both in his identity with God and in his identity with humanity, neither of which the angels share.

Remember that a major part of the message of Philippians 2, found also in snippets and traces elsewhere, is the simple two-movement statement of humiliation and exaltation. This too is evident in Hebrews. It appears in 2:7 and 2:10. It comes back again in chapter 5:8–9, "Although he was a Son, he learned obedience through what he suffered; and being made perfect he became the source of eternal salvation to all who obey him." The descent and arising in the earliest preaching was meant quite humanly and concretely—"You killed him, God raised him." By the time it occurs in Paul's writings, it was already more than this; humiliation and resurrection are seen as ways of God's working. Hebrews unfolds this wider meaning.

The reign at the right hand arises from reference to Psalm 110. This does not mean intercession in the modern sense. As we think in modern terms of the Son being "at the right hand of the Father," in our hymnology for instance, it most often means that he is our "advocate," on our side, pleading our case with the judge. But the person at the right hand of the king is the prime minister. He does not whisper in the king's ear. He governs in the name of the king. This is the meaning that is most central in "sitting at the right hand" in the New Testament, not his being a friend of the believer but his being Lord over the powers of the world.

We find the same link between ethics and obedience we found elsewhere. Remember that the case Paul made to the people of Phillipi, which led to quoting the hymn, was that they needed to be motivated to make them more brotherly together. In Hebrews as well, we find the linkage between the work of Christ and Christian obedience. It is stated especially strikingly in the blessing of 13:20, "Now may the God of peace who brought again from the dead the Lord Jesus, . . . equip you with everything good that you may do his will." The resurrection works itself out in your obedience. This is parallel to things we found in Paul.

But there is one theme that is different from what we found in Paul. This is the clarity and consistency with which one image, one pattern, is worked out. The image is that of priesthood. Priesthood was a divine institution in the Old Testament. Christ is the fulfillment and the end of the priesthood. It is characteristic of a testament, a will, that if you make another one the first one is annulled. Thus Hebrews is using language that was derived from the social and organizational experience of the time, namely, the way one could make a will, and then make another will changing the first one. Making a contract and then writing another contract that changes the first—this language is used to describe the historical succession of God's works. This is another way of making the "new age" argument that there will be no more repetition. There was a testament, and now there is a new testament which dissolves the old. Each testament has its kind of priesthood.

What does a priest do? Through the sacrificial process he purifies for sin. It is significant that Hebrews contains no theoretical explanation of just how sacrifice purifies. That it does so simply is taken for granted. The heritage of sacrifice in the life of Israel is assumed; it is not argued, not explained, not apologized for, not defended. It is simply presupposed.

The priest is not a priest in order to sacrifice. Rather, it is because he is a priest that he can sacrifice. The status of priesthood is more than a job description. He is more than simply the person who carried through certain actions that have to be done because God prescribed them. Jesus is a better priest, and not simply because he is a better victim of immolation. With a traditional view of the atonement in mind, we might think of that as being the obvious thing. Before, the victim was always just an animal; now the victim is a man, not only a man, but this unique man of whom the book's first chapter had said that he is also somehow identical with God. But that is not the point that is being made in the argument about the suspension of the priesthood in the last half of the book. It is not that he is a better victim because he is a divine victim, but he is a better priest because it is himself that he gives. A priest gives something else. A priest kills the animal brought to him by the worshipper. The priest has to purify himself, but Jesus, as the last high priest, gives himself. That is what makes his sacrifice the end of sacrifice. The self that he gives is the self that became like us. Jesus' uniqueness and conclusiveness as priest is not that he lives up to the Old Testament doctrine of atonement, not that he makes up what was missing there by somehow being a little more pure, a little more powerful than the Old Testament priest, but rather that he adds to this priestly process the gift of self and his total humanity, his identification with humanity. He is more than an animal symbolically identified with forgiveness; he is really human and therefore really identified with forgiveness.

What is the victory of Christ in this context? We find a significant shift here. Of all the elements that belonged in the earlier *kerygma* message, the one not emphasized in Hebrews is the resurrection. It is present—for instance in the concluding benediction which we already noted—but it is not at the center because of the choice of image of priesthood as the theme. The real victory of Christ in the language of Hebrews seems to be more at the point of his obedience. In 2:9b he is "crowned with glory and honor because of the suffering of death, so that by the grace of God he might taste death for everyone," and in 2:14b, "he himself likewise partook of the same nature, that through death he might destroy him who has the power of death." Thus death is the victory. Death is not merely the way to victory; it is not the prerequisite to the victory; it is not the thing that people did to him and to which God reacted ("You killed him and then God raised him"). Now it is the suffering of death that is itself what he did. *It* is the victory. One could follow this theme throughout Hebrews. In suffering, in facing temptation, in being human, he saves us: "He learned obedience through what he suffered; and being made perfect he became the source of salvation" (5:8–9a). The victory of Christ is therefore not only at the point of resurrection and ascension. It is already part of the quality with which he accepts humiliation, with which he obeys and suffers. But his victory is not the same thing as moral purity. His faithfulness or obedience, his not sinning in the face of temptation, is not the same as the sinlessness of 2 Corinthians 5:21, "[God] made him to be sin who knew no sin." There it was somewhat a matter of status, but here it is a matter of actually facing temptation and the sufferings of his fate among humanity and continuing to be obedient. Again, this is much like Philippians 2:9—"*Therefore* God has highly exalted him"—Christ's exaltation is the response to his humiliation. It is God's seal on his faithfulness. That connection between his victory and his faithfulness is all the way through Hebrews.

We began our characterization of Hebrews by noting that the idea of fulfillment, an axiom and a way of reasoning within Paul's ministry and teaching, here becomes a theme in its own right. Now we can say the same about the "logic of solidarity." For Paul, solidarity was a pattern of thought, a self-evident postulate. In Hebrews, the divine Son deliberately set out to achieve solidarity, and he did so at the cost of suffering obedience. We are identified with him not because we choose to place our trust in him (as if our faith itself were what saves us), but because he chose to place himself at our mercy. His grace, power, and victory are consummated *in* his humanness, not despite it.

Johannine Christology

We now proceed, more briefly, to the third great theological mind in the New Testament. The Gospel of John begins with a preexistent divine entity called the "Word": "In the beginning was the Word, the Word was with God, and the Word was God. He was in the beginning with God; all things were made through him, and without him was not anything made that was made" (John 1:1–3).

Then the Word became flesh. What is this Word? We are face to face here with a characteristic of John's writing.[1] His writing uses Greek language and imagery. It makes far fewer references to Old Testament patterns, like sacrifice or priesthood, than Hebrews did. This "Word" (*Logos*) is used to say much more than a word in the grammatical sense. In Greek philosophy, "Word" is what we might call reason, something we might call the mind of God, the rationality of God that underlies the universe—there are many different sides of the meaning of the word "Word." It is neither "word" as a grammatical vehicle, nor "word" as a sound, but "Word" as meaningfulness. The *Logos* is an aspect of the divine being *as* meaningful, *as* communicating—"God as communicating."

Elsewhere, in John's epistles, is another favorite Greek philosophical term: *gnosis* or "wisdom." Thus, as Hebrews lives in the Old Testament world, John lives with the Hellenists, yet in the *use* of these terms John does not say what was typical of the day's usage. John says that the *Logos* was preexistent with the Father or with God. We observed before that the concept of "Son" came to reach beyond the earlier meaning of

1. We group John's Gospel with John's epistles for our purposes, without going into critical questions about precise dating and authorship and the like.

the "son" as a member of the family or as someone subject to the Father. "Son" becomes rather a bearer of the Father's authority. Similarly, John says of "*Logos*" more than it meant before. According to him, this Word, the rationality of the eternal divine mind, became flesh. That is not Greek. That is not typical of the way Greek philosophy would speculate about the divine mind or eternal divine rationality. It is not Jewish either for God's self or God's wisdom to become visible. The true God is invisible, and cannot be made into an idol or represented by a graven image. A Jew cannot say, "He became flesh." It would be especially unworthy of God, in the Jewish mind, to be visible.

But this view of the Word becoming flesh is not only a statement of the prologue to John's Gospel. It also becomes the test of faithfulness in the church. One of the questions on our preparation guide was to identify the adversaries or the dangers that any theology warns against. John says most clearly that he is warning against something, provides a criterion whereby his warning can be applied, and says what the warning is about. It is about the denial that the Word became flesh. In 1 John 4:1, John writes, "Do not believe every spirit, but test the spirits to see whether they are of God."

This sounds like 1 Corinthians 12, where Paul says that spiritual utterances are not self-authenticating. They must be tested. By what does one test them? By whether they say, "Christ is Lord." According to 1 John, one tests the spirits this way: "By this you know the spirit of God: every spirit which confesses that Jesus Christ has come in the flesh is of God, and every spirit which does not confess Jesus is not of God" (1 John 4:2–3a).

The concept of coming in the flesh is not just any old affirmation; it is a test statement and a key to faithfulness. It is also the center of our witness: "That which was from the beginning, which we have heard, which we have seen with our eyes, which we have looked upon and touched with our hands, . . . the life was made manifest and we saw it . . ."(1 John 1:1–2a). Grammatically, this is a complex way to begin a letter, yet the author says something simple: "We are the apostles, we are the witnesses to the making visible of God in our life." That is, the affirmation of incarnation is a statement on the authority and the message of the church, and thereby the test whereby you know whether it is correct or not.[2]

Once again, we find something similar to the "logic of solidarity." It is visibly present in the Gospel of John 15:4, "Abide in me and I in you." The same thing is said in 1 John 3:1–2 in the language of Sonship. Not only is Jesus the Son, but John says that we too are sons or children: "See what love the Father has given us, that we should be called chil-

2. Editorial note: The church is the community that bears witness to the incarnation of the Word. Its willingness to affirm the incarnation is the signal test of its authority.

dren of God; and so we are. The reason why the world does not know us is that it did not know him. Beloved, we are God's children now."[3] Thus the concept of being a part of what he is, or manifesting in our life his quality and his nature, is the "logic of solidarity" in 1 John. In fact it is still stronger: if we are in him and he is in us, then there is no room in us for sin. That is why the persistence of sin in the life of the church is a special problem in 1 John 2 and 3. Some sections of 1 John even give us the impression that there can be no sin at all.

As in Hebrews, the Son's identification with our flesh turns around in the form of our obedience.[4] As in Hebrews, the cross is now far more than being killed. It is already a part of the final victory. It can be called "exaltation" or "glorification."[5]

Summary

We have now concluded our survey of the three New Testament theologians, taken one by one. What does it mean for the church to have had these theologians serving at the end of the first generation or at the conclusion of the apostolic age? This review may provide a basis for moving on to try to understand what theology or theologizing should be doing later. We shall ask whether or how the church should keep doing what these apostolic theologians were doing when they started putting the message together in a way that made sense to them and to their age by rising above the particular crisis-related expressions of the first letters to a more systematic and coherent kind of overview. Now we return to compare and contrast them and then move from there to a summary statement on how the theologizing process went on in the early church.

- We have noticed among these authors major differences in style and in logic, for example, in their use of the Old Testament. In John we found no quotes from the Old Testament, but its imagery is there. Its language and stories are presupposed, with reference

3. Editorial note: From the passage Yoder quotes, Christ's Sonship as the basis for our childhood is not evident. Indeed, on reading only 3:1–2a, we could take John to mean that we are the *tekna theou*, "God's children," apart from deriving that status from Christ, the *huios theou*, "God's Son." Yet in 1 John 2:24–25 the author writes, "Let what you heard from the beginning abide in you. If what you heard from the beginning abides in you, then you will abide in the Son and in the Father." The thought continues in v. 28: "And now, little children, abide in him, so that when he appears we may have confidence and not shrink from him in shame at his coming." In both passages we are to abide in the same "him," namely, the Son. The reason why comes in 3:2, for "we know that when he appears we shall be like him, for we shall see him as he is." John's thought is that, because we abide in the Son, "we are God's children now."

4. See, e.g., 1 John 2:18–22, 4:15–17, 3:11ff. (do not be like Cain who slew his brother but like him who laid down his life).

5. See John 3:14, 12:32, 13:31ff., 17:1–5. Cf. Acts 3:13.

to Abraham and his promise and his children, for instance. In the Epistle to the Hebrews there are long quotes, cited in full and interpreted with a sense of their context and meaning. In Paul the quotes are brief and more adaptable; he argues at length on a particular verse or segment of the Old Testament.

- There is a difference among these writers in the centrality of the immediate hope, or what is sometimes called a "future eschatology." In the earliest writings of Paul is a lively expectation of the return of Christ. With the others there is less immediate liveliness or less urgent expectancy to this outlook. There is a movement to other themes, although not necessarily rejecting that expectation. It doesn't relate, after all, to all of the problems the church can talk about.

But what do they have in common, after we have noticed that they differ at many points?

- They have in common, obviously, a reference to *the Jesus history,* whatever the theme being talked about.
- We find all of them using the imagery and *logic of solidarity.* We see "Sonship" in 1 John, the relationship between a priest and his brothers as unfolded at great length repeatedly in Hebrews, the concept of the body of Christ or "being in Christ" or the simple assumption of solidarity as we saw in 1 Corinthians 15 in Paul. These all argue the same thought. We have here, therefore, an understanding, a set pattern, which all three of these authors use some way or other. "The unity of Christ with believing humanity" is an axiom.
- All of them say that *salvation is a unity of a status and a life.* Later theology can distinguish between being saved and acting saved—between salvation before God and salvation among people, between justification and sanctification, or some other way. For all three of these apostolic theologians, to be in God's purposes is the same as to be living in the light. We haven't emphasized this at as much length as the other topics, but it is always there.
- In all three of these writers we find something like the later notion of "preexistence." It is said in different ways and in completely different language. John talks about the eternal Word; his emphasis is on the identity of this Word in eternity. He doesn't quote the Old Testament at all in John 1. Hebrews on the other hand has in the first two chapters a multitude of quotations from the Old Testament; their point is that this Son was working in the Old Testament story. In Colossians there is reference, with another set of words, to the concept of his presence in creation. All of this might

go back to the phrase "equality with God" in the Philippians 2 passage we quoted before, a passage we saw could have more than one possible meaning, one of which certainly included the idea of a *prior* divine dignity of some kind.

In other words, all three of these writers move away from the minimal interpretation of what Christ did which, as technical language developed, came to be called adoptionism. That is the idea that Jesus *became* the Son or came to be elevated to the position of Sonship by virtue of his obedience. This is said in Peter's sermon at Pentecost and it is presupposed at other points, but it is not made into a systematic theory. It is not developed into a full doctrine of how a man who was once just a man became by divine decree something more than a man because he was obedient. (The idea does not go away. It stays around as an alternative view and is systematically elaborated later by Theodotos and by Paul of Samosata.) It is rather progressively undergirded with ideas of preexistence and condescension, of self-emptying, of "taking upon himself the form of a servant," not only in Philippians 2 but also in Hebrews. To say it another way: the phenomenon of Jesus Christ reported in the early story is too unexplainable, too unique (although it is bad English to say "too unique") to have been only another human, like others from the beginning. The idea of Jesus beginning life like other people is not enough to explain what he did. Or, to say it from the side of the monotheism of Jewish Christianity within which the church arose, the idea of a man becoming or being made God is unacceptable.

The only alternative is for God to take the initiative and become a man among humans. The way to state the notion of divine condescension most clearly is the Gospel of John's concept of a distinct entity, not the same as the fullness of God the Father, yet somehow existing independently of the incarnation and prior to it. This concept, which has Old Testament roots (at which we shall look later) as well as Greek philosophical ones, is a way to relate both worlds to one another and still maintain a monotheistic understanding of God, but there is no discussion among these writers about this *Logos* in itself—that is, what "the Word" was doing before creation or before incarnation. All the word does is identify a presupposition. Before there could be incarnation, what must there have been? There must have been a self-revealing divine will that would lack words, yet it is the carrier of meaning.

Now we move back to a summary of what we have learned about the theological process in the New Testament church. Our concern has not been to develop a summary of Christian thought, or of the things we should think. Even when we talked about content and ran the statements made by the New Testament church through our minds, our concern was not to record what that content was so that we could get it straight. Our concern was to observe theology going on as thought—theologizing as a process.

So, to summarize, what was the early church doing? How was the early church thinking? The church gathered around a series of events—the Jesus events—and ascribed them meaning. She confessed those deeds as God's deeds; she proclaimed, affirmed, and reaffirmed that meaning. We saw this most clearly as we followed up the literary clues to the central *kerygma* outline. There, a group of people reported events and related themselves to those events. To judge by the frequency with which these matters showed up on our "grid," we can say that there were, more or less, three degrees of centrality in the way in which this reporting was done.

- First of all, the briefest confession that "Christ is Lord" was centered in the affirmation of the resurrection. That resurrection, however, is not an event all by itself. The Lordship of Christ at the right hand of the Father—to use later language—is not affirmed in isolation. It is linked to our history, which surrounds it, as it were, with a second level of immediacy.
- On this second level, it is said that our history is the fulfillment of the past, that Christ is coming into our history in the future as judge, and that he died right here—"you killed him but we saw him rise." This whole circle of wider testimonies links the speakers and the listeners into the story itself. It links the speaker who says, "We are witnesses." It links the listener who is called to repent, and so this core statement is linked with the whole history of the church and the world to which the church speaks.
- Yet a little further away from the center, a little less frequent, is the level of a number of other statements, like divine Sonship, David's sonship, the mighty works, and the unfolding of the meaning of Christ's death—"He died to deliver us from our sins." These statements that are made once or twice fit, but did not recur and were not reenforced as we went through the various sermons.

What does it tell us, when we come to this conclusion, that the early church gathered around events? It suggests that there is no radical distinction between events and their meaning, no metaphysical distinction that modern people still keep making. Ancient people could make it too. On the one hand are the events as they are. They are the facts; they are old and dead and we deal with them objectively. Then there is the realm of meaning—how one feels about the facts. In much of our lives we try to be careful about the difference. We try to untangle meaning from events. Now we see that "untangle" is what the New Testament church did not do. Not only did not do, not only did not want to do, but could not really have conceived of doing. If things are as the witnesses say, then you must believe them. It is easy to say, "I am a witness." If things are as I am saying, then you should respond. This is not an apologetic stance, in the technical sense of the word. The "apologist" is the person who operates on the assumption that the listener is not convinced. Then he or she deals with the fact that the listener is unconvinced, the doubts and unbelief. We need to have proof. Such is the apologetic process, the process of accepting the listener's need to have proof in order to accept something that he or she doesn't accept. The claim of the New Testament church—"we are witnesses to these things"—and the call to the listener—"you must repent"—indicate that this distinction between meaning and the event-as-it-really-was is false.

What are these events whose meaning is proclaimed as their having happened? They are the work of Jesus Christ. We observed this at the outset and we can still say the same thing. There is no independent doctrine of the Father or of the Spirit. We have not shown that at length, but we could. The earliest creeds of the church were simple statements about Jesus. There are no independent statements about the Father or the Spirit. Statements could be made about the Father, about being the Father of Jesus and having raised Jesus. The first statements that could be made about the Spirit are that it is the Spirit of Jesus or that the Spirit could be sent by Jesus, but such statements are not needed.

The rest of the life of the early church is in continuity with this Jesus story—it does not pick up somewhere else, but it goes on from there. The definition of the apostle is one who is in continuity with that story. The first chapter of Acts reports how the church dealt with the fact that Judas had fallen out of their ranks and stated the requirements of someone to replace him. "One of the men who have accompanied us during all the time the Lord Jesus went in and out among us, beginning from the baptism of John until the day when he was taken up from us—one of these men must become with us a witness to his resurrection" (Acts 1:21–22). So the church gathered round those who could establish the continuity between the earthly ministry of Jesus and the resurrection.

Another element of this continuity is, of course, the collection of the sayings of Jesus. We observed, very briefly, how Paul comments on these sayings. We could watch, at much greater length, the amount of the New Testament that was brought together by the memory of the acts of Jesus, forming ultimately the Gospel documents.

We observed different levels of sophistication in which was first what might be called "the primitive church," the word "primitive" not meaning "crude" but simply "early." Here we encounter the simple resurrection as the basis of Christ's Lordship, the testimony that the Old Testament is fulfilled in him, that a judgment is coming, and that we are called to a sober, suffering, and obedient life. This is the theology of the New Testament church, the church of the first century. Only on the shoulders of this church do we then find something else developing that we can call a more "systematic," a more "self-conscious," or a more "abstract" theology on the part of Paul, Hebrews, and John.

Looking back over this substance, let us think about the sociocultural form with which the early New Testament church did its theological thinking. First of all, with regard to the materials of theological thought, where did they get their language? They got it from the key sermon they repeated over and over again. If you were a Christian, you were somebody who had heard that story and accepted it. But there was also a sizable amount of liturgy, about which we know less. We only find scraps and snippets of it as it was quoted. In Philippians 2 we found a rather sizable quoted segment. Very often it is much less than that. Very often it takes a scholarly hunch even to discern that in a certain place an apostle was probably quoting a hymn or prayer. Then there was the oral reporting—probably fragmentary in the earliest days and then more organized as time went on—the memories of Jesus, the teaching of Jesus, and stories about Jesus.

Why did there need to be theologizing? What is the mandate of the theological process? There had to be theology because there was action in the church, and because there was the danger of false, unbalanced, or improper doctrine. So it was that we read in 1 John 4:1 the warning to "test the spirits." This warning is significant for two reasons. It says first of all that spirits were speaking. There is no expectation that revelation has stopped, that all we have to do is write down the things we know and be done, as if we have our Bible and should need to do no fresh listening from now on. That is not said. Rather, there always will be spirits speaking, but that speech is to be tested because some spirits are of God and some are not. So there is a mandate to test. This is the case as well in 1 Corinthians chapter 12.

Second, there is a mandate to transmit the memory of the church as a human community. People in community have a memory, an identity, which consists in what they know in common. If people know nothing in common they are not a community, therefore there needs to be a teaching process of transmitting the memories of the community. This is not the same thing as testing. It applies especially to the new members. What is it that we believe? What is the story that we remember? It is not only the Jesus narrative; it is also the understanding of the Old Testament. We see in Acts the extent to which reading the Old Testament is what the Christians did together.

Both in order to test as a way of avoiding unfaithfulness and in order to transmit the knowledge of the faith to a new generation of believers or to persons coming in to the rapidly growing church, one needs more than rote learning. One needs more than simply playing back what one hears. If you are responsible for catechism, to teach the essence of the faith to a new believer, you will have to ask what you teach first, what you teach only second or third, and what you teach if you do not have much time. You will have to ask what you teach if the learner is not very able to learn. You will have to ask which learnings are indispensable before baptism. Thus there must be sifting for priorities. There must also be questioning about coherence, about what fits together, what is consistent, what falls into a pattern so that it can be taught more easily. All of this, therefore, is a development of a mandate to think theologically.

Theologizing took place through a great variety of sociological forms. As we read the New Testament we find reference to a considerable number of "offices." The word "office" is already a little more rigid than what was going on then, but there are recurring terms which continue to have the same meaning, referring to functions of communication. There is the *apostle,* the one who has the authority of being a fully authorized eyewitness interpreter of Jesus. The way the apostle proves apostleship is by having witnessed the events he or she interprets. We do not know whether it took more than that, but at least it took that to be an apostle.

Then we find the label *prophet.* The prophet was also a kind of communicator. The word simply means one who speaks forth. Since there were prophets in the Old Testament, everyone knew what it meant to be a prophet. The concept was quite firm in people's minds, and the function of prophecy went on in the New Testament. We find traces of it in Acts and also in Paul's writings.

At least to some extent the New Testament understanding of how prophecy functions under ground rules has background in the Old Testament picture of the office as portrayed in Deuteronomy 13, Deuteronomy 18, and Jeremiah 26–29. Prophecy will continue to be needed, so the office of prophet will need to be exercised. The authenticity of prophecy needs to be verified, not accepted blindly. Part of the verification is related to the past acts of God and older Scriptures, as well as to ongoing experience. The community, moreover, shares in the authentication process (e.g., Jer. 26:16–19). All of these are precursors of New Testament understandings.

There was also the *elder* and the *elder-teacher.* Elder means more than "teacher." It is the function of watching over the life of a group, a moderator or a counselor function. The words "elder," "pastor," and "bishop" seem to refer to the same people. They were elders in the "role" sense; they were recognized for their age and experience. They were bishops in the functional sense of oversight. They were also sometimes spoken of as pastors, that is, shepherds, a symbolic way of speaking of the same function. But some of these elders were teachers and some were not. Those who were teachers then had a kind of institutionalized responsibility for correct doctrine. So there were certain persons who had the assignment of theologizing.

Of course all this communication had a certain social form in meetings. There were what we in modern language call "worship meetings": celebration, adoration, praise, hymns. There were also meetings for catechisms, for learning, for teaching—some kind of school function. We do not know much about how this happened, but it must have happened, because Christians had to learn what they needed to know to be accepted as members. Some of this they learned by watching the worship services. Some of it they must have studied in a more formal way. We have recorded that Paul spent great amounts of time teaching people what they needed to know. Probably they spent most of the time in very small groups. The whole congregational worship process was most often in small groups in houses that had been constructed for other purposes.

Just one example of the theologizing process at work occurs in Acts 18:24–28:

> A Jew named Apollos, a native of Alexandria, came to Ephesus. He was an eloquent man, well versed in the scriptures. He had been instructed in the way of the Lord; and being fervent in spirit, he spoke and taught accurately the things concerning Jesus, though he knew only the baptism of John. He began to speak boldly in the synagogue; but when Priscilla and Aquila heard him, they took him and expounded to him the way of God more accurately. And when he wished to cross to Achaia, the brethren encouraged him, and wrote to the disciples to receive him. When he arrived, he greatly helped those who through grace had believed, for he powerfully confuted the Jews in public, showing by the scriptures that the Christ was Jesus.

Here many kinds of "theology" are described at once. Apollos is versed in the Scriptures; he *had been instructed* in the way of the Lord, such that "He *spoke* and *taught* accurately the things concerning Jesus, although he *knew* only the baptism of John." He was *corrected* and *given* a more accurate understanding by Priscilla and Aquila. He *confuted* the Jews in public. All of these verbs describe theology going on.

So we find great variety of persons theologizing: the apostles, the prophets, and the elder-teachers. We find a variety of social forms: the formal worship, the catechetical conversations, and the debate in public. We find several different kinds of written records: epistles written to a particular church, the general epistles written to all the Christians in a certain area, and a letter that is not really a letter from anybody to anybody in particular, but an essay, a treatise.

What challenges called forth this theological process?[6] The church was in a missionary context in a pagan world. What had to be said to speak to this pagan world? Pagan worldviews and pagan religions centered in "ontology," which answers two questions. First of all was a question of origin. Where did the world come from? Who made it? And so pagan mythology had stories about how the world came to be. The other aspect of paganism was mysticism, especially the mystery religions. People need special religious experiences to get beyond the surface of things and beyond appearances to the *essence* of things, so we are talking not only about religions, but also about the essence of the world as it is. The Christian reaction to this was, first, as Paul did at Lystra and Athens, to make a statement about creation, about providence, and about the God who is at the origin of things. "The unknown creator God is known in Jesus Christ." The first preachers said it that way. The God who made the earth and gave us a place to live has now spoken in the Son, or has now promised to judge the world through a man whom God accredited by raising him from the dead. By the time we get to John 1, Hebrews 1, and Colossians 1, more is said. It is not simply that the God who has made this creation has accredited Christ as the one to come as judge and has raised him. Now there is the affirmation of preexistence, so that creation is no longer something that God the Father does, and the Son does something else, but the Word or the Son is involved in creation as well.

When John 1, Hebrews 1, and Colossians 1 say that the Word or the Son was involved in creation, is this a statement about cosmology? Is this a piece of divinely revealed information we would not have had unless it had been written, and now we know that the Son was there at creation? Is it a piece of information for its own sake, or was it a normal way to express the collision between the Jesus message and this pagan worldview? The pagan worldview centered its speculative concern on origins, and in John 1, Hebrews 1, and Colossians 1 the preacher says Jesus Christ is prior to that. The pagan worldview is concerned to see the reality behind what is visible; especially in Colossians the apostle says that the invisible beings are subject to Christ. Thus, at least in the immediate sense of the missionary experience of the church, these affirmations of preexistence and creation are not given as new information, revealed for their own sake, but they are the normal, appropriate missionary way to state the priority of Christ over the preoccupations of pagan faith.

That is the one side, the mission of proclamation to the pagan world that presupposes the ultimacy of creation and wants to fit Jesus *within* it. The apostles say, "No, we'll put Jesus *above it.*"

6. Editorial note: At this point, Yoder's manuscript includes, "We must step back for a more general effort to grasp something of the challenge into which the church was going."

The other side of the missionary context is the Jewish community that affirmed a God above creation and God working in history, but denied the ultimacy of Jesus within this story. Within the limits of the law as they saw it, the non-Messianic Jewish mind wanted to set parameters for the validity or the relevance of what Jesus has done. "Fine, we'll accept him," these people would say, "as a great rabbi, maybe even in some sense as the Messiah. Maybe we can even accept the idea of a resurrection. But you still have to keep the law, you still have to be good, law-abiding Jews within the limits of the legislation which the Jews have always been trying to live up to." And thereby this kind of person set a limit to the moving of God through history. He or she wanted to make God captive to the cultural system of Judaism. Over against this temptation or this kind of opposition the apostles say, "No, Christ has fulfilled the expectation of the old monotheism that says there is only one God, and he has revealed in His own person the working of God in our time." Thus, in addition to a doctrine of preexistence to place Christ above the pagan worship of creation, we must also have a doctrine of fulfillment to place Christ above the Old Testament story, and this we have in Hebrews and Paul, right in the outline itself. We have it in John in another form, in the debates of Jesus with "the Jews" during his earthly ministry, which is one of the main themes of John's Gospel, more so than in the other Gospels.

There is another form of the pagan worldview, or perhaps just a refined statement of it, usually called Gnosticism. This is the religious or philosophical glorification of insight. *"Gnosis"* means knowledge. The Gnostics had a mystical system, very intellectual but not simply dry and rationalistic, composed of a series of insights by virtue of which they hoped to save people from ignorance. The crux of this insight focused on the point of difference between matter and mind. Ultimate reality is not matter but mind. It is not temporal but eternal. No human temporal material events, no one person, can be ultimate. The ultimacy of Jesus has to be denied not because we know anything more ultimate than he but because we do not, because he was within time, because he was at one particular place and not universal.

This Gnostic depreciation of the material and the temporal is visible all the way through the New Testament. 1 John 4 responds to it when it says that Jesus came in the flesh; 1 John 1 responds to it: We touched him, we heard him, we saw him; that's what we testify to. The anti-Christ is the one who denies this. Hebrews responds to it with its strong emphasis on learning obedience through suffering.

In Colossians and Ephesians the author uses Gnostic language. There are many phrases that were dear to the Gnostics: the invisible God, thrones and dominions and principalities and authorities, things on earth and things in heaven. The language is that of Gnosticism. Colossians uses the language of Gnosticism to rub in the point of incarnation, for example, in Colossians 2:9, "In him the whole fulness of deity dwells bodily." Paul also moves attention away from insight for its own sake—having visions, having knowledge—to that particular kind of knowledge that issued in obedience, especially in 1:15–20. The Gnostic wanted to deal with the invisible, mysterious interlapping of mind and matter. Reality is on the *mind* side, but Paul ties reality down to whether people will be obedient, whether they will live a new kind of life. So Colossians 2:18 rejects pure speculation: "Let no one disqualify you, . . . taking his stand on visions, puffed up without reason by his sensuous mind." Colossians 2:21 rejects asceticism: people who say, "'Do not handle, Do not taste, Do not touch.'" Ascetic discipline was also characteristic of the Gnostic approach. This is all done in the name of what we called before "the logic of solidarity," as in 2:19: "holding fast to the Head from whom the whole body, nourished and knit together through its joints and ligaments, grows with a growth that is from God." We also see this in 3:1: "If then you have been raised with Christ, seek the things that are above."

So we see in Colossians, Hebrews, and John two sweeping affirmations, for which we may use the technical terms *preexistence* and *incarnation.* They come up in different words in different worlds. In all three of these theologians they arise as an extension of the original claim to meet the new challenge. The original claim was simply "God raised him." The wider original claim was, "That's our history, we are witnesses, we call you repent, our life is taken up in him." Now that wider claim is extended in the affirmation of preexistence, which places it above pagan religions; it is extended in the affirmation of fulfillment, which places it above defensive Jewish religion; and it is extended in the affirmation of incarnation, which breaks through the Gnostic idea that it is only worthy of God to be working outside of matter.

We have now noted a number of the central claims of the New Testament theologians, but there are some things they have not said yet. Here we may summarize in three points by citing from Vincent Taylor's writing on the New Testament Christology.[7]

- There is no extended study, Taylor tells us, of the tie between the person of Christ and his work. It is said that he is Lord, and it is said that he died for our sins, but how are these two statements related? It is said that he had to suffer, but why he had to suffer is not said. It is said that he is the Son of God, but why he who suf-

7. Vincent Taylor, *The Names of Jesus* (New York: St. Martin's, 1953); idem, *The Person of Christ in New Testament Teaching* (London: Macmillan, 1958).

fered needed to be the Son of God is not said. With a few exceptions in Hebrews, the accent lies on his triumph rather than on his death. The idea of a death "for sin," of death that was redemptive, is so widespread in the culture of the time that it was not a real problem in the first generation. There are those who think that the idea of a death for sin was brought into the New Testament from paganism—Jesus didn't have that idea, they say, but the apostles did. They got it from their pagan background and had to add it.

The reality is probably the other way around. It was because of their faith that they were talking about redemptive suffering or redemptive death, but the New Testament church did not have to get around very soon to thinking just why his death was saving, why his death was "for sin." The New Testament is clear on his motive, on his obedience. But it does not answer the question, "Why did the Son of God have to die?" This is the question with which the later doctrine of atonement deals. These questions are not dealt with in any clarity or consciousness in the early church. Perhaps it is just as well; we shall see the problems that arise later when we do try to study it.

- Another problem Taylor tells us was not solved is the one we shall come to next in our story, namely, what came to be called the Trinity. The church makes very high claims for Jesus. They call him Son of God, eternal word, image of deity, yet these people are all good Jews, faithful, anti-idolatrous, monotheists. How can one make those high claims for Jesus and still be a monotheist? The adversaries saw this very clearly. Some Jewish adversaries saw very clearly that the claims made for Christ were offensive against monotheism. This is already the case in the Gospels when Jesus claims to forgive, or when Jesus takes upon himself moral authority by saying, "But I say to you. . . ." There were intelligent, perceptive Jews around who knew that was offensive, that it did not fit with Jewish monotheism. The early Christians were just as Jewish, just as monotheistic. When they encountered pagan idolatry and polytheism they were just as offended, yet they seem to have had no problems saying majestic things about Jesus, giving him the title of Christ, talking about him as judging humanity, worshiping him. Later the church will have to put those two things together, and it will not be easy: the high claims of Christ and monotheism.
- There is another question with which we cannot deal at this point, but let us record the fact that it could not be dealt with here. Jesus is a human like others, that much is clear, yet he is also more than other humans. How do those two statements connect? Especially after what we have said about preexistence, what can the junction of these two statements mean with regard to the unique existence of one man within time? A part of the answer is given in terms of self-

> limitation: he emptied himself, he humiliated himself, he learned servanthood, he learned obedience. That is true humanity, but that only sharpens up the problem. The more human was his humanity, that is, the more genuine was his becoming human, the more problems we have with relating this to whatever he was that was more than others. Later we will call this the "two-natures" problem.

Perhaps we can try in a sketchy way to put together something of what we see developing in the christological affirmation. This development is not in the sense of saying something that was not believed before, but of saying more than has been clearly said.

In Acts 2, the first preaching is simply, "You killed him; God raised him." Two statements, two movements. The first one is the life that ends because you killed him, the second is the resurrection. By the time of the hymn of Philippians 2, there is more than this. There is, in the first place, "He emptied himself." The emptying is a general statement made, we could say, prior to the ministry. *Kenosis* is the term we found being used in a technical way. Next comes his servanthood to the death within his human career. Then the resurrection is not actually stated, but is somehow presupposed or taken for granted. After the resurrection comes, "God has highly exalted him and given him the name that one day every tongue will confess" (see Phil. 2:9–11). Away off in the future is the promise of another rising, which is like this glorification but greater because in the present glorification God has raised him and in the future every tongue will confess. Then there must also be a kind of intermediate period of undetermined life (this is taken for granted but is not actually said).

The story develops even further with the concept of the involvement of the *Logos* as Son prior to anything—way back at creation there is an action of God in this One who then came. In between is the period of the Old Testament story about which we have not said much. Somehow we affirm a path from there to here and then we affirm that he will come to judge and then we are affirming the present Lordship. So we see that what began as a statement just at one point has become a view of history. Such a view of history has its ups and downs, and gives to the course of the life of the church a meaning, a rootage in past, present, and future that is very different from Gnostic religion. This gives its character to Christian thought up to the recent present.

But God's care about the time line running from the baptism of Jesus to the ascension gives us one more set of problems. With this we shall wrap up our analysis of the New Testament experience by reaching well beyond it.

We have seen a real movement or growth. We have the core *kerygma*, which was simple. Then we have an expansion into the "primitive theology" of the church, including the *kerygma,* starting with it, but saying many more things about the various titles of Jesus, the Gospel stories, his obedience, and his being the Christ. Third, we found the three "theologians"—each of them rooted in the early church, but speaking different languages, speaking to somewhat different readerships—saying many of the same things or equivalent things, but each going beyond the primitive language. And since then, of course, we keep moving on, and the life keeps on picking up from there and making further circles in every generation.

Now, how are we going to know if this is true? How can we verify these persons' thinking? Up to here they were apostles, so we could trust them, but we have been let in on the fact that the theological process will go on. And what do we do from here on to know if it is true? There are several kinds of logic we can use.

- We can use a position that could be called ecumenical pluralism. This says that everybody is right. As long as you are in some connection with where it started—whatever that connection be, whichever way you branch off—you are still part of the movement; everybody is "in." You keep moving on, you leave the shell behind, and wherever you end up is all right. That will not work! It fails because these people, as they get further apart, are not saying the same thing. They are no longer reconcilable with each other nearly as much as their predecessors were. It is important, as we saw in Paul and in John, that there must be testing; there has to be a verification process. You have to check whether what we say today fits with Christ. Otherwise, if everything is true, then the word "true" doesn't mean anything anymore.

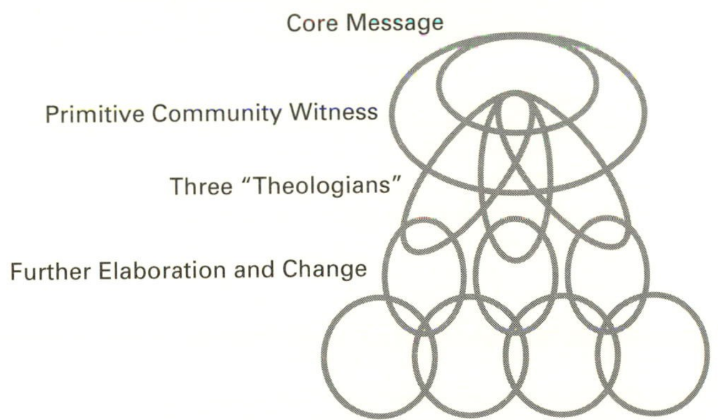

- One alternative is to say only the original is true. But what is the original? In order to get to the "*kerygma*" statement, we had to do literary analysis. Perhaps we did not do that well. Perhaps we missed something or maybe we added something, so we cannot know with certainty what that original account was. Even if we did know, already the New Testament goes beyond it.[8] Is the entire New Testament then the right amount, but then we stop? This position is sometimes called *fundamentalism*. This far and no more. But how do we know exactly where to stop? (We will look soon at the problem of the canon.) Is there really no more than that? Yet when we look at the theology of the fundamentalist, we find that he or she is very concerned about some ideas that only developed in the eleventh century or even only in the sixteenth or the eighteenth. It is not really possible to stop with the New Testament because we are not talking Greek in Palestine.

- Might there be another way of asking the question? Is truth somehow within the awareness of these differences? Can we take the three "theologians" and see what is common to them all? We find them all talking about solidarity. We find them all talking about preexistence. We find them all talking about incarnation. Well, let us say that anything that all three authors saw is right. Might that work?
- Maybe we have to come to the conclusion that there is no one right answer to the choice, "Does the truth stay the same or does it change?" That choice is forced on us by a static view of church and of truth. "Orthodoxy" (the word has many meanings) thinks staying the same is both possible and good. "Liberalism" thinks change both inevitable and good. And (I suggest) they are both wrong. Change is inevitable, so the orthodox is wrong. But change is not always good, so the liberal position is questionable. Change is not always in one clear direction, forward, as the liberal tends to think. So we have to ask—case by case, point by point—which change is faithful? Change is not always faithful. Change is not always unfaithful. We must then discriminate. How do we do that? If the issue is a verbal translation from Hebrew or Aramaic to Greek, then we look in a dictionary. But if the issue is a challenge and a response—a question raised by Gnosticism or a question raised by Judaism, and the response of a thinker to that question—then we can measure and evaluate it, we can test it for truth only in the situation.

How do you ask whether the change is faithful? You have to be there. You have to enter into the process in the life of that community, in that culture, in that language and ask, "Did the respondant hear the question right? Did he or she answer the question in a

8. Editorial note: At this point in the manuscript, Yoder's text reads, "So what is that original account? Already the New Testament goes beyond that!"

way that was a reflection of Jesus?" That is the theological task. In the New Testament church, this is what John, Paul and the author to the Hebrews were doing. It will continue to be our task. This is what it means to be in a community that, far down the road from apostolic times, is answering a new question by building a bridge between that question and the tradition. How do we ask whether they built their bridges right? Is it really an answer? Is it really a faithful answer? Is it an answer that speaks in this age, from this base? That is what we shall see the church asking in all kinds of times, and places, and ways.

Postscript: The Christology of the Evangelists

The outline thus far has been constructed according to the curricular structure sometimes referred to as "block-gap," as contrasted to a thorough survey. We have picked out from the story of the growth of the thought of the early Christians those elements best calculated to make a certain point visible. We now proceed not to fill in all of the gaps but to identify one important additional dimension of the story that was bypassed for purposes of simplicity on our first run through the Gospel materials.

The first chapter of our inductive portrayal of early christological thought focused on titles. It was fitting that we should choose specific titles because they are more solid and less subject to transformation in the course of transmission than are some other kinds of literary forms. But still there is no such thing as a Gospel vocabulary in brute form. We cannot avoid the importance of the fact that the Gospel literature as we have it is the product of a long development over time.

1. First of all were the actual events of the earthly ministry of Jesus. Already when they happened, these events were experienced, described, and recounted through the filter of an uncriticized Aramaic vocabulary.
2. Without any interruptions, the believing Christian community grew through numerous transitions and crises. Through each of these, they bore with them their memories of the words and deeds of Jesus and constantly retold those stories—first of all with a concern not to forget them, but also because they continued to throw light on the faithfulness of the community. The light they threw tended to reflect upon the texts; that is, a text would be retold in such a way that its relevance to a contemporary issue became more visible.
3. No one locality had in its membership all the people who had in their memories all of the extant accounts of the words and deeds of Jesus. Thus as the church grew and Christians scattered, each

place had its own slightly different collection of stories and memories. Some were forgotten. Some were conflated or expanded, often clarified and applied (in the first generation especially, under the oversight of apostles who could vouch for the faithfulness of some adjustment to a new place or issue).

4. Sometime along the way, some of these accounts were reduced to writing. No one can say how, when or by whom the first writing was done. We know too little about the place of the written word in the culture of that time.
5. Along the way, particular accounts of specific deeds or saying of Jesus came to be gathered with others. Sometimes sayings of a same kind were brought together because of a similar subject matter or style, such as chains of parables or the Sermon on the Mount. Sometimes materials were brought together in such a way as to constitute an apparently unbroken narrative sequence.
6. There is no way to know how the above two developments were correlated chronologically. An early generation of modern scholars tended to suppose that written texts existed rather early and that the final editing of the Gospels we now have consisted in the excerpting and conflating, almost as if they were pasted together, of pieces from earlier manuscripts. Another set of scholars more attuned to studies of cultural anthropology, appealing to the enormous memory capacity of story tellers in nonliterate cultures, would tend rather to argue that very large complexes of either narratives or sayings may well have been agglutinated in memorized cycles long before anything was put on papyrus. The conflict between these two sets of reconstructive assumptions is not important for our purposes; it is important to know that both processes happened.
7. Sometime between the years 60 and 100 a few individual writers brought together in a unified literary form something very much like each of the Gospel texts we now have. For the purpose of facing the questions we are interested in it seems to make considerable difference whether it happened about 60 or about 100; but the scholars differ that much.
8. The final redaction was the work of a person who was not a first-hand witness to all of the events in question, and who may actually in some cases have been removed by several stages from eyewitness status.

All of this transmission process can be presumed to have taken place consciously and intelligently. It is therefore meaningful to ask about the theology that was operating or the theologizing that occurred in that transmission process. One set of scholars, quite confident that they are able to determine the part of a particular redactor in the creation of the documents we now have, will then talk with confidence about "the theology of Luke" and "the theology of Matthew." Others are less certain that the redaction process was undertaken by one person rather than by a community, or that it was done self-consciously rather than implicitly. These scholars are less able to talk about the Gospel writer as *a* theologian, but even this latter category of interpreters has to grant that there was *theology* at work in the process that produced our Gospels.

In a complete survey of New Testament thought, what we have done in a specimen way with Paul and briefly with Hebrews and John would need to be done for the Gospels traditors and redactors. We here set that task aside with a good conscience, as something the concerned student will follow more efficiently later in his or her studies, and because the results of such an analysis would not seriously change our present conclusions.

The observation that the Gospel writer was also a theologian, while important to fill out our report, is not the most important observation that needs to be made as we come back to look at the Gospels after having observed the "great theologians." More important is the corrected perspective our second look enables us to gain on the development of Christology itself.

If one were to begin naively with the Gospels, we would understand escalation in christological language, from more simple descriptions of Jesus as a man in the Gospel stories to "higher" predications in the later literature like the Epistles. That kind of assumption enabled a rather simple polarity to arise and become popular around 1900 between the "religion *of* Jesus," reported in the Gospels, and the religions *about* Jesus that developed in the later church, beginning an evolution that climbed on for centuries. Scholarly skepticism therefore finds that the development moves away from the Jesus' simple and modest teaching into increasingly speculative or liturgical developments—which as "moderns" we may properly call into question, as we reach "back behind them" for the most nearly original and therefore more valid statements.

There is a kind of paradox involved when people who prefer not to have a "high" view of Jesus nevertheless espouse the radically skeptical understandings of historical criticism so as not to believe anything but what Jesus himself indubitably taught. That is a modern paradox. A quite different observation matters for our purposes, namely, that "high Christology" is present in the *oldest* documents we have. As a verbally fixed pattern of expression that says something about who Jesus was, we have no source older than the hymn, already in use before Paul wove it into Philippians 2. Something like preexistence and cosmic lordship is already here. As we observed, from there on the rest is simple unfolding. We furthermore observed that such "unfolding" was meant not to maximize the pretentiousness or glory of what the church said about Jesus, but rather to make sure that in the new missionary context the normativity of Jesus, the earthly figure, remained solid. So it can be argued that the evolution of Christology toward the end of the first century and the development of canon through the next two moves toward rather than away from historicity. That makes it important to observe that it was *after* the formulations in the writings of Paul, and very possibly also after the first expression of the ideas we have in Hebrews chapter 1, and John chapter 1, that the early Christian communities found "reaching back" indispensable. That is how they reaffirmed the earthliness of the man Jesus, the story of his doings, and the memories of his own words. The Gospels were not written to give us a Christology less ambitious than that of the Epistles; they were rather written to clarify and hold fast the concrete human content of the faith in Jesus of whom the most exalted things were already being said.

This is a statement about history and about documents, of course. It is not a logical proof. Anyone is still free to believe that the notions of preexistence and ascension are nonsense in terms of a modern worldview, and to choose to tailor a Christology to fit a modern cosmology. But then that should be done on the basis of the truth one ascribes to modern cosmology, and not on the grounds of pretended historically critical recourse to the oldest texts. We only have the oldest texts because of the high Christology. And that same Christology made people, after most of the rest of the New Testament was written, very concerned to hold fast to all they could possibly reclaim about the earthly career of the man they already celebrated as risen Lord.

At this point we cannot close the door on two somewhat more refined alternatives to the criticism suggested above. To deal with those alternatives, however, will only be possible much later in this course.

- One line of debate says that although New Testament "high Christology" is understandable in its context, we must distinguish between it and what was made of it several or many centuries later, as it came to mean to many people that Jesus was no longer genuinely human. That is a worthwhile question that we shall need to debate later.
- Or it is possible to say in a broader sense that when the early missionary witnesses turned their aggressive proclamation into the thought framework of the Hellenistic world, they embraced too many assumptions of that worldview? Thereby they denied something essential of their Hebraic background, and became either too broad and uncritically open to the surrounding world, or too narrow in identifying Christian thought with a Hellenistic worldview, to the exclusion of possible similar adaptations in other cultures.

Each of these criticisms will have its place later. Now we note only that it is confusing to link them, as is often done, with an effort to drive a wedge between Jesus and Paul, or between the high Christologies of the later New Testament writings and the simple self-understanding of the Rabbi Jesus of the Gospels.

Collateral Readings

Now that chapter 5 has spoken of the "systematic" quality of theological task, it is time to begin coming to grips with your collateral texts.

1. Decide for yourself in which order, if you were going to study or teach all of them, you would want to approach the following topics:
   a. The virgin birth of Jesus
   b. The person of the Holy Spirit
   c. The existence of God
   d. The authority of the Bible
   e. The nature of religious experience
   f. The resurrection of Jesus Christ
   g. The nature of proof in matters of religious conviction
   h. The humanity of Jesus Christ
   i. The deity of Jesus Christ
   j. The importance of the church
2. Then analyze the structure of your collateral texts, observing the following for each of the above themes:
   a. Where in the sequence of the book is it dealt with?
   b. How much space is it given in proportion to the total text (percentage of pages)?
   c. Does it matter where it comes? Does the sequence of themes appear to be important to the author?
   d. Are there any of these themes that the author does not deal with directly? Can you tell why?
   e. Are there important themes to which your author gives more attention than to those above? Which? How much space?
   f. Does the author discuss directly the reasons for having the material organized as it is?
   g. Can you see any correlation between the above and the author's denominational loyalty, or the author's place on a scale of liberal-to-conservative?
   h. What use would your author have for our inductive exercise of watching the early church theologizing? How does your author use Scripture?

From now on, accompany each topical study with a cross-reference to what is said of each theme in the collateral texts, and where.

Readings on the Task of Theology

The other commended sources of alternative orientation concerning the task of theology are the books *God Who Acts: Biblical Theology as Recital* by G. Ernest Wright and/or *Eyes of Faith: A Study in the Biblical Point of View* by Paul Sevier Minear.

1. What is the author's intention in writing the book? Does this include an attempt to speak to
   a. practical issues?
   b. academic concerns?
   c. intellectual problems?
   d. church hassles?

To what extent is the author's intention reflected in the plan or outline of the book?

2. Is the author arguing against some "wrong" position(s), i.e., does his or her intention include a polemic? To what degree is the book characterized by such a polemic?
3. What does the title of the book mean? What does it exclude?
4. Wright observes that 1890–1910 was the "greatest age of biblical scholarship on Christian history" in spite of some questionable assumptions.
   a. What were the questionable assumptions?
   b. What made the period so great?
   c. Do those things that made biblical scholarship of that time so great help the author carry out the intention of the book?
5. What does the author mean by the following terms? Does he or she use them consistently? Why are they defined as they are?
   a. History
   b. Event
   c. Faith
   d. Theology:
      i. Systematic
      ii. Biblical
      iii. Theology of recital
   e. "Being" or "activity" of God
   f. "Being" or "activity"/"work" of humanity
   g. Revelation
   h. Knowledge
   i. Religion

6. What is the relation between the "acts" and "word(s)" of God? Between "event" and "interpretation?"
7. What, according to Wright, is the bridge between biblical history and us?
8. "Theology may perhaps be defined as the discipline by which the church, carefully and with full knowledge of the risk, translates biblical faith into the nonbiblical language of another age."[9] Evaluate this statement in the light of previous study, class discussion, and *Preface to Theology* chapters up to this point.

9. G. Ernest Wright, *God Who Acts: Biblical Theology As Recital* (London: SCM Press, 1952), 108.

PART

2

Post-Apostolic Theology

6

Historical Development (c. A.D. 50–150)

Preparation Guide (for chapters 6 and 7)

Read all your collateral systematic theology texts and answer the following:

1. Is the Nicene Creed or the definition of Chalcedon cited?
2. If so, what kind of authority do they have? Is their phrasing and substance binding? Is there discussion of the difference between phrasing and substance?
3. Is there any explicit discussion of the authority of the creeds?
4. Is any attention given to the early christological controversies or to the Councils of Nicea or Chalcedon (or others) as historical events?
5. Is attention given to significant shifts in Christology from the Gospels to the Epistles, or difference in emphasis between New Testament writers?
6. How does the author's treatment of Christology compare in balance and in content with the early church's preaching?
   a. What place (position, relative space) is given the resurrection and the earthly life of Jesus?
   b. How many elements in the *"kerygma"* outline figure in the systematic treatment?

Background Readings as Needed:

Bethune-Baker, J. F.	*An Introduction to the Early History of Christian Doctrine: To the Time of the Council of Chalcedon.* 1903.
Dorner, I. A.	*History of the Development of the Doctrine of the Person of Christ.* 1861–63. 5 vols.

González, Justo L. *A History of Christian Thought.* 1970–75. 3 vols.
Harnack, Adolf von *Outlines of the History of Dogma.* 1893.
Kelly, J. N. D. *Early Christian Creeds.* 1972.
Kelly, J. N. D. *Early Christian Doctrines.* 1960.
Pelikan, Jaroslav *The Christian Tradition: A History of the Development of Doctrine.* 1971–1989. 5 vols.
Seeberg, Reinhold *Text-book of the History of Doctrines.* 1977. 2 vols. in 1.

In this second unit we move out of the New Testament period, but shall still follow history through the early post-apostolic period. For this chapter we shall concentrate on the transition from the age of the biblical writers into the age when we can begin to follow church history with some clarity. We ask, what kind of period are we getting into? What is changed about the context of theologizing now that we are beyond the age of the apostles?

We have only dealt with one topic in the Bible—christology—and we will continue to follow this same topic. We could, of course, have followed other themes—covenant, ethics, the nature of God. We chose Christology partly because it was central but also partly because in the next period it is the topic of the most visible development and debate.

The next section is thus both the same and different, as we measure what the churches do. It will be the same in that there must be theology. There has to be a thought process that must relate the traditions to new problems.

The word "tradition" comes to be used as a technical term. When Paul said, "I gave to you what I have received," he used the verb *paradidimi,* but soon we have the related noun, *paradosis* (tradition, that which is given over). This total tradition—the stories about Jesus, the hymns of the church, and the simple creeds like "Jesus Christ is Lord," will have to be related to new problems, just as Paul related them to new problems in his time.

But there is a structural difference in the situation in which the church is now working. There are no more apostles. From now on the *paradosis* is always second hand. Nobody with a firsthand memory of what Jesus was like remains, no firsthand witness to the totality of that earlier life of faith, so it is easier to lose one's balance. It is easier to lose one's sense of perspective on the relative importance of different topics. It is no longer possible, with a kind of self-evident and automatic feel for appropriateness, for an apostle to say, "That doesn't fit with my memory of Jesus," because nobody has any memories of Jesus that are not secondhand. This is the case as much in the year 120 as in the year 220; in fact, for reasons we shall see a little later, perhaps even more so. The church is scattered, Christians are all relatively new to the faith, the faith is relatively new to the culture, and there are no fixed limits to the literature that is considered apostolic. The writings of Paul, Hebrews, and John are not at the center of the canon because there is no canon.

Before we go through the history, we should remind ourselves why we are still reading it. Most theology texts follow other approaches. You are now reading systematic theology texts. Do your authors pay much attention to historical sequence in the development of thought? Normally not. Normally they pursue one of two other kinds of principles of orientation or organization. The approach may be topical and logical-deductive, beginning at place from which the other statements follow logically and unfolding one statement from the preceding one. Or it may be an apologetic approach that begins from the reader's point of view and tries to convince him or her from there. Why do we stay with the historical treatment a little longer, after having watched the Bible develop in the history of the apostolic church?

- First of all, we follow the time line because we want to see how the process of continuing doctrinal development is still like the development of the New Testament. The church still speaks to problems arising out of her history, not simply out of speculative talk. Neither is someone playing with ideas and trying to be consistent. This is not the idle development of a system of something that makes sense, nor is the theological process a scholar simply attempting to classify, itemize, synthesize, and organize a bunch of biblical texts in logical sequence—for example, by taking the texts apart from their original literary form and arranging them in a logical order. The material from systematic theology comes from history and is something we need to learn by looking at the history. When we forget that history—when we chop it off and begin with the sixteenth century, with the time when someone in the Middle Ages develops a doctrine of atonement, or with the modernist controversy in our century—and lay out a set of logical truths or convictions, we forget that the origin of this entire body of propositions was the experience of the church through time.
- Another thing we shall observe, especially in this early period, is that the church's thought about Jesus is still central to the problems with which it deals. Christology is not simply central to the first generation—where people *began* with their faith centered on Jesus—but it continues to be central through our period. The problems of the church center on who Jesus was and how Christians should understand his uniqueness, authority, and mission.

We begin now to describe the immediate post-apostolic age, the latter years of the first century and the first half of the second. Then in the following lecture we shall return specifically to the christological debates as they developed and led to the conclusion of the Council of Nicea.

Our first subsection, then, will be post-apostolic theology, or the Apostolic Fathers. The term, "Apostolic Fathers," has traditionally been used to deal with those writers in the early church who were of the generation that knew the apostles. They remained in some kind of living touch with the apostolic generation. What is the center of the faith of these people?

The Apostolic Fathers

The writing just after the apostolic period exhibits a different tone than what went before. One description says that the faith these people express—or the theology with which they deal—can best be described as discussing God's call to new life, a new kind of life in obedience to revealed truth. God's wants have been revealed in a new kind of life, as well as in the church's call to live this new kind of life. Ethical problems related to the meaning of obedience need to be debated immediately. Later, we shall talk about the difference in tone, preoccupation or mood between both this period and what went beforehand, and this period and what comes after it. Let us try to describe it first.

An early debate concerns whether sins committed after baptism can be forgiven. Peter's preaching already affirmed a link between baptism and forgiveness of sin. His was not a sacramentalistic view of the water working as a spiritual mechanism, but he did link baptism with forgiveness. How then is one forgiven for sins committed after baptism? A key to the life of the early post-apostolic churches is that they had to struggle with the problem of whether or not one can be forgiven. This is a sign that they thought of the Christian life as a life in which normally one would not need to be forgiven. Normally, one can stop sinning. God's revealed truth has taken us into a new way of life and helps us—by teaching, the Holy Spirit, and the congregation—not to sin anymore. What if we do sin? Study and debate developed about whether one should delay baptism until just before death, so that the baptism could cover all one's sins. Or, in exceptional circumstances, might there be another forgiveness? *The Shepherd of Hermas* reveals, as special revelation, that *once more* after baptism can there be forgiveness, but only once. This reinforces the idea that the Christian does not sin. Of course, this idea has attestation in the New Testament itself, especially in 1 John. What it means is subject to all kinds of explanations and redefinitions, but 1 John 2:6 does say, "He who says he abides in [Christ] ought to walk in the same way in which he walked." So you do not have to sin, for if you are in him, and if you abide in him, then you do not habitually sin. The one who commits sin is of the devil. "No one born of

God commits sin" (1 John 3:9). That statement is the kind emphasized in the next generation.

If God wants to bring us into a new way of life, then our works please God. The work of martyrdom especially pleases God. So we have, for instance, the example of the bishop Ignatius, who wrote a number of epistles at the beginning of the second century. He wrote to the church in the city where he was likely to be executed, and asked them not to interfere with his martyrdom. Perhaps they could have interfered (somehow, they could have appealed to the authorities or could have tried to help him escape), but his message was: "Please don't: I want to be martyred, I want to share in the death of Christ by dying myself." Works, especially this kind of works, can have merit.

What, then, is the meaning of grace? If God asks of us a new kind of life, and we can live this new kind of life—if we can perform what God asks of us—then what is the meaning of grace in the theology of these people?

Grace is God's help. God helps us obey by giving us grace, and grace comes to be—in a connection with Greek thought—a kind of energy, enablement, or possession one can have as help in living the right kind of life. Grace is a kind of fuel or force, as over against the other spirits that work upon us, and as over against the flesh. Grace is an energy, a working power that helps us to obey.[1] So this is one center: God's revealed truth calls and enables people to live a new kind of life.

The second center is a concern for immortality. Humanity is mortal because we are not pure spirit, but grace can give us the status of immortality. Grace can change us. Remember in 1 Timothy the pattern of duality between flesh and spirit, angels and nations, the world and glory. We are in the world, in the flesh. We are therefore mortal, but we may be made partakers of immortality through the work of grace. The immortality the second generation Christians were concerned to possess is not so clearly rooted in Easter. It is rather the status in which we live the new kind of life. It is because we have this new life that we are already living in immortality.

This is neither totally different from nor not radically contradictory to the statement of the apostle Paul that "we walk in newness of life," but for Paul this meant sharing the resurrection, while for the later apostolic fathers it entails keeping the rules or living in the new power of grace more than it is the sharing of the resurrection nature. It is a difference of tone, perhaps, more than of substance, yet it is a visible difference.

In these fathers is less profundity of statement about Christ than in the New Testament theologians we read before. They call Jesus "preacher," a

1. A good survey is given by T. F. Torrance, *The Doctrine of Grace in the Apostolic Fathers,* in which, if you are interested in pursuing the matter further, you may see something of this non-Pauline tendency in the life of the second generation church.

term we would not find in the writings of Paul or in Hebrews. There is no problem in how he relates to the Father, no problem involved in talking about his divine nature. The Holy Spirit is named, but there needs to be no discussion about whether the Holy Spirit is a person or not, whether the Spirit is part of the divine being or not. The name is there but no problems are encountered. The death of Christ is not too central. Atonement is not a concern; that is, why the death of Christ was a death "for our sins" doesn't need to be debated. The cross is a moral model. Ignatius wanted to die the way Jesus did. Sometimes, but not always, the new holy way of life that God calls us to live can be described apart from Jesus in terms of virtues, truthfulness, and morality.

What should we think about this concentration on morality and immortality? This is not the way the apostles preached. It is different from Paul, and especially so as he has been understood in Protestant history since Martin Luther. Some say that this kind of Christianity that concentrates on morality and immortality is Judaism with a little less ceremony, without the ritual and the Old Testament readings. Others say this is Hellenistic religion with a little revelation and moral discipline added.

But how should we understand the non-Pauline character of the apostolic fathers as they concentrated on morality and immortality, on living a good life and overcoming death? Protestant theologians (a good example of this is Thomas Torrance) will say, "We know that Paul told us that we are justified by faith. Therefore we don't believe morality is the main thing God wants. We want to be obedient, we want to be moral, but that is neither the center of God's concern nor what theology is about." From their perspective Paul's message is the starting point that Luther then clarified because the Catholics had forgotten it. Now, the Protestants say, we see how soon they began to forget. Already in the early post-apostolic age Christians fell away from the message of Paul. There was growth toward Catholicism. Of course, the Lutherans maintain that as a loss, while Catholics can start at the same point and claim it as a gain. This was the initial development of the strong "Catholic" emphasis on overcoming death and on a Christian way of life.

If we have a clearer historical perspective, which is what we want in this analysis, we do not need that debate. The preaching of the apostles underlay the life of the New Testament church *before* the work of Paul and his colleagues—the author to the Hebrews and John. The New Testament church had liturgy and a Christian way of life *before* the "great theologians" of the New Testament. These elements lived on after the "great theologians" with little change. They formed the major background of the thought of the apostolic fathers. That is, the church was living; the church was planted all over the Roman world. The church had its character, thought patterns, ways of life, and simple cultural expressions in the lives of simple believers and local leaders *before* Paul, *before* his writing derived its particular theological emphasis from the struggle with Judaism. And the church had its character *well before* Paul's emphasis was further narrowed, made more precise, and systematized by the Reformation. The apostolic fathers wrote to particular issues; they did not seek to be typical or balanced, and therefore they are slanted as sources. They dealt with the things that came to them, just as Paul had been doing. They did not try to represent everything. Therefore they are not fully fair samples of the life of the church. They do not fall back into "Judaism." They simply represent the normal tendency of ordinary people—as true of people in the nineteenth or the twentieth century as in the second— to see in religion a preoccupation for the problem of mortality and the problem of morality. This does not fall away from the message of Paul, it simply deals with a different agenda.

A further new development in the life of this generation is the apologetic concern. Christian spokespersons begin to attack non-Christians and non-Jews directly and debate with them the nature of true faith. Why is Christianity right? Can we commend the faith to those who already have a faith as better than their faith? Paul did this in Athens, in Acts 16. Or can we only proclaim the story and let the chips fall where they may, so that some will believe and some will not? By the middle of the second century, Christian thinkers (some of whom, of course, received a degree of education before becoming Christian) began to pick up the challenge to prove that the Christian faith represents the most intelligent position. They began to argue that intelligent, Greek thinkers ought to accept Christianity because it is noble and good, because it meets the requirements of an intelligent person's questioning. In the second century a school of writers develops whom we call the apologists. They clearly still speak of the faith that has roots in the Old Testament and the Jesus story, but they no longer base the faith in that history.[2] They claim it as the most intelligent religion for Greeks: "Christianity speaks to your questions and reenforces the insights of your poets."

Yet they do not sell out to the unbelief of those to whom they preach. They maintain elements quite different from Greek speculation and from Gnosticism. They keep the Old Testament story, events, God breaking into human affairs, and the importance of the election of the people of Israel. They keep the rejection of multiple deities and idolatry. They keep the casting out of demons and spirits and retain Scripture's lack of interest in speculation about different levels of reality, about the spirit world in between this world and God. They differ from the Gnostics also in affirming that creation is good. Not only do they consider the polarity of spirit and flesh overcome in that humanity is saved, but

2. Editorial note: Yoder's text reads, "But that is not where they base it anymore."

they argue there was no polarity in the first place because the world was not evil. Matter is not bad. The world is orderly. The world is good. The world is the theater God has made to conduct affairs with humanity. In all of these ways, then, the apologists did not sell out to the Greeks with whom they spoke, and especially not to the Gnostic Greeks' system of speculation about truth and being, yet they used Gnostic language. They talk, for instance, about redemption as overcoming corruptibility. Humanity is corruptible. We will die. We change. Change and decay are symbols of evil that Christians are also willing to use. Humanity must take on immortality and the incorruptibility given in grace in order to be saved. Or, to use another Gnostic image, humanity is in the dark. Our reason is darkened and only truth will illuminate us, so the language of illumination, with darkness as a symbol of evil, is also taken over from Gnosticism.

The concept of the *Logos,* or Word, somehow not the same as Jesus but behind him and active in creation, develops at greater length. This was a Gnostic concept as well. Many levels of intermediaries who transmitted the divine energy down to where humanity could grasp it and be helped by it stood between God and humanity. In the middle of the ladder of levels and rendering it systematic was the *Logos,* the rationality of creation. The *Logos* helped the prophets. The *Logos* helps us. The *Logos* was in Jesus, but this *Logos* has a certain identity behind Jesus. There is not simply, as John 1 says, a revelation taking on flesh among humanity. Underlying it is the concept that mattered more to the Gnostics, a link in the chain of different intensities of reality.

These samples only point to the different atmosphere in which the apostolic fathers wrote. It is a natural difference—one that is not surprising, one for which we have no reason to scold the New Testament successors. They faced a new set of questions, and they did it with the tradition that they had.

Let us look at this same age from the perspective of the problem it creates for church order. In addition to putting some of the same questions we have asked in another way, this calls for another set of developments. The New Testament church had many kinds of leaders in the local congregation, many kinds of ministries. The basic office, very clearly from the book of Acts as well as from Paul's writings, is the apostle. Apostles traveled around, accessible to all the churches. They were the authorities; they knew about Jesus. But then they died. Where is then the final authority in the life of the church? One of the earliest documents we have testifying to the life of that early church is the *Didache.* This book is not, as its title says, the teaching of the twelve apostles, but a very early testimony to the form of the church's life, including statements about worship patterns and other matters. On the one hand it concentrates on the local congregation's need to solve the problems of church order, define heresy, and name ministers. On the other hand it deals with itinerants, people who travel around acting somewhat like the apostles, though they are not apostles. They have revelations. They give teaching. They make demands on the congregation. The *Didache* asks, "How are we going to deal with them?" The answer is very simple. If a prophet says, "The Holy Spirit has revealed to me that we must have a banquet," and then eats nothing, he or she is a true prophet. But if the prophet eats, then he or she was not a true prophet, but just ordered a meal for himself or herself. If a prophet asks, you give him or her enough food to travel to the next place, but give no more food than that. The prophet is not true if he or she wants more. Somehow the ministry of those who claim authority must be tested, and the *Didache* applies functional tests, tests that center on how prophets operate, rather than on the incarnation. Such rules of thumb can perhaps help to tell the difference between a genuine prophetic visitor and another, but they will not solve the long-range problems of church order.

The resident episcopacy, or a bishop in each city, developed as the longer-range solution. At first this bishop was not a theological problem. The definition of church does not make issues of whether there is a bishop, what he (or she) is called, or how many of them you have. Those will be very important issues much later.

The Greek word for bishop, *episcopos,* means "overseer" or "supervisor." The pattern for resident episcopacy developed along the following lines. First, one of the several ministers who served the church of a city became the presiding member of that group of elders. From presiding he then rose further to a different level of office. When the city began to be considered the capital of its province, the bishop presided over the surrounding countryside too. As congregational membership in the larger city increased, the church subdivided into parishes or quarters, and the bishop came to be in charge of many congregations. This process was gradual and reached no conclusion in the first two centuries of the church, although it moved in a centralizing direction.

The whole church of the city elected the bishop, even if it was a large city with numerous congregations. The church gathered for a mass meeting in which a new bishop would be chosen, but increasingly, the bishop could act without the church. He was not simply the spokesperson for the church or the moderator of the church. This development followed the cultural slant where, under the Roman government, each city was the capital of a province. Each city had an administrator named by Rome. Increasingly, there was a churchman for each of these political units. This process begins by the year 100; we could say there was an incipient episcopacy evident in the letters of some bishops like Ignatius of Antioch and Clement of Rome.

By the middle of the second century the episcopacy is clearly and visibly established. The churches therefore needed to deal with derivative issues that appeared only after the episcopacy was in place. For instance, the question of succession arose. If a bishop dies, who replaces him? Does he choose his replacement before he dies? Or is there a new congregational election? Does he ordain his replacement before he dies so that his replacement receives authority from him? Or does someone else ordain a new bishop? Those are all questions one can ask only after the bishop's office has been well defined.

The next level is the problem of the archbishop. If there is in every city a bishop who might disagree with other bishops, who decides among them? Who rules over them? Before the end of the second century another parallel to Roman administration begins to develop, namely, the appointment of superbishops or archbishops in the cities that are more important.

But we can stop here for our purposes. The development of episcopacy has much to do with the doctrines of church and sacraments. It also comes to determine who has a right to define doctrines, but for now it adds little to our study of Christology.

7

The Christology of the Apostles' Creed and the Canon

SYMBOLUM ROMANUM, as in use ca. 340

Πιστεύω
I believe

1
εἰς ((ἕνα)) Θεὸν (πατέρα) παντοκράτορα (*creatorem caeli et terrae*);
In ((one))* God (the Father) Almighty, (Creator of Heaven and Earth);

2
καὶ εἰς ((ἕνα κύριον)) Χριστὸν Ἰησοῦν, τὸν υἱὸν αὐτοῦ (τὸν μονογενῆ),
And in ((one Lord))* Jesus Christ, His (only-begotten)
τὸν κύριον ἡμάς
Son, our Lord,

3
τὸν γεννηθέντα ἐκ πνεύματος ἁγίου καὶ (*natus est*) Μαρίας τῆς παρθένου,
Begotten of the Holy Spirit and (born of) the Virgin Mary,

4
τὸν ἐπὶ Ποντίου Πιλάτου σταυρωθέντα (*passus est, mortuus*)
Crucified by Pontius Pilate, (suffered, died)

5
καὶ ταφέντα, (*descendit ad inferna*)
and buried, (descended into Hell)

6
(καὶ) τῇ τρίτῃ ἡμέρᾳ ἀναστάντα ἐκ τῶν νεκρῶν,
(and) risen the third day from the dead,

7
ἀναβάντα εἰς τοὺς οὐρανούς,
Ascended into Heaven,

8
(καὶ) καθήμενον ἐν δεξιᾷ τοῦ πατρός
(and) seated at the right hand of the Father,

ὅθεν ἔρχεται κρῖναι ζῶντας καὶ νεκρούς·
whence he shall come to judge the living and the dead;

9
καὶ εἰς τὸ ἅγιον πνεῦμα
And in the *Holy Spirit, (the communion of saints),

10
ἁγίαν ἐκκλησίαν (καθολικήν),
the Holy (Catholic) Church,

11
ἄφεσιν ἁμαρτιῶν
the remission of sins,

12
σαρκὸς ἀνάστασιν, (ζωὴν αἰώνιον).
the resurrection of the flesh, (life eternal).

( ): absent in early form, added later to form SYMBOLUM ROMANUM.
(( )): present in earlier forms, dropped by 340.
*- "One" used with "God" in Coptic and Egyptian forms ca. 500.
- "one" used with "God" *and* "Lord Jesus Christ" in most Greek forms from 325 (Athanasius) on, whereby "our Lord" is not used.
- the 340 Greek text reads either "the Holy Spirit" or simply "Holy Spirit"; otherwise Greek forms vary between "one Holy Spirit" or "the Holy Spirit."

Another dimension of the adjustment to the post-apostolic situation is the development of brief normative statements like the creed. We observed one creed in the very earliest texts: "Jesus Christ is Lord." There are other very simple statements. Some are twofold: Jesus was Son of God and son of man; he was justified by God, crucified by humans; "You killed him, but God raised him up." Such two-phrase statements were the nucleus of the later creeds or confessions.

This kind of creed had numerous uses:

- There was, of course, the baptismal use. "Do you believe?" had to be asked of a candidate for baptism. The candidate had to learn at least to say, "Yes," or, more likely, to repeat the statement. If it was a simple statement like "Jesus Christ is Lord," even an illiterate new Christian could say it with meaning.
- There were confessions like this in hymns.
- There were confessions like this in the context of persecution. We noticed 1 Corinthians 12 may have been read in the face of persecution.
- There were places, probably, where the creed had a special significance for evangelism. This was perhaps one of the ways Chris-

tians could simply proclaim "Jesus Christ is Lord" and let people take it up from there—public witness.

- There were apparently exorcisms in which the proclamation, "Jesus Christ is Lord," was used to cast out spirits or struggle with an evil power in the human community.
- And there was the confession at the Lord's Supper.

In the New Testament term *epikaloumenos* we find brief traces of the centrality of *confessing*. An *epikaloumenos* is literally "a confessor," "one-who-calls-himself-by-the-name-of," or "one-who-invokes-the-name." Before the Christians were called Christians they were perhaps called *epikaloumenoi,* "callers upon the name." In Acts 9:14 and 21, Ananias says in his vision of Christ sending him to Paul, that Paul is feared by "all those who call upon thy name."[1] Paul's conversion was called "calling on his name."[2] This is also the verb used to talk about a person having a surname. Simon was *surnamed* Peter, he had a "further name." A Christian is one who proclaims and professes the name. "Those who *call upon* the Lord from a pure heart" in 2 Timothy 2:22 are not all those who pray sincerely. They are all whose confession that "Jesus Christ is Lord" is genuine. The same verb, in Acts 25:11, is also a legal "appeal," that is, calling on a higher court to help.

Gradually the simple statement, "Jesus Christ is Lord," expanded into twofold statements, and then into statements that referred to the Father or the Spirit as well. Then, with reference to baptism, the statements were developed into a kind of learning outline. We turn now to the so-called "Roman Creed," an early form of the Apostles' Creed. In the late third or early fourth century the outline is already relatively full. We shall analyze it as a document of the development of the function of creeds in the life of the church.

The Apostles' Creed

As far as we can tell, the Apostles' Creed was a baptismal formula. A candidate for baptism stated this creed as her or his confession. It was brief enough for an illiterate person to learn it by heart. It was full enough that, if one knew all of it, he or she had an outline of the essentials of the Christian faith. Ours is the form in which it was used in Rome, although very similar forms must have been used in many other places.

The Roman symbol came to be called the Apostles' Creed. A legend developed in the fifth or sixth century that once the twelve apostles gathered and agreed, each would write a sentence of the creed. That

1. See also Acts 2:21, 15:17; 1 Corinthians 1:2; Romans 10:13; James 2:7
2. Acts 22:16b.

twelve-ness is somewhat artificial, especially in that the eighth and twelfth sections each consist in more than one statement.

Let us make some structural observations about this text:

- Note the threeness in the use of the preposition "in" following "I believe." It occurs in the first line, in the second line and then in the ninth line. Those three, "I believe in" statements, are called the three "articles."

  I believe in the Father,
  in the Lord Jesus Christ,
  I believe in the Holy Spirit.

- Next, observe the evident centrality of the second article. It is much longer. Its statements are much fuller. Whereas the statements under the third article are all phrases that make no grammatical sense—the third article is just a list of nouns—the second article is made up of participles, some of which have to be translated by clauses. All of them describe Christ: begotten, crucified, buried, risen, ascended, and seated. It is linguistically uniform, in that all the participles stand in the same grammatical relationship to the name "Lord." It is also primitive, in that this is the way the earliest creeds seem to have been put together. There is thus reason to suppose that the second article was the nucleus around which the rest of the creed gradually developed.
- Reference to the Father is not much more than a prologue to the statements about the Son. It consists of only one line: "One God the Father almighty." The phrase, "creator of heaven and earth," was added later.
- One also has the impression that the statements in the third article are only an epilogue. They are not participles, just phrases. There is neither grammar nor logical construction, but only a string of nouns. The Holy Spirit is not always the object. The church, remission of sins, resurrection of the flesh, and life eternal are all elements not intrinsically belonging only under the Holy Spirit. They fall into a catch-all section at the end, for which "Holy Spirit" was the title. It is not clear whether these various elements are objects of the preposition "in" (I believe in the Holy Spirit, in the Holy Catholic Church, in the remission of sins), or whether there is some other grammatical relationship (such as "I believe *the* Holy Catholic church, *the* remission of sins"). You cannot diagram it grammatically.

The centrality of Christology therefore remains clear, as in the earlier confessions. It shows in the narrative character of the middle section, whereas there is no tense, time, or narrative in the first and third articles. It shows in its literary unity of participles all modifying the same noun. In this sense the Apostles' Creed parallels the earliest *kerygma* and the simplest confessions. It is still fundamentally a Christological document, with something coming before and some other elements gathered at the end.

There is some uncertainty about the word "one" that appears in the beginning of the first and second articles. It is marked in our text with double brackets because it was dropped later. "I believe in ONE God the Father, and in ONE Lord Jesus Christ." It was in the earliest texts, but by the time the texts are used in the fourth century, it is no longer present. What does this mean?

It seems that the inclusion of "one" began in the earliest writings of the church as a part of its antipolytheistic thrust in the age prior to Constantine when paganism was still around. Perhaps it was stated about the Father and was then carried on from there to refer to the Son as well. "One Lord" echoes "one God the Father." Of course, by the fourth century, when most people were Christian and there was no live polytheism or counter-religion, and when the church had more or less merged her monotheism with Greek philosophical religion, it was not very meaningful to say, "There is only one God." By definition God is one. It is no more meaningful to say, "There is only ONE Lord Jesus Christ." So with the passage of time, this adjective was no longer needed in the West. In the East, the movement was somewhat different. There the literary parallel, "one God, one Lord, one Spirit," was maintained to reflect the argument about the Trinity and the three persons being one.

We noted a parallel to earlier preaching in the centrality of Jesus, in the fact that the second article's participles give the core of the creed a narrative character, but there are also some visible differences.

- There is no Old Testament story. Where the apostolic preaching glanced back to the prophets and the promises of the Old Testament, where John's Gospel and Hebrews continued that tradition, the creed now glances back to creation: "God the Father Almighty, Creator of heaven and earth." The element of creation is not in the earliest Roman Creed, but it is soon added, and we shall observe the change it makes.
- A second change lies in the way the early confessions included the call to forgiveness. They presupposed not only the need for repentance, but also a context in which conversion was a real possibility. In the Apostles' Creed, forgiveness of sins is under the Holy

Spirit, but not grammatically related to it. The third article is a catch-all of things that one also believes. Neither does the creed refer to the life of Jesus. The Gospel stories filled out the early *kerygma* by reference to his birth. In the creed the reference to the birth is expanded and given proportionately *more* attention than in the Gospels: "conceived of the Holy Spirit, born of the virgin Mary."[3] Then the creed leaps immediately to "Crucified under Pontius Pilate." So there is not, in the entire creed, an echo of Jesus' call to repentance. The person confessing this creed is already a believer, already asking for baptism, but he or she no longer really assumes that the world is being called to repentance. By this time we have had Constantine. The pagan world is moving under the control of the church, so the concept of the minority church, calling people to listen, repent, believe, and receive forgiveness, does not quite fit. It is not needed, and so it is not surprising that it is not in the creed.

- Third, in spite of the fact that the creed's outline has a temporal quality in the narrative character of its series of participles, the "fullness of time" theme is missing. No Old Testament prophecies are fulfilled, even though they would have been helpful in the debate with Marcion, which we shall soon discuss.

The Father-Creator element substitutes for the Old Testament story in the creed somewhat similarly to Paul's reference to the creator at Lystra and Athens, but it is not the same.

Moving the reference to creation into the first article of the creed creates a significant difference from Paul.[4] The meaning of "Father" is now changed. When Jesus spoke of "the Father," it was "our Father" to whom we pray; when the early preachers spoke of "the Father," they meant the "Father of Jesus who raised him from the dead" or the "Father by whose adoption we (with Jesus) become sons and daughters." In the creed, "Father" means Creator, and thereby it deviates from the New Testament, where in John 1, Colossians 1, and Hebrews 1, the Son or the *Logos* was the agent of creation. This distinction will have considerable significance in the unfolding of theology across the years.

- More reference to suffering is added. The early church simply said, "You killed him." The original creed had "He was buried" and its Latin adaptation added "He descended into hell." Resurrection still

3. The extended reference to Christ's birth (only begotten, begotten, born) is also proportionately greater than in the early preaching. Perhaps that comes from the Nicene controversy; perhaps it comes from somewhere else.

4. Notice that in our text the reference to creation is in parenthesis and in Latin rather than in Greek. This demonstrates that it was a later addition and not used yet in the middle of the fourth century.

dominates among the participles—"is risen, ascended." But the additions to the early preaching give more total attention to the sufferings. This shift of accent will continue through the Middle Ages.

- Another new phrase is the first one after the Holy Spirit, the *communio sanctorum*. There are two possible English meaning for the Latin. *Sanctorum* is a genitive plural. If it is taken as neuter, then it means, "sharing in the holy things," and thus refers to the sacraments. If, however, *Sanctorum* is masculine, then it means, "what the saints have in common." Which is more likely? Its place in the outline is where there might have been a reference to baptism in an earlier form of the text. That would then indicate that we refer (instead of simply to baptism) to all the sacraments—especially the Lord's Supper, which would then be understood as having been added to the outline under this heading. That fits with the developing importance of the sacraments in the early medieval church. The Lord's Supper is no longer a simple supper. Baptism is no longer the obvious portrayal of newness of life. We now have speculation about the meaning of the holy things (the *sancta*) and how it is that Christians gather to share in them. So the critic could see in the insertion of the text, "the sharing of the holy things," a trace of the development of sacramentalism, superstition, and speculation in the medieval church.

  The other possible meaning arises out of the observation that this phrase was apparently added first in the West. That is why it is in Latin and not in Greek. The church in the West incorporated in her life, by taking over pre-Christian forms, a special amount of attention to the so-called "Cult of the Dead." The dead were not worshiped, but they were honored. In the very earliest church buildings a special segment was set aside for revering the memory of the dead. The fact that *"communio sanctorum"* comes just before the name of the church in the creed might indicate that the reference is to the church's inclusion of dead saints and the angels. It is clear in any case, that the *communio sanctorum* as the fellowship of living and dead saints is the meaning toward which later the understanding of the creed moved.

There are other additions:

- The church is now an object of belief: "I believe the church."
- The church comes to be called "catholic." This clearly reflects debates in the fourth century between the church that was everywhere—universal, catholic, in that sense—and local churches.
- The last addition is the phrase, "life eternal." What does this mean? Because it comes after "resurrection," does it mean more

than resurrection? Is it simply a repetition of the meaning of resurrection, or is it something else? One question, of course, is what "life eternal" meant in the third and fourth centuries. Another question ought to be what it should mean now if we continue to say it. It seems that *at that time* it simply reinforced the statement on the resurrection. When the time-centeredness and history-centeredness of the Hebraic witness of the earliest church were being lost, then the idea of eternal life might have seemed to imply more than the idea of resurrection (although in the New Testament church it would have been just the other way around). So adding "life eternal" may be just a paraphrase or a repetition.

We have moved through the substance of this creed. Earlier we examined what it meant that creeds had to be developed to be used in liturgy, teaching, and acceptance of members into the church. Next we can move to development of doctrine beyond the creeds. But before we do that, we have one piece of parenthetical study to address—a topic which has not come up before in our outline, but is clear in this creed and can just as well be dealt with here as elsewhere. Wherever we deal with it, we shall be somewhat outside of the outline because there is no one normal place for it to fit in. That is the reference to the virgin birth.

The New Testament story is clear. There does not seem to be much ground for dispute about the record. There are two birth narratives in the Gospels. Each of them refers to the virgin birth as a meaningful part of the story, but without special emphasis, surprise, or shame. It is just part of the story. That is the first unambiguous part of the record.

Second, the three great New Testament theologians appear to pay no attention to this concept, or to the Gospels' report. There are snippets and phrases where, *if* we presuppose *great* importance given to the concept of the virgin birth, we can *perhaps* find it echoed in Galatians, Hebrews, or John, but nowhere is it argued. Nowhere is it clearly affirmed. Nowhere does anything depend upon it. Nowhere else in the New Testament is it strategic. Not only is it absent in the three great theologians who developed the idea of the incarnation at great length, but it is not present in the other parts of the New Testament literature either. We did not find it in the *kerygma* of the early apostles when we tried to discern what they preached. It is not in the "primitive" epistles.

There is a difference, then, when we move from the New Testament to historical theology—be that medieval orthodoxy, Protestant orthodoxy, or that of the apostolic creed with which we are working right now. In historical theology the affirmation of the virgin birth is clearly present, as it was in the Gospel birth narratives, but it is also given much more emphasis than it had in either the birth stories or the apostolic theologians.

The first meaning it came to have in systematic theology takes its strongest form in the later Eastern church. Incarnation itself becomes the means of our salvation. For the Greek Fathers (to whom we will refer again later in the course), we are saved not so much because Jesus died for us as because God became human for us. The phenomenon, the metaphysical event of God becoming human is the root of our salvation. Because Jesus was really a man, he accepted the full price of humanity, including death, but this death was the outworking of what really mattered—the incarnation itself. So the event of Bethlehem really matters more than Golgotha in this theology, and the virgin birth is the point at which that metaphysical event is identifiable or even datable.

The "Western" medieval view was different again. Its genesis was earlier, but this view dominated the Middle Ages. According to the medieval church sinfulness is transmitted to us from our parents through bodily procreation. Because we come into being from parents, they passed their sinfulness on to us.

In order to have a sinless nature Jesus had to have a sinless origin. In order to be free from the contamination of original sin, in order not to be a sinner like everyone else, the birth of Jesus had to be metaphysically different. This is the explanation of virgin birth that dominates medieval Roman Catholic thought. Jesus had to be born differently from others because he had to be sinless. He had to be born of a virgin to be preserved from the stain of original sin. If such logic is pushed back another generation we get the doctrine of the immaculate conception. This refers, not to the conception of Jesus, but to the conception of Mary, who also already had to be free from sinfulness by virtue of the way in which she was conceived. Where are we now along the story? The New Testament does not make much of it, but theology does, in the Middle Ages especially.

Contemporary theology often negates or rejects both the concept and the report of the virgin birth for a number of different reasons that we must untangle. In the first place, it is *negated on the grounds of philosophical presuppositions*—things like this just do not happen. After all, modernity adopts a scientific view of things. The world operates according to laws. Exceptions do not happen. Miracles do not happen, so obviously this exception did not happen. This brings to bear upon a particular narrative report a set of philosophical presuppositions that declares the virgin birth impossible regardless of who was there, the quality of the witnesses, or the reports of who could observe or report upon it. Miracles do not happen. This is a report of a miracle. It therefore could not have happened.

The second negation comes from those who hold that the concept of a virgin birth is *theologically not wholesome*. There are various reasons for this. One is that it supports the false view of sin operating in the Middle Ages—the idea that sin is especially connected with sex or vice versa. Another view argues that it is problematic to maintain that sin is especially connected with the body as over against the spirit or the whole person. You cannot focus sin in certain kinds of behavior, in the animal part of us, or in the lower part of human nature, so that freedom from sin means rising above our animal nature. All of this is theologically unwholesome. Therefore, we should reject the idea correlated with it, namely that Jesus' birth is in any way unique.

There is also the *Docetic* view of humanity. Jesus, according to the witnesses we have been reading so far, was a real man. But according to much Christian piety, he was not a real man. He was not really tempted, tired or weak. He did not get impatient. And so it is that much Christian piety, poetry, and art has given us a picture of a Jesus who was not fully human. This links up with an understanding of his birth as unique and miraculous. So in order to guard *against* the unwholesome theological dangers that lie in a *Docetic* view of the humanity of Jesus, some people who say we must reject the virgin birth.

Still another line of thought concentrates on the cultural variety and difference between our age and the age of the Bible. The New Testament was written, to say it moderately, in a *prescientific world.* Its mode of thought, the type of literature it is, does not mean to be scientific. So when the New Testament tells us that there was a human being whose birth was not like the birth of other human beings, the writers are saying something they want to say. But they did not mean to tell us that Jesus was a *biological* exception. They did not mean to tell us that the rules of human existence were broken. This is not that kind of literature. This is not scientific literature; it does not mean to record scientific impossibilities. The notion of the uniformity of nature is a modern notion. Since it could not be affirmed in the New Testament church—neither could it be denied—there must be some other meaning to the story. It has some other point and needs to be understood as some other kind of communication.

There are then at least three negative arguments: it does not happen, it supports an unhealthy theology, and it takes New Testament literature to be more scientific than it needs to be. The primary argument is that most of the rest of the New Testament does not say much about it.

Contemporary conservative theology is sensitive and defensive about these challenges. Instead of examining them and judging whether some of them have weight, most contemporary conservative theology has aggressively risen to defend this traditional doctrine in something like its medieval form. Again, on a number of grounds it has come to be a symbol of the issue of biblical authority. If you doubt at this point the Bible's reports, then you are challenging in general the reports of the Bible. Thus the debate of the past two centuries about the whole issue of biblical authority and revelation very often centers on this point. A person who affirms the simple, literal understanding that seems to arise out of these two birth narratives is one who believes the Bible. A person who challenges this is one who does not believe the Bible.

A second line of defense sees behind the issue even more than a test of biblical authority. The virgin birth is a test of whether one accepts the absolutizing of the modern worldview. The scientific worldview tells us the universe is closed. Exceptions do not happen. Miracles do not happen. Flukes do not happen. Christians, however, are people who believe there is a person-like higher power who made the world and can change it, therefore Christians must deny the scientific worldview. They can accept it for modest purposes, for engineering purposes, for purposes of driving cars and trains and building computers, but they must deny its ultimacy by affirming the possibility of miracles. The virgin birth becomes one of the best samples of the issue of miracle versus the scientific worldview. This is another traditional clash in which many Christians take sides.

There is the further argument that the miraculous birth of Jesus proves his deity, over against either a naturalistic and humanistic view of Jesus that says he was a good rabbi—perhaps the best of all rabbis, but after all, just one rabbi beside others—or a Jesus to whom we choose to give as much authority as he merits or wins. Traditional Christian theology has always affirmed more than that. It seems to make sense to connect it with the report of his unique birth. It would be appropriate for the only God-man in history to be born this way. It would be appropriate for the denial of Jesus' divine Sonship to be linked with the denial of his birth. Certainly in the negative form we can agree that those two denials hang together. So it seems logical to conclude that the two affirmations belong together, and that affirming Jesus' miraculous birth is demanded by the affirmation of the incarnation. Either incarnation demands the virgin birth, or the virgin birth safeguards the incarnation.

A final conservative Protestant argument, which relates to the medieval view of which we spoke, is that Jesus had to be different from birth in order to be our Savior. In order to be freed from the sinfulness that is part of all humanity, he had to take his relationship to humanity from a different point of departure than the rest of us. This does not have to be connected with the Middle Ages' crude and carnal concept of original sin. Any concept of original sin seems to imply that people are sinners because they were born of sinful parents, into a sinful society. If Jesus can break this vicious circle, if he can stand outside it to free us from it, if he will not be the prisoner of it, should he not come into human life in a different way? Is it not appropriate that his standing above the world to save the world be reflected in his unique origin?

The reasons indicated above are the most current and evident ones. There are others, which I note without further evaluation:

- The possibility, once realized, of a sinless humanity symbolizes or proclaims the perfection of the church or the reality of salvation even when each of us seen severally is a sinner.
- If the miracle of the incarnation saves us, we must know when it happened. If Jesus came into being gradually, organically, we have no way of dating the saving event.
- Confessing the need for such a miracle tests our seriousness about the totally desperate lostness of our fallen state.
- The miracle of heavenly flesh assumed by the Son or Word is the guarantee of the possibility of our own sanctification.[5]

The purpose of this course is not to provide solid answers to hotly debated issues in the history of theology. Any answer that could be suggested at this point would be premature. It would short-circuit weighing the pro and con arguments. But since the Apostolic Creed brought the virgin birth to the surface of our study, we should at least try to clarify the nature of the question.

First of all, this is a question of history. It is a question about what really happened. It follows from this that answers from grounds other than history are inappropriate. Some of the main grounds cited for denial of this traditional doctrine were philosophical, for example, the modern philosophical commitment of the scientific worldview that says things like the virgin birth do not happen and therefore it could not have happened. That is not a statement about history. It is not based on going back and checking what really happened on the only grounds we have; namely, the witnesses. It is a philosophical denial and as such is illegitimate. Philosophical grounds may raise a question. They may make belief difficult. But the belief is no more difficult than the philosophical assumptions themselves are questionable.

But if we reject philosophical grounds as a final basis for decision, we must also reject them as a basis for affirmation. It is striking that some of the conservative defensiveness on the point has also been philosophical; that is, it argues about the logic of things rather than about the witnesses.

How we take the reports of the virgin birth is not really a test of biblical authority. It is not a test of whether we believe the Bible. It is rather

5. No literature survey is offered here. The strongest defense of the classical tradition is J. Gresham Machen, *The Virgin Birth of Christ* (New York: Harper, 1932). A careful recent review is Raymond E. Brown, in his *The Virginal Conception and Bodily Resurrection of Jesus* (Mahwah, N.J.: Paulist Press, 1973).

a test of hermeneutics—how we understand the Bible. The question is not whether Matthew and Luke say that Jesus was born of a virgin. We know that. The question is what they mean by it. What they mean should not be presupposed to be the same as what a medieval Christian, a sixteenth-century Christian, or a nineteenth-century Christian thought it meant. Certainly the majority of the New Testament's silence on this point is not strong support for the idea that the virgin birth had to mean what orthodoxy thought it meant, so we must reject the idea that the issue of virgin birth is automatically and always a test of whether people accept biblical authority. It is rather a test of hermeneutics. What did the Gospel writers actually mean by this report? Did they mean it to be biological reporting or did they mean something else?

A second inappropriate philosophical argument (and it is widespread in practice) sees in the virgin birth the test point at which we affirm the deity of Jesus. It is quite possible in New Testament thought or any ancient thought to affirm deity without linking it to virgin birth. In fact, this is done all the time. The prologue to John and Philippians 2 are familiar examples. Every statement of Jesus' deity in the New Testament is unconnected to discussion of the virgin birth, so it is possible to affirm deity without the virgin birth.

It is also quite possible to affirm virgin birth without deity. Heretics like Paul of Samosata did. The pagan religions of the time did as well. The idea that a particular divine savior figure was born with a mother and without a father can be found in pagan parallels all over the ancient Near East. This also undercuts the idea that the report is meant to defend a deterministic worldview. In the evangelists' worldview, miracles did happen, but virgin birth did not mean that this person was a god. It just meant he or she was uniquely favored, or perhaps a mixture between deity and humanity. It is not proof of metaphysical uniqueness in the ancient mind for someone to be born without a human father. Neither is it necessarily the case, in logic or in the biblical view, that to be born without a human father is necessary to be sinless. That association comes from the Augustinian depreciation of the body's natural drives and needs, but there is no logic for saying that a person born without a human father is any less likely to be a sinner. It is not needed for supernaturalism; it is not needed to save the concept of miracles. You can have the concept of miracles and not affirm that the virgin birth was one. All this indicates that we must first of all set aside the assumption that we can solve this problem on general philosophical or theological grounds. It is not that kind of a problem.

If some "intent to prove" must be attributed to the writers (rather than simply an intent to gather together all the stories that they had heard), the birth narratives would rather solidify Jesus' humanity. They give Jesus a family and two hometowns. They explain that his family and even cousins (Elizabeth, John) were modestly aware of his mission. He is comparable with Samuel, Samson, and John in having a mission from birth, recognized by Simeon and Anna. These items, not the absence of a human father, are the concerns of the texts.

The next consideration to which we must turn, if we are asking questions about history, is whether there are explanations for the silence of the rest of the New Testament. It is not in the kernel of apostolic preaching. Can we understand why it might have been left aside? There are considerable dangers of *Docetism* in the early church. Traces of that danger are present in the later writings of the New Testament. There are already people for whom Jesus was not quite a real man, with reference to understudying the meaning of resurrection as well as his earthly ministry. To have made a point of this kind of unique origin—assuming it to be true—would get in the way of the rest of the story. It would play into the hands of those who wanted to make of the Christian faith another mystery religion, another kind of Gnosticism.

There is a further consideration, especially in Luke's report. More than once Luke's early chapters refer to Mary remembering things, "storing them up in her heart." This might fit with Luke's report that he did research, checked into documents, and went around looking up the sources. He told Theophilus that he did checking before he wrote his Gospel. It is conceivable, and scholars have played with this hypothesis, that a particular set of reports in the early part of Luke's Gospel went back to the memory of Mary herself, and which she did not pass around. They did not become part of common Christian tradition until Luke (or somebody before him) looked her up, received them, and then was able to pass on some of her private memories. This is just a possibility, but a historically meaningful one.

Another aspect of the historian's concern for looking for witnesses is to remember that the introduction of this idea late in the life of the church would have needed to be explained. If we assume it was not a true report at the beginning, then how did it get in? We cannot figure out any very easy hypothesis for explaining how such a report would have arisen so late. Emil Brunner suggests that it was cut from whole cloth to unfold of the doctrine of the two natures. That is, if Jesus was God and a man, he must have been born this way. But as we saw, this does not follow. It is not necessary for a God-man to be born in this way. In fact, later invention would have had hard tests to meet. There were apostles, and after them people who remembered the apostles, and had a concern for not letting impossible things get into the report. The New Testament church had no taste for the fantastic. They saw clearly to reject other documents that played with the fantastic and the imaginative. Those texts were systematically left out of the New Testament documents.

Before the end of the first century, anti-Christian polemics made use of the virgin birth as a ground for mockery, claiming that if Joseph was not Jesus' father, a Roman soldier named Pandera was. The ease with which such slanderous use can be made of the report is further circumstantial grounds for its not having been "made up" and inserted later. It can even be claimed that we see in Matthew's account the sign of a tacit embarrassment that the early witnesses felt at this point. The genealogy of Matthew 1 lists four other women:

Rahab, a Canaanite prostitute (Joshua 1);
Tamar, who posed as a prostitute to fool her father-in-law into fathering her child so that he would have a posterity;
Bathsheba, wife of a foreign general, whom David took from her husband, first by adultery and then by having him killed (2 Sam. 11); and
Ruth, foreign, re-integrated into Israel by a strange courtship ritual. There is even a reference in the Ruth story (4:12) to Tamar's offspring Perez. Ruth's husband Boaz was the son of Rahab.

Thus for anyone remembering the stories, Matthew's inclusion of these women, paying no attention to any other mothers, points to a strangely interlocked succession of cases where the marital relationship was irregular. Why did Matthew lift this out, if not to signal that the abnormality of Jesus' familial context was in line with earlier precedent, or even with a divine pattern? Why would he have made that point, if not because the coming birth account was also irregular?

Any historical question partakes of historical uncertainty and permanently has that character. It is not possible to answer a historical question with absolute certainty, but only with historical certainty. There are always the problems of hermeneutics. What does the text mean? What is the real meaning of the witnesses' testimony? And there are always tests of the value of the witnesses. Did this person see what he or she reports? Does he or she have any reason to report inaccurately? To distort or slant the report? We will never get an answer to these questions that is not subject to historical uncertainty.

Quite apart, then, from any debate on a doctrine of the authority of Scripture (which we have said is not a legitimate concern to bring in at this point), we can say on the short range only two things. First, that the only sources we have on the virgin birth affirm it, and second that we cannot think of any especially plausible reason that anyone would have had to invent it, since it is not a very helpful idea in the ancient near Eastern world. It is not unique. It does not prove anything. There is some plausible reason not to falsify such a report, and good reason not to propagate it even if it were thought to be true—so that perhaps something of the silence is explainable. As an initial introduction to the historical problem, this is where we shall have to leave it for now.

It is not a cop-out, but our first duty at this point, to deal with a narrative text as historians by testing whether the witnesses are credible and otherwise leaving it at that. Abandoning the historian's role for that of the philosopher or the natural scientist and ruling on grounds other than the record that certain reports cannot be true is always logically possible, but it means preferring some other worldview to that from which the sources spring—an uncongenial background for fairly reading any text.

Another exercise, quite fitting for the historian, is to argue on general literary and cultural grounds that Luke and Matthew did not mean to be affirming what the older Christian orthodoxies affirmed and defended. To test that hermeneutic alternative is not our assignment.

It is yet another matter to suggest that there is no point, in a modern missionary situation, in insisting on the intellectual offense of a virgin birth as a touchstone of faith or as the central miracle. Nowhere does the New Testament give it that centrality.

We followed the thought of the early communities so respectfully and descriptively that there has been no point at which it was either fitting or imperative to step back from the earliest witness of the apostles to ask what doubting the testimony to the resurrection would do to the entire construction. It is evident that the resurrection and the virgin birth are quite different in the place they have in the early witness. They are, however, nearly parallel in the problems of credibility they place before the modern skeptic with a commitment to historical and natural scientific patterns of interpretation and doubt. What credibility do the resurrection reports have when looked at with the standards the doubters applied in the case of the virgin birth? The parallelism between the two "miracles" is greatest when put in the context of modern debate about the notion of miracles as such. Both reports describe events of the kind that normally do not happen. As such they are parallel. The questions of credibility they raise are analogous. They differ of course in the social nature of the event. Most of the appearance reports in 1 Corinthians 15 were public, therefore the absence of any ancient documentation of evidence that would count against it, such as anyone reporting having found the real body of Jesus in a tomb or any credible ancient document reporting fraudulent actions on the part of the disciples is a weighty silence.

It is not our place to discuss psychological or logical credibility in depth. It is common-sensical to argue that the disciples had at the outset no vested interest in proving such an unlikely event. They had been predisposed to despair and disbelief, rather than oriented in a way that favored fabrication of false evidence. A leadership team knowing they had fabricated false evidence would hardly have produced the New Testament story, but this level of hypothetical debate about credibility is the apologetic background to the historical debate rather than its substance.[6]

We turn next to the issue of the canon, which is the last of our statements about the nature of the post-apostolic age.

The development of church order responded to a real problem. Who guarantees the identity of the church? Who ensures that the next generation's church will be faithful to this generation's ministry? Bishops developed, and then archbishops, to deal with this. The apostles were gone and they had to be replaced by some kind of person.

They also had to be replaced by some kind of statement, by the creed as a guide. Many more writings gather around the creed and the apostolic writings. Every generation had new questions. Someone was creative. Someone answered those questions and wrote a document. As these documents gather around the earlier documents, the lines between them blur. Every time you try to clarify something, you add another voice to the medley. The church was always faced with the same heresies that were present in the New Testament age. There was the Ebionitic heresy, which we have noticed in passing, but perhaps not by name. The Ebionites were Jewish Christians or sympathetic Jews who concentrated on Jesus' humanity. Their Christology allowed Jesus to be Messiah in the sense of a technical title, but kept him within the framework of Judaism, dissolving Jesus' uniqueness into a sub-case of history in general—one more rabbi, one Messiah, a man among others whose authority over us is not absolute.

6. The following bibliographical suggestions may guide the student desirous of following the matter further. Gordon Kaufman and Brunner are the contemporary theologians who have worked the most seriously in a systematic context with doubt about whether the resurrection reports are to be believed straightforwardly. J. C. Wenger does not attend to the issue.

Raymond E. Brown — *The Virginal Conception and Bodily Resurrection of Jesus.* 1973.

Van Buren, Paul — "Easter" in *The Secular Meaning of the Gospel: Based on the Analysis of its Language.* 1963.

Fuller, Reginald H. — *The Formation of the Resurrection Narratives.* 1971

Harvey, Van Austin — *The Historian and the Believer: the Morality of Historical Knowledge and Christian Belief.* 1969.

Ladd, George Eldon — *I Believe in the Resurrection of Jesus.* 1975.

Perrin, Norman — *The Resurrection According to Matthew, Mark and Luke.* 1977.

Ramsey, Michael. — *The Resurrection of Christ: A Study of the Event and Its Meaning for the Christian Faith.* 1961.

Selby, Peter — *Look for the Living: The Corporate Nature of Resurrection Faith.* 1976.

Wilckens, Ulrich. — *Resurrection: Biblical Testimony to the Resurrection: An Historical Examination and Explanation.* 1977.

The Gnostic or the Docetic approach on the other hand tended to dissolve Jesus into one more example of revelation. These two tendencies always bother the church. As the bulk of documents increases, as the number of answers to these questions increases, the church's attempts to find its way grow more and more chaotic. As a response to this, the canon gradually develops.

The word "canon" means a "rule" or a "criterion." The canon develops as a criterion for the acceptability of writings. The canon lists those writings that belong and ought to be accepted as Scripture. By transfer the word canon comes to mean the body of writings themselves, not just the list.[7]

The first canon was developed by a man who was later condemned as a heretic. Marcion was active in the middle of the second century. He wanted to distinguish clearly between Paul and the other writings, and between the Old Testament and the New. As Marcion has been interpreted since then, he was against the Old Testament and anti-Jewish. He contrasted the God of the Old Testament with the God of the New. He wanted to excise all the Jewish traces from the New Testament as well. Although there may have been something of this to his position as it developed, it did not start there. These were not his central concerns. He simply wanted some solid footing amidst the growing pluralism. It started simply with his desire to know, in this vast mass of literature that was developing, where the court of appeal was. What is the criterion that can show us the truth in this pluralistic mess of many kinds of literature that says many things, and even contradictory things? How is the church to find its way? Marcion says, "Let us do it by distinguishing between the authoritative literature—mostly the writings of Paul—and the rest." The so-called "orthodox" church, which rejected Marcion's approach, still had to respond to him in the same language. This meant drawing up their own list, which in addition to Paul had the other Epistles and the Gospels. This list was relatively solid by the year 300, although its fringes were not final for quite a long time (for instance, with regard to the book of Revelation).

What does it mean when we make a canon, creating a list and saying, "These writings are our Scripture and others are not"? The traditional meaning, found especially in Roman Catholic apologetics, relates to a debate between Catholics and Protestants. The Protestant says, "The

7. See F. W. Beare, "Canon of the New Testament," in *The Interpreter's Dictionary of the Bible: An Illustrated Encyclopedia Identifying and Explaining All Proper Names and Significant Terms and Subjects in the Holy Scriptures, Including the Apocrypha, with Attention to Archaeological Discoveries and Researches into the Life and Faith of Ancient Times,* vol. 1 (New York: Abingdon Press, 1962), 520–532; A. C. Sundberg, Jr., "Canon of the New Testament," in *The Interpreter's Dictionary of the Bible . . . Supplementary Volume,* (Nashville: Abingdon, 1976), 136–140.

Bible is the only authority, the church is not." The Catholics respond, "No, the church is the final authority because we made the Bible. We gave the Bible its authority." Traditional Roman Catholic apologetics says that the church ruled on the authority it chose to give to Scripture. The church first wrote Scripture in the first century. Then the church in the second and third centuries said, "That is the Scripture to which *we* chose to give authority." This argument will not work. It will not work because recognizing the canon did not *give* authority to these writings that they did not have before. Rather, a line was drawn including only those writings that were assumed *already* to have authority. They did not deal with whether or not these writings had authority, but asked whether they were apostolic. They did not even deal with whether the writings were authentic. The letter to the Hebrews was left in because it was (wrongly) assumed to be a writing of Paul. It was not, as far as we know, but it was apostolic—it came from the apostolic age. It was a valid witness of the first generation church. So setting up a canon is not granting authority to texts that had no authority before. It is rather the recognition by the church that the texts are of such status as to already have authority over us.

The second hole in the older Catholic apologetic line is that there never was (or at least we find no record of) an official action whereby a church agency—a synod, a bishop, or a pope—took action to say, "Now we give authority to these Scriptures." We have rather lists—more than one—of different ages, that simply record the texts we now accept in our New Testament.

Another loophole in this apologetic idea is the fact that the list was never *fully* clear. The bulk of the outline was clear by the 300's, but there continued to be, all the way until the sixteenth century, a small group of texts in the list called the *antilegoumenoi,* "those which are spoken against." This meant 2 Peter, Revelation, and sometimes some others—texts that until the time of the Reformation were not accepted as canon by everyone. Of course, there was also another group, which we call the Apocrypha, which was accepted by Catholics but never by Protestants. So in the recognition of the canon the church precisely does *not* take and claim authority and then confer authority on this book in a legal sense, as a Parliament gives authority to a law that is passed, or a dictator gives authority to a decree that he signs. It is the other way around. The church recognizes the *limitation* on her authority by saying, "Those are the writings that stand above us. Those are the writings to which we cannot add. This is the body of literature under which we stand and from which we take orders."

So we see, beginning in the development of the canon, what later church history refers to as the concept of "restitution," that is, reaching back for criteria. The church is no longer as simple a stream moving through history as was the apostolic generation. This movement in history recognizes the need for standards, criteria, and places to go back to for judgment; we need something by which to test ourselves. That cannot be *all* of our history because it does not all say the same thing. It must be our earliest history. It must be the writings of the apostles and no others. What are they? Well, probably these. Then we have our canon. So the development of a canon is the beginning of the church's self-critical concern to judge herself by her origin.

This restatement of the meaning of the canon as the beginning of concern for renewal, or for judgment of the church by her origins, saves us from some other misunderstandings of what it might have meant. It was not a revealed canon. Some fundamentalists seem almost to think that the identity of the canon itself is a subject of revelation. There is no basis for that. It was not infallible. Those who drew up the canon thought Hebrews was Pauline, and it is not. It was a judgment applied to an imperfect text—parts of John's Gospel were left in and probably do not belong in. John 8, for instance, is probably a true story but it does not belong there in the text. The canon is not a final ruling. As we saw, up until the sixteenth century there were variations, and there still are between Protestants and Catholics. It did not include a ruling on the Old Testament. We have no Christian statement on the Old Testament canon. Christians took over Jewish traditions. It was never decided by any church. So the canon is a human, historical thing, fuzzy on the edges. But the *meaning* of canon is still fundamentally significant, because it indicates why we need to go back to this book—not because of any doctrine we have immediately of how the book was written but because it is the record of the point to which the church must go back if she is to be the church, if she is to test herself for being the church by reference to where she came from. It is that understanding of canon to which we shall constantly need to be returning and by which we shall constantly need to test ourselves. Later, at the end of the semester, we may find further things we can say about biblical authority.[8]

Beyond the sample represented by the problem of the canon, perhaps we can take a broader look at how we tend to read our history. We

8. We might test the concept of canon by a hypothetical question. If in the sands of Egypt we were to find a parchment that was very clearly another letter of the apostle Paul, written to the church at Alexandria, it would not be a part of the third century canon. Neither would it be a part of Martin Luther's canon, but it would be an apostolic writing. What place would that have? This is a good point at which to test our understanding of the biblical canon as that body of literature under whose judgment the church stands and on which it stands to be renewed. To pursue further this theme, see my "The Authority of the Canon," *Essays on Biblical Interpretation: Anabaptist-Mennonite Perspectives,* ed. Willard M. Swartley (Elkhart, Ind.: Institute of Mennonite Studies, 1984), ch. 17.

read history over a time line. That makes sense. We have learned, and the Bible has taught us, that God works through history. The passage of time matters. What develops in the passage of time is important in God's purposes, so we draw a time line and follow that line through the centuries. Here a heresy branches away from the church. The main line goes on. There is the division, for instance, between the Donatists and the Catholic tradition that was right, so it goes on. Later the Eastern and Western churches divide. Then the Protestant line continues when Catholicism branches off. And so we go on.

On the naive level we can see quickly that this is inaccurate because it is only *one* line. As a matter of fact, there are many lines. The Christians who stand at some other point can just as well read the whole picture with their line as the continuation, so we really ought to have a "tree" we could read from every direction, taking every line seriously (see sketch.) That is the superficial shortcoming. But there is something still more wrong with assuming that this line just goes on. We need more dimensions because in every age there is the choice between faithfulness and unfaithfulness, so we need one line that represents the norm and for every group another line that wiggles, wanders, and gets more or less unfaithful. Then there would be points at which that erring position is called back to the norm. "Back to the norm" means restitution and renewal. Marcion tried to do this. He said, "Our church is getting confused. It is becoming pagan. It is mixed up with several concepts of God, so we will have to go back to the norm, the preaching of the apostles, and slough or pare off everything that is not a part of that." When the second and third century churches said, "No, Marcion, your canon is too small, we have the right canon," they did the same thing. They were reaching back to the norm, to the standard, from which the deviations were to be judged.

Part of the lesson of the church's history is that this keeps happening. As there is wandering, there is also renewal. There are various ways in which the church is called back to her norm. It is neither simply a matter of one line going on and being right, nor of all the lines continuing and being right together—no ecumenical pluralism where you say, "We need all these lines." It is rather a matter of how the church is either unfaithful or restored to faithfulness. If God continually restores the church to faithfulness—it happens in the Reformation and with the Anabaptists, John Wesley, Marcion, and in between with Francis of Assisi—then that pattern of reaching back to the norm is a fundamental element of our church history and of our theologizing.

In Mennonite history, the man who wrote the *Martyr's Mirror,* Thieleman J. van Braght, had a view we consider naive of how there have been "Anabaptists" all through the centuries. *Martyr's Mirror* is a collection of Anabaptist martyr reports from the sixteenth century, but

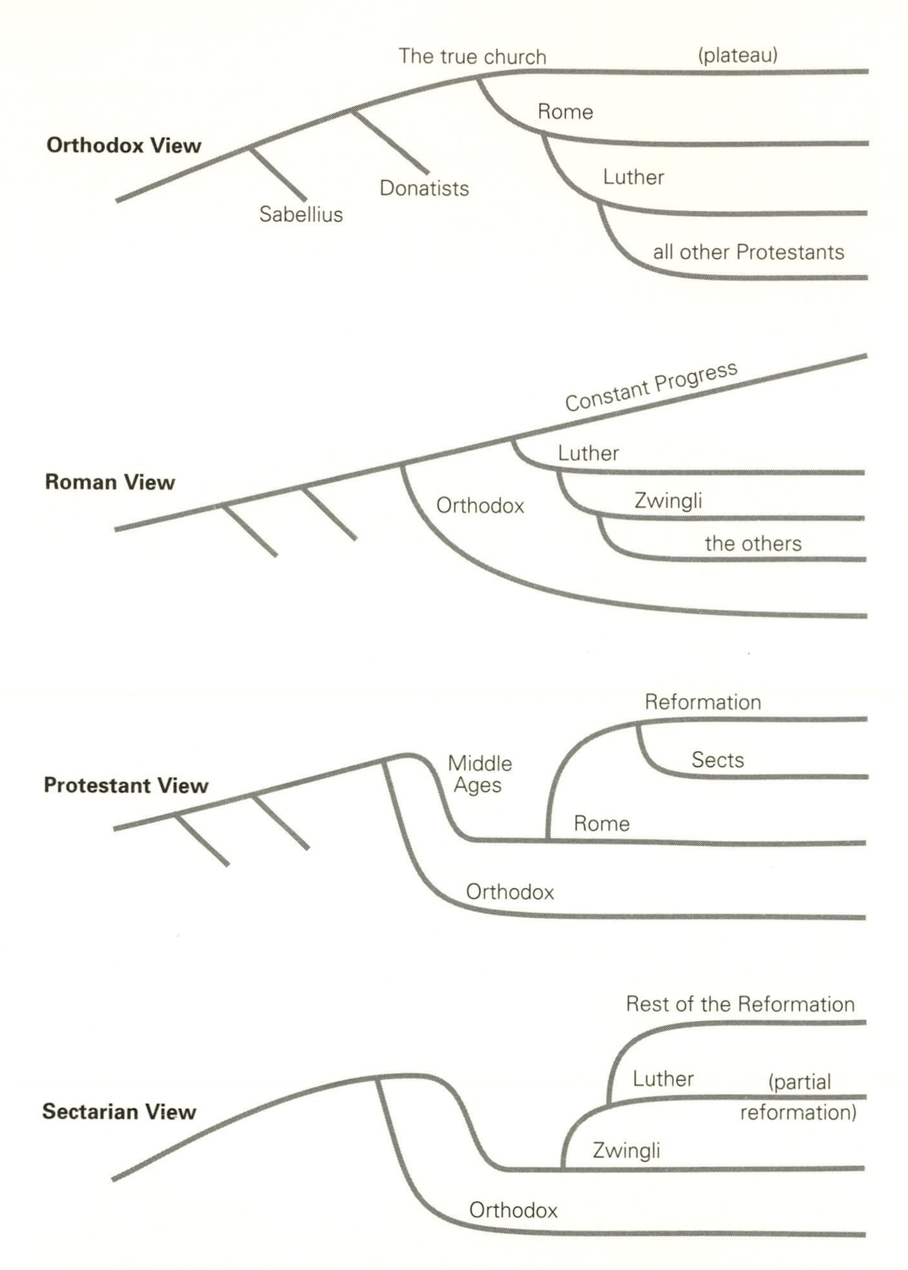

it mattered just as much to van Braght to include as the first third of the book, martyrs for believers' baptism from all the centuries. He was naive in the idea that these people were somehow all connected, so that the fourth century believers' church people got their idea from the third century and passed it on to the fifth century. This idea of an underground channel of apostolic dissent will not hold historically, but van Braght is right in the sense that we find theologizing where Christians reach back to the norm to restore the faithfulness of the church. Faithful theology is not simply a matter of being in a stream that comes from the beginning. It is rather the process within that stream of calling it to judgment, checking, and testing it with the origin, of going back to where we came from to see where we got off track.

8

The Trinity and The Council of Nicea

Preparation Guide

Read all your collateral systematic theology texts and answer the following:

1. What place (sequential position, relative space) is the doctrine of the Trinity given in the outline?
2. Is this doctrine as such a revealed truth, or a solution to problems arising out of understanding revealed truth?
3. Is there a discussion of possible other views (e.g., Arianism, Modalism) and their strengths and weaknesses? Is the doctrine of the Trinity treated as the result of doctrinal development?
4. Is "person" defined? How? Is it held by your author to be an adequate term? A necessary one?
5. Does the author discuss the interrelations of the three "Persons" of the Trinity among themselves? Does he or she discuss the difference between the "economic" and the "ontological" concepts of Trinity? Does he or she mention in this connection *circumincessio? Circuminsessio? Perichoresis?* Appropriation?
6. Does the systematic theology text you use illustrate the concept of "Trinity" with modern analogies or arguments?
7. Does it try to make "threeness-in-oneness" an understandable idea by the use of analogies, illustration, or logical redefinitions?

We have observed the transition from the apostolic age to the life of the church beyond apostolic times, and have said something about the framework in which that church had to think. We still have a long way to go before we can see the church of the Middle Ages—or of the present—communicating, testing, debating, and theologizing. On the library shelf in section 230, or in the books listed for collateral reading, you find texts that claim in some way to have the completeness of a finished system of theology. This gives us some picture of the bulk and the kind of material dealt with under the heading of "theology."

But how do we get from here to there? How do we get from the New Testament and early post-New Testament church to the present where there is a sizable additional bulk of vocabulary, topics, and debate to be handled under the heading of "theology"?

The first major step beyond the New Testament level into which we have to move has come to be called "dogmatics." This term has a different meaning in theology from the one it has in lay usage. In ordinary, lay, colloquial usage, "dogmatic" is a bad word. A dogmatic person says what he or she thinks without listening to you or to your question, but *dogma* as a Greek root simply means something that is placed solidly. A dogma is a statement of the church that has been defined. Any statement that has been defined is in some sense dogmatic, but especially those creeds that have been given formal status by major councils of the churches are dogma. The discipline of "dogmatics" (as distinct from other things you do in theology) is the discipline of interpreting these documents and examining how dogmatic statements develop. These later statements have a more precise character as *dogma* than did the Apostles' Creed, which we examined as a testimony to the liturgical life of the church, and which was not elevated to the status of dogma by a particular church council.

To understand what happened in the third and fourth centuries, we need to think back to the phenomenon of getting off the track and getting called back, to which we referred in the preceding lecture. This is the phenomenon of heresy—positions and doctrines held to be so wrong that they need to be explicitly condemned, such that anyone holding to those positions needs to be excluded from Christian fellowship. In the New Testament persons are excluded from the fellowship, or exclude themselves, on the ground of what they thought as individuals. In 1 John, for instance, the writer mentions "anti-Christ." Such persons had been members of the Christian community and were no longer members. Perhaps it was revealed that they had not ever really been members, even though it seemed they were. Paul refers in his letters to persons who he says have "made ship-wreck of the faith." But in the third and fourth centuries we move to *groups* or *categories* of persons: "Those who say that . . . [and then we find a formula, a condensed statement], let them be anathema." Whatever kind of person would say that, this category of person, is condemned automatically.

The fact that the church developed this process of defining dogma and excluding heretics makes special problems for our work as historians:

- It means that for those who were condemned, we have only secondary sources. We have no writings of Marcion or Nestorius in any faithful form. We have quoted statements from them who were condemned, but their writings were not saved or recopied. They may even have been burned. Now this is not a fair way to read anyone's biography. Not only are our sources limited, but history accentuated these polarizations and tensions unfairly by looking for critical differences. Marcion and those who condemned him, as well as Nestorius and those who condemned him, agreed on many of the things that mattered most, but history has recorded the differences and made them test cases and samples of wider differences.

- From that point on the person's name begins to point to a peculiarity at that test point.
- Then we confuse the nuances of his or her actual thought with the place of the idea in the history of thought, and with the place in logic of the position. So when we say, "Augustinianism," "Nestorianism," "Marcianism," or "Montanism," we do not mean simply what some person actually thought. Certainly we do not mean everything he or she thought. We mean the idea we have chosen as most peculiar to him or her, to represent special emphases or peculiar mistakes. That makes it very hard to be fair with the story.

Furthermore, we have some special problems of method in dealing with this material in lecture form. This is probably the most complex material with which we shall deal in the semester, as far as both vocabulary and logical intricacy are concerned. It is not easily clarified in presentation or even by further free discussion. We shall have to bear with the limits of lecture playback of the struggle in the church and hope afterwards to see it more clearly from the other end of the story. This will necessarily involve a certain amount of complex definitions of unfamiliar vocabulary that might make these few hours more difficult than the rest of the semester.

At the end of our New Testament reading the church was left with an unsolved problem. We said that was probably good. The early church had a high view of Jesus, such a high view that they could speak of him in terms normally reserved for God alone, and say about him things that you could not normally say about any human. Yet this early church was rigidly, loyally, and Jewishly monotheistic—both denying that there could be two Gods or more than one God, and denying that the true God could be seen in human or any other visible form. The New Testament church did not stumble over the built-in opposition between these two sets of ideas for a number of reasons. For one thing, the concept of adoption or exaltation was used in the earliest church, that is, the idea that Jesus was a man raised to his position by virtue of God's approbation of his obedience. That seemed to be an answer for a while.

There was also a partial way to avoid immediate trouble with this difficulty because the earliest Christians were so clearly Jews. When they talked about the one God—there is only one God, invisible, not wanting to be worshipped in temples—this was no philosophical Absolute or unique metaphysical being irreconcilable with this one man Jesus. It was rather the God of their story, the YHWH of Old Testament history. They were not bothered by the philosophical difficulty of putting *this* absolute deity together with the humanity of Jesus, but as the Jewish background receded and the church became more accustomed to speaking Greek and thinking in Greek categories, then the problem of relating this jealous and zealous monotheism of biblical faith with a high view of Jesus arose. Is there one God after all or are there two? Three? How do we connect Jesus with the only God?

Two centers of intellectual life developed in the church. We shall observe their differences once in a while, although we cannot pursue them in any full, historical way. On the one hand is the city of Antioch, the base of the missionary activity of Paul. It continued to be the center of the life of the church in its corner of the Mediterranean. Antioch was not an ancient cultural center in the way Alexandria, Corinth, and Athens were. The way the Antiochenes theologized was simpler, more modest and exegetical. They read one text at a time and asked what it meant; they read the stories and asked how they happened. Their sense of how to understand the biblical texts in the second and third centuries was still Hebraic, historical, unphilosophical. The other center was Alexandria—a city of ancient and proud intellectual heritage—represented, for instance, by the Jewish philosopher Philo, but also by many pagan philosophers. This was the center of academically integrated and systematic knowledge. It was also the first place the early church set up a systematic schooling process, where people would gather full-time around a teacher and order their thoughts for teaching and coherence.

The debate to which we shall turn reflects in one sense the difference between these two schools, although it is not that simple. It has its element of church politics, in which the polarization of these schools (and their respective bishops) makes a difference. There is also a difference in theological approach, but we shall not tell the story that way in the beginning, although we might come back and look at that dimension of it.

We need to watch how the early church dealt with the interrelation of the high claims made for Jesus and the high claims made for the one true God in the Jewish tradition that the early church took over without any question.

We begin by returning to a concept we found in John's Gospel, for which there is more history than we at first noticed. The concept is *logos,* or "word," which we will find being paralleled by "wisdom," *sophia* in Greek or *chokma* in Hebrew. Wisdom is almost a person in the part of the Old Testament we call "the wisdom literature." Proverbs 8 states this most strongly, and is so representative a text that it is worth reading at some length:

> Does not wisdom call,
> does not understanding raise her voice?
> On the heights beside the way,
> in the paths she takes her stand;
> beside the gates in front of the town,
> at the entrance of the portals she cries aloud:
> "To you, O men, I call,
> and my cry is to the sons of men . . ." (Proverbs 8:1–4).

"Wisdom" speaks in the first person, telling humanity how wise the words are:

> I, wisdom, dwell in prudence,
> and I find knowledge and discretion.
> The fear of the Lord is hatred of evil. . . .
> I have counsel and sound wisdom,
> I have insight, I have strength.
> By me kings reign,
> and rulers decree what is just;
> by me princes rule,
> and nobles govern the earth. . . .
> The LORD created me at the beginning of his work,
> the first of his acts of old.
> Ages ago I was set up,
> at the first, before the beginning of the earth.
> When there were no depths I was brought forth . . . (Proverbs 8:12–24a).

Thus "wisdom" is personified in dramatic form in the proverbs. Wisdom is the first of the acts of God, the first creation and therefore before all creation. Wisdom is the coherence of creation. Through wisdom kings know how to rule. It is through wisdom that the skies are firm above and the water stays under the earth. Wisdom is thereby the agent of God in the rest of creation. This wisdom is divine; it partakes of the nature and authority of God. It is not simply a tool or a reflection of God. It (or rather she) seems to be a part of God.

The things the Old Testament said about wisdom can be carried over and said by the New Testament of the *Logos*. In speculative Greek philosophy *logos* already has some of these meanings. So the two heritages could work together. Both the *Logos* and the first creation could be affirmed as preexistent, the agency of God in creation, and divine in character. All the prologue to John's Gospel adds is that this entity became flesh and dwelt among us. It does not indicate any philosophical problem with the chain of equations that says the *Logos* is equal to God, somehow becomes human, and in between is the order of creation. This chain of connections or equations is not unthinkable. It does not seem to jeopardize the unity of God. In all of this the Greek and Jewish traditions are nearly parallel.

Greek thought about *logos* has another dimension, however, which comes from the linkage of *word* and *reason*. Rather than the wisdom that makes the world make sense, this is reason as what makes thinking make sense—sequence of thought. On one level we could say that *logos* is the principle of rationality or the principles of order in the universe. The universe is orderly—it has hierarchy and the dependence of effects on causes. That reasonableness of the universe is its *logicality,* its *logos*-likeness. In Greek thought the *logos* is not God. It is below God and dependent upon the world because it is the rationality of the world. If there were no world, there would be no *logos* because *logos* is the order of the world. But if *logos* is not God, neither is it human. It is all through creation, especially where creation is most orderly—like in the stars or the law of gravity—not where creation is irregular and erratic, as in earthquakes or humanity. It is universal, so it could never be especially in one particular human. This speculation about the *logos* will ultimately, when unchecked, issue in Gnosticism's concern for seeing into its order and peering into the hierarchy of things. What is higher and what is lower? How do things interlock? How are things derived from what came before? These are mysteries; they are not empirical things one measures, but things perceived through mystical insights. The mysteries reach *toward* God but not *to* God. So Gnosticism never gets to God; it studies the search for God.

But now we link *logos* and *sophia:* one more Hebraic, one more philosophical. Both of them, somehow fitting together, are affirmed in the New Testament. This *whole heritage* is attached to Jesus already in Colossians 1, Hebrews 1, and John 1, and before them in Philippians 2.

Are there other New Testament testimonies to the presence of this thought independent of those texts we already know? First Corinthians 8:6a: "For us there is one God, the Father, from whom are all things and for whom we exist." This may be a quotation, although Paul does not identify it as such. The concept of preexistence is present elsewhere as well. 1 Corinthians 10:4 talks about a "supernatural Rock," that followed the children of Israel—"and the Rock was Christ." That is a difficult figure of speech, but is obviously saying that Christ was present in some way with ancient Israel.

We could find more texts, clearly by Paul himself and not only pre-Pauline, in which allusions to the Hebraic concept of wisdom are undeniable. But Christian testimony does not simply "pick up" philosophical thought about the *logos* and Hebraic thought about wisdom in God's creation. It brings it to earth. This too was beginning in the Old Testament. Proverbs are a very earthly set of rules about how to live, how to be prosperous, how to be wise, and how to be honest, so already in the context of Proverbs 8 wisdom was becoming human, becoming material, and becoming secular. But in John 1 and the other passages in parallel, the newness is that this wisdom became flesh. Yet by becoming fully human, by living among us, the *Logos* did not become any less divine, because John also says the *Logos* was "with God"; the *Logos* was divine. So whereas in Greek thought *logos* was a halfway thing—neither quite God nor quite human—the prologue to the Gospel of John pushes both ways, and affirms identity at both ends. This makes our intellectual problem all the worse.

How can we maintain the unity of God in monotheism? That is the one end of the problem. Or say it the other way: How can we keep the humanity of Jesus? Certainly the Bible wants to do both. If we push in the direction of the unity of Jesus with God, then Jesus is just God's visible self-revelation. That is what we call a theophany—God's visible self-revelation in a way that has no character of its own. How is Jesus then distinct from the Father? How is he then distinct from other theophanies? Genesis 18 recounts the story of Abraham having three visitors to his tent—that was a theophany. Elsewhere in the Old Testament there are apparitions. Isaiah saw a vision of God. How is Jesus different from *that* kind of appearance of God? The earliest church kept the difference by saying, "subordination and adoption," but that does not affirm enough.

So we have two lines of thought. We can say strong things about Jesus, but then we have a potential threat to monotheism, or we can say strong things about the Father and then deal with the problems of how real Jesus could be and how necessary his work can be.

We may assume that Jesus and the Father were one, and then we are not taking Jesus' own story seriously. We can affirm that they are different—then we cannot be sure we have one God in mind. The *Logos* must be both in the world (if he is not he cannot save us) and distinct from us (again, if he is not he cannot save us). For Jesus to be the *Logos* he must both be equal to God (sharing God's capacity to save us) and different from God (or he would not be the *Logos* among us). This is an intellectual problem. A problem we have because of words. You could say that if we refused to use the words we have been using we might not have the problem, but the church of the second and third century had to use their words. We have to respect the problem they had with their words even if we come to the conclusion that we have better words and do not need to stumble in the same way.

We begin to watch the church work at this problem by labeling the schools of thought that developed. We have to remind ourselves continually, however, that reporting on schools of thought in the ancient world is hardly ever fair. We do not have all the facts. The facts we have are slanted by the reporting of those who won out in a given controversy. Nevertheless we can report some of these typical answers, not claiming historical fairness but only that they represent the logical problem.

Monarchianism

There are, first of all, answers to this problem that we classify as "Monarchian." Their first concern was with the unity of God, with monarchy. They interpret the unity of God in such a way as to relate God's oneness to the work of Jesus. One subheading under this is the *Ebionitic* kind of Monarchianism. The Ebionites were a group of people who emphasized Jesus' humanity at the cost of his authority. Jesus was another holy Jew. This position was represented by Paul of Samosata in the controversies into which we are moving. Again, he is known only because he is pointed to as a representative of this kind of heresy. We have no way of knowing whether we are being fair to him.

The Ebionitic heresy in the time of the New Testament denied the preexistence of the Son. It said that Jesus was just a man whom God used. The later Monarchian position has that same concern for the full humanity of Jesus, and perhaps correlates to the school of Antioch. It accepts a high doctrine of the *Logos* and the uniqueness of Jesus. It does not deny the incarnation or preexistence, but it still is concerned to safeguard the historical character of Jesus as more than a theophany.

So they move in the direction of saying that *logos* is in Greek what the face of God is in the Old Testament. It is clear that we read about God's his countenance—"the Lord lift his countenance upon you." What does that mean—the face of a God who is invisible? (Moses also saw God's back once.) It means God's presence or way of self-manifestation. God is a God who makes God's own self known. Then *logos* means that aspect we see when God makes God's self known—the Father as manifesting himself. Not only do we have reference to the God's countenance, but we have the story of Melchizedek, who is very difficult to explain, and according to Hebrews seems to be superhistorical (7:4). But all of these appearances of God, all of these faces of God, do not create a second deity or separate personality. They are simply the principle of self-manifestation in the person of God—the one God, not a separate thing at all. Not a separate personality, not a separate consciousness, but just that side of God, the face, the self-revealing quality of God.

For the Ebionites, this *logos,* this quality of God, is in all humanity. It is especially in Jesus, uniquely present in degree, but it is not equal to him because Jesus was a real man. The *Logos* of God simply used him much more than others, more than us, and more than anyone before him. The *Logos* used him uniquely, but still the *Logos* was not a person. It was the self-revealing quality of God, using as a vehicle Jesus, who was a real man.

This is a logical position. It keeps monotheism and it keeps the humanity of Jesus. But it affirms less than the New Testament, even less than Proverbs 8, in that Ebionism has no room to affirm a distinct character, quality, or identity carried by this *logos*/wisdom independently of and prior to the historic event that all our texts affirm.

The other form of Monarchianism came to be called *patripassianism.* The roots of this label are the words for "suffering" and "father." This view, in order to maintain the unity of God, admits of a certain analogy to the Docetists who went before, and has some correlation with the school of Alexandria. There is one God. The only distinction within God can be within the way God chooses to do things, and the word for this is "economy" in modern English, or *oikonomia,* which is the Greek word for stewardship—how you manage your household, how you do things, administration, implementation. So any distinction within God is purely *for purposes of implementation* and no distinctions exist on any other level.

The Docetism to which we referred in an earlier lecture was concerned to defend God's purity and immutability or unchangingness. It said Jesus was not real because God only *seemed* to be in Jesus. In the late second and third centuries the concern is not to defend God's immutability, but God's unity. So in Jesus, God's own self works. In Jesus, God's own self suffers. In Jesus, God's own self dies. The death of Jesus is the work of God's self for us. This is a very powerful position on the level of piety. It enables one to take the work of Christ with utter seriousness—no less than God was at work among us; the work of Jesus *is* the work of the Father. But if you take this position seriously then again the concept of preexistence is meaningless, and Jesus' humanity is not genuine because he is after all God just taking this shape in order to work among us.

So neither of the Monarchian positions, the patripassian or the Ebionitic, fits the New Testament witness. In observing this we are talking about the documents without committing ourselves to specific systematic-philosophic concerns. There is the threat of pantheism—if the revelation of God is the same as God, then God is everywhere. Or there is the threat of deism—if God is not the same as Jesus, then God only ever reveals actions or edges, God's hand or face. Both schools of thought, which were concerned first of all to safeguard the unity of

God, one from above and one from below, so to speak, fail to permit us to take seriously the texts, especially with reference to the humanity of Jesus and the preexistence of the *Logos*.

Tertullian

Perhaps we should try a system that starts at the other end. We might begin by working out seriously an understanding of the distinct existence of the Son. What would that position look like if unfolded and set up in debate? The church father Tertullian, who was active around the year 200, is a good sample of how such thought went on. Tertullian was a debater. He had been a lawyer before he became a church leader and writer. He began by arguing with the classic Docetic position, which said that Jesus must not have been a real man because God only *appeared* in him. Because God cannot change, God could not have ceased to be God in order to become flesh, and God's appearance in Jesus must only have been an appearance. It could not have been God's real presence because that would require God to change. God would have had to become subject to time and space. God would have had to become finite. God would have had to become visible, and none of that is possible. By definition it is unworthy of God.

Tertullian argued that God differs from us precisely in that God can, as we cannot, change and remain the same *at the same time*. Is this just playing with words? Perhaps. But playing with words matters if you are a debater. It is unworthy of God to cease to be God. Humanity cannot change without ceasing to be what it was, but God precisely can change and still remain what God was, therefore it is possible by definition for God's true self-manifestation to come among us in the form of a man.

But it is unworthy of God, the Docetists went on, to enter into flesh, to be visible, to become touchable, or to compromise with human existence and all that is unworthy about human existence—its dirt and suffering. Tertullian argued that if the particular God whom we seek is the God of the Bible, then God is the God of grace, and chooses graciously to do that which is below, beneath, and unworthy of God. That is the meaning of grace—God deals with humanity in a way they are not worthy of. It would have been worse yet for God just to *seem* to be there. It would have been worse if God had fooled us by making us think that Jesus was a man when he was really just an appearance.

That was Tertullian's argument with the traditional Docetism, but he also argued with the later stage—with the updating of Docetic concerns in the patripassian position. He tried to prove not that God can accept change, but that the *Logos*, the Son, is distinct from God as such, God the Father.

In the philosophical use of these words at that time there had already been a distinction between the *Logos* by itself and the *Logos prophori-*

kos, as reaching out or in action. "*Logos*-as-such" would be when we think about it in our worldview. The *Logos*-active would be those times when the reasoning, creative quality of God is making things happen in God's creation. This distinction is desirable philosophically in order not to make the *Logos* the prisoner of the world. The *Logos prophorikos* is only real when we look at the world and see the world as the reflection of the logicality of God, but the *Logos* is *Logos* by itself even when this is not happening. The *Logos* is itself when we do not see it, independently of our perceiving its action. Only thus understood is the *Logos* not the captive of creation.

Tertullian takes this idea and turns it around. He pushes that distinction back into the definition of God. In God the *Logos* is the potentiality of revelation. It is the aspect of God that is ready for revelation. God was looking forward eternally to revelation and incarnation. Tertullian even uses the concept of "training"—God was in training, God was practicing, learning, getting ready in the Old Testament; when God created the world the *Logos* was practicing this self-revelation. In the Old Testament theophanies, in the Old Testament prophecies, God was, or the *Logos* in God was, practicing self-manifestation. Now in Jesus the *Logos* is fully known, fully real or actual. The process of *Logos*-speaking, the Word-being-spoken, has come to this conclusion. There is a divine Son before creation but already then he is destined for incarnation. In fact that is his nature, to be destined for incarnation. In God the Son or the *Logos* is the tendency toward, or the potential for, revelation. Precisely since God is our God, the God of the Bible, the God of revelation, and the God of Jesus, therefore the potential for revelation—this tendency to reveal, this intent toward self-manifestation—is a part of the divine nature and not just an accident, afterthought, supplement, or appendix. God is by nature a God who has an identifiable tendency toward self-manifestation. That is the *Logos* in God.

By defining things this way Tertullian keeps the preexistence of the *Logos,* keeps the concept of the *Logos* independent of the world (neither simply *prophorikos* nor the captive of the world in which it is the structure). He also keeps the distinction between God-as-absolute and God-as-self-revealing, thereby this *Logos* has its identity before the present—before Jesus.

This is the real beginning of the doctrine of the Trinity. In fact Tertullian seems to have coined the word "Trinity" himself. It is significant that he begins to replace the word *Logos* with the word *Son,* which is a more widely used biblical term, although both occur in the New Testament. He begins to find ways to overcome the idea that *distinction* and *unity* are opposite. Ordinary language use implies that "the Father" and "the Son," God and Jesus, or God and the *Logos,* are either the same or not. Distinction and unity are alternatives. Two realities cannot at the same time be distinct and the same. Tertullian begins to work with words in order to find ways to assume that distinction and unity are not necessarily opposite. He seeks a way of affirming distinction and unity at the same time without being silly or contradictory. He tries to develop patterns of thought, vocabularies, and logic that permit him to say what the biblical text demands must be said: the elements of preexistence, distinctness, and monotheism.

Origen

Tertullian's contemporary in the Eastern part of the church was a more philosophically and speculatively inclined Alexandrian named Origen. Origen does some of the same things as Tertullian, and tries to make some of the same cases in somewhat different language. He does it more speculatively. If it is good for God to have a Son, and obviously it is because God chose to have one, then it is good forever for God to have a Son. "Have-a-Son" is not simply a stable status of sitting there being a father. To have a Son is to generate, to beget. If it is good for God to beget a Son, then the Son is eternally present with the Father, as the ray of light is eternally present with the light source but clearly dependent upon it by sharing in its nature, not independent of it, but of the same nature.

The difficulty with this argument is that, as far as playing with words syllogistically is concerned, it would work for the world. God needs a world. God wants a world. It is good for God to have a world. We know that because God made one. So if it is good for God to have a world, God must have had a world eternally. God must eternally make and have a world. Origen actually taught this. The church rejected it later. How could they reject one and not the other? The logic is the same. The difference is a problem of church politics.

But it is significant that Origen, like Tertullian in a different form, tried to find a way to say that God can at the same time be the one only true God and yet somehow mediate between God and the world. God can somehow be related to the world, because in God the relationship between the whole and the parts is different from us. For us, for matter, for our thinking, for our mathematics, to divide is to multiply, or to multiply is to divide. You cannot get more pieces without separating them from each other. You cannot separate pieces without having more pieces. That logic works with our world of matter. But Origen, like Tertullian, tried to find a way to say it does not have to be that way with God. Origen's attempt is less successful than Tertullian's because "generation" is still subordination. The Son, the light beam, is still less than the light source. The God behind the Son is higher than the Son just as the God behind the world is higher than the world. So in a sense Origen just pushed the problem back a notch. If you have a God who generates and a Son who is generated—a God who begets and a Son who is begotten—is there behind both of them yet something else? A divine essence as such? If not, do you have two Gods and polytheism after all? So we are still stuck with the danger of polytheism.

Sabellius

Let us say we have accepted this idea of the Trinity, threeness-in-one. And now we want to find a way to come back and affirm oneness more strongly after having accepted threeness. A man named Sabellius does this.

Sabellius accepts the language of Trinity but states it with renewed concern for unity. He catches again the concern of the Monarchians. He wants to say that Jesus is truly God, that Christianity is not deism—a distant God who just sent us a message or a messenger. He wants to find God working in Jesus and in the history of the Bible story, but not all over the place. He does not want pantheism. He develops a way of doing this that we can reflect in a diagram. God is a monad (A) and utterly one, having no form because the form comes from the world. The world holds out its molds. When God enters the form "Law" (B) then God is really present to the world as Law. Then the monad moves on to be present in the form of "Jesus" (C) and then (D) as the "Spirit" giving many gifts.

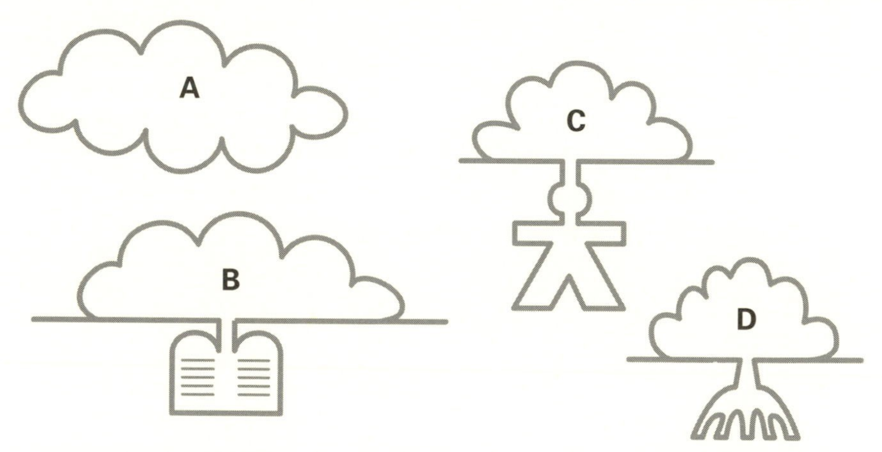

God is one. For oneness Sabellius even uses the word *monad* for the one eternal, indivisible unity. He also uses the words *Logos* and Father for that. God is truly a monad, the *Logos* and Father. But the world gives to God a certain form to take on.

There is for instance, the form of "the Law." This is a human form. God comes toward the world in the form of laws and conforms to these terms. What I have called "form" is *chreia* in Greek, a "need," an "opening," or a "mold." God takes the form of a mold that the world provides.

Later God comes in the form of the man Jesus. This time the world holds out a human form, and so God is manifest validly, wholly, in that shape—the shape the world provided. Later still, the world will prepare more and different shapes, and God will then be known in the form of the gifts of the Spirit.

First, we have the way the Old Testament first sees God. God came in the form of Law. Then we have the way the disciples perceived God—in the form of Jesus. Then we have the way the continuing life of the church perceives God—in the form of the gifts of the Spirit. But all the time it is one divine being who comes in the shape the world is able to perceive because the world has a mold like that. God as a whole—the living one God, is this total unity. So the real distinction that matters is not between Father, Son, and Spirit. That is a secondary distinction. The real distinction is between God in unity, and God as perceived (in threeness). The distinction is between "in the mold" and "out," not between Father, Son, and Spirit. God as a whole is one. God as a whole creates the world and then uses it as a vehicle of self-revelation within the shape it provided. These are the three ways in which God is made known in the world, the three molds or "modes." Sometimes Sabellianism is called "modalism."

What does this do for our problem? Is this a solid position between the two weaknesses of Monarchianism, which is either pantheistic (with God everywhere) or deistic (with God not quite present)? It looks better at first. The true God is truly present in Jesus, in the gifts of the Spirit, in the Old Testament revelation. Surely this is true revelation, so it seems to answer the intellectual problem of dealing with the concept of revelation without jeopardizing the unity of God.

But let us test it at the same textual points where we tested the others. What about the concept of preexistence? Well, that won't work at all. Before God enters a mold, God is just a timeless, shapeless blob. There is no preexistence of anything. The existence of the Son, or for that matter even the existence of the Old Testament God—as of course with the existence of the Spirit present in the church and the gifts—is always conditioned by the fact that the world provided that shape. God as such has no shape. God received that shape from the world, so there is no preexisting Son, but only the Son when the shape of Jesus is there. There is no continuing work of the God of the Old Testament because *that* God is succeeded by the Son when God's formless unity moves into another of its various shapes.

When the monad—the God-essence—takes on the form of Jesus Christ, from where do we get the limit of his humanity that he imposes upon himself?

If the limits of his humanity—the shape of Jesus—came from the world, then we could be Ebionitic after all—then the humanity of Jesus is prescribed by the world and it won't save anybody. If, on the other hand, what Jesus was like came from something within God, then there must have been a division within God and God is not one after all, so we did not solve that problem as well as we thought.

Yet another difficulty: When the monad has moved on from one mold to the next, do the former shapes cease to exist? Does the Son no longer exist or function once the Spirit works?

The Sabellian picture works better with the concern about revelation than it does with a concern for atonement or for salvation. The image of light is the one that Sabellius liked because he could say that each of the modes is illumination. Each of these is God's self-revelation. We have no record of what Sabellius said about the cross or about how God's activity on the cross was salvific. Perhaps the record is simply deficient, but it is characteristic of this view, which fails to take seriously the preexistence of Christ, that it then has difficulty saying strong things about God acting in Jesus' death.

Another testing point we may find fruitful in an effort to understand the development of this problem is Jesus' humanity in the sense of growth. Luke tells us that Jesus was a baby and then a boy and that he grew up. He "grew in favor with God and man." Some of these views have great difficulty accepting the idea that he should have grown. After all, he was the Son of God to start with, and God neither changes nor grows. So we can always test for Docetism in particular theologian's comments on those passages, especially in Luke's Gospel, where we find reference to the growth of Jesus. There is no growth in Sabellius's view of the Son. God is either there in Jesus, that is, in the form of Jesus as he is, or else God is absent in Jesus because God is over here being Spirit or back there being the Law.

Let's try to back over the history we have summarized thus far with a capsule statement in another set of words. These theologians safeguard the unity of God. They want monarchy in that sense, but to do so they have to emphasize deity. This tended to be Docetic or patripassian, making the historic reality of Jesus' career questionable, and the test they cannot meet is in the passages that deal with the growth of Jesus as a person, or with his being tempted, or making decisions, or with his suffering.

The other alternative to save Monarchianism is subordination, which tends in the Ebionitic direction. Then the problem is how the work of Christ can be of any saving value. The test for that is whether these theologians can deal with the texts that deal with preexistence. Sabellius says that threeness comes from the world, not from God. So that is really a form of subordination. But, Sabellius says, "No, all three are revelation, the Son no less than the Father. The oneness of God comes from God 'as such.'"

Sabellius lost out—partly for church political reasons but partly because of the logical arbitrariness of his explanation of threeness. It could have been four. That is, he could have added creation back before the Law, and the *chreia* called "gifts of the Spirit" is a kind of grab bag. There is something artificial about his position. Tertullian and Origen had both said more by saying that the desire for and tendency toward self-revelation, the urge to manifestation, and the move toward incarnation is in the character of God. They said something much more fundamental than Sabellius, for whom God as such had no shape at all. So the inadequacy of Sabellius is not corrected by his combining the weaknesses of both kinds of Monarchianism. He does not provide a real revelation of God coming to the world in order to save it.

The next stage begins with the debates of the fourth century. We move from the intellectual to the institutional, and from schools of thought into the story of church politics.

We begin with the thought of Arius. His concern is not the same as that of the preceding century. In the debate we have been examining the concern was for the unity of God. Arius's concern is God's transcendence. In the fourth century an age of toleration and accommodation begins. There was still, in the early part of the century, some persecution of Christians, but it soon ended. The church was increasingly able to accommodate to the culture of the surrounding world. Her membership increasingly included people whose transition from paganism was not a radical conversion, but rather a matter of moving over a little to a superior religion. After all, within the pluralism of the Roman world, people were always moving from one religion to another. A religion that was superior was one toward which people would gravitate. The vision of a God who was working among humanity for its welfare was very respectable as over against some of the crude deities of the Greek pantheon. People could move to this religion without having a deep sense of sin and therefore also without having a strong sense of the need for God to break into the world to save them.

It follows that the pressures toward affirming the uniqueness of Jesus and toward a definition of the saving work of God in Jesus, pressures which would emphasize Jesus' deity, were weaker than they had been in the earlier centuries. The concern for the dignity of God as such tended to be stronger.[1]

Arius accepted the phrasings current after Tertullian. He talked about the Trinity, but he renewed concern for Jesus' subordination to

1. There is some parallel in sociology, in culture, and even in theology between Arianism in the fourth century and Unitarianism, which arose out of the Congregational churches in New England, in the nineteenth century.

God as such, which was characteristic of an earlier age. There are two ways in which to state the subordination of the Son to the Father with which Arius is concerned. First of all, one may say it in terms of time. Origen had said that the Son is begotten by the Father.[2] To Arius' mind, begetting or *generation,* is an event, and events are in finite time. But God is above time. God is before time. God is not limited by time. Therefore, Arius is supposed to have said, *"There was a time when the Son was not,"* namely, before the beginning of finite time.

The other way to put it is in terms of causality. God is the pure cause. God is the first cause and the only first cause. The Son cannot be made out of God—that would be Sabellian modalism. The Son is just another shape of the Father. Arius rejects this because then the Son is not genuinely Son and God would have comprised the character of the "first cause."

But neither can God need the Son eternally in order to be God, as Origen had said. If God needed to have a Son, the divine independence, sovereignty, primacy, and unity would be destroyed. When God chooses to create a Son and a universe, it must be a free choice if God is to be God. So, *if* the Son cannot be made out of God *and* the Son cannot be eternally a part of God, *then* the Son had to be made like the rest of creation, out of nothing. So the key phrase is: *"The Son was made out of nothing."* These two statements, snippets from the writings of Arius, are the battleground in the period of history to which we turn.

Arius was a priest in Alexandria. The bishop over him was Alexander of Alexandria. Arius accused his bishop of being Sabellian by saying that God made the Son out of himself, and thereby falling into a heresy that had already been condemned. Alexander, being bishop, silenced or deposed Arius, but instead of simply accepting the reprimand, Arius left the diocese and found other bishops and friends to support him.

Alexander refined the traditional argument in response to Arius, saying that although one thinks of beginning (or begetting) as an event in time, it does not imply a prior time. You cannot talk about a time before time, which is, of course, what this sentence tries to do. Before time it wasn't time. Perhaps you can conceive of absoluteness without time, but you can make no statements about "before time." Alexander also turned to logic, the logic of the pun, asking whether Arius' objection to Origen—that God is not always a God with *Logos* or communication as part of the divine character—meant that God was once speechless? Can you conceive of a God who would be a higher God and who would be

2. Editorial note: Origen also maintained that the Son is *eternally* generated by the Father. Therefore, Origen himself did not conceive of generation as a necessarily finite activity.

without communication, without *Logos* (*alogos*)? This kind of argument was thrown back at Arius: Can you imagine a speechless God?

In debating, Arius made his position more offensive. He not only said that the *Logos* was subordinate in the eternal creation, but he pushed even more strongly the limits of what he was willing to say about Jesus. Arius said that Jesus earned Sonship by his obedience, so preexistence is not really needed in order to understand the New Testament. He thus dismantled not only the systematic, dogmatic, and philosophical statements of the second and third centuries, but began to go back and challenge some of the things that the New Testament itself had said.

The Council of Nicea (325)

In the midst of this mess, the emperor Constantine convened the first Council of Nicea. This was not the only issue that needed to be dealt with. It is the main question we remember, but there were many other questions. Constantine had put an end to the persecution of the church a dozen years earlier, and by 325 was concerned that his church be unified so that he could count on it for support in his effort to unify the empire. If Christians squabbled among themselves, then they could be little help to him in running the empire. Constantine's interest is unity. Not yet baptized, not a Christian in the formal sense of the word, he convenes the Council of Nicea, to which bishops from all over the empire are summoned. Alexander is still the bishop of Alexandria, but he is beginning to be aided and almost replaced by Athanasius, a figure we will see more of later. Right now Athanasius is secretary to the bishop of Alexandria, but is also named as secretary of the conference at Nicea.

Constantine not only convened this meeting, he made its decisions by dictating at crucial points what wording they were to use—this despite the fact that he was not yet a baptized member of the church. The decision took the form of a creed, a statement like the Apostles' Creed but extended at certain points with phrasings that say what needed to be said in order to clarify the substance of the debate. This demanded additional statements of two kinds. First of all it demanded extension of the statement about Christ: "I believe in one God, the Father Almighty, maker of visible and invisible, and in one Lord Jesus Christ, Son of God, only begotten of the Father, who is of the nature of the Father, God of God, Light of Light, very God of very God, begotten, not made, being of one substance with the Father." So it adds statements about the being of Jesus, and later turns back to the rest of the earlier creed: "made flesh and died, suffered and rose," and the other elements. But the crucial additional statements about Christology are near the middle, "begotten, not made."

This is an obvious response to the discussion about the creation of the Son and "being of one substance with the Father." Here is the crucial word *ousia,* meaning "substance." So if *ousious* means "being of substance," and *homo* means "the same," *homoousious* then is "being of the same substance." If we just add one letter to *homo, iota,* then we get *homoi,* meaning "like." So *homoiousios* is "being of like substance." The difference between the two words was all that mattered in the debate. Arius said that the Son was of *like* substance with the Father. The Athanasius-Alexander crowd said "of *the same* substance with the Father." The emperor Constantine made the decision and ruled, "We'll say it without the *iota.*" This has been characterized as the battle over a diphthong, but it is one word that makes a big difference in definition: "of the same essence, substance, nature, with the Father." This is the expansion of the creed that made of it a new dogma.

The other change that was made added a condemnation at the end:

> Those who say that there was when He [the Son] was not, [this is a direct quotation of the phrase from Arius], and that He was not before He was begotten, and that He was made out of nothing, or that He was made out of other persons or substances or flesh, that He was created, that He was changeable . . . [there follows a list of other statements, also from Arius] such a person, let him be anathematized by the Catholic church.

This is then what we call the Nicene Creed, with an extension of the statements about the unity of Christ with the Father and his being begotten not made, and at the end with a specific condemnation of the people who teach these particular phrases that are to be rejected.

The text was not immediately recognized as the "Nicene Creed." They did not put it in the newspaper the same evening and report it as such. It was significant for the time simply as a document of the political tug-of-war that went back and forth during the next generation.

Arius and his party were on top several times. They had more friends in the imperial court. Athanasius was sent into exile, sometimes as far away as Europe, several times before the thing finally settled down in a solution both political and theological. Until a century later the Nicene phrasing was not really recognized and given creedal status. There was another council in Constantinople, in 381. From its archives the bishop of Jerusalem found the Nicene text in a slightly modified form and quoted it in Ephesus in 431. Because the creed's first formal use was 381, 1981 was proclaimed the "Year of the Second Ecumenical Council" and anniversary of the Nicene Creed by Patriarch Dimitrios. But it was not recognized as dogma until it was quoted in 431, even though it was adopted in 325. The Council of Nicea kept the creedal form and the use of participles to make the major points, but it bent the creed so as to make of it the instrument of the particular point being argued right at that time.

For a full fifty years the tug-of-war went back and forth. Arius had a lot on his side. He could appeal to the Antiochene school's rejection of speculation, so he found allies there. He had political friends, especially in the imperial court. There were a few emperors and court counselors between Constantine and Theodosius who were very clearly on his side; partly this was for practical reasons, because his theology fit the empire. If you lower your concept of Christ, then you can raise your vision of the emperor because the *Logos* was in both Jesus and the emperor. We saw way back in Proverbs that kings reign by the wisdom of God. If Jesus is a little smaller, the king will be a little higher, and that is just what Constantine and his advisers wanted.

A further factor for Arius was the new converts moving into Christianity for its respectability, popularity, and intelligence. It is an edifying and high religion, but these people prefer a simple monotheism and do not want to bother too much about Jesus in particular or about the Jewish-Hebrew strain of Christian thought.

Arius was also helped by the fact that the other tradition, now called "Athanasian," was mixed up with popularization, the ignorance of the common people, the search for the mysterious typical of popular piety, and the asceticism of the monastic movement, which had already begun in Egypt and looked down on culture, civilization, and intelligence. Arius had a lot on his side, but Athanasius finally won out. He had become the representative of the movement that made a higher claim for Jesus and accepted the Nicene phrasing as the best way to say it. He won partly because the churches in the West backed him. They had not been in the debate, but when they heard about it they took his side. After he was exiled to the West, he was able to keep up his friendships there. He won partly because of his moral power, his staying power, in spite of exile, whereas Arius always seemed to let his convictions depend a little on how much support he got. Athanasius had less support in the court but more popular support. This meant that when the emperors changed he came out stronger. Another reason was that with the passage of time Athanasius' friends and disciples worked out with clearer logic the language they used to state the doctrine of the Trinity as it was finally developed.

Any doctrine, but especially a doctrine of this kind, is basically a set of assumptions about how we should use words and rules about what certain words ought and ought not to be used to mean. So we come to the point where we can line up these terms, compare them with one another, and see in the interrelation of "just words" what the doctrine was about. We have here three columns of words that are somehow related and somehow different. The relatedness and the difference will be what we shall work on.

		B	A
Greek	*Ousia*	*hypostasis*	*prosopon*
Latin-based	Essence	substance	person
English	being (nature)	basis	face

The words on the first line are Greek. *Ousia,* as we observed, comes from root "to be" and means "essence." *Hypostasis,* like substance, comes from the roots "to stand" and "under"; so we could restate it (bottom line) as *basis. Prosopon* is a word that has several kinds of meanings, but the root meaning is the mask that is worn by an actor in a theater or a "personage"—personage in the sense not of an individual with personality, body, and spirit, but a figure in a drama. We can call this a "face." It is that which you see. On a theater program even today we sometimes read at the top of the list of characters the title *dramatis personae. Persona* in this sense means a figure in an act. Here we have in Latin, Greek, and modern English, equivalent words for "face," a "personage." We might say "role" in contemporary sociological language. By filling out our equivalents on the grid, we have Greek, Latin, and English, but with the same root meaning in each column. The doctrine of the Trinity in a very simple sense is just a set of rules about which of those words you use for what.

In the early Greek debates it was assumed that *ousia* and *hypostasis,* essence and substance, were the same. That would not make much difference in modern English either. *Being* and *basis* point to the same general concept. Both of these tend to mean "what a thing really is." Whether you call that its essence or substance is really not a significant distinction.

Sabellius said there is one divine Being and therefore there is one divine substance. He said *one* about both of these. But there are three faces, three persons in the sense of face, masks, molds, figures, or apparitions, so Sabellius drew the line at "A"—one to the left and three to the right. Arius disagrees. There are three substances because the Father and Son are really substantial. Of course there are three "faces," but there are also three substances. Since "substance" and "being" have the same meaning, there must be three essences too. So the *ousia* of the Father and the *ousia* of the Son cannot be the same. These are the two logical positions that both assume substance and essence are the same. So you say with Sabellius (line A), "One to the left and three to the right," or you say with Arius, "Three of everything."

The new answer, the new set of linguistic conventions, was worked out in the latter part of the fourth century by the three great Cappadocians, Gregory of Nyssa, Gregory Nazianzus, and Basil of Caesarea.

They were all from Cappadocia and worked together in unfolding, linguistically, Athanasius's position.

Look at the relation of the two right columns. Sabellius had used *prosopon* in a superficial way. When God has three of these, God is not really very three but still mostly one. The Cappadocians argue that we must say there are three *hypostases* in order to avoid the superficiality of the threeness of masks and faces in Sabellius. God is three in more than faces. There is a real, *substantial* threeness to God. Therefore we must say there are three *hypostases* but still one *ousia*. The three—Father, Son, and Spirit—are one in their essence. To be quite simple, the doctrine of the Trinity in Greek simply means that you use the word *hypostasis* for what there are three of. Then you use the word *ousia* for what there is one of. You simply affirm that that is what the word means from now on. You draw the line between threeness and oneness at "B."

But this looks different from how it looked in the West where Latin was used. The fact that the roots of these words are etymologically equivalent does not mean they have the same meaning. In the Latin world the distinction between essence and substance is very hard to make. On the other hand, *persona* comes to mean not only a mask or a role but also something more substantial, like what we mean in the modern word when we talk about personhood or personality. *Persona* does not mean that much yet, but it is beginning to evolve in that direction. Thus, it does not strike the Westerners as superficial. So the Westerners, instead of saying that there are three substances and one essence, tend to draw the line at "A" and say there is one substance and three persons, but that means that in Latin, and then later in French, English, and German, they used *persons* where the Greek uses *hypostases*. The equivalent for purposes of theological translation will no longer be the equivalent on the basis of etymology, but it will be this equivalent which we will use in our theological talk. It means that when we watch each other from East and West, the Westerners always think that the Greeks are affirming three gods, three substances. That is the danger of tritheism. The Greeks looking to the West will perceive the Westerners as affirming only three faces, and that this is the danger of modalism or Sabellianism, so the West fears tritheism and the east fears Sabellianism.

The solution then is a mere verbal formality, but it is a verbal formality that meets a need and answers a question. It safeguards the New Testament content with at least a degree of success in a quite different thought world.

What is the New Testament content? It is that Jesus, the Word in Jesus, is genuinely of the character of deity and genuinely human, and that his work is the work of God and yet the work of a man. The Nicenes try to say this not in narrative but in ontological and philosophical language. Now I said this is only a verbal formality. Correct. But to say that it is "only verbal" is no reproach in the Greek language culture. Words are the only tools you have to deal with truth. The problem was verbal in the first place.

But if being "only verbal" is no grounds for reproach, is there something else wrong with it? Can we say, as Nels Ferre does for instance, that this doctrine of the Trinity does not talk about God as love anymore? He is right that we do not find the word *agape.* But, as over against the distant God of Arius who is so far away as not really to be working among humanity, this is a way to affirm the love of God. Nicea says that God is really present not only in the distant Father but also in his Son, and also in the Spirit. This is an affirmation of love; this is the way to say "love," in the language of ontology. Over against a God who needs the world, who is bound to the world, who is dependent on the world to be who we know God is, this is the way to make the statement that God's being among us is free grace. Arius defended the purity of God, but he made Christ a halfway thing. Sabellius defended the validity of God's work, but he made Christ a transient thing. This new definition avoids those two dangers—Christ is not just a transient thing, but REAL. He is not just a mixture, but this divine *hypostasis* genuinely became a man.

So, although we can defend this definition as not strange or foreign to the substance of the Bible, and in fact as defending a biblical concern in nonbiblical language, it is clear that *in form* we are moving farther and farther away from the Gospel story. The form of the confession is still used, but it has been so padded out with statements about the essence of Christ that one recognizes no narrative to it anymore. One is not driven to think of the movement of time, of God doing something among humans in a given time and place, as being very important.

So we have moved away from the narrative form. In the subject matter we have moved away from the resurrection. It is still affirmed in the creed, but it is not the subject of debate. The debate is about the eternal status of the resurrected one. With continuing cultural change there will be room for still further shifts. Recall the diagram of the *kerygma* in the early church and the several theologians. Each time one movement built upon another, it required a more involved inquiry to decide whether the new form expressed the same faith as the old. In that sense, with Nicea we are still moving away from the biblical center in mood, in style, in content. The next move, when the word "person" is given a modern meaning, might be even further away.

What does the word "person" mean in modern usage? It means a center of consciousness, a will distinct from other wills. When we talk about three persons, we talk about a reality that is best portrayed with three human figures, three wills, or three consciousnesses. This actually happens in later Orthodox thought. They draw pictures of the Trinity. You find icons in art collections with three human figures just alike. Of course, the Father and the Spirit are not really like that, but we know what the Son is like. And since the Son, the Father, and the Spirit are the same, we can draw it that way.

The notion of three "personalities" is a new import into the doctrine of the Trinity. Trinity does not mean that. It means three roles, three modes, three ways of acting. Modalism is wrong if by it we mean what Sabellius meant, namely that God will move in and out of several roles and never be all three in one. But mode, or "way of being," is probably the best way to say today what the doctrine of the Trinity originally meant. (Karl Barth and Gordon Kaufman use "mode.") In modern language "personality" means being photogenic, having a "good image," getting along well with people, or being integrated. All of these descriptions of personality as the character of one consciousness or will are then taken to mean that there must be three consciousnesses or three wills in God. This emerges, for instance, in an especially complicated form, in the Pentecostal movement's discussion of the personality of the Holy Spirit. A "person" is thus and so, and the Holy Spirit is one of the three persons of the Trinity. Therefore the Holy Spirit, seen apart from the Father and the Son, must have the characteristics of a person. We have to recognize this as a deformation of the doctrine of the Trinity. It is not only a modern deformation. It is present already in Islam.

The strong anti-Christian, pro-monotheist Muslim movement focuses to a considerable extent on the tritheism Mohammed thought he perceived in the Christians with whom he dealt. He may have been right, as regards those Christians. "Christians say there are three Gods. There is but one God." This is the Muslim creed. This antitritheism may be partly explained as a misunderstanding of the "three person" language of the Trinity. We have to learn "three persons" did not really mean three personalities.

Now that the Trinity is official doctrine, another point of deformation arises if we think that God's self-revelation of threeness-in-oneness is *itself* something that saves us. We find the extreme form of this in some medieval Catholic teaching, which says that there are some truths you can know by reason and some truths you can only know by having them revealed to you. It happens that the truth that God is three persons is one that can only be known by revelation. It is truth, a thought content, a piece of information about deity that we know because it was given us by special supernatural revelation.

As a matter of fact, it was not given us by revelation. That you should say, "*Hypostases* are what there are three of and *ousia* is what there is one of," cannot be given by revelation. It is something the Cappadocians figured out in the fourth century. That there is God the Father, that there is the Son, that there is the Spirit—and that these three are the same—*that* much we can find in the Bible, but not as information having been revealed. How to connect them in a form of words in order to keep from tripping over the differences was worked out later. The doctrine of the Trinity is the solution to an intellectual difficulty that arises if we accept the statements of the Bible. It is not itself a revealed truth, but the solution to the word problem we get into when we accept revelation in Jesus, the continuance of that revelation in the Holy Spirit, and hold to monotheism at the same time.

Is the doctrine of the Trinity valid in other cultures? This is being talked about considerably right now (1970), especially because of the rabble-rousing literature written by Bishops Pike and Robinson. Perhaps, as they say, we cannot ask the modern mind to be bothered with ancient Greek literary forms. But the problem the doctrine of the Trinity seeks to resolve, the normativity of Jesus as he relates to the uniqueness of God, is a problem Christians will always face if they are Christian. The doctrine of the Trinity is a test of whether your commitments to Jesus and to God are biblical enough that you have the problem the doctrine of the Trinity solves. It may be that there will be other solutions, words, phrasings or ways to avoid tripping over the problem the way the Greeks did. But we shall have to examine them with the same commitment to the man Jesus, and the same commitment to the unique God that they had, or else we shall have left the Christian family.

Your preparation guide refers to the question of the Nicene Creed's authority. This synod or council accepted this document and condemned the people who did not accept it. What authority does that have for us? Strikingly, many Christian groups and thinkers, who in principle refuse to grant the Catholic church any right to set up a normative interpretation of the Bible (or certainly to teach anything above or beyond the Bible), still give the Nicene Creed and its trinitarian statements equal authority to the Bible. If we look back at the politics between 325 and 431, at some of the theologians' methods and motives, at the personal quality of Constantine, or if we ask in what sense he was a Christian when he dictated this dogma, then we have to be dubious about giving this movement any authority. If we call into question the acceptance of Hellenistic thought forms foreign to the way the Bible thinks, which fit with neither the Hebrew mind nor, for that matter, with the modern mind, then again we have to challenge whether the creed does us much good.

To make of the Nicene Creed a *creed* to use for liturgical purposes, and not to make creeds of the other things decided at Nicea, is an example of the peculiar selectivity of history, where we pick out the things we like and drop the rest.

It is understandable for the high church tradition to have picked out the Nicene tradition, because the king was finally on that side. Therefore the Nicene Creed, or the later creeds, have some kind of hermeneutic authority, not theoretically about the Bible but practically *above* it in application. For the Believers' Church tradition, and for modern reading of the story, it seems that the only claim of the Nicene Creed is to have provided the best answer to an intellectual problem. The doctrine is not authoritative, but the claims of Jesus who creates the problem are. The doctrine is not supernatural truth, supernaturally communicated for its information value. It is not learning what the Holy Spirit gave to the Council Fathers of Nicea because there were bishops assembled from the whole world at the invitation from the Roman Emperor. It is valid because it reflects the serious struggle of people, within their language and culture, with their commitment to an absolute God and to a normative Jesus.

This way of recounting the development of alternative views of the Trinity has an apparent logical sequence. Any particular view is more clearly understood when it is seen as constituting a response to the view mentioned before it. It should, however, not be thought that just one line of development existed in which one view succeeded another. Neither should it be thought that there was just one population in which such a conversation went on. The total Christian community in the early centuries was enormously varied and enormously scattered. Many kinds of people held many kinds of views without either the convictions or the communication techniques that would have made them thrash out every difference with each other. Thus the clarity of types in logical sequence which is useful for our purposes should not be misunderstood as an actual description of what went on.[3]

Now we skip ahead of the chronological sequence for a look at some recent treatments of the doctrine of the Trinity. Our intent is not so

3. Since these lectures were prepared, additional studies by Alan Richardson and Jaroslav Pelikan have made these developments more accessible. See Richardson, Alan, *Creeds in the Making: A Short Introduction to the History of Christian Doctrine* (1964) and Pelikan, Jaroslav, *The Christian Tradition: A History of the Development of Doctrine* (Chicago: University of Chicago Press, 1971–1989); *The Development of Christian Doctrine: Some Historical Prolegomena* (New Haven: Yale University Press, 1969); *Historical Theology: Continuity and Change in Christian Doctrine* (New York, Corpus, 1971). The present account should not be understood as a substitute for serious reading of the history. It is offered rather as a way to get into an understanding of why the problems were problems and why the conclusions reached were felt to be conclusive.

much to report on them or to agree or disagree with them as to identify the points at which they differ from what we are talking about. Check them with your other texts.

- There are modern *psychological* doctrines of the Trinity. Some accept the old language and, in order to make sense of it, modernize it, so they talk about "three persons" in the way I said earlier the developers of the doctrine did not mean to. Then they talk about what a good thing it is that community, communion, multipersonality, and different ways of doing and perceiving things are in God. Those things make God bigger. This is interesting speculation, but it cannot claim to be based on the doctrine of the Trinity in its origin.
- Another line of thought, pursued with great poetic creativity in the Middle Ages, is the *vestigia trinitatis,* the vestiges or traces of the Trinity. If God displays a characteristic and God made the world, then perhaps the world displays the characteristic as well. Ever since Augustine people have been looking for threeness-in-oneness: the light source, the light beam and the illumination; the spring, the river and the mouth of the river; the mind in memory, the mind in will, and the mind in reasoning. You can look anywhere in the world—you can look in the human personality—and you can always discern threeness in oneness. They are the same and yet not the same. And so it is that God—Father, Spirit, and Son—are three and yet one. Such a claim is simply poetic as far as I can see. It is fun but it proves nothing.
- Karl Barth pushed this thought a little farther by saying that revelation bears the marks of Trinity.[4] If you claim that there is such a thing as revelation, it must be triune. You have the one who reveals himself—the Father. It is not revelation if you do not have that. You always have the one who is the means of revelation—the Son. It is not really revelation unless you have the Son who is the same as the Father. If he is not the same as the Father, it is not the Spirit's real revelation as "revealedness" in the church that receives it. It is not real revelation if you do not have that. That revealedness must be the same as the Father or it is not real revelation. If there is revelation, there must be a revealed, the revealer, and the revealedness—the Father, Son, and Spirit. Barth worked this out at great length, but it can be found earlier—in Hegel, for instance. Gordon Kaufman follows it.

Now what this proves, if you want to be logical, is only the "economic" Trinity. *Oikonomia* means administration. Theology has

4. Editorial note: See especially, Karl Barth, *Church Dogmatics*, vol. I, pt. 1 (Edinburgh: T. & T. Clark), paragraphs 8–12.

> long made a distinction between the economic Trinity (Trinity as we see God at work in the world) and the ontological Trinity (Trinity as God in God's self). Logic says that Barth may have demonstrated that we *perceive* God working in three forms—Father, Son, and Spirit. We cannot conceive of real revelation without that, but maybe that is simply a limitation of our perception. Perhaps God as such is just one. But Barth turns the argument around again: If God has been revealed truly (for otherwise it would not be revelation), then the economic Trinity must be the same as the ontological Trinity. God as such must be the same as what God revealed God to be, so if God has revealed threeness-in-oneness, God must *be* threeness-in-oneness. This modern development has a certain relationship to the ancient logic and the ancient debate but is not really the same thing.

As we survey the efforts at modern understandings of trinitarian thought, we observe two different structures in conflict. They interlock, overlap, and sometimes lean on each other, but they are different.

- We could call one of them the *historical* trinitarian structure. The Father is the God of the Old Testament. The Son is Jesus who called the God of the Old Testament "Father," and is spoken of in early New Testament terms as being exalted, rewarded, and adopted by the Father. The Spirit is present in the church in gifts. Characteristic of this "historical" Trinity is a lack of speculation about deity as such, about metaphysics. It is further characteristic of this view that it is very difficult to distinguish between the Father and the Spirit because the Father is Spirit. Jesus said so in John 4:24. The Son's humanity distinguishes him from the Father and the Spirit. He is man, and the Father did not take on human form. The weakness of this view is that it does not explain the New Testament texts that talk about the *Logos* as preexistent.
- The other structure of thought about the Trinity can be called *philosophical/ontological.* The Father represents God "as such"—God as absolute, God as unrelated. The Son represents the eternal *Logos,* the revelatory principal in God. The Spirit represents God in human awareness, in the community, in the church. You remember this from Tertullian and Karl Barth. What is the difference between these two structures? Why the shift from one to the other? The development of the *Logos* cosmology, whose concern was to defend the transcendence of God by placing the *Logos* as intermediary between God and the world, accounts for part of the shift. Partly, too, it arose to handle preexistence, which this view can talk about while the other could not. The concept of preexis-

tence developed in the early church theologians in order to save the preeminence of Christ and his finality.

The difference between these two views is most visible at the point of asking who the God of the Old Testament was. For the historical view, which we can maybe also call "biblical" in that sense, the God of the Old Testament seems to be the Father to whom Jesus prayed.

For the philosophical/ontological view, the God of the Old Testament seems to be already a working of the *Logos,* already a working of the revealing dimension of God, and therefore of the second person. And so theologians working radically with the concept of the ontological Trinity say that the God of the Old Testament, YHWH, is the *Son* of the orthodox Trinity. This strikes people as peculiar. The other pattern of putting things together seems more congenial when one begins from the biblical end. So we have in the doctrine of the Trinity a peculiar movement. One end is the naive historical-biblical Trinity that cannot deal with the concept of preexistence affirmed in the biblical documents. The other end is a clear systematic theological/ontological Trinitarianism, but it has the peculiarity that God the Father is untouchable so that the second person must already be working in the Old Testament. Somehow that does not fit either.

Other Canons of the Council of Nicea

1. The general rule that a eunuch may not be a priest does not apply if the castration took place against his will and after his ordination.
2. A clergyman guilty of a grave moral offense shall be deposed, if he had been baptized and ordained too hastily.
3. No woman shall live in the house of a priest unless she be his mother, sister, aunt, or a person free of all suspicion.
4. A bishop is appointed by all the bishops of a province; if that is not possible, at least by three.
5. A person excommunicated in one diocese shall not be admitted in another. All bishops of a province shall meet semiannually to review whether some excommunications were too harsh and to confirm that the others are still in force.
6. The exceptional, ancient custom is confirmed, whereby the bishop of Alexandria is patriarch over the metropolitans of Libya, Pentapolis, and Thebes. Also recognized as patriarchates are Rome and Antioch; similar rights (of oversight over other metropolitans) belong to other (unnamed) eparchies.
7. The bishop of Aelia (Jerusalem) has special (unspecified) honor but not at the cost of the rights of the metropolitan of Caesarea.

8. Novatian clergy (*cathari*) may be readmitted to the Catholic clergy without reordination.
9. If it becomes known that before ordination a priest had been guilty of a major crime, the ordination is annulled.
10. Same provision as (9) for those who had denied the faith (*lapsi*).
11. Exceptional possibility of restoration for *lapsi* under the persecution of Licinius.
12. Exceptional rigor of penitence for those who at their conversion had left the army but then returned to it.
13. Do not deny the sacrament to a dying person. If a person who was under discipline receives the sacrament on his deathbed and then recovers, he is still under discipline.
14. The time of discipline shall be shorter for the *lapsi* who were only catechumens at the time.
15. There shall be no more exceptions to the rule that a bishop may not move from his diocese.
16. A priest may only be ordained in his own diocese and may only serve in the diocese where he was ordained.
17. A priest who lends money at interest shall be deposed.
18. Deacons shall not administer the Eucharist to priests, nor sit with them.
19. If Paulinians wish to be reconciled to the Catholic church, they must be reordained and rebaptized.
20. On Sundays and from Easter to Pentecost prayer is to be offered standing, not kneeling.[5]

5. Karl Joseph von Hefele, *History of the Christian Councils—to A.D. 325*, vol. 1 of *A History of the Councils of the Church: From the Original Documents* (Edinburgh: T. & T. Clark, 1894–1896).

9

Chalcedon and the Humanity of Jesus

Preparation Guide

1. What place (relatively how much space, and where in the sequence of topics) is given by your authors to the doctrine of the natures of Christ?
2. Does the author use such technical terms as essence, *hypostasis*, begotten, *enhypostasia*, and *anhypostasia?* With or without definition?
3. Is there a discussion of the Definition of Chalcedon as representing development in history?
4. In what sense was Jesus fully human? Is this a problem for the author?
   a. Is the concept of *kenosis* used? If so, what limits did it involve?
   b. Did Jesus possess (could he have utilized) the divine attributes of omnipotence, omniscience, omnipresence?
   c. Was Jesus really tempted to sin? Was sinning an open option?
   d. Did his thought or his understanding of himself change or develop in the course of his youth? His ministry?
   f. Did the boy Jesus really grow? Is there reference to Luke 2:40–52?
5. Is the deity of Christ argued by biblical proof texts? By inference? Otherwise?
6. Is the virgin birth an important issue? Does it guarantee Jesus' deity?
7. Is the nature of the resurrection body discussed? How was (is) it like or unlike our body? On what grounds is this said?

8. Do the systematic and contemporary texts pay attention to critical issues in the interpretation of Gospel sources, such as:
   a. Whether the Gospels all agree?
   b. Whether they are historically accurate in their portrayal of Jesus' self-understanding?
9. Does your text deal seriously with the challenge that says the whole discussion is meaningless on the grounds of modern understandings of reality?
10. What proportion of the text is given to the theme of the resurrection?
11. What proportion is given to:
    a. The earthly work of Jesus?
    b. The events between the cross and ascension?
    c. Things like the Gospel reports (teaching, healing, and calling followers, announcing the time has come)?
12. Do Chalcedon and Nicea have equal importance? Equal authority?
13. Is the Council of Chalcedon discussed as an event, e.g., its politics and procedures?

We now are ready to move on beyond the point where Nicaea became "dogma." This took a hundred years. In 381 at Constantinople there was some slight rephrasing of the Nicene Creed. Later that wording was found in the records of the 381 meeting and quoted in argument in the council of 431. From then on the identity of the three persons of the Trinity is orthodox belief, and the Nicene-Constantinopolitan phrasing was final.

Now where does the problem of pneumatology lie? The question of Nicea had been the relation of the Father and the Son. They talked about the Trinity, but there was no real question about the Spirit. Let us stop a minute to ask why. Part of the answer is that, as any debate takes on momentum, one finds one's self sloughing off certain parts of the problem. The Spirit was a problem that took other forms. The Montanists in the late second century, and the Donatists in the third and on into the fourth, made a point of the working of the Spirit and dealt with it on the level of church organization, piety, and ethics. Somehow it did not become a theological issue. It would have if the concept of the Spirit being cosubstantial with the Father and the Son had been taken very seriously.

One could in fact argue that the problem of the Spirit's identity is a greater problem intellectually; you don't have in the Spirit the distinctness from the Father that you obviously have in the Son because he is a man. The problem of the character of the Spirit arose later in the debates around the *filioque* clause. The very fact that this is a Latin phrase demonstrates that it comes later. This is the one word whereby the Latin version of the Nicene-Constantinopolitan Creed says that the Holy Spirit proceeds from the Father *and from the Son*. The Eastern church prefers to say that the Holy Spirit and the Son both proceed from the Father alone.

In what sense is the Spirit of God in the world independently of the Son? This is not only an issue with a long history, it is the subject of debate today in discussions about the mission of the church. How is God at work in the world? How is the Spirit of God at work in the world? In many ways? In other religions? In human insight? Or only in relation to Jesus—to his name or the message about him? None of those issues were debated at any length in the fourth and fifth centuries.

Now we turn back. Having seen how the church has affirmed the unity of Jesus and the Father, how do we relate the Son of God to the man Jesus? The more the doctrine of the Son as divine *hypostasis* is settled, the more difficult the relationship that he has to the man Jesus becomes. The Arian view of the *logos* raises no special problems for the man Jesus because the *logos* is subordinate to the Father, but the stronger the statement we make about the deity of the Son, which is what the Trinity is about, the more problem we have about the relationship between the divine and human natures of the Son. We now turn to that. The debate actually ran parallel to other debates, but it surfaced and came to conclusion later. It was especially fueled by the conclusion of the Nicene debates. That is why we move on to it now. It was precipitated but also made more difficult by the concept of being faithful to the creeds, which only could begin to matter now, when there was a creed to be faithful to.

Again we turn to analysis in terms of theological types or "schools." Such analysis, we have seen, is always questionable, but is the only way we can do it on short notice. What are the logical options? What are the possible ways to put together the possible answers to this question? We see these options represented partly in the variety of schools and cliques.

There was, again, the Alexandrian school with pre-Christian roots. Apollos, who seems to have been quite a rhetorician, represented it in the New Testament. The Alexandrian Christians were clearly not Gnostic, but the conversation and conflict with Gnosticism marked them. They therefore made strong statements about a speculative definition of deity—statements we find reflected in John 1 and Colossians, speaking of Christ as the Son and as present in creation. But yet, answering the Gnostics, they say that Jesus came in the flesh. In Jesus Christ then, according to the Alexandrian thought, the *logos* takes on humanity to redeem the race. He did not become so much the particular man Jesus, but rather identified himself with humanity. This is especially fitting—unavoidable we could say—because in Greek *anthropos,* the word "human" does not permit us to distinguish between a given human being and humanity in general, so God became (generic) humanity. It is more important that God entered into humanity than that God was found identified with this particular Jew from Palestine.

Then you have to debate how divinity could be particular in Jesus after we said it came into humanity. If this man Jesus is sinless, if he is God's presence, how different does that make his humanity from ours? The Alexandrian school expresses a position that is reflected today in the tendency to equate the finite and the sinful. After all, both are imperfect. To be finite, to be limited, is to be imperfect. To be sinful is to be imperfect, and how can God accept imperfection? How does God accept limitations? The clearest problem with this view is found in the exegesis of passages that deal with movement and humanity in Jesus. Luke 2 says that the boy Jesus grew and then moves on to say that the man Jesus was tempted. He was anxious, he was worried, he was tired, and he died. All of these—growth, temptation, anxiety, fatigue, and death—are characteristics of imperfection. They are not very far from sin. In fact, it is because of these weaknesses that we sin. How could Jesus have participated in these imperfections? The Alexandrian answer is that this is all only the human side. The *Logos* in itself cannot grow, be ignorant, or tire, so it is only the human side of Jesus. And yet real humanity involves these things. To grow is, for a human being, inseparable from sin. To be an individual is for a human being to be involved in imperfection.

Accordingly, salvation for humans, according to this Alexandrian line of thought, is to receive and take upon one's self the thing God did by coming into humanity. As God became human, so humans become God. This is called *apotheosis,* or deification. Humanity becomes God. The Alexandrians did not say this quite so crudely, and Greek Orthodox theology echoes them even today. Human salvation is participation in deity—not just divinization, being made somehow Godlike, but deification, being made part of God. Humanity as such is changed. The change begins in Bethlehem where God becomes human. It changes for me when I am baptized, and it continues to change for me as I partake of the sacraments and become more and more God-in-the-world. But fundamentally it happened in the incarnation. That the early Jesus grew, made decisions, was tempted, tired and died, is less important than that God became an infant and later ascended into heaven as the God-man.[1]

1. This helps illuminate the growth in importance of the virgin birth issue.

Origen took one extreme of this line of thought and was later condemned for it: If God became human for humanity, then God must have become angel for the angels as well. With regard to Jesus it was not easy to avoid the distortions of the Alexandrian line of thought. It finally leads to the position we identify with Apollinarus. Apollinarus was an Alexandrian who simply pushed the concern not to allow Jesus' humanity to interfere with his deity to its logical conclusion.[2]

If Jesus is a man and yet different from others, how is he different? Humans, in addition to body and soul, have *spirit* or *mind*. In Greek this is called the *nous*. Apollonarianism contends that the spirit of Jesus was the *Logos* of God. The rest of Jesus was just like the rest of us, but Jesus had a divine mind instead of just a human mind that understood God like any other human would. So at the point of the *mind* of Jesus, Apollinarus was consistently Docetic. The mind of Jesus did not grow, did not make decisions, because it was the mind of God.

This raised problems in the details of debate for Apollinarus. Did Adam, before he fell, have an unfallen human mind? If so, how was the unfallen human mind of Adam different from the mind of God? But we are not debating in so much detail with Apollinarus that we should bother to enumerate his weaknesses.

In the Alexandrian school salvation is imitation. Even the term *mimesis*, imitation, is used. Imitating God does not entail ethics the way it does for the Anabaptists or for some modern liberal Christians. The imitation of God means allowing the same thing happen to us that happened to Jesus. I imitate Jesus in that I let the divine Spirit take over my mind through the sacraments, teaching, and worship. What really happens to save humanity is a divine transaction in which humanity is taken up into deity. Here Scripture is simply a teaching technique; it is not revelation. In fact, even cross and resurrection are simply teaching techniques, parables, because everything of consequence happened before that. The cross and resurrection are just the way this divine taking-on-of-human-form-for-its-salvation unfolded and worked itself out. But if it had not happened, if there had been no Calvary, what really mattered had already taken place in the incarnation.

The other school, we said, was Antioch, as old as Alexandria, but not based on a pre-Christian philosophical heritage. It was less academic, less speculative in its style, more Hebrew, more historical, more grammatical, more rabbinical, and more interested in reading particular

2. Remember, very often what we say about a heretic, as representing a theological *type*, might be unfair to the person actual was and his or her real concerns. The position we are describing may not reflect Apollonarus's considered views, but *Apollinarianism* has this position. Charles Raven's *Apollinarianism: An Essay on the Christology of the Early Church* (New York: AMS Press, 1978) is the best book on Apollinarus.

verses understanding what they mean, reading particular narratives and asking what really happened. The Antiochenes feared Modalism, just as the Alexandrians feared Ebionism, a too-human Son of God. Antioch was concerned for Jesus as a man and for reading the story in such a way as to safeguard that true humanity. The center of Antiochene thought is the humiliation and self-emptying of the divine we find in Philippians 2 or Hebrews 5:8–9: "He learned obedience through what he suffered; and being made perfect he became the source of eternal salvation to all who obey him."[3] The growth, temptation, and suffering are all real, human experiences. His obedience as a man is our salvation. Our obedience as women and men is part of his work of restoration. Antioch could talk about *apotheosis* or deification too. But we are not made part of the divine being by transubstantiation, by being taken up into the miracle of incarnation turned around. We are not deified in Christmas, sacraments, or insight. We are made part of the divine character by an act of will, by obedience, by faith, by accepting the gift of the Spirit, by living in the world as Jesus lived in the world, and by sharing in his humiliation (Phil. 2) and suffering (with Hebrews). Over against Apollinarus, the Antiochenes argued that when Adam sinned he sinned as a whole man—his body, spirit, and soul all sinned. It was not just his mind. So humans must be seen as wholes, not just as minds. Therefore, we must have more saved than our minds. So Jesus must have been more than we are at every point and not just in his mind. The *Logos* is fully present in Jesus, but within his full humanity, not replacing a part of his humanity. And the self-emptying of God in the suffering of Jesus was more important than the emptying which was involved in the incarnation. That, we noted, may have been the primitive meaning of Philippians 2 as well. Then the death and resurrection of Christ really matter most. The death was the real defeat of Satan, and the resurrection was a real new creation.

Both of these schools meant to be trinitarian. Both of them meant to affirm all the things that Nicea made orthodox, but they certainly differed. Again the issue was soon dealt with on the political level. That is what made an issue serious in that age of the church.

3. Editorial note: Instead of a direct quotation at this point, Yoder's manuscript reads, "He learned obedience through his suffering, that he might make perfect his brothers," and adduces Hebrews 2 as the chapter reference. Hebrews 2 does not mention that Christ learned obedience, which we take to be Yoder's point in the text. Hebrews 2 both notes that Christ was made perfect through suffering, and associates suffering with brotherhood in verses 10 and 11: "For it was fitting that he, for whom and by whom all things exist, in bringing many sons to glory, should make the pioneer of their salvation perfect through suffering. For he who sanctifies and those who are sanctified have all one origin. That is why he is not ashamed to call them brethren."

By the fifth century Constantinople had replaced Alexandria as the second center of church power and teaching authority. Antioch and Jerusalem were both older bishoprics, but not cultural centers, and especially not political centers. Alexandria was the oldest of course, first by history and by momentum. It was the throne of Mark, and Mark was the favorite of Peter. But in 381 Constantinople had been named as the second Rome and was becoming increasingly a church center because it was a political center, so people were looking for a way to play Alexandria and Constantinople off against each other as centers of church power. Alexandria tried to defend itself as more orthodox.

Nestorius was an Antiochene theologian who was called as patriarch (archbishop, metropolitan) of Constantinople in 428. He preached a series of sermons in 428 and 429 against patripassianism and Docetism, that is, against theologies that did not take the humanity of Jesus seriously.

The symbol of this became a term still used as part of Catholic piety, even in the West: *Theotokos,* which roughly translates as "mother of God." Literally, is should be translated "bearer of God," and is a term used for Mary. Nestorius can accept this. He can accept calling Mary the mother of God because her son was the Son of God, but it is dangerous. He pointed to the dangers, and because of them would rather not have the term used. One of the dangers is worshipping not only the man but also the mother. There was left over in Egypt from pre-Christian times a mother worship that reflected the cult of Isis and Osiris. Nestorius saw the danger of turning one's attention away from the humanity of Jesus, which he affirmed, to a special privilege for the mother. He was not against Alexandria or anybody's official teaching, but he was against the popular abuses to which this teaching opened the door.

Cyril, bishop of Alexandria, was interested in undermining anything that happened at Constantinople. He thought Nestorius's moves gave him a chance. Cyril argued for the oneness of Christ's nature after the union of the divine and human. ("After the union" became a technical phrase.) That is, you can think about human nature and divine nature separately before the incarnation. But afterwards, there is but one nature: the human nature (Jesus) is swallowed up in the divine nature. It is somehow still there but not really. You can still "recognize" it. (That is a technical term too—"recognize," or discern.) If there has really been incarnation then the human nature really is not the one that is operating. It is the divine nature, because Jesus is now omnipotent, omniscient, eternal, and so on. Cyril wanted to avoid making Jesus just another Old Testament prophet. The Old Testament prophets had the Spirit of God in them. That is not enough for Jesus, so he accused Nestorius of separating Jesus as the Son of God from the Son—the Eternal Son in the Trinity—and teaching "two Sons." That way to say it sounds funny, so it made a good debating point. This is one of the polemic slogans: Nestorius was accused of teaching that there are two divine Sons, the human son and the divine Son.

We shall skip the politics. The story here is much more complicated than Nicea and went on for twenty years. Some bishops called synods and voted before the other party arrived. Others came to the synods with soldiers and monks as bodyguards—and the monks were usually rougher than the soldiers. There were efforts at mediation and mutual offers to resign. Then the offers were withdrawn, and they debated what the offer had been. Both parties called on the pope as a mediator. By calling on the pope to mediate, they heightened his power. This kind of appeal was a major factor in contributing to the development of the papacy.

Both parties grew increasingly radical, in both their political methods and in their language. Finally Nestorius resigned. The extremes went in several directions that we shall not bother to debate or even report, but on the level of formal decision, we jump to 451, the Council of Chalcedon. (Councils are all identified by the places where they met.)

Chalcedon (451) again prepared a creed following the apostolic or Nicene outline, but again made changes at the point of what was at stake:

> We confess . . . the same Son, our Lord Jesus Christ . . . begotten of the Father before the ages according to deity, but in these last days begotten, for us and our salvation, of Mary the virgin mother of God *Theotokou* according to humanity . . . recognized in two natures, without confusion, without change, without division, without separation.

That does not make much of a sentence in English, but it is a good sentence in Greek. Two elements are nonetheless clear in the translation: "begotten of the Father before the ages according to deity" and "in the last days for us according to humanity is recognized as having two natures." These two "natures" are said to be unmixed, unconfused, undivided, unseparated. You cannot divide and separate them. They are not mixed. They are not swallowed up one in the other. They are united, but they are two natures.

This is a statement, in other words, of the distinctness of the natures in their unity—which is Nestorius's position in terms of actual content. But on the level of politics, Nestorius was defeated. He had been condemned by an earlier synod and that condemnation was never revoked. He resigned for the sake of the peace of the church, thinking that Cyril would withdraw the charges at the same time, but he did not. Politically, things remained polarized. Although the Council of Chalcedon took Nestorius's position in substance, everyone present was finally forced to make a statement condemning Nestorius as a person, so he stayed banished. Then his party divided on whether or not he should have defended himself. The position of the Eastern church was Cyril's—that is, the deity swallows up the humanity. This is still the case today. Two natures are affirmed but in such a way that the divine absorbs any individual human reality.

A rather large group of churches left the fellowship of orthodox churches because of the Chalcedonian formula. The formula itself says "two natures." These new groups are called *Monophysite* because they affirm only "one nature." They took more radically the position that the human nature of Jesus was gone, swallowed up. Now there is only a divine nature; at least there is no more human individuality. All around the eastern edge of the Roman Empire, churches broke off as national units, partly for nationalistic reasons but partly for theological reasons, because of their desire to have a stronger vision of the deity of Jesus. They still are separate from the mainstream of the Eastern Orthodox Church, which talks about two natures but still really believes the way the Monophysites do, but they left because of the words of the Chalcedonian formula itself.

On the other side are the Nestorian churches that were pushed out, especially in Syria and east. During the following several centuries these Nestorian churches were far more vital and missionary, far more Christian in changing their culture and in moving out into the wider world (going all the way to China), but in recent centuries they have dwindled out. Both the Nestorian and the Monophysite churches created mostly national units around the eastern end of the empire. These positions, apart from the political details, were really quite close. Both said that the divine and human natures are distinct. Both said that the divine and human natures are united in Jesus. Both affirmed a real humanity and a real *Logos*.

In terms of the basic schools, the Antiochenes were stronger. They took the Nestorian line on the historicity and individuality of Jesus. The Chalcedonian position was really clear only in negation—not mixed, not confused, not divided, and not separated. Hosts of technical terms were developed in order to safeguard the things on which the council had compromised, but the life of the popular church went on being Monophysitic, that is, affirming such a swallowing up of humanity in deity that it did not really matter what kind of man Jesus was. He really did not grow up because he was born God. What really mattered was the birth, and the resurrection just spelled that out.

How do we evaluate this two-nature controversy given this hasty overview? First, it was a test of Nicea's seriousness. It was because of what Nicea said about the deity of the Son and about the unity of Son and Father that this next debate had to happen. If it had not happened, it would have shown that the Nicene statement was not serious.

We can again say that it was the cost of accepting Greek garb. Modern critics will refer most sweepingly of all to Chalcedon as verbal baloney. It imposes itself only when one accepts a bunch of verbal definitions that do not have to be accepted. And yet, we have to ask, does that mean you would not have had those same problems in another world or culture, or would you just have them in another shape? Again, as in the case of Nicea, they were not piecing together biblical texts—here one that said Jesus is man, and here one that says that he is the Son of God—trying to make them fit, and deciding that because they fit it is true. They were solving a problem that came out of the encounter of different frames of reference and sets of definitions. They tried to safeguard what a Christian has to say to be faithful to Jesus and still say it in the terms of the culture in which they were speaking and as answering the questions that it raised.

Perhaps we can say that culture raised the wrong questions. Yet if you say that any culture raises the wrong questions, you of course have to ask whether ours raises the right questions. Was it not really the business of the church to speak to that culture even if its questions were wrong? Is the definition of Chalcedon perhaps a way to say to *our* culture that *its* questions are wrong? What happens to our culture's questions when you say we must affirm that after the deity he is begotten of God before our world, that after the humanity we discern in him two natures, and that these two natures are neither mixed nor confused, neither divided nor separate?[4]

The meaning of Jesus' humanity varies enormously from one theological system to another. You should watch in your own sources what Jesus' humanity means according to the stance of a given theologian.

As we have seen, for the Alexandrians, birth mattered most. That he

4. Students interested in pursuing the notion that Chalcedon may be affirmed as proper adjustment to "Hellenization," while doubting on the same grounds that it should continue to be helpful, may be interested in Leslie DeWart's *The Future of Belief* or Paul Van Buren's, *The Secular Meaning of the Gospel: Based on the Analysis of Its Language* (New York: Macmillan, 1963). Both call into question not only the christological formula, but also the concept of God as immutable, impassable, etc., that lies under the formulation of the problem. A more critical evaluation by (the later Archbishop) William Temple is quoted by Van Buren: "The formula of Chalcedon is the confession of bankruptcy of Greek patristic theology. The Fathers had done the best they could with the intellectual tools at their disposal" (34). In response to Temple one might suggest that a "confession of bankruptcy" might be a morally proper conclusion if it is truly the case that certain tools do not fit certain tasks. As John Martin Creed indicated in *The Divinity of Jesus Christ: A Study in the History of Christian Doctrine since Kant* (Cambridge: University Press, 1938): "The negations of one age may in the context of another age defeat the very aim they were originally designed to subserve. Thus that conception of two natures and two wills functioning side by side, which we find so strangely inapplicable to the Jesus of the Gospel texts, was, in the context of fifth-century thought, directly calculated to reserve the imperiled truth of the real humanity of the historic Christ" (121).

was all human is all that matters about Jesus. It does not much matter what kind of human he was. We could say call this a doctrine of salvation by birth. That statement is not quite true with radical consistency, but it is implicit. Revelation could have been done just as well otherwise. We can get revelation from a teacher, a book, an icon, or a sacrament. In fact, we do. And therefore the book, the sacrament, the Bible itself, and other forms of revelation—even the church—are for the most part on the same level. None of them matter enormously. What matters is that God had to become human. When that happened, we were saved.

The Roman tradition—speaking now on the level of the kind of popular culture it creates—sees Jesus Christ as exalted Lord and coming judge. He is the one who gave the command that there should be a church and empowered his apostles to empower their successors to be the church. He now reigns. When he returns he will judge. Revelation is neither in him nor in the book. It is in the church he mandated to work in the world. God could have forgiven arbitrarily. God could have said, "Humanity is saved," and by fiat we would have been saved, just as God said, "Let there be light," and there was light. So the choice of God to use the humanity of Jesus is an arbitrary choice. We do not ask it to make sense. God could have done otherwise, but chose to do it this way. We are thankful for God's choice and we see that it makes sense this way, but it could have happened otherwise. So the humanity of Jesus is part of God's gracious choice, but why God HAD to choose it, why it made *sense* that God did it this way is not terribly important. We affirm the human nature of Jesus but it will not matter much for our thought. What kind of person he was will again matter little.

For Protestantism, and (I would suggest) for the New Testament, the humanity of Jesus matters more than that. God is in some sense personal. Humanity is in the image of God: person, will, communication. If humans are persons, and God has chosen to want us to be persons, then there is no other way of God's dealing with humanity than in person. The humanity of Jesus is the necessary prerequisite to whatever God wants to do with us. It is not an arbitrary afterthought, but neither is it itself the miracle of salvation. It is the vehicle, the bearer of the possibility of an encounter between God and humanity.

Protestant thought, then, centers neither on incarnation nor on the authority given to the church to administer grace, but on what Jesus did as a man, giving himself. God is seen not so much as transcendent and Jesus is seen not so much as reigning, but as the self-giving God and the self-giving Jesus. His humanity matters not only as how he came to us—the clothing he had to wear to get to us. The revelation of the obedience that God wants of us also matters.

A sideline in the debate about the two natures becomes important within the Protestant movement in a difference between Lutheran and Calvinist thought. It is interesting because it demonstrates that Lutherans and the Calvinists in the sixteenth and seventeenth centuries were as hung up on words as the third and fourth century Greeks could be. The term is *communicatio idiomatum*. An *idioma* is a characteristic, that which is idiomatic is characteristic of a language. The characteristics in question are those of the divine nature and the human nature. The human characteristics of Jesus are, of course, that he had a body, that he was temporal, and so on. The divine characteristics are eternity, omnipresence, omnipotence, etc., but if his natures are related in the incarnation, united somehow and yet distinguished somehow, we have to have rules about what we are going to say about whom. When you talk about what Jesus does, how do you know when you are talking about God and when you are talking about Jesus as man? You had better not say the wrong thing because then you would be confusing or separating the natures, which Chalcedon disallowed.

There are three kinds of *communicatio* that have to be distinguished if you are careful. You can say of the whole person of Jesus Christ something that is really true only of one of the natures. You can say the "Son of God was born and died" or that he suffered. Well, that is not really true. The man died and suffered. The man was born, but the Son of God only participated in that through the sharing of the characteristics through the incarnation, so at this point the characteristics we affirm apply only to one. We could turn it around. We can say things about the human nature that are really only true of divine nature. Jesus was omnipotent. Jesus was omnipresent. It is good to put those two side by side because the omnipotence is something which, for Orthodoxy, we see him practicing in the miracles; the omnipresence we do not.

But you can only go that way. You can give to Jesus divine attributes because that is the meaning of the incarnation, but you cannot go the other way around. You can't talk about the blood of God because God has no blood. You should not say God suffers.

Unfolding these distinctions becomes extremely complicated as you try to be careful with their logic. The Lutheran and Calvinist theologians of the seventeenth century had time to be very careful. If your collateral text is Lutheran or Reformed, you should look *communicatio idiomatum* up. The point is to indicate that this problem kept working because people were trying to be serious with the two-nature doctrine. The Lutherans and Calvinists differ because the Calvinists say that you can never say, "God is here in the bread." Luther said, "Why not? If omnipresence is a character of God, then omnipresence has been given to Jesus and he can be anywhere he wants to be." Calvinists said, "The body of Jesus is in heaven. He went to the right hand of God." Lutherans said, "Of course. But he's omnipresent. The human nature of Jesus has taken on the divine character of omnipresence. Therefore he can at the same time be in heaven and in the bread."

A final word now about the problem of the place of creeds. For Catholic tradition it is clear. The creeds *are* the history of the church. The Spirit led the church, as it had been authorized by God through Jesus in the Spirit, to work and to speak in Christ's name. So when the church states dogma in a creedal document, it is authoritative. Protestantism has been ambiguous about this. The Protestant movement began with a debate about the authority of Scripture, and said that only Scripture is authoritative. Yet the Protestant fathers were themselves products of the Catholic Middle Ages. They assumed that the creeds were identical with the Bible, and therefore there is no problem of choosing between them. Everything in the creed is in the Bible. The creed is a handy summary of the Bible. The church fathers who defined the Reformation—Luther, Zwingli, Calvin—saw no real problem with this.

The radical reformers, especially Servetus and Socinus, did see a problem, but not because they tried to be rationalistic or unbelieving. They began as biblicists, and the doctrine of the Trinity is not in the Bible. The doctrine of the two natures in its Chalcedonian form is not in the Bible. They began simply by saying that if a doctrine is not in the Bible we should not require it of each other. It may be a solution to an intellectual problem, but it is not taught that way.

The Anabaptists were in between the radicals and the Reformation leaders. They assumed the Apostolic Creed—the called it "The Faith," *Der Glaube,* as did most people. But they did not give it any final authority. A conversation was recorded between a Catholic priest and three Anabaptist women who were in jail. They were unenthusiastic about debating with the priest, but he kept asking what they believed. They said they did not believe in baptizing babies because it was not in the Bible. "Well," he said, "there are lots of things that aren't in the Bible that you do—it doesn't say in the Bible that you should take a bath." They said, "We've been jailed for six weeks, we don't bathe here." He kept trying to find out sincerely what they believed: "Do you believe in the Apostolic Creed?" They answered, "When did Jesus say that?"

So although most of the Anabaptists would have accepted this as part of the tradition and not debated it much, they gave the creed no dogmatic quality. They gave no special importance to the fact that the church had made decisions about phrasing in the fourth or fifth century. This is a significant question that modern fundamentalism, and American Mennonites within modern evangelicalism, have not thought through. In what sense are we bound to doctrinal definitions of the fourth century, or the fifth, or the sixteenth? Is it only in the sense that they are useful documents of how the church struggled to keep the centrality of Jesus straight in the language of their time? Or do we, without thinking, take over from fundamentalism, which took it over without thinking from Calvinist Orthodoxy, which took it over without thinking from the Middle Ages, the idea that there is a certain amount of post-biblical dogmatic substance that all true Christians have to believe?

Probably, if we were to be fully honest, we would need to challenge more clearly the Catholic axiom that assumed the authority of the councils and therefore of the creeds. We would need to challenge it more clearly at the point of automatic authority, while being still quite interested in listening to that history, learning from it, and sympathizing deeply with what it tried to say. But it must mean something to us that the Arians and the Nestorians—each in their own age—were less nationalistic, less politically bound to the Roman Empire, more capable of criticizing the emperor, more vital in missionary growth, more ethical, and more biblicist than the so-called orthodox churches of the Empire. At the most, these creeds fruitfully define the nature of the problem with which we are struggling. They are helpful as a fence, but not as a faith. A doctrine that says we "perceive the divine begetting of the Son, eternally according to the deity, and according to the humanity perceive the two natures as neither mixed nor separated," tells us something we should not say. We should not say they are mixed. We should not say the human nature is lost in the divine, or vice versa. We should not tear the two apart and have two Jesuses walking side by side, then one of them leaving and the other one staying, or the one dying and the other ascending. We should not say with Arius that we know of the time when he was not, or that we know out of what the Son was made.

The creeds are helpful as fences, but affirming, believing, debating for, and fighting for the creeds are probably things on which a radical Anabaptist faith would not concentrate. Yet that gives us even less reason to join with Bishop Pike and Bishop Robinson in fighting against the creeds. The creeds are part of the only history we have. It is a fallible history and a confused history. A lot of dirty politics were involved in defining the creeds, in explaining their meaning, and still more in applying their authority, but this is the history with which God has chosen to lead a confused people toward at least a degree of understanding of certain dangers and things not to say if we are to remain faithful.

PART 3

Systematic Treatment of Christological Themes

10

The Structure of the Discipline

Preparation Guide

Read in your texts about the nature and language of theology and the structure of Christology.

1. Has your collateral author a treatment of Christology apart from the Trinity, two natures, and atonement? If so, what are the other headings and what space are they given? Where is it? Under what headings and in connection to what themes?
2. Does your author discuss the relation of the prophet, priest, and king as figures in Old Testament faith and life?
3. What place does your author give to the resurrection?
   a. Is there a need for discussion of its really happening, its historicity, its mode?
   b. Is it an issue for historical investigation only or does it recur in a fundamental way in the discussion of other issues?
   c. Could the rest of the book have been written without it?
4. Is attention given to significant shifts in Christology from the Gospels to the Epistles, or difference in emphasis between New Testament writers?
5. How does the author's treatment of Christology compare in balance and in content with the early church's preaching?
   a. How does it compare with the place (position, relative space) given the resurrection in comparison to the early life?
   b. How does it compare with the number of elements in the *kerygma* outline that figure in the systematic treatment?
6. Are the words "dogma" or "dogmatics" used? With or without definition?

7. Is the substance of theology itself the *content* of faith (i.e., its object, *what* one believes) or is faith something else that theology prepares for or explains or safeguards?
8. Is theology "systematic"? Is "system" defined?
9. Is ethics part of theology?

Now we move to the third section of the course, following the sections on biblical and early church history. We move to the classical or systematic treatment of themes in Christology.

First we played back the New Testament uses without systematic classification. Then we observed the unfolding of ancient doctrinal debate. Now we turn to the treatment you find in systematics textbooks, especially as derived from Protestant theological writing, which began in the sixteenth century but reached its peak in the seventeenth and eighteenth centuries.

On each of these levels we have defined the discipline of theology by watching it happen. We did this in the New Testament and again in the next period. We can summarize by saying that theology always had a double function. On the one hand, it sought to transmit the heritage without deforming it. Theology seeks to protect the transmitting or the transplanting of the heritage against deformation. It therefore is alert to heresy, to problematic ways of speaking, and to wrong ideas. On the other hand, theology speaks to the questions that arise in a new context.

Obviously, if the task of theologizing is done well, we always perform both functions. But we should be aware that when we read history we notice the latter, the change, more. People do not bother to write new treatises that say the same old thing. When something is written or debated, it is the new side that is discussed. Many of the old statements are still made, many of the old hymns are still sung, many of the old themes are still preached, but they are not given the same attention. So there is constantly in reading the history of theology an imbalance in the direction of paying attention to change and not to stability. We must recognize and make allowance for that.

That our attention goes to what is novel can move us away from the center with which we began as we read the story at the same time that the church at large is perhaps closer to that center. Remember the sketch of the core *kerygma,* the rest of the primitive thought of the New Testament church, then the theologians, then the second and third century, and so on. Many of the things Christians thought in any period had been said before, but they did not have to debate those things because they had them in common. So the focus of attention in debate, and in the statements of dogma, was on elements farther from that center than was the focus of attention in witness and worship.

Another summary remark is that the value of dogmatic statements like Nicea and Chalcedon is of greater negative than positive importance. Look at Chalcedon: "unmixed, unseparated, unconfused, undivided. . . ." That affirms very little. But it is clear, and you can argue it was necessary to make those negative statements. Even in Nicea the point was negation. You should not say, as Arius does, "There was a time when he was not." Neither should you say that the Son "was made out of nothing." We shall often help each other by reminding ourselves that the clarity and utility of a theological statement is sometimes greater on the negative than affirmative side. Affirmation may be nearer to the center; the negations may have to do with contemporary rephrasing.

Again, these doctrinal debates deal far more with the general *idea* of incarnation than with the particular texts that speak of the Word becoming flesh. This is at least characteristic of the Hellenistic world; it might have been different with the church expanding into another culture. They developed the *concept* of God coming into human form. They did not debate much about interpreting particular biblical texts or elements of ancient preaching one way or another. That is healthy in the sense that it gives us a broad perspective from which to face new problems. It is healthy in that it gives us a sense of theology providing an orientation, stance, and way of facing up to general issues, but there is also a danger in focusing on the general rather than on the particular. The example with the two natures was the inability of the majority position up to Chalcedon to deal with Jesus as really a man, especially as reflected in the debates about Luke 2, where there are reports of his being a child and growing and learning. How can the eternal, omnipotent, omniscient Son of God grow and learn? The Apollinarian tendency, which is in a sense the main stream of Eastern Orthodoxy, cannot handle Jesus' humanity, historicity, growing, thinking, and deciding as seriously as Luke's Gospel does, so the particular and the general need to be kept together by a constant return to the story itself.

The oscillations between the particular and the general, between the negative and the affirmative, between change and fidelity build an increasing body of doctrine as this motion continues in the life of the church. There are statements, writings of the early church fathers, and the creeds that have special authority, all of which need to be remembered and taught. A Christian thinker in the fourth century cannot just learn the Bible; he or she must know something of what has been taught since. And since you cannot think about or know it all, or at least cannot teach it all to everyone, then the theological process becomes a profession, a teaching profession in the church. It must be more and more organized, more and more selective.

Most of the teaching by the teacher of the New Testament congregation (the *didaskalos*) was probably rote learning. He or she taught people the kernel *kerygma,* certain sayings of Jesus, and certain Old Testament passages that had a special relation to Jesus. Instruction was probably oral with very little by way of organized teaching techniques and very little written. But of course, with the centuries it was possible—even unavoidable—to have a much more academic and organized process involved in the life of a church. It became necessary because there was more to teach, because there must be selection there must be organization. So which themes, which substance, which books, and which topics are worthy of the most attention? This rapidly develops into some kind of system that steps back from the material to ask how it fits together.

It is possible to teach without a system, just as it is possible to write a history without any major emphasis. Historians use the terms "chronicle," "annals," or "archives" for historical writing that tries simply to report everything in order without analysis, but the real writing of history goes past the reporting to find tendencies, trends, emphases, currents, causes, and effects. It asks which events were more important and which were less. So it is also in thinking. It is possible just to play back every thought that comes to you, but if you really use your mind on the material you are learning, you begin to notice patterns. You begin to establish inter-relations. You will find general themes and subordinate themes. You will identify issues that do not really exist or are not really important. This is the origin of what we now call systematic theology. It is a process in which teaching *includes* attention to coherence, system, and organization; to distinction between major and minor themes; and to distinction between what you ought to say first and what you ought to say last in order to be thinking straight. The term "systematic theology" itself stems only from the post-Reformation period, but the concept of systematizing thought already begins with the later church fathers.

The center of Christian teaching soon came to be the creed, though not immediately, because, as we saw in the story, the creeds were not creeds to start with. When the Nicene Creed was adopted at Nicea, it was a political document. It was another century before it began to be dealt with as a creed in the sense of normative theological statement. But once there were a few of these creeds in the background, then they provided the center for systematizing theology. If the Nicene Creed has established something, then that is something you ought to notice your own construction of a theological system. So it was with the doctrines of the Trinity and two natures—these themes became central. When a systematic theological treatment is dominated by themes from the creeds, we call it "dogmatic," in a technical sense dealing with dogma.

"Dogma" in modern language is almost a swear word, or at least a smear word. You call somebody names who disagrees with you, or whose style you dislike, by saying that he or she is dogmatic. In technical usage it simply means dealing with a statement that was fixed at a certain time. It comes from the verb stem that means to set or to place, to peg down, to make a point. A dogma is that body of statements which has been pegged in the history of the church, and dogmatics is an analysis of the thought of dogmatic statements.

We have noticed that it was normal for the church to develop a conscious theologizing process, but by following this we paid little attention to the social context of theology. From the New Testament up through Tertullian, theology went on in the persecuted church. It was quite clear in the New Testament, and it was quite clear for Tertullian, that Christians are a minority, separate from the rest of the world in important ways, who behave differently from others and have a separate ethic. They work socially with each other in a way different from other people, and they have a distinct community. They live in a society controlled by a pagan organization and dominated by a pagan thought world. Christians thought as a minority in an unbelieving world, and they considered this normal. The clash with the non-Christian world was a part of the standard situation in which Christian thinking was to be done. So in the early church fathers' thought were always elements of argument, polemics, and mission, of facing unbelief and challenging it, whether it be in the form of confusion or unfaithfulness within the church, or of the actual non-Christian stance that was the official position of the government and most of the people.

The change in the early Middle Ages, of which we may consider Augustine the sample, is that now the church is established. The church has taken over the empire, or vice versa. The pagan organization, in the sense of cult and temples, has been defeated, but now the church has to replace the function in society that had been provided for by the secular, pagan state, and the pagan cult. Christianity took over the religious functions of pagan religion that provided for the religious needs, desires, and appetites of the whole population. The nature of Christian worship changed in order to provide for everyone, not just for decided disciples. The nature of Christian ethics had to change because you have to be able to run society now according to your ethics. The Christian statesman became a very important person, whereas it would not have occurred to the church of Tertullian's time that a Christian would ever be able to be a statesman. Pagan thought was rather sweepingly brought into Christian thought. There were philosophical issues the Christians had not thought about before. Would they take over the way intelligent pagans thought about those issues, and more or less baptize it? Augustine himself, for instance, is neo-Platonist in his philosophical orientation.

The entire process has a clear impact on theologizing. The pagans who became Christians in great numbers after Constantine could not be expected to give up their crude or primitive (or elite) understanding of the services that religion ought to render to society, so such celebrations as Christmas and Halloween annex pagan rites. Such concentration on the nature cycle as is shown by the meaning of medieval Easter, the blessing of the fields, the flocks, and the fishermen's boat; the whole complex merger of Christianity with nature religion and culture religion changed the meaning of theologizing more than people noticed at the time.

Yet the memory of paganism remained. The church in the early Middle Ages was not persecuted, but people who know remember that the church *was* persecuted. The memory of the reality of paganism remained part of Christian thought, at least on the edges. So it was still thinkable that Christian faith is alternative to unbelief, and even though unbelief had no profound place in the system, it was still there.

This changed in the late Middle Ages. We might think of Thomas Aquinas as representative of this. Theologizing became the business of people who had nothing else to do. Certain monastic orders concentrated on nothing but teaching, maintaining the heritage, maintaining libraries, and organizing the body of knowledge into a coherent whole. The writings of Aristotle were rediscovered through the Arabic world, which had preserved them. Organized scholastic forms developed. Universities began in some of the major centers (Thomas himself was in Paris).

What could be called an encyclopedic concern began to develop, attempting to see everything as part of one cycle and to teach everything as part of a whole. This was based on trust that everything humanity can know could be put in a single framework. Everything would have its place, including the physical sciences and the biological sciences—or what was known of them—and all of philosophy and history. Everything had its place in the outline of the perfectly educated person, whose business is to lecture on everything and teach students how everything is in its place.

The world was closed geographically. There was an Islamic world, but people were not expected to talk to it. The break with Eastern Orthodoxy was complete. So Christian thought was limited, for the part of history that we are talking about, to Europe. There were a few Jews around, but they were not considered any challenge to Christian faith, so Christian thinking was systematized without any reference to unbelief or mission. Of course, there is no persecution. Christian faith is simply all the truth; all knowledge is theology. All learning is the business of theologians because theology brings together all intellectual disciplines. You can subdivide them, but they are all different kinds of theologies. Law is part of how God wants the world to be operated. The natural sciences are a discussion about how God created and maintains nature. Theology is the point at which all thought coheres. The debating, then, is not between belief and unbelief, but it is the clash of schools, options, and systems within Christendom. "Christendom" is the word for Europe. It is a geographic expression. The theological process is one of organizing everything, ultimately, beginning with the most basic way of putting together a total worldview, which is expected to be coherent and speak to every issue with authority because there is but one body of truth. There is one Christian culture, and theology exposits it; theologians explain its unity.

This had to change with the Reformation and confessional division. Then each country had an established religion. Since it was different from the next country, the elements of debate and controversy became more important because the vision of a Christian universe, *corpus christianum,* was gone. There was the same intensity of debate as in the early church, except you had it against other Christians instead of against pagans. Then, the seventeenth and eighteenth centuries not only pulled different Christians apart, but other disciplines also began to pull out from under the church. The natural scientists no longer assumed they were a branch of theology, but went and took their readings themselves. The linguists, or the historians, began to work at their own intellectual discipline without assuming that it was part of the great coherent whole dictated from above by revelation.

We shall not deal further with these shifts in the social context of theology, but it makes a great difference to have noticed them. Very often the substance of a theological debate, for instance between the Calvinists and the Lutherans, is considerably illuminated when we are aware of the differences in the social function of theologizing from one age to another.

One of the new characteristics of the period into which we move is the great diversity of positions. In the New Testament there was diversity in unity, but we could see that the major emphases were parallel in different languages. Especially remember that the three great theological strands of the New Testament developed the same concept of preexistence in the encounter with Gnosticism. After the New Testament period, we followed a history of debate, but we always saw one side coming out on top. It happened for political reasons, but there was a right answer at Nicea and at Chalcedon. Now we shall move into the realm of continuing systematic debate where there is no longer any evident right answer. Your collateral readings are partly intended to make you aware of that. You will observe how differently different sources see the same topics. We shall use other ways as well to become aware of the diversity of positions.

What should we do about this diversity of positions? What should we do in general as Christian theologians? What should we do specifically in a "preface" course? If in this course we were to settle rapidly on the one "right answer" and say why this is the right answer to any one of the debatable questions, then you might quite possibly wonder, "If that is the right answer, why was there such a problem? If it is so clear, why did all these other people debate so long about it?" If it were possible to give the right answer and explain why it is the right answer as simply as one would have to do in a course of this limited length and depth, then would we have really seen why theology is needed in the church? Why not just have somebody give us the right answer and go on to more important things?

In addition to this, of course, if I sought in the lectures to give the one right answer, some of you would probably say you do not want to be indoctrinated. If, on the other hand, we leave the question dangling, then some of you will say, "He doesn't know what he thinks. He is evasive. We can't get any help, or he is unsure of himself. He is afraid to commit himself, or to say what he thinks."

So what *should* we do? Some say that the right answer for the whole church is to have a great variety of positions. There is no one right answer to most questions. Pluralism is the right answer. Pluralism consists in the claim that all the answers are right. If it is the case, then we need to survey them all, notice the strengths, and perhaps weaknesses, of each, then let them all stand side by side, and be happy in that richness and diversity. That is an understandable position with certain cultural values, but remember that part of the function of theology was always to guard against the serious possibility of wrong teaching. Certainly the New Testament thinkers were clear that there was such a thing as wrong teaching. Although several teachings might be in some sense right (four Gospels, three "great theologians"), we still need to recognize that being wrong is possible.

So ultimate or absolute pluralism is hardly justifiable in the total life of the church, although perhaps relative pluralism is a good way to overcome some kind of cultural narrowness. That is why we use many different collateral texts in this course. To the extent that anyone can do so, I can say that on the three big questions which we shall discuss—atonement, eschatology, and revelation—I have definite ideas about the right answer, or at least about which answers are better than others. In fact, in earlier years, when this material was part of the outline of a year-long course on the senior level, we spent some time together working out what seemed to be the most nearly right answer, but in this lecture series I shall not try to answer those basic questions with the right answer. The reason for this is not evasiveness, but that this is a preface course. Our purpose is to demonstrate the necessity and the fruitfulness of studying in a given field, not to cut off the study by telling you which conclusions you must come out with. Perhaps we should discuss whether that is a satisfactory way to run a course. At least it is the way this outline is set up.

We concentrate, as in the other periods, on Christology—just one segment of systematic theology, especially since Protestant orthodoxy a tendency to outline Christology under the heading of the "three offices" or "threefold office" of Christ has developed. *Office* is meant in the technical sense. It is not a room where you talk to someone at a desk; it is a function. The "threefold office" describes the work of Christ as the work of a prophet, priest, and king. In the Old Testament the life of Israel was marked by these three functions. They were the three primary dimensions of the relation between Israel and God. They were the functions for which there was anointing. Anointing symbolically imparted the mandate of the spirit. Deuteronomy 16 to 18 describes Israel's prescribed social organization and the functions of the prophet, priest, and king—in addition to the judges. (There would have actually been four functions in that passage, but the judges were not anointed. They were a level of congregational or village organization). The prophet and priest were the offices of leadership in Israel, and Deuteronomy predicts there will also be kings.

Recent biblical scholarship accentuates the contrast, or even the conflicts, among these various offices. On the one hand is prophetic religion, while on the other is priestly religion. The prophet is the spokesperson for God's justice and the changes God demands. The priest advocates the status quo, and calls down blessings of God on things as they are by going through sacrificial or sacramental rituals. This emphasis was very strong in Old Testament scholarship in the thirties and forties. Today it is less strong. Scholars now say that both prophets and priests, and even in some sense kings, ideally or properly belong in the same community of Israel, so when the prophet criticizes the priest it is because he is not being a good priest, not that he should not be a priest. When the priest opposes the prophet, it is because one or the other of them is not being faithful rather than because the various functions are intrinsically antagonistic. There is a difference, but the difference has been overdone.

You might ask whether your collateral sources think these functions in the light of Israel are related to the use of the same terminology for Jesus. All three of these functions were picked up in the New Testament as ways of describing what Jesus fulfilled. The word Messiah really means prophet, priest, and king because it means the anointed one. In the Old Testament all three of these offices were the subject of an anointing, but increasingly messianic language, already then and especially as it developed later, had to do with the king. But Hebrews also sees Jesus as the priest, the high priest, the ultimate high priest, or the one priest properly so-called who brings to its accomplishment the concept of priesthood in his sacrifice—not just of a victim but of himself. We have, although only very sketchily, noted the record of the expectation of "the prophet." We referred to this in John 1:21 when we discussed New Testament Christology. John the Baptist was asked first if he is Christ. He denied it. Then Elijah? He denied this too. Are you the prophet? Again, he said no. "The prophet" is one of the figures of messianic expectation which Jesus in some sense fulfills (compare Acts 7:37).

The next thing to say about all three of these functions is that they apply in discipleship. This theme is underdone in mainstream theology. I doubt you will find in most of your systematic books a reference to discipleship or ethics. But even if you did, it is doubtful whether your authors would derive their ethics from the things they say about Christ, so that the Christian would share in prophecy, priesthood, and reigning. Yet this is clear biblical language.

First Corinthians 12–14 discusses the function of prophecy in the life of the church. The concept of Christians reigning with Christ has mostly future dimensions, but it cannot quite be demonstrated that it is only future. Second Timothy 2:11 says, "If we have died with him, we shall also live with him; if we endure, we shall also reign with him. . . ." This hope is clearly future, but it is a future that matters for now. You already ought to behave as if that were your expectation. In Ephesians 2:4–6, the hope seems to be present. "God, who is rich in mercy, . . . even when we were dead through our trespasses, made us alive together with Christ . . . and raised us up with him, and made us sit with him in the heavenly places in Christ Jesus." "Sitting at the right hand of God" is the description of Christ's present Lordship in which Christians somehow already participate. Ephesians 1:20 said it about Christ: ". . . the immeasurable greatness of his [God's] power . . . according to the working of his great might which he accomplished in Christ when he raised him from the dead and made him sit at his right hand in the heavenly places." And 2:6 says that we sit with him.

Christians also share in the priesthood established by the Christ's work. Revelation 4 and 5, with the vision of the Lamb that is worthy to receive power and to open the scroll, praises the Lamb because he ransomed humanity for God from every tongue, tribe, people, and nation and *"made them a kingdom and priests to our God"* (5:10). Originally this was a kingdom *of* priests (see Exodus 19:6 and Isaiah 61:6). It expressed the idea that the whole people of God was to be a priestly people (see 1 Peter 2:9) with the access to God's presence a priest has, that represented other people before God. If what Christ did as divine Son he also did as a man, and as the normative human who calls others, the disciple is somehow to share in whatever it meant for him to be priest, prophet, and king.

This "threefold office" emphasis was first developed with great care as the outline of Christology in the Protestant world. It was not a strong medieval emphasis. It is used in Protestant orthodoxy. This points to another dimension of the threefold office outline that is not emphasized in your collateral texts but that probably was quite important when Protestantism began using this outline: a *polemic* implication. To say that Christ is king in the Protestant-Catholic debate of the sixteenth and seventeenth centuries was first to say the pope is not. This is to say that the church should leave "reigning" to the working of providence or to the working of Christ at the right hand of God. Therefore the management of history is not the business of the church. This is not a systematic or a dogmatic theological statement in the narrowest sense, but it is a significant part of the polemic implication. We can see likewise that to say that Christ is priest affects the doctrines of humanity and salvation. It says humans cannot save themselves but that one who identifies with them can save them. To say Christ is prophet also affects to the Catholic doctrine of the teaching authority of the church. Each element of the threefold office touches on an aspect of the polemics in the Protestant-Catholic debate. It thus serves as a criterion of balance, completeness, and coherence more than of truth. It helps to ask "Have we forgotten anything?" rather than "What shall we say?"

Before following this threefold outline in the pattern that organizes our material, let us look at some of the limitations it has *as an outline.* When we look at the texts that use this outline, we find that it is a somewhat superficial principle of organization. How can we talk about Christ under these headings? Sometimes the division is temporal. Jesus was the prophet until his passion. In his ministry he taught and was in that sense a prophet. Then he was a priest in his death and up to his resurrection. He gave himself as a sacrifice. Then he became king when he was called to sit at the right hand of God. This pattern of organization does not differ substantially from another kind of organization, which we find in Calvinist literature, but shall not follow. It deals with "two states" of Christ—his humiliation and his exaltation. Philippians 2 is divided this way. He humbled himself and then he was exalted. "King" is the same as exaltation, and "prophet" and "priest" are his humility. This will not quite suit either. For one thing, the teaching work or the prophetic work of Christ continues in the life of the church through the Spirit after the passion events. The intercession, or priestly function, continues at the right hand of God. This makes the prophet too narrowly a teacher of love and truth and prediction—as if truths by themselves were enough and Jesus is a prophet, just like all the other prophets, in that he tells us true things—instead of thinking of Jesus himself as revelatory or as revelation.

It is understandable that the more systematic theology texts prefer to make the offices simultaneous, so Karl Barth says that Christ as king means the divine exercise of sovereignty in which God chooses to move toward humanity. God comes down, but comes down because God as sovereign has chosen to condescend to humanity. So Christ as king is the doctrine of the incarnation. Christ as priest moves in the other direction. Christ as priest is the true human moving towards God to reconcile us with God. So Christ as priest is atonement. Christ as prophet is the fact that the double movement from God to humanity as kingly and the movement from humanity to God as priestly is itself revelation. Therefore, in all of it Christ is prophet.

Other earlier European theologians used some of the same language but put the labels on a different place. Christ as prophet is the movement from God to humanity because that is revelatory. Christ as priest is a movement from humanity to God. Kingship is the presupposition and the total of the two. In order to do that, Christ had to be king.

In our case we shall not bother with diversity in outlines. We shall stick closer to the earlier meaning of the language in each of these headings. With regard to kingship, for instance, we shall look at the concept of the kingdom as it has its place in the earthly ministry of Jesus, in the Old Testament, and in the early church. From there we shall unfold what is the most significant thing to say about Christ as king.

But this survey of the variety of ways to use this threefold outline is helpful because it tells us not to take it seriously. Do not think that there is any structural protection in having these three points. If there were, then we would have to stick with them always. But that is not what they are good for. The threefold office is simply one way of classifying the material, one way to remind yourself to check whether you have missed anything, or to check for balance, completeness, and coherence. It is not in any sense a sacred outline. It neither guarantees that, when we have said everything under these three headings, we are finished, nor that we are right.

But it probably does provide a better way to balance our treatment than some of the other principles of classification people have used. One of the other principles is the idea of Trinity, especially clear in H. Richard Niebuhr, who says that a theology concentrated too much on Jesus is out of balance because it fails to attend to creation and history. A theology that concentrates too much on the Father is out of balance because it fails to attend sufficiently to redemption. A theology concentrating on the Holy Spirit is out of balance because it does not attend enough to the fixed revelation of the past. So, according to Niebuhr, we need to use the concept of Trinity as a source of balance in a theology that gives equal time to Father, Son, and Spirit. If we take that back to our Nicene discussions, we observe that it is a form of Sabellianism. It assumes that what makes God *God* is the monad underlying the three states, rather than the clarity of the revelation in history. The threefold office outline, whatever is wrong with it and whatever its limits, is still more helpful as a reminder or principle of organization than some of the others.

Notice in the outline that we shall treat each of the three topics on two levels. With Christ as king we shall treat eschatology, with Christ as priest, atonement, and with Christ as prophet, revelation. In each of these cases the second topic is much narrower than the first, and yet is the one on which we shall spend more time, because that is the form in which this issue has been debated. On each case we shall first look at a wider circle with a minimal statement and then concentrate on the theme within that wider circle and watch the debate. We shall do this, as I said, in a pluralistic way, by observing a variety of positions, contradictions, options, and schools of thought. We shall not learn, at least not in class, to get the right answer, but to know how many different possible positions there are that might be counted as answers, and how they relate to one another.

A reminder about vocabulary may be in place. We saw that the label "dogmatics" is generally used in the continental languages, but not in English, where the word has taken on distasteful connotations. The replacement is usually "systematic theology." This substitution is confusing, since the literal and disciplinary meanings are not the same. "Dogmatics" deals with the deposit of history. It takes seriously its historically fixed character. "Systematic theology" is more concerned to test inner logical consistency, clarify first principles, and reason coherently from them. In doing so it may be selective or disrespectful of the original context in which a question or an answer had meaning.

If we filled out the spectrum of theological subdisciplines, we would also need to itemize:

- Symbolics. The direct exegesis of creeds (*symbolon* is Greek for creed).
- Philosophical theology. The interaction between systematic theology and the language and values of one's surrounding culture as expressed in its philosophy.
- Apologetics. The portion of philosophical theology which seeks to interpret or commend or defend the faith in the face of unbelief, skepticism, or neutrality.

11

Christ as King: Last Things

Preparation Guide

1. Does your author think of the "last things" as an event or events in temporal history? Does he or she discuss a sequence of expected events at or just prior to the end of history as we know it? If such events are predicted in any detail, what position does the author see as the alternative or the adversary, and what are the issues?
2. How is the "end" related to our time and calendar? Is it the next thing that will happen or are there prior "signs" that must first occur? Or is it not really chronological at all?
3. Why does God let history continue? (Compare to question 8.) What is God waiting for or trying to achieve? Why did not the world end sooner?
4. Is the concern of eschatology primarily
   a. a sample of issues of method (hermeneutics, biblical authority);
   b. a sample of issues of philosophical orientation (time/eternity, myth, mechanism, closed universe);
   c. a projection of contemporary realities; or
   d. an indirect way of dealing with one's philosophy of history?
5. In what sense does Christ reign now and in what sense is his reign a future one? Is this discussion part of a description of the work of Christ or does it come elsewhere in the outline? In what sense did Christ fulfill or not fulfill the Old Testament expectations of messianity?
6. What is the present state of the dead? In what terms does your author discuss the general resurrection and judgment? Is there

one judgment or none or several? Is judgment an event in its own right or merely the unveiling of what already was?

7. Are persons to be judged by their works? By their faith? How do the two relate?
8. What hope is there for human civilization? Is human endeavor, work, social development, etc., worthwhile? Is it worthwhile spiritually? Eternally? If so, how does this value correlate with the progress of Western civilization? With liberation as a social goal? Is the coming judgment correlated with social collapse or atomic catastrophe?
9. What of the reality of hell; what is its significance? If the author leans toward universalism, what are his or her grounds? If the author rejects universalism, does he or she recognize that it has some biblical grounds?
10. Does your author deal with the idea that Jesus or the New Testament writers first expected a very early end of history and then had to adjust to a disappointment?
11. Is humanity immortal? What does that mean? Why?
12. What is said of *individual* hope for the hereafter? Will individual identity persist in eternity?

Sources for Further Reading

Boettner, Loraine. *The Millennium*. 1957.

Erb, Paul. *The Alpha and the Omega: A Restatement of the Christian Hope in Christ's Coming*. 1955.

Glasson, Thomas Francis. *His Appearing and His Kingdom: The Christian Hope in the Light of Its History*. 1953.

Martin, James Perry. *The Last Judgment: In Protestant Theology from Orthodoxy to Ritschl*. 1963.

Ryrie, Charles. *The Basis of the Premillennial Faith*. 1953.

Smith, C. Ryder. *The Bible Doctrine of the Hereafter*.

Winklhofer, Alois. *The Coming of His Kingdom: A Theology of the Last Things*. 1963.

We could proceed in any sequence in dealing with the three "offices," prophet, priest, and king. This time we shall begin with king. The king, like the prophet and the priest, was a standard figure of Old Testament society. "King" was, like prophet and priest, a title Jesus took on in a particular way in the New Testament. For "king," as for the other titles, we shall first look briefly at its broader meaning and then concentrate at greater length on a subtheme. The theme of eschatology is much narrower than what it means to say Christ is King, but that is the theme our readings intensively survey. First, we take a brief look at the broader part of affirming the kingship of Christ.

In the Old Testament the king was the expression and personification of Israel's identity, yet he was an ambivalent expression. It was not always clear that it is a good thing to have a king. From Moses through Gideon in the ancient story, Israel had no king. A number of reasons for this are worth reviewing. Partly—sometimes it is said literally—it is because YHWH is the King. There is something about the covenantal structure of Israelite society, something about the way the people function with their priesthood, their prophets, their judges that means they do not need any other king than God. Often the Old Testament tells us that this is the point at which Israel is to be different from other nations. The characteristic of the other nations that Israel should not follow is that they have kings.

When Israel did come to choose a king, part of their motivation was the desire "to be like the other nations." Jotham's fable in Judges 9:7–15 makes a striking statement of the low view of kingship in the period just after Gideon. Jotham told the story of the trees' demand for a king. They thought the olive tree would be a good king, but it was busy producing oil. They thought the fig tree would be a good king, but it was busy making good sweet fruit. They tried the vine, but the vine was busy making people happy with grapes and wine. So they tried the bramble bush. The bramble bush was happy to take over as king because it had nothing else useful to do. This fable graphically portrays the view some voices in ancient Israel had of secular kingship.

This does not mean that ancient Israel did not have a social structure. It does not mean we could find in ancient Israel a background for a New Left anti-institutionalism, which thinks that a society would operate without structure. But ancient Israel had a different *kind* of structure. They had "the elders in the gates" of the villages. In every community, every village, and every clan was a collective leadership of a few respected wise people who spoke for the community and made the decisions. In addition to these, there were charismatic "judges," the men or women, like Gideon and Saul, on whom the Spirit of God fell in a unique situation of crisis. They were chosen to this ruling function, but always *ad hoc,* always in the face of a need, not because they had been selected for it or sought out on the basis of some recruitment or election process, and certainly not because their father had ruled.

The ruling function carried out by these elders and judges overlapped very clearly with the priestly and the prophetic roles. Samuel was all three. He is sometimes referred to as a prophet; he functioned sometimes as a priest; and he moved around from place to place functioning as a judge. Similarly, of course, this had been the case with Moses himself.

But the king was accepted, yet still with reservations. Deuteronomy 17 is part of a passage where the four offices of Israelite society are described—the prophet, the priest, the king, and the judges in the gate. This section warns against kings, because of the danger that they might not keep the promises Israel had made. "When you come to the land which the LORD your God gives you, and you possess it and dwell in it, and then say, 'I will set a king over me, like all the nations that are round about me'" (here the theme is conformity, like Mennonites wanting to be like the Presbyterians):

> You may indeed set as king over you whom the LORD your God will choose. One from among your brethren . . . not . . . a foreigner . . . Only he must not multiply horses for himself, or cause the people to return to Egypt in order to multiply horses. . . . He shall not multiply wives. . . . nor shall he greatly multiply for himself silver and gold.

He shall not accumulate wives, cavalry, or money. Thus the kingship was accepted, under conditions. The narrative in 1 Samuel 10 corresponds to this set of prescriptions in Deuteronomy 17.

This of course means Saul, then David, and then the divided kingdom. Two different concepts of succession operate within this kingship. In the north there is an effort to maintain the sense of the Spirit of God falling upon a man and making him the king. To use the modern language of the sociology of religion, the king is "charismatic," not in the Christian sense but in the sense of Max Weber. People rise up because of their personal qualifications, because of the kind of leadership they provide. In at least every second or third generation, or sometimes every couple of months, there is a change of dynasty in the Northern Kingdom, much like the change from Saul to David. David takes Saul's place, not by being his son but by pushing him away, by displacing him, and by being a stronger leader than Saul was—by having more "spirit." So every few years in the Northern Kingdom a new dynasty replaced the old. But they were not really dynasties. There were at the most two or three generations during which a king would be strong enough to determine that his son was also going to be king. But the norm was the other pattern, that of the charismatic usurper.

The southern kingdom, Judea, held to the dynastic concept rather faithfully. But both kingdoms were finally subject to a negative verdict—God turned down the whole thing. What it means for God to want a person to be God's prince and servant, is defined, by the time we get into the prophetic period, by the figure of the servant of the LORD in the latter part of the book of Isaiah. Here the "servant of the LORD" is a technical term; it clearly means a kingly figure. Scholars differ as to whether it means one person or a type, whether it is strictly future, or whether there was a prince in exile in Babylon to whom it was spoken. They differ in the extent to which they think this man englobes the fate of all Israel in his peculiar redefinition of what it means to be God's servant. But in any case, the kind of king God wants is a servant. Isaiah 42, 49, 52, and 53, say that the kind of king in whom God is pleased will bring God's righteousness to the ends of the earth. That is the language of Isaiah 42:

> He will not cry or lift up his voice. . . .
> He will faithfully bring forth justice.
> He will not fail or be discouraged till he has established justice in the earth.

It is a political figure, a kind of king, but a suffering king. Of course, in the New Testament this came to be one of the most striking prefigurings of Jesus' own servanthood.

So kingship in the Old Testament had a long and speckled career. It was not universally a good image, but was suspect. The greatness of David is looked back to as a kind of ideal age. The greatness of Solomon, which is honored in the wisdom literature, is dubious from some other perspectives because of all his wives, horses, and gold.[1] Then there is God's principled negative judgment on kingship expressed through Jeremiah, and the redefinition of what kind of a man God wants to represent God's people in the Suffering Servant.

We have sought to situate the variety of meanings of "king" in Old Testament usage. In the New Testament we encounter Jesus as "Messiah," the one anointed to be king in the Gospel story. We find it in Matthew 16:15–16, the story of Peter's confession. "Who am I?" "You are the Christ."

Jesus makes clear, as the Suffering Servant image had begun to, that the coming king is the Suffering Servant. Yet he picks up the Messianic expectation. He does not tell the Jews, "You were expecting a king and you should not have because what you really need is something else." He does not say, "You are expecting a king and I am not a king." No, he says, "You do right to expect a king, but expect a different kind of a king." He claims that this is the fulfillment of the Messianic expectation rather than its rejection. He says that God will conquer, but not by restoring David.

After David's reign, Israel degenerated and collapsed. They renewed their efforts in the Maccabean times, but collapsed again. Now Jesus will restore Israel, not to Davidic kingship but by identifying kingship with suffering. One kind of fulfillment would let the old vision of David be the norm. Jesus would return Israel to Davidic kingship. But instead

1. The reason the wives are an offense is more political and cultic than sexual. Many of Solomon's marriages represented political alliances and the wives brought their idols along.

the movement is reversed. Jesus claims he fulfills the promises. He is the son of David. So Jesus answers the question, and does not dodge it, when he says, "The kind of ruler I came to be is the servant." We have dramatic statements of this in Matthew 20 and Luke 22:

> The kings of the nations rule over them,
> but you shall not do that,
> you shall be one another's servants,
> because I came as a servant.[2]

This is his redefinition of the meaning of kingship. He did not say "king" is a bad word. He says it is a concept some people have misinterpreted.

We could discuss at some length where Jesus got the idea that he was to be king by being a servant. This depends on Jesus' self-consciousness, and also on the Gospel texts themselves. The texts themselves give the impression that the first statement to this effect became clear at his baptism.

Jesus makes clear in the passages already referred to not only that this is the kind of king he will be but that his disciples are to be this kind of servant as well. This is the way, not to renounce greatness, but to be great. "Whoever would be great among you must be your servant, and whoever would be first among you must be your slave." This is not a rejection of the vision of power that the Israelites had. It is a redefinition of it, and it is more than a matter of language. It also has to do with our contemporary discussion about the political. Did Jesus take a nonpolitical or apolitical position? *Or* did he take a *properly defined* political position? That he uses the word "king" and parallel terms, and then redefines them seems to make it most appropriate to say that he tells us what a proper political position is, rather than that he takes an apolitical position.

When Jesus says, "I am the king, but the servant kind of king," he fulfills the hope of the Jews. I suspect most of your background reading and thinking and listening to Sunday School teachers about the hope of the Jews has assumed that the Jews were wrong. Jews usually are wrong in those takes on the story. They wanted a king and Jesus did not want to be a king. He had to struggle and struggle with them to get them to see this point. Finally they killed him for refusing to be the king they wanted. Well, that may be understandable on the elementary Sunday School level, when you have to use words with the meaning that they have for your audience, but if we want to read the biblical literature properly, that is a backward use of language. Jesus did not say he

2. Editorial note: This is the author's translation.

did not want to be king. He said: "I want to be *this* kind of king." That fulfillment was relevant, for instance, to the Zealots who were looking for a king and from whose ranks he found many disciples. It involves a different way of living. In Luke 4, Jesus begins his public ministry by proclaiming, "The *kingdom* of God is at hand: now you are going to live differently. The law will be fulfilled—the law of jubilee. And this will mean you will handle money, sex and marriage, conflict, and power differently from the way people generally do." The coming of Christ as King is the fulfillment of a social hope.

We could go into much greater length into the ethical axioms or the spiritual axioms of this hope. Now we must limit it to some brief hints.

- One of the axioms in this new arrangement is that it parallels God's original intent. This is most striking in Matthew 19 when the Pharisees are discussing whether divorce is permissible. Jesus conceded that there seems to be room made for divorce in Deuteronomy, but he says that was a concession—a concession made for the sake of the hardness of human hearts. "But from the beginning it was not so." In other words, *"from the beginning"* is the original standard Jesus has now come to restore. One of the things Jesus says about his kingdom, one of the axioms of the new order of relations among people that his kingship establishes, is that things will be as they were meant to be. Things will fulfill the creative intent of God.
- Another axiom is divine sovereignty. This is most strikingly described in the passages in the Sermon on the Mount that deal with prayer, anxiety, and taking thought for the morrow. It is assumed, as the point of these teachings, that God is in charge. God watches over the birds and the lilies. Why do you think you have to bother God with a lot of words when you pray? Why do you think you have to bother with economic security? These are the kind of things the Gentiles are concerned about, but your heavenly Father knows your needs, so *you* seek the kingdom and God will take care of the rest.
- Another axiom is that obedience is possible. Concessions to disobedience and imperfection are no longer needed. There do not have to be systematic adjustments to the fact that we know people will not keep rules. We do not have to lower the target as, for instance, traditional Catholic ethics does in one way or Calvinistic ethics does in another way, in order to adjust to the fact that people do not or cannot do as God wants. Perhaps God does not even want their obedience because then they would be proud. Here there is no prior adjustment to the impossibility of obedience. The Sermon on the Mount's radical statement about how it will be

when Christ is king assumes that it can be that way. We can do God's will.

Now we skip to the early church's reflection on the concept of kingship. Remember from our vocabulary study that *Lord,* another word for the one who rules, replaced *king.* We saw that the confession "Christ is Lord" is the primitive creed—the oldest confession of faith—and that this refers not simply to a title, but also to a function. The powers are subject to him. In 1 Corinthians 15:25ff., he reigns over the powers of this rebellious creation until all of them are rendered submissive. The language of principalities and powers is particularly Pauline language. It sounds strange to the modern reader. Yet in spite of great changes in worldview between Paul's time and our own, if we read him carefully, we can understand what it means that Christ is reigning over rebellious powers. We find it has an appropriate application to a lot of contemporary problems. God uses the power structures of this world and society in spite of themselves for God's purposes. Christ, reigning at the right hand of God, ("prime minister" in modern language—the executive) carries out the purposes of the one who is sovereign. His function is ruling over the rebellious structures of the universe for God's purposes.

In the Old Testament we have this vision already in Isaiah 10. Assyria is called in by God to chastise Israel. This does not mean Assyria is good, but God uses Assyria, in its rebellion, as a punisher, "the rod of my anger." But Assyria, because it will be proud of its success, will also be struck down in turn. This use of the power structures of the rebellious creation under God's providence ("providence" is the scholastic technical word for what the New Testament called the Lordship of Christ) is the concrete meaning of Christ's Lordship. For instance, the early church can say, because he is Lord over those who persecute us, we can remain faithful in our suffering. Those who persecute us are permitted to do so because that is somehow part of Christ's purposes. Therefore we can accept martyrdom as the way to serve him, knowing our obedience will ultimately be vindicated. We can be faithful in persecution because we know it is not the last word. We know that those who are now destroying us will fall as Assyria did. In Revelation 13, for instance, the image of evil is the two beasts. The first one makes war on the saints. A "call for the endurance and faith of the saints" is the last thing said about it in chapter 13. This is the way it is. The persecution of the saints is the meaningfulness of the present situation under Christ's lordship, therefore we can be obedient in spite of the fact that it does not pay, in spite of the fact that the rewards of obedience are not visible. We can obey because of the Lordship that we confess.

Christ as King rules for the sake of the church, despite his suffering. Revelation 4 and 5, the first vision of John, is of the gathering of the church. The scroll represents the meaning of history that can be opened only by the Lamb. The Lamb is praised because of his worthiness to ransom persons for God from every tribe, nation, or kingdom, and make them a priestly kingdom to reign on earth. *To reign. To share in his kingship.*

The Lamb brought together this priestly kingdom. That is the answer to the question, "What is in this scroll?" "What is the meaning of history?" It is said in another place as well that the meaning of history is somehow the hidden working of the Lordship of Christ through the church. In Ephesians 3, Paul designates as his special message

> to make all men see what is the plan of the mystery hidden for ages in God. . . . that through the church the manifold wisdom of God might now be made known to the principalities and powers in the heavenly places. This was according to the eternal purpose which he has realized in Christ Jesus our Lord.

The place of the church in the history of the universe is the place where Christ's lordship is operative. This is where it is already clear that he rules. The kind of ruler he is is a suffering servant kind of ruler. The church is moving history by her servanthood. Most of us still think that the way to move history is not by servanthood but by some other kind of rule, but the church is the instrument through which God is moving history by servanthood, in the extension of doing that same thing in Jesus.[3]

The fact that God extends Christ's reign in a hidden way through the powers and in a visible way through the servant church is the reason for history. This is why time goes on. You have in your question sheet a question that may have seemed strange when you first met it—why doesn't time just stop? Why does God let history continue? What is still going on that has to be done? In the key places where we find a New Testament answer to that question it has to do with the gathering of the church. At the beginning of Acts, for instance, the disciples are gathered around Jesus before the ascension. They ask, *Now* are you going to restore the kingdom? He says, "That is not for you to know, but I give you the promise of the coming of the Spirit and the mission to Jerusalem and Judea and Samaria." This very familiar passage on the promise of the coming of the Spirit to make them witnesses answers the questions of the disciples such as, "When are you going to set up the kingdom?" It

3. This is a very sketchy summary of the meaning of the affirmation or confession of Christ's present lordship. If you are interested in this concept of principalities and powers as the language of Paul's philosophy of history, the little book by Hendrik Berkhof, *Christ and the Powers,* is a good simple introduction.

does not sound like an answer, but it shows that the question is poorly phrased. In Matthew 28, what we usually call the "Great Commission" is introduced by the statement of Jesus, "All authority in heaven and earth has been given to me." This is a statement of lordship, the meaning of ascension. "All authority has been given me. Therefore as you go, as you baptize, as you teach, make disciples." Matthew 24 states the temporal quality of God's concern even more clearly in verse 14: "This Gospel of the kingdom will be preached throughout the whole world." But it is clear that the meaning of the duration of history—why it does not stop—is the church's proclamation. The preaching of the gospel is why time does not stop. This then is the meaning and the content of his kingship. Kingship is ruling over history so that this can happen.

Characteristic of most of the biblical language with regard to hope, rule, and the passage of time is a strong emphasis upon the meaningfulness of the historical process. This is significantly different from the Platonic worldview in which time is a disadvantage. There, the eternal is genuine. Our wearing out and getting old represents the passage of time. Essential reality is the nontemporal, therefore the most essential hope is a nontemporal hope, so it is rather crude to talk about Christian hope or about the passage of time. Really we want to get out of this time scale into eternity where there is not any time scale. Imagine a graph on the blackboard. We could represent time as movement along the graph line by line, year by year. As long as you have your eye glued right at the board you will only see one moment at a time, but if you get off that board—out of finite time—then you can see the whole thing. That is how God, not being temporal, sees time. Similarly, we too will no longer be temporal when we are free from our bodies and time and enter into eternity. Time really does not matter. It is part of the prison in which humans are lost. That is the Platonic vision.

Alternatively, the Bible tends to speak of temporality and sequence continuing even beyond the present world. Once in a while we find a phrase in the New Testament describing the departed saints as "asleep." Now this does not literally mean that they are sleeping. It means that, although they are not in the present shape or state of existence, those who are no longer with us are still doing something that takes time. There is an intermediate state between death and the end. Despite the many jokes told about St. Peter letting people in at the pearly gates, you do not, according to the biblical picture, immediately find yourself in "eternity" when you die. Rather, you find yourself waiting in an intermediate state for which one of the old words was "paradise." "Paradise" does not mean eternity. Jesus said to the man crucified beside him, "Today you will be with me in paradise." He just meant, today you will be at the place where the dead wait until history reaches its conclusion. The dead also wait for history to reach its conclusion. In Revelation 6 we have a picture of the martyrs. What are the martyrs doing? They are not already rejoicing in the heavenly throne room. They are not already sharing in the glories of heaven. No, they are under the altar. Revelation 6:9 reads, "I saw under the altar the souls of those who had been slain for the word of God. . . . They cried out with a loud voice, 'O Sovereign Lord, holy and true, how long . . . ?" Those who have died in the faith still wait until the number of their fellow servants is complete. So the meaning of time is so important that we cannot even accept the Platonist assumption that when you die you become eternal. No, when you die you are still temporal. You are still waiting for the world to be brought to God's purposes. No one enters into this fulfillment until the entire universe enters into it. This is what Paul meant when he said (in Philippians 1:23, for instance) he would just as soon die and be "with Christ." This did not mean infinite eternity. It meant this intermediate state. Time matters. The historical process matters. It matters so much that even those who are no longer in it still wait for it.

It is not surprising then that in Ephesians 6 and 2 Corinthians 4 we encounter the language of warfare, that is, of conflict-ful, meaningful, and purposive movements of forces in history. It is not incongruous or surprising that the book of Revelation ends with a new earth. It is very different from many cities we have heard of, including the old Jerusalem, but it still is a city and not a cloud. It is still most meaningfully spoken of in terms borrowed from historical experience. So it is also that time is not unlimited. We do not have all the time in the world to get done what needs to get done. Things are coming to a head in the biblical language. Your salvation is nearer than when you first believed.

Our heading here has been the three offices of the classical Christology, but in orthodox dogmatics there is very little reference to ethics under these headings. In the Bible, however, ethics is always present. We are to share in Christ's reign. We are to share in his priesthood. We are to share in his prophet-hood. The way we reign with him, as we saw in Matthew 20, is to share in his servanthood because that is the way he defined kingship. We are to be servants because he came to serve. This speaks directly to a contemporary ethical debate. The major axiom in modern ethics, ever since the Middle Ages, is that you ought to do what will make things come out right. Proper behavior on your part is the behavior that will produce, in the total social mechanism, results that will be good, or less evil. This is a mechanistic kind of utilitarianism. You do something that makes the mechanism of society work to bring about the greatest good to the greatest number. Such good action—making things come out right—has been the model.

But if the cross is the way to be Lord, if we are supposed to have in ourselves the mind that was in Christ Jesus (Phil. 2), and if the way he was minded was that he did not count self-determination as a thing to be grasped, then Lordship comes through self-emptying and servanthood unto death. That is the way to be Lord. You do not get things to come out right by reaching for the controls. You do not manage things by getting the steering wheel in your hands. This whole pragmatic management/lesser evil/best results approach to being human is challenged to its core when servanthood is made the key to our ethics.

Another key to New Testament ethics, especially clear in Peter, Paul, and James, is the acceptance of subjection. This is not palatable to modern men and women because we do not see it through Christology or through the fact that Christ suffering is the way he became Lord. We see it as the subjection of a convict, or a coward, or someone who is unconvinced, sheepish, doubtful about him or herself, with no self-confidence. But the subjection (more precisely, "subordination") of Jesus to us, the Romans, scribes, Pharisees, Herod, and Caiaphas was his loving freedom. It was the way he chose to be sovereign in the world. He was so strong that he could deal that way with human hatred. He could proclaim victory over the bonds into which he let himself be put because of the freedom with which he had accepted those bonds.

Modern psychology shows us that our rebellion often takes the shape of what we rebel against. Marxism tries to overthrow the tyranny of capitalist materialism by turning materialism against capital. Anti-Communism does the same when it uses the tools of the enemy. So with the rebellion of children who talk back to their parents in their own terms. They try to affirm their freedom by rejecting submission. Because Jesus chose subjection instead of having it imposed upon him against his will, and because he accepted that free subjection as the measure of his love, instead of as a limit on his will and self-determination, he proved that he is not the slave, but the Lord, of what he bowed to. If we knew this and could work it out, if we could think in positions of originality, it would be the key to a whole different way of looking at ethics in society.

We must identify the nature of the shift we will make to the narrower sense of the meaning of kingship. This topic is traditionally called eschatology. The creeds stated that Christ is now "reigning at the right hand of God, whence he shall come to judge." Coming to judge was not at the core of the earliest preaching. Remember that on the induction grid only one of the sermons of Acts refers to judgment, namely, Peter's speech to Cornelius. Later we saw it in Paul's sermon on Mars Hill. From then on it had a clear and solid place. The future, the outcome, of the present reign of Christ is judgment. Biblical literature clearly gives us this picture of the unfolding of events. It would take a little longer than the time we have remaining to describe these events with any degree of detail. Let us only scan their sequential character, as the way kingship unfolds at the end, the way it breaks through, the way it becomes final that Christ is King.

- The present state is characterized by three facts: Christ is reigning in a hidden way over the powers; the church is the visible organ of his servant sovereignty; and the departed saints are with him, waiting.
- Then there is the *parousia* which is usually translated "return." It does not mean that literally. *Ousia* simply means "being," and *parousia* means "being nearby." So parousia really means presence. But since Christ is not here now his presence will mean a return. Thus logically it is not really wrong to render it "return," even though linguistically it is not correct. So Christ returns. "As he went, so he shall return."
- Then is the resurrection of the body. This one detail of this sequence is clear in the creed at the very beginning. It is already the topic in 1 Corinthians 15 and 1 Thessalonians 4. This is the resurrection not of Jesus but of all people.
- Then there is a judgment. This will be the subject of a later lecture.
- Then there is the restoration of earth—that is, a new earth, and a new heaven—and there is eternal darkness—hell.

This entire sequence is described not only in the book of Revelation, but also in the teaching of Jesus and in some of the writings of Paul and Peter, in imagery that varies but not enormously. It has the character of describing events in continuity with events we know about now and somehow come at the end of the history we are now living, and yet they are events we cannot conceive as coming at the end of history we are now living. So what does that mean? What can it mean? What are the questions of hermeneutics? What are the options? What are the several ways to interpret this kind of language?

The concreteness of the problem is reinforced by the awareness, worked out especially in the writing of Oscar Cullmann, that *immortality* is not the New Testament way of speaking of Christian hope. There is no expectation in the Bible that humanity has a nature or essence, which is intrinsically immortal and unable to die. The doctrine of the immortality of the soul is a non-Christian doctrine that has been picked up by certain Christian traditions. We could perhaps make a case for its appropriate use in certain contexts, but the idea that humans are divisible into two parts and that the body will fall away and the soul will live immortally, as well as the idea that the soul or any portion of a person is intrinsically worthy of immortality, are both unbiblical ideas. The New Testament talks about the resurrection of the body. "Body" does not mean only the physical organism but the wholeness of the person as *incorporated,* which comes from the Latin for "embodied." The person as a whole dies and the person as a whole is raised. That is the only way we know personality. The idea that a soul would be more pure if it did not have a body is pre-Christian, Greek, and not biblical.

Our purpose here is not to spell out the argument at great length but to say that the biblical affirmation or expectation is the resurrection of the body. This continued to be said at even as late a time as when the creeds were formulated in the second, third, or fourth centuries.

There is also to be some kind of judgment. The New Testament really uses two kinds of language about judgment. On the one hand is the judgment of God upon sin and human guilt, for instance, in Romans and Galatians with reference to condemnation. In this context we are judged not by our works, but by our faith. Those who believe undergo judgment not on the basis of what they did, but on the basis of the work of Christ on their behalf, whereby they are freed from condemnation. That is a clear element of the New Testament. In Luther's language, that is the Gospel.

But the eschatological passages in the New Testament continue to refer to judgment on the basis of works, even in Paul. What is the relationship of these two kinds of judgments? One obvious solution, working for harmonization, would be that two kinds of judgments are to be expected at two different times (if we can continue to use the language of time in speaking of this kind of future). One strand of interpretation clearly makes this claim. First, is a judgment on the basis of belief, which must happen before the millennial period (which we have not identified yet), so that the saints can reign. That sorting out must have taken place so that the believers—whose status is righteous on the basis of their faith—can be on the right side. They can be resurrected before the period of reigning, while the others can be deferred for a later resurrection and judgment.

Second is the judgment before the great white throne described in Revelation 20:12. This is on the basis of works. Here all evil persons will be rewarded with the evil results they have merited. And, sometimes in the same movement, sometimes distinct from it, there will be discrimination, or the weighing out, of relative recompenses for those who are saved.

This neat harmonization of the concept of "forensic justification" in Paul with eschatological justification by works probably does not hold water exegetically. It feels strained. It is not our business here to settle that completely. I suggest it is significant that most eschatology texts do not make that harmonization. The term "forensic justification" needs to be defined. It comes from the same root as *forum,* which is not just any public square but a tribunal. *Forensic* justification is when someone is declared righteous by a judge, when a court acts and declares, "You are now pardoned. Your sentence has been commuted." That concept of justification—that a sinner is no longer to be dealt with as a sinner—is, according to Protestant theology, found in Romans and Galatians. Although it is a striking omission, very few of the texts relate this to judgment on the basis of works, which clearly dominates the eschatological passages. All of the ways of harmonizing them are a little stretched.

Another element of this expectation is a restored earth and heaven. There will be some kind of human society, "new Jerusalem" in the language of Revelations 21:2. "New Jerusalem" is, of course, Old Testament language that is picked up in the New. It is unclear whether physical nature—plants and animals—are also to be restored, but there are hints of this. There will also be "new heavens," whatever that means, "heavens" being the abode of the invisible powers. Remember that Philippians 2, one of the very earliest literary testimonies found in the New Testament, talks about every knee bowing and every tongue confessing, *on earth, under the earth, and above the earth.*

Finally, there is the ultimate abiding state of eternal death or eternal life. How do we relate this kind of expectation to the rest of reality? The outlines, as I have traced them, are widely accepted by interpreters with all kinds of theologies as being what the texts say. But how do we relate this to our world, to the thought of the nineteenth and twentieth centuries, to the twenty-first century, and to our worldview?

The language of the biblical picture seems simple and clear. It is of course not philosophical language. It seems to be ordinary language, the kind of language that anybody talks on the street, about the past, the future, skies, mountains, and stars. It seems to predict an end to the temporal process, an end in the strictly temporal sense. That is, *when* it happened would be on the calendar and after that there would not be a calendar any more. It is an end that is not pre-datable, and cannot be fixed with precision, but is expected soon. "Soon" means, for the New Testament writers, a sort of urgency and priority. For example, when talking about marriage in 1 Corinthians 7:31, Paul says, "the form of this world is passing away." Some things are not wrong in themselves, but we shall not bother with them because of the transitory character of the present arrangement. *Soon* has to do with priority, making most important those tasks that most need to be done while there is still time. Language like that—"while there is still time"—is the most appropriate portrayal of the understanding of the imminence of what is to come.

But there is also a concept of delay. Although it will be soon, it will not be right away. Some things have to happen first, though precisely what must happen is not clear. Matthew 24:14, "This Gospel . . . will be preached throughout the whole world, as a testimony to all nations," is just one expression of the concept that the time passing between now and then is meaningful. It is not like sitting and waiting for an earthquake; it is not a thumb-twiddling time. During this time the church has a mission, and it may be (although this is a very faint hint) that *when* it happens will depend on the church's faithfulness. The end, it seems clear, is both the destruction and the fulfillment of our present human history. It is said even in terms of the geography of our present earth. It is the fulfillment of human effort—civilization and history. That means human effort is meaningful. There is a place in God's plan for our effort, work, service, and generosity. Matthew 25, where the nations will be judged on the basis of whether they fed the hungry and took care of prisoners, is one example of the expectation that how we behave now makes a difference for this ultimate fulfillment. Pursue the matter as you do your reading. The preparation guide asks whether human endeavor is worthwhile. In other years most students reported that the texts they used did not seek in their eschatology sections to give any ground for the value of our present work. The New Testament, however, certainly does. Human effort is meaningful because what God is going to do will be the fulfillment of human efforts, of human history. And yet, because earth will be destroyed in its being fulfilled, no goal that we could fix, no product that we can bring forth, is itself ultimate.

Now this picture of time's movement, end, fulfillment, or stoppage was not philosophically problematic for an ancient or New Testament audience. They did not have an understanding of the permanence of matter, the preservation of energy, and the uniformity of nature, which are fundamental to the scientific view of the universe and have much to do with how our minds operate. Nothing was inconceivable about a powerful force from outside moving across the face of the earth, changing its shape, and making things stop. It may very well be that the visions of the book of Revelation, which talk about the sky being rolled up and the stars falling down, were understood even by John to be dramatic visions and not prewritten photography. But there are certainly elements in the New Testament expectations that seem to be meant as predictions of how the end will look to people experiencing these events or describing them in ordinary language. The point is that *then* this kind of intervention from outside against the rules of the material and historical process was no problem. It was not something that the readers of the New Testament had to swallow hard to think, stretch their minds to conceive, or sacrifice their intelligence to believe.

The pagan religions had seen world history starting this way. The Old Testament story can be read in the same vein, with the story of God picking up dirt to make Adam and the rest of the Genesis story. There was no philosophical or cultural problem; there was no problem of imagination or incompatibility of worldviews. It was not hard to believe, in that cultural sense. This is the first thing we have to recognize when we relate that worldview to our own. We are impressed with the difficulty of making that connection. The readers of the New Testament were not, so we do not understand them if we think their problems were our problems. In order to properly understand them, we must not impose our problems upon them. We still have to work with our problems, but we are not doing a fair job of reading the documents if we think that our problem is the one with which they struggled.

For ancient people, the problem was not whether there could be divine intervention in history, in an ordinary "lay" sense. What was novel for that world—what was Christian as over against pagan, or what was biblical as over against the Gentile understanding—was that the God who intervenes in that way is only one God and works consistently. The world looked to ancient people, and it still looks to "primitive" peoples in some parts of the world, to be the theater where several gods are acting. Some are on our side and some on the other side; some are fighting each other. The idea that a unity of divine will acts consistently—that the God who works is the only God and does not want us to honor other gods, but intervenes in history for our sake, making us a people in fellowship with God—took a lot of believing. This was the real content of meaning to the people to whom this testimony was addressed. This was the novel thing about New Testament eschatology: instead of several gods using the world as their playground, or their battleground, there is one God who uses the world as the theater of divinely purposeful action. God specifically wants to gather a group of men and women to operate meaningfully within this context in fellowship, with God and with each other. That was what was hard to believe. That was what the New Testament story said. That is what the New Testament eschatology said that mattered then.

Today, "divine intervention" is a philosophical problem in its own right. Our culture has been so formed by Christian history and by the impact of Christian ideas that it is not hard for us to conceive of the unity of God. It is not impossible for us to conceive of God as consistent or as good. It is not hard for us to conceive of God as caring about people and wanting fellowship. It is not at all difficult for us to conceive that the purpose of God might have been, specifically, to use history—including the natural universe—for the purpose of having a place where men and women could grow in fellowship with God and with each other. All of that is thinkable, even self-evident for us, but we do not notice that it is what was new in the New Testament. On the other hand, we have trouble with the idea of divine intervention, of God sticking a finger into the machinery to keep it from working the way it otherwise normally would.[4]

4. The standard phrase for this image is often not fully understood. You will find in the literature the phrase *Deus ex machina*. Often this phrase is used wrongly. It comes

The simple way to handle this question is to ask, "Are you going to believe it or not?" You must *believe,* if you accept biblical authority, and then there will be no problem. You believe that that ancient worldview is still right and that the worldview or scientific uniformity that does not reckon with intervention is inadequate. The scientific worldview might be good for what it works on, but it is insufficient. It only works on scientific questions and make no room for what the Bible says must happen in certain realms or events.

For now let us not assume that is an adequate answer. (We will return to the question again when we talk about biblical authority as a topic.) This is, incidentally, not the same position as the orthodoxy of Protestantism of one or two hundred years ago. It is only since the nineteenth century that people have the idea that to believe the Bible means not to believe modern natural science or modern philosophy of science. The orthodoxy of the eighteenth century did not conceive of biblical authority as revelation as over against the spirit of the times, the way modern fundamentalism sometimes does. Just as it is improper to assume before we start the shape of the opposition between the modern scientific worldview on the one hand and believing the Bible on the other, so it is also inappropriate to assume it with regard to our question of a temporal end. The New Testament does not affirm a temporal end to things as something we must believe over against a mechanistic, natural-law, or closed-system view of nature. It affirmed a temporal end in the framework of a worldview where everybody assumed that divine forces stuck their fingers in, and that what was going on at the time was not the only possible arrangement.

The laws which now obtain, with regard to gravity or the atomic weight of oxygen, might be different—ancient people would assume—if some divine personage wanted them different. When Acts 1, for instance, pictures the ascension, it is not over against the aerospace scientists who now know a lot about how you get off the ground and to where you can get if you go that way. There is no intention in the New Testa-

---

from the language of the theater. The *machina* does not mean a mechanism, as you might imagine an automobile mechanic reaching into the engine to adjust its timing. The *machina* in a theater is the place up above and behind the curtain, where they move the scenery around. There are balconies and catwalks and pulleys and lamps to be used by the people you do not see behind the scenes in order to make the lights go on and off, the weather happen, or whatever else happens in a play. It was characteristic of certain ages of the theater, when the idea of omnipotent deity was part of the cultural equipment, that when the playwright put the cast in an impossible situation and had not figured out ahead of time how to make it work out, "God" would come down from the *machina*—in the form of a person with a robe on—make some omnipotent statements, and things would come out right. God would reach out to change people, or the date, or whatever was needed to make the play come out right, so the technical meaning of this term is the intervention into a play of a personage from the outside who had unlimited power to make things come out differently from the way they ordinarily would have.

ment to set up one worldview over against the other and tell you which one is right. The New Testament simply speaks in its own culture.

Now what are the solutions to our present predicament of arguing against contemporary worldviews—whether it be that of the scientist who thinks he or she can explain everything mechanistically, or of someone else in the modern age or in another part of the world with a primitive animistic worldview? We may argue, for instance, that the way secular people see this world is not big enough to contain spiritual reality. We may argue that the "spiritual" is another dimension that modern people do not have the tools to deal with. We may argue that miracle is a possibility that modern people have no grounds logically for rejecting. We can carry on this argument with considerable effect. It has some logic in its favor, but to make this argument basic is to depreciate, for the purposes of all further conversation, the reality of the ordinary world in which our neighbors live. The Bible spoke to its neighbors in their ordinary language. It did not tell them their ordinary language was wrong. It did not tell them their worldview was wrong. It did not tell them it was right either. It just said, in that language, some fundamental things about the character of God and God's intention to make history come out right.

If, then, we argue against the reality of the world in which our neighbors live, or against the adequacy of their ordinary language to be the vehicle for talking to them, then we do in our time what Gnosticism did, not what the apostles did in biblical times. The Gnostics, instead of talking to people in their own worldview, told them they ought to get an insider's worldview. "There are just a few of us who know how it really is. So if you want to understand our language, take special lessons so that you can share our insight. If you go through a special process of initiation, if you learn our interpretation of the inner structure of the universe with all its *aeons* and powers and *logoi*, *then* you will finally be able to see the truth." This was Gnosticism, and it was the primary adversary of all three of the great theologians in the New Testament. Over against that, they developed the strong emphasis on what came then later to be the concept of preexistence. They affirmed the priority of Jesus—Jesus as now Lord—over all the systems of speculation about where the world came from. This was, we saw, basically an anti-Gnostic approach. So, if the basic thing we try to say to modern people is, "Your worldview is wrong; you need to learn a foreign worldview that we have in our book here," the missionary impact will be that of a modern Gnosticism and *not* the impact the New Testament testimony had.

So much for an effort to pose the question. Now let us look at some of the traditional answers. Let us be clear that this is a philosophical question rather than a theological one, in the sense that we are talking about the meaningfulness of our language. We have to talk about that first before we know what we are talking about as the real nature of the biblical affirmation.

First let us sketch some of answers to this question that groups of people have stated in the past. They did not state them strictly self-consciously as philosophical answers, but rather as ways of reading the Bible. Some of these answers are respectable in some circles and others are respectable in other circles. Probably this is the area of all theology where it is most easy to be disreputable, and where it is most possible to have the impressions: "What in the world are they talking about?" "How in the world can one talk that way and be Christian?" or "How can they take that seriously?" So we will have search more here than with atonement or revelation to find ways of taking seriously the strangeness, difference, and foreignness—not only of context but of thought pattern, structures and forms—of the various people to whom we shall listen.

One logical extreme, which we must take seriously here even though from certain cultural perspectives it is easy to be impatient with it, is *dispensational premillennialism*. One reason some have difficulty taking this position seriously is that they associate it with their own youth and with the particular cultural orientation of certain people who represent it. Another reason is that this position uninhibitedly has the courage to face the option that the Bible and the worldview of our times might be fundamentally at odds, and in such a way that the decision of Christian faith includes the willingness to look foolish from the perspectives of other respectable worldviews.

To seek to understand seriously the dispensational stance, we begin with its basic axioms. The first of these is that it is not fundamentally difficult to discover the "literal" meaning of a text. When we talk about the literal meanings of a text there are no insuperable linguistic or philosophical difficulties involved; everyone knows what a text means. The basic hermeneutic axiom is that all texts are to be taken literally.

The second axiom, no less fundamental, is that the entire body of Scripture is on the same level in regard to both principles of interpretation and authority. All of the literal statements of the entire Bible can and must be interpreted as part of a coherent whole with no contradictions or shifts in meaning along the way. For eschatology, this means especially that all texts of a predictive type, whether in the Old Testament prophets, the Gospels, the Epistles, or Revelation, are part of the same consistent system of information and must be interpreted in such a way as to make them all fit.

Before moving on to sketch the "schedule" that results from this approach, one more key concept, the "dispensation," must be identified. All history up to the present is divided in distinct segments with varied characteristics. As a technical term, "dispensation" labels one of the several different arrangements that have obtained for the regulation of God's purposes among people. It renders the Greek *oikonomia,* arrangement, set-up. Adam was created and placed on earth with a particular assignment, which he failed to fulfill. Then God started again and placed Adam in another history with another set of obligations and promise and recompense. Again he failed. God started again with Noah with a new covenant, a new set of rules and promises. Again humankind failed. God started another arrangement with Abraham, with a new covenant, a new set of promises and conditions under which people were to live to serve God. This failed again. Thus the scheme of a series of "dispensations" set up by God, in which humanity again and again fails and God has to begin over, is the standard pattern of salvation history.

Most original about the dispensationalist structure, however, is how it applies to the beginning and the end of the work of the church, which is a kind of "parenthesis" between the coming of Jesus and the fulfillment of the promises of the Jews. If the Jews had accepted Jesus in his first coming, there would not have been a place for the church. Since they rejected him, the next dispensation, that of the church, was inserted, and it has its own meaning. Yet when the "church age" fulfills its purposes, we will have to go back and pick up the promises to the Jews who were left dangling. They will then be fulfilled, as the prior commitment of God. Thus we see that, in addition to the apparently more basic assumptions of the literal meaning of Scripture and the unity of the entire body of teachings, an instrumental tool of interpretation is added: One way to harmonize things is to put them into separate categories and in sequence so that any apparent contradiction can be explained on the grounds of the difference of levels or ages. The difference in ethics between the New Testament and the Old or between Jesus and Paul is, for instance, explained on this basis. The Sermon on the Mount is a description of how to live in the millennium, but because the Jews refused Jesus, it does not apply today.

Now we return to the eschatology proper. When this approach is taken a pattern of expectation unfolds that can be described as follows. First of all is a picture of the world situation just before the triggering of the end events. The present historical system will develop, without major shifts, in an evolutionary way until it finally reaches this situation just before the end. The situation is characterized by the presence of Israel as a people in the land of Palestine (see Ezekiel 36:24, Jeremiah 31:8, and Amos 9:14). Second, it is characterized by a unified world governmental system made up of then federated kingdoms (see Revelation 13:7, 16, and 17:17). Third, within that politically united world there will also be a completely apostate world church (Revelation 17). Cultural development will be marked by increasing wickedness (2 Timothy 3:1–5).

When all these conditions have been met, the sequence of more precisely definable end-events described in various prophetic passages of Old Testament and New will begin.

a. There will be the "rapture" in which Christ will come from heaven, and, while still in the sky, will call unto himself his own, that is, those who believe in him.
b. History will not have ended. The life of society will go on but with oppression and suffering or "tribulation." This will be a period of seven years.
c. Sometime at the beginning of or during the tribulation period the believers who are elsewhere with Christ will be judged according to their works. Whether they are saved is not up for judgment, since they are saved by faith, but there will be a variety of rewards according to what they did on earth.
d. Israel, living in Palestine and not accepting Christ as Messiah, will enter into a covenant with anti-Christ, the leader of the apostate world church in its alliance with world government.
e. Anti-Christ will break the covenant with Israel.
f. The later half of the seven years of tribulation can be called the great tribulation. During this period Israel will be in distress, sharing the suffering now that anti-Christ has turned against Israel.
g. The distress will coincide with people being commanded to worship the image of the anti-Christ.
h. People will need to flee Jerusalem in a hurry.
i. Many will be deceived by false Christs.
j. The conflict will turn to victory when the angel Michael arises.
k. Jesus will come back to earth in glory with the saints in an appearance that is called their "revelation."
l. The forces of good (the angelic hosts and the saints of Christ and Israel *now believing*) will meet the forces of evil in the battle of Armageddon. This is the same thing as the "day of the LORD" in Old Testament prophecy—the time when the LORD of hosts ultimately crushes every enemy in a literal military encounter.
m. Heavenly bodies will be rearranged.
n. There will begin a reign of one thousand years during which Israel will be fully restored to sovereignty and the promises of the Old Testament will be fulfilled in a renewed Davidic kingdom.
o. Satan will be cast into the lake of fire, a place of continuing temporal punishment, not annihilation.

p. The nations will be called to the judgment before the great white throne. To enable this there will be the second resurrection. The first resurrection at the time of the rapture had been for the dead saints; now all (the rest) are resurrected (that is, those who died as unbelievers) to a final judgment on the basis of works.
q. God will create a new heaven and a new earth.

It should be no surprise that with this concern for detailed integration of passages from different places into one scheme, variations in the scheme can arise from differing applications of the same assumptions. One of the variations pays more attention to the details of the events before the end. In Revelation 2 and 3 letters are directed to seven different churches. Some interpret these not simply as seven different locations in Asia Minor where there were churches at the time of John the Seer. Rather, they see them as seven ages through which the church will need to progress and degenerate, so that by calculating where we are along that line of development we can know how near we are to the end. It is also possible in Mark 13 to see an idea of the sequence of events before the end.

On the other hand, there are both warnings against thinking that the end is imminent, and there are also statements to the effect that when the end comes it will surprise people who have not been looking for it. How can the same event be at the same time clearly predicted and unpredictable? Thus there are tensions that lead to various ways of combining the two elements of unexpectedness on the one hand and signs and prerequisites on the other.

- One of the variations interprets the rapture as coming after, not before, the seven year tribulation period. Then it becomes identical with the "revelation" or "appearing" of Christ in triumph. This has the advantage of explaining that the church will continue to be present on earth during the tribulation period, which would seem to be part of the picture in other New Testament predictions of tribulation for the church.
- Another way to solve that same problem is to speak of a partial rapture. Not all Christians will be taken up at the time of rapture, only those who have a particular understanding of eschatology, "those who have loved his appearing." Those who expect the end will not be surprised, because they have discerned the signs of the time and know what they are looking for. Others will be surprised and will not share in this first triumph, as a result of which there will continue to be a church present in the period of tribulation to bring the message to the Jews.

Now we step back for perspective and ask again in more detail what the assumptions about the nature of reality and the nature of language are that find their consistent expression in this approach. I said before that the two assumptions are the unity of Scripture and the literal intent of the texts. But to be more critical, this great concern for creating a coherent system by bringing together passages from many different times and contexts does not take *any* of the texts literally in the *strict* sense. To assume that a passage from Daniel and a passage from Revelation deal with the same event is to say that the text of Daniel could not be straight and meaningful for its original writer or readers. The entire approach seems to the outsider to mix arbitrariness with overemphasis on minutiae in a way that makes it hard to know which images are more important than others. For instance, the figure of one thousand years is spoken of only once in all of Scripture but it becomes a key concept; many of the other segments of Revelation or images of Daniel do not get the same attention.

Despite the avowed intention of most premillenialists—and despite specific warnings in the biblical texts—this entire approach has undeniably contributed to the particular preoccupation with prediction, calculation, and finding our place on the schedule that has frequently been refuted by events, has discredited fundamentalism, and has moved the church away from her primary concern.

One part of the unspoken lack of self-critical capacity that goes with this understanding of being "literal" is the tendency to modernize texts into saying things they cannot possibly have originally meant. For instance, the prediction that "every eye shall see him" is taken to mean that there will be worldwide satellite television coverage of the second coming in the sky over Jerusalem, or the peculiar animals of Revelation 9 are taken to be modern flame-throwing tanks. The effect of the entire approach is to shift attention from the resurrection, discipleship, mission, and the present reign of Christ as Lord to ever more detailed elaboration of the system of inside information about how events will unroll in a period for which we are, after all, not responsible.

This approach does, however, have some significant implications for the present.

- It adds a distinct dimension of motivation to the missionary work of the church in that the Gospel preached to all nations (presumably meaning reaching all cultural units rather than every individual) is a prerequisite of the end. Since we want the end to come, we not only devote primary concern and the cream of our resources to missionary work, but we are also guided by this view as we make priority decisions within that work. We are more concerned to reach new tribes, even if this means very small isolated groups in central Africa or South America or New Guinea, than to reach increasing numbers of people in place like Calcutta or Tokyo where the church is already present.

- Another implication is special concentration on the Jewish people as objects of witness. This is partly so there may be a basis for their conversion at the proper time in the tribulation period; it is partly so that prior to the tribulation the unbelieving Jews may be held fully accountable for their hardness of heart; and it is probably also partly because the Jewishness of the imagery in the literature that the dispensationalist takes so seriously makes him feel at home in conversation with Jewish culture, with its preoccupation with the law and prophets, temple sacrifice, and the feast days.
- Still another policy implication is that, since there is no intrinsic connection between our attempt to improve the world and the coming of the end, and since there is not much time left, Christians will have little interest in schemes or programs for relative improvement of the social situation. Things will get worse, not better. That does not mean we try to make them worse, but we place practically no hope in their improving. Effort in that direction is therefore wasted, whereas effort invested in reaching the nations may actually "hasten the Lord's return."

Beyond the confusing effects of nonfulfilled prophecies and the question of misplaced emphasis, it would seem that the two most basic difficulties in taking seriously the dispensational premillennial approach are:

- On the one hand that it makes of the clash between church and world a clash between mentalities or cultural levels, as if "faith" were a matter of believing things that clash with one's sense of reality, and
- On the other, that in order to take history seriously it is broken up into small pieces that are discontinuous with one another, so that Judaism must be put on the shelf in order to have the church, and then the age of the church will again be set aside when Judaism is restored.

The interpretation of the promise of Israel that is the most basic to dispensationalism is the one that most literally takes the language of Ezekiel and Daniel, rather than the one that takes the most literally the Gospels and Epistles. It seems to be the claim of the New Testament that the same Christ is Lord—past, present, and future. That the Lamb who was slain is worthy to receive power seems to mean that the cross, the stance of the church, and discipleship will not at some future time be rescinded when God reverts to terrestrial kingship as the way God always really wanted to structure people. So while trying to take time and place very seriously and literally, there is not a readiness to believe that the movement from Galilee to the cross was a forward movement and a fulfillment. We should rather accept the position of the unbelieving Zealots at that time who in some sense were right when they felt that what Jesus said and accomplished was a defeat and a denial of their hopes rather than what they should have accepted.

Despite all that seems strange or even unthinkable to genuinely secular minds in this whole approach, we must insist that this is not in itself ground for rejecting the whole stance. There is, after all, something unacceptable to any mindset in a message of death, resurrection, and coming judgment. We can object if the way this strangeness is unfolded makes it seem like a body of Gnostic secrets, but we cannot in principle object simply on the grounds that it looks foolish. Something about the gospel always looks foolish to a certain kind of human wisdom, and ought to. Probably what is questionable about dispensationalism is not so much the fact that it looks foolish to the wise of this world as the fact that it fails to look weak to those who seek for signs and powers.

A little closer to the center of the spectrum of varied views is *non-dispensational premillennialism.* Here the preoccupation with putting all of the fine details on the schedule—the key techniques of separating epochs and shifting from one economy to another—is laid aside. So too is usually a detailed concern for rapture and tribulation, but one still expects a series of events that at the same time stand in some kind of continuity with our current history and also bring it to an end. This approach has traditionally in the past been labeled as *"chiliasm,"* a word based on the Greek for "one thousand."

The label "chiliastic" is used by historians to describe many persons and movements across the centuries who have expected some triumph and earthly kingdom, whether exactly for one thousand years or not, to be initiated by specific divine intervention. It has in common with the preceding view a "literal" expectation, but with much more flexibility as to detail and with readiness to consider many more elements of the prophetic vision symbolic or poetic. Some chiliastic movements have expected the new age to be introduced partly by the initiative of the select group of the faithful. In other cases it was to be brought about completely without human assistance.

One more step in the progressive deliteralization is the position usually called *amillennialism,* although that negative description is hardly a substantial way to identify a position. Here the expectation that there will be a specific terminal to the temporal sequence remains. Time will come to an end in some sense, but no particular form of earthly fulfillment is to be expected, and neither is any preoccupation with the calendar or the details of the transition from the present regime to what follows. There will be judgment and there will be eternal rewards, but by the nature of the case we can say nothing meaningful about the transition from one order of things to the other. All of the apocalyptic language in the various prophetic writings says in different ways different things about the very same "end event," namely the shift from present chronological history to eternity.

This is probably the position held by the majority of the Mennonites and Protestants. J. C. Wenger is probably correct in saying it is held by "all major theologians and denominations." It is not quite clear whether this is in itself a strong recommendation for the idea, since at many other points we would disagree with the "major theologians and denominations." They are more committed to one normative worldview than I, less committed to discipleship, more ready to identify Christianity with culture. It could be argued that all "major theologians and denominations" are still under the impact of Augustine and that therefore their tendency toward Hellenism cuts at the historicity of fulfillment. What does it mean to say that God is fulfilling history, if at the same time God must stop it?

One more step in the same direction of deliteralizing is the position sometimes called *postmillennialism.* It looks toward a fulfillment of God's kingdom-building purpose in history, a kind of millennium that we shall attain by progressive development rather than by catastrophe and a new divine intervention. In traditional Protestantism the expectation of a millennial kingdom in continuity with the present temporal process was not an alternative to the idea of the return of Christ. Rather, the return of Christ was expected at the conclusion of the millennium. This is why it is called "postmillennial." The return of Christ follows the millennium. This position in the past has been held by a major segment of the conservative reformed tradition and by Catholicism.

In recent fundamentalist debate, the postmillennial position has been confused with optimistic theological liberalism because both expect progress in history. A fundamental difference should, however, be clarified. Traditional postmillennialism still expected the return of Christ and some kind of end to the temporal process after the millennium. Theological liberalism did not necessarily do so. All of these views, in other words, are still, in varying ways but to the same degree, "transcendentalist." They all take seriously a conception of ultimate reality that makes it possible for divine causality and divine agency to claim sovereignty over, and interfere with or even bring to an end to, the universe and the sequence of events we call history.

Thus far we have surveyed the "transcendentalist" position on the scale of various positions that in one way or another work seriously with the concept that the temporal process will end. We spoke of the premillennial views, dividing them into dispensational and nondispensational, then of the amillennial and the postmillennial. Each of these four arose within classical or traditional Christian movements. All of them in some sense or other conceive of the working of God "above" as meaningful. For all of them, in order to be theologically correct, one can and must speak meaningfully of an end to the historical process.

Now we turn to another set of positions that might be called *immanentist.* In these views, whatever the meaning of the language of expectation *in the Bible,* its meaning that *for us* must be conceived of and understood properly *within* the system of historical process—within what we call time, space and body. Even though the language of the texts talks about the end of time and the end of space, what it means, at least in order to correlate with modern talk, must be moved within the system.

Humanity is the creator of value. Increasingly, through a kind of evolutionary process—the evolution of institutions, the development of science and so on—humanity will make history come out right within history. This then reproduces in a new form the expectation for history of the traditionally postmillennial position we saw present in both Catholic and Reformed forms, but doing it without any concrete conception of the overarching or intervening work of God. Whatever God does, God does immanently—using the laws, techniques, and resources of historical process to bring history to its conclusion. Those resources of course can include evolutionary development—development that goes beyond where it started. This kind of thing has been brought to a new degree of vigor and excitement in certain Catholic circles with the thought of Pierre Teilhard de Chardin, who combines some evolutionary anthropology with Catholic theology. Teilhard de Chardin was a paleontologist by profession, and created a new vision of how God will to bring all human history in a social evolutionary way to a millennial realization. His vision of millenial realization is not what you would normally think of when you read about a thousand years' kingdom, but it can be understood as a translation into immanent terms of that expectation. Simpler forms are in the "secularization theology" of Harvey Cox and Arend van Leeuwen.

The second, and biblically more serious, position within this same category is designated usually by the phrase "realized eschatology." The phrase goes back to C. H. Dodd and Albert Schweitzer, in different ways. If in Dodd's book *The Apostolic Preaching and Its Developments,* which we used at the beginning of the course, you read more than was assigned, you will remember that the end of the book already moved into this problem. We dealt then with the preaching of the *kerygma* outline, the Jesus narrative, but the book continues by asking what happened to this outline in the other writings in the New Testament and specifically in John's Gospel.

The slogan "realized eschatology" represents the claim that already in the New Testament the temporal expectation of which we have spoken was reinterpreted (not to say "corrected") so that it does not, according to the most mature view of the New Testament, look forward to an end of temporal process. This process of correction, redefinition, or change of focus can be observed within the New Testament. In the very earliest recording of the New Testament, for instance Matthew 10, Jesus expected that the end of the world, or the establishment of the kingdom, would come in connection with the first preaching trip of his apostles.

He sent his disciples into Judea on a preaching mission, saying, "You will not finish visiting the cities of Judea before the end comes." Then he changed his expectation. Albert Schweitzer especially develops the concept of a changing expectation on Jesus' own part. Next, Jesus expected the end to come at his own death, but it did not come then either. The earliest preachers in the apostolic church then taught it would come "soon." In First Thessalonians 4:15–17, Paul talks about "We who are alive at his coming." Paul expected himself to be in on it. Later this was not such a live expectation. In Philippians we have the testimony of Paul's meditating on whether it is better for him to stay alive and keep working or to go to "be with Christ," which does not mean the coming of Christ but rather his own death (1:23). In 2 Timothy 4:6 he says, "The time of my departure has come." By the time of the writing of 2 Peter, the early church is struggling with the fact that the end still had not come. So there we have the discussion of a thousand years in God's sight being as a day, and a day as a thousand years.

But there was one more step of adjustment, according to Dodd and those who follow him. That is seen in the Gospel of John, which transforms this entire language of expectation into the claim that in the coming of the Spirit counselor in the life of the church, everything has happened that we were waiting for. We have fulfillment in the life of the church. The Spirit in the church is the answer to the whole problem. It is the coming of everything that was to come. The return of Jesus is in the form of the Holy Spirit and that is, at the latest, at Pentecost. Or perhaps even, according to John 20, it is complete in the resurrection itself and the presence of the resurrected Jesus in the upper room breathing on his disciples and saying, "Receive the Holy Spirit." That is all that was needed by way of "return." So what is left? It is the church itself as the returned presence of Christ—the present reign of Christ in his body or the presence of God in Christ in the church.

The claim here is not a modern, critical, or unbelieving claim, which would say: "We choose not to believe the Bible when it says that something is coming." It is rather an exegetical claim. The New Testament itself, with the passage of time, in the movement from the earlier writings to the later writings, tells us that this language of expectation—promising that which is to come or speaking of him who is to come—has been refined and redefined *not by us but by the apostles* as an early way of saying that in the presence of God the Spirit in the church, Christ has returned to his people to fulfill all the promises of his presence. Then, with regard to the historical process, we are not waiting for anything more in particular that is still to come.

Rather, everything in the life of the church is in a sense the second coming. Every act of service, every act of victory, every act of reconciliation, every empowerment *is* Christ returned to save his people. We do not look ahead in the historical sequence for some final fulfillment of the promise. This understanding of the presence of the Spirit in the church can base its claim at least on some strands in the witness of John's Gospel.

The other form in which something almost identical is said I would label *existentialist*. We find this in the writings of Rudolf Bultmann, for instance, when, instead of talking about the church, he says many of the same things about "faith." Instead of saying that Christ returns in the Spirit to create the church, to come to the church, to make the church alive, Bultmann says that the Spirit comes to me. Christ's promised return is the fact that I find faith, that I can understand myself in a new way, that I can see life differently, and that is all that is going to happen. Of course, that experience puts me into the church, so the difference between the immanent fulfillment in the believing person and that located in the presence of the Spirit in the church is not enormous.

Last, we may identify here as *dualist* another position that says both that there is an end and that there is not. Here one distinguishes between the individual and history. One can then speak of the end of time as that which happens to each individual. The end is therefore real because it happens when each one comes to an end, that is, at the individual's death. As I suggested before, we could conceive of the passage of time as a line running across the marks in a graph where your life has its ups and downs as time passes, and then you come to your point of death. The lines go on but you are not there anymore. You have gone off the graph. And where are you when you are off the graph? Well, you are in eternity. So that is the end for you.

There was a point in the development of Karl Barth's theology when he wrote a commentary on 1 Corinthians 15. In that he gave the impression of that meaning of the second coming or the resurrection. For me the beginning of eternity is my death—which is also therefore my resurrection. Thus, when you say "eschatology" or "the end" you mean "the point at which I get off of the process of history." The process goes on—we do not expect it ever to stop. But for me, it is the end. It is ultimate in the negative sense that I am not involved in the process anymore. All of the language about Christ coming to us is another way of saying that we go to him, and that however the end comes, it is Christ we meet. Of course, you can talk about it as if time were to end there. As far as I am concerned, it did end there. But this is not a statement about historical process; it is a statement about me and my relation to the historical process.

This spectrum is not exhaustive, but it is representative. These are the options that people have resorted to to put things together and establish some relationships between the worldview that they operate on when they drive their cars down the road and the worldview that they operate on when they read the Bible.

Without suggesting which of these positions is right, or even suggesting why some of them are wrong, let us back away from the outline and think of it not with a view to an immediate answer but in order to see it is a sample of a problem of *hermeneutics*. Hermeneutics in the wide sense asks how you interpret meaning. What is the meaning of meaning? How do you go about handling meaning?

There is first of all the level of *literary* hermeneutics. How do you understand the meaning of a text? The literature with which we are dealing here is called apocalyptic literature. It includes, but is not limited to, the book of Revelation and Mark 13. This literature is the most difficult to interpret in the Bible just from the points of view of literary style, vocabulary, allusion, and the relationship between what the writer says and what he means. With some literature you have no difficulty knowing what it means because the language is so much like your own. Each sentence seems to be put together in a way that you can tell what its content is. Then we talk about "literal" meaning. In other cases we talk about figurative meaning. But if we looked carefully at language, this two-sided key that we thought at first made sense turns out to be a false key too. "Literal" is not really a meaningful adjective to use at this point. All language is literal (that means written with letters). All language is also figurative. It is not the thing itself; it is always some kind of a picture or pointer. Erik Routley, the writer of one of the books on Christology, says that we run astray every time we say, "This is 'figuratively true' of Christ but that is 'literally true' of him." All language is figurative. This applies even more massively to the hermeneutics of prophetic literature than it does to the hermeneutics of dogmatic literature.

When I tried to illustrate the one end of the spectrum we *called* "literal," I used the imaginary case of TV photographers being taking footage of the end times. But that is figurative—it is a picture. Anyone knows that what a photographer makes is only a picture. There are some ways in which this picture corresponds very clearly to what happens. There are also quite a number of ways in which the picture a photographer gets does *not* correspond to what happened.

So all language is figurative, but language still varies enormously in how consciously it uses its figurative character. A scientific textbook and an engineering handbook have disciplined their figurative character so that the writer and the reader have very little difficulty in meeting on the meaning of a figure. The more technical it is, the more figures it has. The common person cannot read calculus because of the different figures it has, and the way this figurative technique operates is different in each science or in any given branch of mathematics. Our difficulty is that the way the figurative character of language operates in the Bible's apocalyptic literature is not disciplined for us in the same way. When you read about the sky being rolled up as a scroll and a third of the stars falling, what do those things mean? What do they mean literally? Nothing in our world. What do they mean figuratively? Even to know that, we must find extremely complicated ways of getting ourselves into the cultural skin of the writer or of the readers to whom he or she was writing. For this kind of literature, that is extremely difficult. The historic and cultural reference is a part of any text, but this kind of text is the hardest to pin down. We are told in the book of Revelation: "Now pay good attention; this person whose number is 666 or 616 (depending on the text) is a man." The author clearly tells us about somebody living in the Roman Empire of his time or just around the corner, and the readers will obviously know who that is if they stop and think. But today, we obviously do not know who that is if we stop and think. We need an extremely complicated thinking process even to have wise guesses about who it might have been. All of this eschatological literature had *some* kind of contemporary reference. We must assume that unless it explicitly says it has none. But what that reference *is* is the hardest to know for this language, at least in part because the author intentionally hid the meaning because he did not want it to be accessible to an unbeliever or persecutor who happened on one of these texts.

Another demonstration of the fact that this literature is very hard to pin down hermeneutically is the paradox of fulfillment in the New Testament. Jesus very clearly claimed to fulfill the general expectations and promises of the Old Testament prophets. Then when his story was written up by the apostles, by Paul, by Matthew, he was also seen as fulfilling specifically yet many *more* texts, expectations, and promises, but the fulfillment was always different from what the people who were expecting fulfillment expected. It never turned out that it fit the recipe. It was not what the people had thought, people who thought they had understood. Fulfillment is always a surprise, but if it is the nature of this literature that, when what it predicts happens, the people who were waiting for it are surprised, then what does that do to our capacity to read literature that purports to be talking about our future?

One of the rules about interpreting literature is cross-referencing. Interpret Scripture by Scripture. Interpret the marginal themes by reference to the major themes. This again is a criterion that cuts both ways in our specific case. Some argue that the Gospels tell the stories of Jesus himself while the Epistles speak about him clearly in rational, expository language. Taken together they form our solid ground in the Bible. In order to get to the fringes of the Bible, to the prophetic literature of the Old Testament or the book of Revelation in the New Testament, we have to move *from the center*. In the Gospels, while there is reference to an end and a coming judgment, and in the epistles, while there is reference to the return of Christ, there is very little detail about the rapture, a thousand year kingdom, a restored Jerusalem, or the many other details you find if you read the book of Revelation with a millenialist interpretation. So the rule starts with the simple, the sure, the clear, and the basic. It moves away from the concern for detail that is especially found in the premillennial systems. It moves toward one of the less precise—perhaps the amillennial or one of the immanentist—approaches that do not make so much of concern for the details of the historical process.

But you can say it just as well the other way around. The Gospels tell us about Jesus. The epistles tell us about the life of the church. But the prophetic and predictive apocalyptic literature of the Bible tells us about revelation and prophecy, and if you should go to the center for each kind of literature, you might choose the book of Revelation. It was placed at the end of the New Testament to finish the process. It is the capstone, the culminating revelation. That is where we go for what is clear. Of course, we should not expect what Jesus or Paul said about the end to be clear, because the clarity had not come yet. So the rule that you interpret what is not clear by what is clear does not help either. It is a vicious circle (or a gracious circle). There is no self-evident way to find what is the center from which the rest comes.

In the history of exegesis it is thus not surprising that less progress is made in this topic than in most other topics. With regard to many of the disciplines of biblical interpretation, we can say that scholars are making progress. You do not see much debate today about the authorship of the book of Hebrews, for instance. The idea that Paul wrote it simply does not stand up in any school of thought if you read the critics. There are other examples. There are doctrinal emphases that in the sixteenth century were limited to Protestants, which are now agreed to by Catholic biblical scholars because they are in the text. If you read the text carefully, you make progress in getting together, in having a more common interpretation, for instance, of the concepts of grace or justification by faith. But apocalyptic literature is one area in which there is no history of progress, no growing clarity in the realm of exegesis. That is no reason for not being concerned about reading this kind of literature, no reason for writing it off as hopeless. All the more reason, in fact, for being conversant with the variations of interpretations and the different schools. It is just another illustration of the fact that the hermeneutics of this kind of literature are difficult.

Looking at the problem this way, bringing to the surface of our awareness the fact that it is a problem not simply of belief but of hermeneutics, should help us a little. Many, especially many dispensationalists, reject the hermeneutic problem as not a real problem because of their assumption that what constitutes the proper literal reading of the text is unchallengeable. If you do not read the texts the way they do, you don't believe. There is no hermeneutic problem; you just have the problem of getting along with all these unbelievers!

But if we do face honestly the existence of the hermeneutic problem and its special delicacy with regard to this theme, does that in itself teach us anything? It probably ought to teach us at least a degree of modesty about the promise of someone who has one key that will unlock everything. Such "keys" are the concept of dispensation or the periodization of Revelation 2 and 3 as identical with the course of church history. This kind of clever key has to be taken with great skepticism. Haste to harmonize and to answer all the problems by having a way of putting everything in its right box is one recourse against which we ought to be warned.

So much for the problem of what I called literary hermeneutics. But there is a much wider, deeper problem of *philosophical hermeneutics*. Literary hermeneutics asks, "How do I interpret the meaning of this text?" Philosophical hermeneutics asks, "What do you mean by meaning? What is the meaning of the question of meaning?" One subdivision of that question is the one with which we began, namely, "What is the relationship between our history and its limits?" We can talk about our history because we are in it. That is where language comes from. But what does it mean when we are within our history and we talk about its limits? We talk about what goes beyond, what is above, what transcends. When I say, "My history has a limit," what am I saying? Am I saying anything? Am I saying something about history itself, or am I saying something about something beyond history? If it is beyond history how can I say it? If it is within the history I am talking about, then I am not really saying it is limited, because I am still able to talk about it. As far as I can reach I can still talk about it as my history. That is one sample way of stating the problem of philosophical hermeneutics.

Another is the constant interrelation of form and substance. Substance is everything we say. It is in a certain phrasing, a certain vocabulary, within a certain set of assumptions and certain imagery. But *what* I say is not quite the same as *how* I say it. That is, we distinguish between the substance and the form. The words I use are not quite the same as what I mean. So we have the picture, for instance, of the kernel and the husk, or of the way something is said over against the real meaning of the communication.

If we try to keep the kernel and drop the husk, then what shall we say about eschatology? Shall we, for instance, say that all that this eschatological language of the New Testament means is that "God is love, God is personal, God cares for me, God builds community, there is only one God, and God works in history?" Is that the kernel? And the husk is all of this detail about the new Jerusalem and the thousand years? If the kernel is these biblical theological affirmations about God being love, monotheism, forgiveness, and Christology, then we are with one of the immanentist views. If that is the case, then in the post-Christian world we do not have anything to say that the world has not already heard. In fact, these sentiments are so widespread that most of our civilization assumes that God is on our side, whereas in biblical language God is very often on the other side. That there is only one God is assumed in our culture far beyond the membership of the Christian churches. So if we keep the kernel and not the husk, then do we really have anything to say at the point of eschatology? Or are we really just rephrasing in eschatological language things that could be said better in other language without the interpretation problem?

On the other hand, we could say you cannot separate the kernel and the husk that way. The vitamins are on the edge, it is really the peeling that has the nutrition value; this is what they say at least about rice and potatoes. We keep the husk because that is the reality! You must continue to believe in a man coming back from the sky. You must continue to believe in the stopping all-of-a-sudden of the temporal processes. But then we are proclaiming to our world events unrelatable to the reality with which people live, in a way the New Testament was not doing when it made the same promises. Thus we shock modern people at a point where the New Testament did not shock ancient people. The New Testament proclamation was shocking because it talked about resurrection and judgment and monotheism, but not because it talked about a man coming out of the sky against the rules of physics (anybody can believe that). Neither was it shocking because it talked about the sky rolling up as a scroll and a third of the stars falling (anybody can do that). What they could not believe was that God would put a seal of approval on a man who was killed as a criminal, by raising him from the dead and promising that he was going to come back and judge the world. So that if we make the point of preaching husk, then we are saying to the modern world, "Your worldview is wrong, your culture is wrong, you can't hear the Gospel in your culture. You will have to learn the language of a past culture in order to hear what we have to say." And then we find ourselves (and Christian apologetics has been found) making defensive use of what Colin Williams used to call the "eerie edges of existence." You appeal to the things you cannot quite explain yet—the psychic phenomena that do not fit into a scientific worldview, the personality weakness of someone who cannot quite stick it out, or the sense of guilt you have when you really have not done anything you should not have done. You look for the gaps around the edges around the manageable world and say that is where God still is. "See, you don't have your world all put together. God is there around the edges. God is in the gaps." So we have a defensive, apologetic use of the places where the modern worldview does not hold still or cohere. We look for the weak seams and tug there, to argue against the modern worldview. Is that what we want to do? Do we want to jump on people (or their cosmology) when they're down? Or is there some other way of relating the biblical claim to modernity?

It is not the purpose of our preface course to give answers. We shall stay with this specimen only a little longer, as a demonstration that the problem we are talking about—although it is a real problem—is also partly the creature of our own cultural development and our own philosophical estrangement. We think in terms of systematic, logical options. Either everything is to be taken very literally or everything is to be taken atemporally, or everything is to be taken in terms of an evolutionary process that finally succeeds, or everything is to be reduced to the way I come to feel my authenticity. We think in terms of systems and definitions. We want to make things make sense by backing away from concrete cases, specific images, and specific propositions and making general propositions or universally valid images. That sharpens our problem rather than helping solve it.

This observation does not tell us which of these approaches is right, but I think it tells us something that is wrong about all of them. The amillennial view, according to Wenger (and I think this is quite correct), has been held by most western theologians. It says that the ultimate fulfillment of the purposes of God for history will be an end to history, but an end that has no duration to it, no time, space or body to it.

It will just stop and then there will be eternity. The fulfillment will have about it something like a new Jerusalem coming down from heaven, something like a man returning from the sky, something like a judgment, and something like a bottomless pit. But it will all happen at once. Then it will be over, and we will be in timeless fulfillment. The idea that fulfillment is timeless is itself the most clearly nonbiblical of these positions. It is Platonic. It creates the problem of how you move from a temporal system to an atemporal system. Eternity is not having time anymore. It is getting off of temporal boundedness. A blackboard has only two dimensions. The room has three dimensions. When we get off the board into the third dimension we pay less attention to that limited universe in which there are fewer dimensions. Time does not matter. Eternity is not temporal. It is atemporal. The difficulty with that view is that it is Platonic. In biblical thought, the eternal is not atemporal. It is not less like time, but more like time. It is like time to a higher degree. The kingdom is not immaterial, but it is more like reality than reality is. If real events are the center of history—certainly the cross was a real event, certainly the resurrection is testified to as in some sense a real event—then the fulfillment and culmination of God's purposes must also be really historic. The God of the Bible is not timeless.

In the old debates about the Trinity, one of the ways of stating the question that Tertullian and Origen discussed was whether God was ever speechless. Was God ever without the *Logos?* The answer was: "No, God from eternity had the *Logos.*" We must say essentially the same thing about temporality if we are to understand the biblical vision of history. We cannot conceive of an atemporal God reconcilable with the biblical vision of God. We can conceive of a hypertemporal God who is more temporal than we are, who is ahead of us and behind us, before us and after us, above us in several directions, and who has more of the character of timeliness and meaningfulness in movement rather than less.

Then the millennial positions seem more fitting in one way. They take time seriously. They expect time to go on in fulfillment of God's purpose. They can make sense out of a concept of a thousand years, whether they take it in a strictly chronological sense or not. But when you read this kind of description soberly you cannot help getting the impression that, especially in the extreme dispensational form, the interpreter has too much confidence in his or her capacity to extrapolate from this point in time. The dispensationalist moves farther in the same direction as what we have been talking about, and assumes that it will be the same later.

In 1 Corinthians 15:39–44, while Paul talks about the resurrection of the flesh and thereby makes us expect something like ourselves and our bodies, he also makes the point that it will be a different kind of body:

"Not all flesh is alike . . . . There are celestial bodies and . . . terrestrial bodies . . . . So it is with the resurrection of the dead. What is sown is perishable, what is raised is imperishable. It is sown in dishonor, it is raised in glory. . . . It is sown a physical body, it is raised a spiritual body." If you can call them both "bodies," the physical and the spiritual body must have something in common. But Paul's point is that they do not have everything in common. You cannot simply extend the lines of our present sense of history and say the future will be like that.

What are the other options? The optimistic postmillennial view trusts to something within the process—Christian leadership, Christian social insight, cultural evolution, or the power of God—to make the world better and better with power from within. That seems to make sense in some ways. We all are happy with the fact that we have medical services and travel facilities that did not exist a hundred years ago, to say nothing of the time of Jesus.

But at the same time, both our own experience and biblical language make us think that the world is not going to make itself essentially better that way. Only with resources from within, or even only with the working of God from within the world, as it gets better it is also getting worse. We have more doctors than we ever had before, but there are also more people starving to death than there ever were before. Many observers of history hold the general impression that all that can save the historical process will be an intervention, something that does not rise out of the process itself. It would be as much within the process when it happens as the resurrection, but would have to be as irregular, as unexpectable, and as untypical of the process as the resurrection was. And what is said about this evolutionary view would also have to be said about the other immanentist views. The assumptions that the universe is closed, that we know where its edges run and nothing is ever going to come in over those edges, do not fit the biblical understandings of creation and providence, at least as we could normally read them.

I point to some elements at which people in the heat of debate on this particular question do not usually look. If you ask what kind of end we look forward to, then these are the questions that we need to ask.

The New Testament says more than the traditional eschatological debate does about the dimension of partial fulfillment now. Christ *will* reign, but he *already* reigns in some sense. This is not the same as the classical postmillennial view because we do not say a golden age is already here. But there is a hidden rule—a providential governance of history in which Christ as risen Lord is already active and which Christians can share in, reigning with him, sharing his hidden rule, and sharing the hiddenness of his rule by suffering as he did in his earthly kingship. This is just one sample of a wider pattern.

Paul Erb's book, *Alpha and Omega,* is organized around the formula of partial fulfillment. Whatever God ultimately wants, whatever God has promised, God is already doing in some sense. There is already in some sense a victory of good. It is said in the Bible; you can see it in history. That victory of the good must come to a culmination, which will be more of the same. There is already a reality of fellowship among people. It is incomplete and imperfect. It must come to a culmination. Erb does not answer the basic question, but is a helpful statement of how much can be said without answering it. There is a fitting pattern of expecting more of what is already given in the life of the church. In one sense of expectation, we should almost agree with the realized eschatology theme; not that we have all that is to come, but that we have do have something of what is to come. What we have is of the same character as what is to come. Thus the Christian communion service in the early church was a foretaste of the banquet of the Lamb.

One of the questions in your reading outline asks, "For what is God waiting? Why hasn't the end come yet?" In the Jewish tradition, God waits to find one perfectly obedient person. When that one is found God will fulfill all God's promises.

The premillennial pattern, especially in its dispensational form, says that certain scheduled events have not yet happened. We are not yet to that point along the sequence of expected events. There is not anything that we have to make happen. Meaningfulness is not in the historical process itself, but there are certain landmarks, and God has kept counsel as to where those landmarks are and when we will get there. So we are waiting. What we do while we wait is not a meaningful part of the fulfillment of the promise.

Augustine had an answer that was a little more concrete than this. God made the angels so they would stay the way they were. God did not give them complete free will. So, when some of the angels fell into rebellion, they could not be saved. They were not made in such a way that they could repent. Thus, there were vacancies in heaven. History has to go on until there are enough saints to fill the vacancies the angels left in heaven. Now that was a clear answer. But if 144,000 is the number of angels, we have probably already taken care of the gaps, so there is some doubt about whether that is an adequate answer.

Sometimes it is said in terms of patience, anthropomorphically. There is reference to the times of God's patience and the ending of God's patience.

The postmillennial approach says, "We have not gotten there yet. There is really nothing that God is waiting for. It is our own fault that we have not gotten that far, because reaching the end is up to us." So what are we waiting for is not really a question in the same sense.

According to Cullmann, the reason the end has not yet come is God wants to unroll a specific purpose within history. Not just passing certain landmarks at the other end, but something must happen in the historical process: time itself is meaningful, and lost time is meaningful. Urgency is a necessary note in the church's work because the mission of the church is meaningfully related to the end of time. When the church has done her work of reaching all the nations, then the end will come. This seems closest to New Testament language, but again, of course, it simply sharpens the problem with which we have been dealing.

One last subject comes as a kind of footnote. It could have come somewhere else in the outline, just as we discussed the issue of virgin birth when we were talking about the creeds although it could have come at another point. The subject is hell. Can we say, must we say, that God's ultimate victory will really be victory and ultimate—in the sense that no creature can finally and permanently resist God? So that the end will always for everyone be salvation? Or can we, and must we say, that those who turn their backs on God's reconciliation can stay that way and can permanently resist God? The latter would seem to follow from the historicity of revelation, that is, from the fact that God puts real choices to people. When they have made their choices they are made and not reversible. When that choice is no, God respects that negative answer. Now why does God respect that negative answer? Because it is the negative answer of a creature to whom God lovingly gave freedom. It was an expression of love to create persons who could turn their backs on God. Persons who could not have turned their backs would have been lesser persons and it would have been less an act of love to create them that way. Then, the picture we should have of hell is not torment as punishment for broken laws, but rather, leaving people in the isolation from God and from humanity that they had chosen. Thus the book *The Great Divorce,* by C. S. Lewis, says it very well by describing hell as where the people are who do not want to be in God's fellowship. It is not our business in this context to spell out the relation between that and the well-intentioned pagans who never heard the Jesus story, or sub-normal minds, or infants who have no basis for responding to any proclamation. Those discriminations would also have to be discussed. Now we are speaking about bindingness of historical choice for those who do make a historical choice that is negative.

Yet we must be fair to *universalism,* the concept that God's triumph will in the end after all overcome all resistances of all humanity. Today it sounds very often like an antimissionary and maybe a humanistic position, yet it has its historical origins within the evangelical movement. The Universalist denomination, which only recently merged with Unitarians, was a pietistic and evangelistic denomination. It is pietism that reckons with the logic of God's omnipotence, lined with loving intention, and says that God cannot be defeated in the end. Portions of the New Testament text seem to support this. There is a valid testimony involved in this vision that pietism or radical evangelicalism had of the triumph of grace. God's grace will win in the end.

Christians should not base their doctrine of hell on anything but the fact of humanity's rebellion. They should not base it on a doctrine of double predestination, saying that God wants to hurt some people, that God chose from all eternity which people to leave in the condemnation they had earned. The only reason for hell is that people persist in a rebellion for which there is no good reason. It is not our business to argue it, to use it as an evangelistic tool or to prove it to people. It is just the seriousness of being human that the choices that you make are final choices, permanent choices, and God will respect that. God loves creatures that much. This does not correlate with our outline. It could be said within the context of any particular eschatology. But it probably does fit here too as background to what it means to say that God will triumph in the end. Part of God's triumph includes the promise not to bulldoze or to steamroller people who have chosen to resist.

12

Christ as Priest: Atonement

Preparation Guide

1. Is there a discussion of
   a. Priesthood as a function in the life of Israel?
   b. Sacrifice and its meaning in the Old Covenant?
   c. The relationship of the priest in Israel to the prophet? To the King?
2. How does the author label his or her view of the atonement? Does he or she refer to other views?
   a. If so, are they looked at as having each its element of a validity, or is there but one right view?
   b. If there is one right view, does it seem that holding the right view on this matter is more a test of having developed in the course of history, having predecessors? Does he or she look at its relation to other schools? Or is his or her own view simply identified with the Bible's view?
3. Where in the outline is atonement treated?
   a. Is it part of Christology or Christian experience?
   b. Is it tied to the resurrection, to personal appropriation by the believer, or to the doctrine of the person of Christ?
4. If certain views of the atonement are rejected, is it because
   a. They are unbiblical,
   b. They fail to respect certain basic dogmatic concerns such as the justice of God,
   c. They are unacceptable to modern people, or
   d. They do not really explain why Christ had to die?
5. Note any significant divergence between the different collateral texts.

6. Is the believer a priest? In what sense? Does Christ's priesthood have meaning for ethics?
7. Is there any cross-reference to the way modern psychodynamic views of human nature handle guilt?

Possible Supplementary Readings

Clark,Theodore R. *Saved by His Life: A Study of the New Testament Doctrine of Reconciliation and Salvation.* 1959.

Denney, James. *The Death of Christ.* 1951.

Forsyth, Peter Taylor. *The Person and Place of Jesus Christ: The Congregational Union Lecture for 1909.* 1901.

Hengel, Martin. *The Atonement: The Origins of the Doctrine in the New Testament.* 1981.

George Stuart Hendry, *The Gospel of Incarnation.* 1958.

Knox, John. *The Death of Christ: The Cross in New Testament History and Faith.* 1958.

Leon Morris. *The Cross in the New Testament.* 1965.

Moule, C. F. D. *The Sacrifice of Christ.* 1957.

Paul, Robert S. *The Atonement and the Sacraments: The Relation of the Atonement to the Sacraments of Baptism and the Lord's Supper.* 1960.

Taylor, Vincent. *The Atonement in the New Testament Teaching.* 1958.

Wolf, William J. *No Cross No Crown: A Study of the Atonement.* 1957.

In the sequence of treatment of the threefold office of Christ, we now move to the priestly office. Just as the kingly office concentrated on eschatology, so in the discussion of the priestly office will be largely focused on the doctrine of the atonement. Yet not all of the work of a priest is centered in reconciliation.

The function of a priest in Israelite society was not only to work for forgiveness or reconciliation. He was also the leader or spokesman of the congregation in praise and intercession. Not all of the reconciliation the priest brings about is through any particular sacrificial process. Before we accept centering the concept of Christ's priesthood on the doctrine of the atonement, let us remember that (as was the case for Christ the King, and as will be the case for Christ the Prophet) the function of a priestly personage is wider than that one debatable question.

In the book of Hebrews the doctrine of Christ is focused upon the concept of the perfect priesthood. Hebrews 5:8–9 speaks of how Jesus shares the characteristics of every high priest. One characteristic is being chosen among his brothers. Christ shared the characteristic of not choosing himself but being called by God just as Aaron was. "Although he was a Son he learned obedience through what he suffered. Being made perfect [having come to the culmination of what he was called to do], he became the source of eternal salvation to all who would obey him." Also in chapters 2 and 8, Hebrews talks about priesthood as the overarching generalization for all Christology. This is just as systematic and biblical a Christology as one that concentrates on the *logos* and revelation, or the other organizing concepts current in the later life of the church.

To be a priest is to be a representative human. This is the theme of Hebrews 5. Becoming a representative human involves abandoning certain divine prerogatives on God's own part. This is the analogy in Hebrews to *kenosis* in Philippians 2. Christ's sacrifice in Hebrews 9—and herein he differs from other priests—is himself. The element in Christ that corresponds to the ritual purity of the priest is his sinlessness.

Orthodox Reformed and Lutheran theology of the seventeenth and eighteenth centuries made a distinction between active obedience and passive obedience. Christ's active obedience was that he did what God told him to do. He was a good man. His passive obedience was that he accepted the suffering that was his predestined path. But in neither case was there any very specific concentration on whether he could have sinned, or on what it meant that he was free of sin. Currently, a challenge is being addressed to the concept of sinlessness. You may have met it in some of your readings on Christology. It is most clearly stated by Nels Ferré. Ferré says that one is not really human unless really tempted. And one is not really tempted unless that temptation has a hold on him or her. So Ferré talks about the "unsinlessness" of Jesus. He does not say "sinfulness" or "guilt," but the "unsinlessness" of Christ, as a way of affirming how deeply he was genuinely identified with humanity. In another sense Reinhold Neibuhr, and in still another sense Dietrich Bonhoeffer, talked about Christ as becoming sinful by being involved in the historical process and by being part of society.

Before we move to the atonement theme in its narrower form, we should verify how, just as the other offices have, so also the office of priesthood has a meaning for believers in solidarity with Christ.

The Reformation was especially loud in its anti-Catholic polemics at this point. The "priesthood of all believers" was a polemic against the idea of the mediatorial office of the Catholic priest, against the idea that we need a priest between God and us. We saw that each of the three offices of Christ has its polemic thrust. Now the priesthood of all believers can foster individualism. The high priest has access to God. Every priest is authorized to do his sacrificial, sacramental duties to have access to God. If we are all priests then we all have access to God and we do not need each other. This notion has developed in recent Protestant thought but was certainly not involved in the biblical phrasing from which it took off. Priesthood is, in biblical thought, collective. Moses spoke about a "kingdom of priests," and Revelation 5 picks up the phrase again. That is, Israel and the church are to have—as peoples—a priestly function, rather than being a group of individuals each with his or her own priestly status. The function of a priest is not to have access to God. That is a presupposition of his function, an aspect of his work. The function of a priest is to mediate for others. So to be priests is to be bridges between others and God, not to be persons of privilege who can get along on their own. Especially in the present ecumenical discussion of the theology of mission, this concept of the priestly people has become quite fruitful. It is a privilege to be elected as a priest. It is a privilege for an entire people to be a people of priests. The purpose of the priestly people in the language of 1 Peter 2 is "to proclaim the virtues of him who called you," to be the tool of reconciliation between others and God.

We now turn to the doctrine of the atonement more narrowly conceived. It is one of our classical debating themes around which there has been a great amount of concern and conversation. It is certainly worth extensive attention.

A brief detour is needed on vocabulary. The root of the word "atonement" seems to have been authentically the still visible English derivation from the composition, "at-one-ment," meaning literally (a) "to bring back into oneness." Then the linguistic equivalent would be "reunion" or "reunification," and the semantic equivalent would be "reconciliation."

But then the meaning of the term shifted. It somehow came (b) to include all of the wide field of meanings related to the saving work of Christ in response to sin, however understood, so that it could include reparation, vindication, propitiation, satisfaction, and so on. Instead of being one answer among others to the problem of sin, it became the label for the field of discussion of many answers to that problem.

Yet the development did not stop there. Somehow the term came in popular parlance to designate more narrowly the dominant view in the above set, namely (c) reparation, making things right, or satisfaction. When "atone" is used to denote something a human being can do about an offense he or she has committed, it bears that meaning.

When "atonement" is used to designate the subfield of systematic theology, it continues to function with sense (b) above, and that is the usage in most of this text. Recourse to the original etymology (a) is special pleading: it clothes a valid thesis in the form of a semantic game or a definition. The thesis is valid but to make it by reconstructing etymology is a diversion. It may reasonably be argued that the popular domination of the equation of atonement with reparation (c) is so strong that we should abandon the technical usage (b). Arguments of that kind would make almost all technical language questionable. They would undercut as well whatever new and "better" term one would attempt to replace it with. The "better" term "reconciliation" is just now also under a cloud in some circles, because in the judgment of some theologians of liberation it has been used to cloak the avoidance of confrontation and social change. So for the purposes of this text we shall keep "atonement" as the name of the field.

While we are looking at semantics it might be pointed out that most of the other terms have also undergone some kind of evolution. To "repair" or make reparation means to make things equal again. The root is the same as the one we have in the term "peer," someone who is one's equal. Yet in mechanics to repair means to fix something again the way it was. In politics it means to compensate by some kind of payment or performance for an evil that was done. Which of those meanings do we have in mind when we talk about "reparation" in the discussion of the work of Christ? Which of them do we have in mind when we talk about the ministry of the church to criminal offenders?

J. C. Wenger's text enumerates six different ways of interpreting the work of Christ. Wenger gathers together the biblical textual material in a systematic way. We need not redo his survey but can rather pass to classifying what we find in one form in Wenger, namely, six different ways of describing what Jesus did.[1]

- The first is *victory over the powers of evil,* stated with special clarity in Colossians 2:13b–15: "God made (you) alive together with him, having forgiven us all our trespasses, having canceled the bond which stood against us . . . . He disarmed the principalities and powers and made a public example of them, triumphing over them in him." (Or "in it," in the cross—depending on the translation.) Christ conquered the powers. We will return later to ask what that means.
- The second concept Wenger lists is *victory over the flesh,* or over death, a victory in which we share. This extends the meaning of the resurrection. We die with Christ, we rise with Christ, and we live a new life. We have victory over self. This is what the cross does.
- Third comes the concept of *substitute suffering.* Here the understanding is that humanity is in the objective status of guilt. Humanity ought to suffer. Christ takes this suffering on himself by proxy.
- Fourth, Wenger lists *reconciliation in the name of the Father,* "God was in Christ reconciling the world to himself." To be reconciled—

1. J. C. Wenger, *Introduction to Theology: An Interpretation of the Doctrinal Content of Scripture, Written to Strengthen a Childlike Faith in Christ* (Scottdale, Pa.: Herald Press, 1954).

when you break the word down to its roots—means to be brought back into council, into a relationship of communication and sharing. To reconcile means to reestablish a relationship that was there and was then broken by the turning away of one of the parties. The idea is not that humanity is separated from God and Jesus is on our side, taking our side before God. God is in Christ, reconciling us to God. Not the Son versus the Father, but humanity separated from God. The work of Christ is God's initiative to restore a relationship.

- The fifth concept listed by Wenger is a *revelation of love*. The cross reveals God's love. God is love. God seeks to bring people to that knowledge. How is this done? It is done through Jesus. In addition to the text Wenger lists, one of the standard simple statements is 1 John 3:16: "By this we know love, that he lay down his life for us."
- The sixth of Wenger's concepts is that the death of Christ *reveals the righteousness of God*. This is a concept that can be broken down into two meanings or two branches of subconcepts. What does it mean that God is righteous? Or what does it mean that God's righteousness is revealed or made known? It can mean "punitive righteousness." This is what we sometimes call "justice" in modern language. It means the punishment must fit the crime, that every crime must receive a fitting punishment, and that each must receive what he or she has coming. God's righteousness is like this; it needs to be vindicated by being made clear that all crime is punished.

  The other concept fits more with the Hebraic word for righteousness—*tsedqah* or *tsedeq*—which is not so retributive or punitive as it is "setting things right." Righteousness is what makes righteous, what makes right. It can be called justification, which makes things as they ought to be. The cross is then not the vindication of God's righteousness by punishment, but the revelation of God's right-making and justifying character.

If we seek to be still more thorough in combing through the New Testament, we can find other atonement concepts. These six (or seven) are among the concepts that have been most fully elaborated in later Christian thought, but there are at least three more undeniably present concepts that stand in some relation to the death of Christ:

- There is (eighth) the literal use of the word *"ransom"* in Jesus' own words in institution of the Lord's Supper—"to give his life a ransom for many." A ransom is what is sacrificed or turned over so that something or someone else can be restored to freedom.

- Ninth, the major gap in Wenger's list, and a major challenge to our own understanding, is the portrayal of Jesus' death as a *sacrifice* in some continuity with the blood animal sacrifices of mosaic legislation. These celebrations combined in various proportions the following elements:
  a. The blood of the victim sprinkled on objects and on persons to sanctify and purify;
  b. The choice portions of the victim's body being burnt up, offered to God in heaven as a pleasant odor;
  c. Other portions of the body of the victim being eaten, celebrated, and constituted a communion of the worshipping people; as well as
  d. A means of economic support for the priesthood.

Hebrews simply assumes, without explanation, that this ceremony was effective for forgiveness, and goes on to show how Jesus as both priest and sacrifice culminates and terminates the sacrificial system. But how?

- Tenth is the concept of *adoption*. We are made children. This is most clearly said in Galatians 4. The description is less clearly linked to the meaning of the death of Christ, but it yields a very clear description of what it is that God does for us in salvation.
- Eleventh, the term *"redemption"* is different in its literal meaning from the others, although very often in modern language it seems not very different. To redeem is to buy back. It is a little different from ransom, in that what you buy back is something you owned once. Then you mortgaged it or put it in hock; you lost possession of it. Now you buy it back by paying for it and it is again yours. This we have literally in the language of Romans 6:17–18: "You used to be the slaves of sin. Now you have been bought by God and now you are the slaves of righteousness." The statement "you are bought with a price" is made twice in 1 Corinthians.

We have eleven key concepts, all of which are used in the New Testament to say something about what Jesus did and how we are saved in him, but now we must move beyond accumulating phrases to a doctrine of atonement. This is the topic on which there probably is the greatest variety of formulation of any theme debated among Protestants. There was never a creedal definition on the matter, neither do particular denominations line up, nor do traditional doctrinal statements, organizations, or confessional documents that make an issue of the doctrine of atonement. The closest approximation to that would be modern fundamentalism, which, however, does not write its creeds in a fixed form.

What is a doctrine of the atonement about? What does the doctrine of the atonement try to say? What questions does it try to answer? It talks about the death of Christ for us, but what does it try to do? It is not enough that it should say that Christ's death is costly or tragic or moving. A doctrine explains something. The doctrine of the atonement has to explain why Christ's death was necessary. Why did it have to be this way? Why was it appropriate that it should be this way? If it was inappropriate, if it was not necessary, if it did not have to be this way, then it does not make sense. So how does it make sense that God chose to work to save humanity in this way? Perhaps if we broke the issue into subquestions we could ask, "What does it mean to be lost, and how does the death of Christ deal with lostness? Why did it have to be this way? Could it have been done otherwise?"

Jesus simply said, when he predicted his suffering, that according to the Scripture it had to be. Buy why did it have to be? What was the logic of its having to be? We ask this question when we develop a doctrine that goes beyond the simple repetition of biblical language, establishes connections, and asks for reasons. The first thing the doctrine of the atonement must do is answer the question, "Why did Jesus have to die?" The second thing it must do is to do justice to all the biblical language. We have eleven phrases or concepts. We could say, "I like number six," or "I like number three," and drop all the rest. That would not be theologically legitimate. To do justice to the biblical material we must not simply choose on the basis of taste, feel or history. We must find a way of weaving them all together. We must find an expression of the meaning of the death of Christ that fits with them all. Or at least we must find one that is not contradictory to any of these kinds of languages.

There is another reason that it would not be enough to choose among the ten or eleven images named above. Since theology continues beyond New Testament times, there is no reason to be limited to images from the original texts. Nor do the ten images listed all count as answering the questions that a doctrine of the atonement must answer. Some do not render evident why the death of Jesus achieved what it did. Some do not show why his death was indispensable toward that end. Nor does the list exhaust the main themes that have become the most important in cross-referencing Christian thought to other value systems:

a. Propitiation, offering something to an offended deity to render him propitious, friendly again;
b. Expiation, the discharge of a debt to the moral order that demands some time or some kind of suffering, pain, or payment;

c. Reparation, a restoration of balance to make up for damages done; and
d. Penalty, the infliction of a prescribed suffering.

These concepts, when taken coarsely, overlap considerably; when analyzed closely they differ visibly. Each is involved in the effort to understand the cross. None seem to be directly biblical.

We might suggest that a further desirable characteristic of a doctrine of the atonement would be that it should link in some necessary and critical way—without which something would be missing—to other important issues in Christian thought. We found that the concept of incarnation—the real presence of God in Jesus—mattered very much to biblical theologians and to the early church. So, for a doctrine of the atonement to be solid and meaningful, to be the needed link, it ought to coordinate somehow with incarnation in its double meaning of genuine humanity and genuine divine presence.

In the believers' church stream of church history, we find that it is important to keep in view God's call to discipleship and the wholeness of salvation, which is not simply something done for us "out there," but is done to us and through us. It would help if the doctrine of atonement included that. Any theory or set of logical answers to the questions we ask here ought to be suspect if it neither needs nor is based on the rest of the New Testament. So we are not asking for one simple way of answering the question; we are asking for an answer that fits best within the framework of the rest of biblical and historic Christian thought.

Before suggesting a "right answer," as we did with the doctrine of the last things, we begin again with a spectrum of the major traditional answers to this question. We shall not try to be complete. We can speak only to the representative or the typical major lines of thought.

- The oldest of these, speaking now not only of a biblical phrase but also of a theory, is the one Gustaf Aulén, the Scandinavian theologian, calls the "dramatic view" in a work that carries a dramatic name, *Christus Victor.*[2] Here the language is of conflict and victory, of the battle or the duel. The cross was a struggle between Jesus and his enemies, or between God and God's enemies in the person of Jesus. Behind the Romans and the Jews were spiritual powers and principalities. There is growing respect today for this element of dramatic struggle in the description of the meaning of the cross. The victory in this struggle is not simply that Christ

2. Gustaf Aulén, *Christus Victor: An Historical Study of the Three Main Types of the Idea of Atonement* (New York: Macmillan, 1960).

died. We need the resurrection to make this into a finished view, and of course that is faithful to the New Testament preaching. But it is not quite clear why there had to be a death. Why could God's victory not consist in his not having to die, or in his having to die but not dying anyway? So, although it is certainly the case that much of the language of the church fathers and the New Testament in this mood of conflict and victory, it is not certain that it gives us a doctrine of the atonement that explains why there had to be a cross.

- The next system to be filled out at some depth is one that took off from Jesus' own language and developed the concept of ransom. Ransom, as spelled out, means that you ask, "Who is the prisoner, why, under what conditions, and how did the death of Christ buy freedom?" Satan thought—and it was a logical thing for him to think—that the Son of God would be a good trade for the people Satan had in his power. Humanity was in Satan's power because he had misled them. He had brought them to sin. When they sinned, then they were his slaves. He had kidnapped them, so to speak. Then Jesus gives his life as ransom for the lives of all those whom the devil had taken captive. The devil assumes it is a good trade because this is the Son of God and these others are only humans. But then when he gets into the hands of Satan, Christ cannot be held. Death cannot hold him down, as Peter said in Acts 2. He rises, he pulls away from the hands of Satan. Satan was fooled.

  This system soon wore thin because thinkers decided they did not respect it. This was partly because it granted certain rights to the devil. It assumed that he has something coming, and that even God has to pay what the devil has coming. Then there is the element of fraud: the devil was fooled, he thought he was getting something in return for the people he was giving up and he did not. God deceived Satan. Thus, although this was the first system to be worked out with some kind of logical clarity in the second century, it turned out not to be respected for very long.

- The next concept of the atonement is not listed in this form in Wenger, but came to be very important, especially in the early Eastern church. Humanity is saved, not really by the death of Christ at all but by his birth. Human nature is given immortality. Jesus is not just one man's obedience or revelation of God. What happens in the incarnation of the Word in Jesus is rather that human nature is taken over by the divine nature. Not simply this one man Jesus, but humanity is taken into the Divine being. Human nature is given immortality by God coming into human nature. This kind of approach is respected today in some Anglican circles, but it is also very much the theology of the Eastern Orthodox church. God comes into humanity and shares the humanity's lot even to the point of death. Because God shares in the human situation new life is possible. This incarnational theology has evident connections with social ethics. It supports the concern to get out into the world where people are and take that world seriously, and of course incarnation is biblical language.

But in the New Testament, incarnation is not interpreted in relationship to the death of Christ. The death of Christ is not simply that he shares the human lot and dies his own death, that he shares our mortality. The death of Christ is different from the way we die because it was not merited, because it was innocent. The death of Christ is also different in its social meaning and in its centrality in his work. Christ said his death is a part of what he came for. Also the social meaning of his death as a criminal, as someone condemned by the Roman government, is in no sense typical of all human deaths. So the cross is not really explained by this incarnational understanding of atonement. People who hold this view can link it very well with the cross, but the real salvation of humanity comes, for them, at some other point. Cyril of Alexandria is exemplary of this view: "Having been born of a woman according to the flesh, he took to himself the body he had taken from her in order to take root among us by means of an indissoluble union and to make us stronger than death and corruption." Athanasius said as well, "The word became man in order that we might be made divine." This change of status by virtue of the incarnation really means that the death of Christ, although unavoidable, did not matter in the sense that we would have been lost without it. It had to be because people all die and because he was to die this way, but we were really saved at Bethlehem.

- The next view traditionally listed on the calendar of development through the centuries has come to be called the "moral influence view." Its medieval representative was Abelard. Sometimes it is called the "subjective view." It is widespread in modernity, but it started in the Middle Ages. Humanity has lost its way. God is not mad at us, but we are selfish. God is love. God's purpose is to forgive us, and that forgiveness is ready and waiting. It always has been. God is that kind of God from all eternity, so God does not need to be propitiated, appeased or satisfied. Humanity needs to be ready to be forgiven, but we are not ready. We are self-centered. Our hearts are turned inward upon ourselves. We are turned away from God, rebellious, angry, closed, and twisted. We need something to happen that will make us willing to accept being forgiven. The death of Christ is the example, or it is the dramatization; it makes God's love for us serious in our experience. God loved us just as much before the cross. God loved humanity just as much from all creation. But the cross makes it show, makes it visible, stops us in our tracks, and makes us pay attention to what has always been. The drama of this self-sacrifice on Jesus' part makes us willing to accept the forgiveness that God has always wanted to offer to us.

This is one of the serious theories to which we shall return, but let us first put to it the question with which we began: Why was the death of Christ necessary? Was there no other way to show love? Why was it that the death shows love? If the death was necessary for our welfare, then Jesus' willingness to accept this death is a sign of how far he was willing to go for our welfare. But if the death did not do anything for our welfare, then his willingness to accept death is not especially meaningful.

If I am sitting on the dock at the edge of a river and see my neighbor jump off the dock to swim after a drowning child, then this is an act of love, because the child needed to be rescued. The child was really out there and would really drown if someone did not come to help. So when my neighbor runs the risk of drowning himself in order to save this child, the risk is for the sake of the real contribution he will make. If he dies in that effort to save the life of a child, I know he gave his life out of love for that child. But if the child is not drowning, if the child knows how to swim, has a life preserver or a boat, and my neighbor risks his life by jumping off the pier, that is not a sign of love because it was not necessary. It was neither functional nor needed. So unless we know why Jesus had to die, and how his death helps us, the fact that he was willing to do it does not testify to any special degree of his love. Thus the subjective view, in its strictest logic, does not quite answer the question. If it is the case that we needed the death of Jesus, then his willingness to go to this extent is a testimony of his love. But if we did not need it, then how does he testify to his love in doing this unnecessary thing?

This might be the place to insert, as a kind of parenthesis, reference to some contemporary re-formulations of problems of the atonement. Most of them are branches of the subjective approach. There are *psychiatric views*—reference being not to the psychiatric profession but to a way of looking at humanity that psychiatry has brought into the modern consciousness. This way of seeing human nature as sick in the soul is a metaphorical way of saying that the thing that is wrong with us is in our psyches and it is well described as guilt. This then really rephrases the understanding of sin as "selfishness." The center of the meaning of what is wrong with humanity is humanity—obviously. Christ changes what is wrong in the psyche. One example is the writing of Lewis Sherrill, the late professor of pastoral theology, whose book *Guilt and Redemption* is an effort to link the traditional theological categories with a psychiatric understanding of human nature.[3]

Guilt is a subjective state. That I am guilty is something that I feel. It is in myself. If I feel guilty before God it is the result of my unbelief. I feel guilty because I have not believed, because I have turned away from God, or because I have not trusted God. Because my unbelieving ways make me unable to trust God, the vicious circle of guilt and unbelief results in broken community.

Now Christ comes to me as a doctor figure and tells me I should look away from myself and love God. He speaks a word of condemnation—I should look away from myself. Yet he calls me to look away from myself and to love God, and this is a word of promise and justification. To love God means to forget self-justification, to forget my pride, guilt, and confidence that I can help myself and to turn toward God. But to do this, I must repent. To do this I must break through my self-concern. But I cannot. I am locked up in it. Someone else must break through my defensiveness, because I cannot. Someone must come to me who takes up my hostility. Repentance has to mean my own decision, but someone has to tell me it is my own decision. Someone has to push me into this decision of my own to accept God's love, and that will be someone who, who bothers me, who interferes with me, against whom I react, and who takes up my hostility and absorbs it. By absorbing it, that person testifies to me that his or her love goes even that far. This is psychotherapeutic language and it can, in a sense, explain Christ's death. Why does Christ have to die? Because a therapist or counselor who helps a person get out of the shell of defensiveness must absorb the hostility of that defensiveness. He or she must be rejected or even destroyed by the defensive person. This then still rephrases the view according to which lostness is in the person; the lostness is subjective. Although by using modern language, it seems more convincing, it still places the problem within humanity's own soul and psyche rather than at a point where God had to act.

- Next we move to the view to which we will need to pay the most attention. This is the view technically linked with the word, *"satisfaction,"* whose formal classical statement goes back to the medieval theologian, Anselm of Canterbury, one of the truly great minds of the Middle Ages. Later, we will see that this view needs to be divided into sub-types. But for now, we will try to say what these various subtypes have in common.

3. See further discussion of this topic in chapter 8.

"Satisfaction" comes from the Latin meaning, "to do enough," "to do what has to be done," or "to do what is demanded." What is demanded? God is Holy. Sin offends God's holiness and that offense demands satisfaction. It is something like the punishment in a court. Something needs to be made right when people have sinned against the holiness of God.

But the only satisfaction possible is death because that is the nature of guilt. This is the arrangement God made with humanity at the beginning: the soul that sins, that one shall die. So the only satisfaction possible is for each to die for having offended the righteousness of God.

But this penalty is "negotiable," to use a term from the commercial world. That is, another can pay it. It is not uniquely personal in that only I can die the death I owe to God. A death is a death. So, conceivably, someone else could suffer for me, just as someone else could pay a monetary debt. But no one who had a debt of his or her own can pay mine, because there is no one who has an extra life to give. Everyone has to die for his or her own sin. But if there were to be a sinless human, then he or she would not have to die for sin. Then if that person were to die, that death would have the quality of being transferable. It could be applied to someone else's guilt. And if, in addition, this person were not only innocent, but were more than human, were an infinite kind of human, then logically, it might be possible that his or her death could apply to many people, or to all humanity.

This is the explanation of the incarnation for Anselm. At the beginning he did not really try to develop a new doctrine of the atonement. He asked what the reason was for the incarnation. His book was, *Cur Deus Homo,* "Why Was God Man?" or "Why Did God Become Man?" The answer is, "So that there could be this kind of a saving work." So that there could be this kind of human who, being human, could die the kind of death that humans have to die, but by being innocent could apply this death to others and by being infinite—that is, by being divine—would be able to multiply the accessibility of this merit enough for everyone. God became human so that this one man could be blameless and yet dying, willingly, could credit his death to those others who became eligible for that credit. There is no disrespect involved in using financial language. It is the best image Anselm had.

Who would benefit from this work? In the Middle Ages it was the people who accepted the sacrament. In the Protestant period, of course, it is those who believe.

Before itemizing the strengths and weaknesses of this view, we should note the variations within it in order to avoid tripping over differences later. Three at least can be distinguished. For our purposes in the rest of the argument here, we can deal with this as if it were but one position. Yet the three ought to be noticed. There have been times when the distinctions among them mattered considerably to some people.

- First is satisfaction proper in the narrow sense, in which we would think of "God as the plaintiff." Using the language of the courtroom, humanity is guilty, and God sues for damages. God was offended and hurt by humanity, and God's suit is not for punishment but for compensation, as in a damage suit. It is not punishment that fits the crime, but it is rather compensation that makes it public, that recognizes there has been offense and guilt and that it is our fault. You cannot calculate exactly how much damage can be asked for, but something at least is demanded. In this case it is death because that was the kind of offense. The cross takes the place of the life that God laid claim to because of the nature of our offense.
- The next view, within the general satisfaction family, is called more precisely the "penal view." Punishment here should be understood in the narrow sense. Here God is seen not as a plaintiff in a damage suit but as judge and prosecutor in a criminal proceeding. Humanity broke the law and should be punished. God is the judge who makes the decision but is also the accuser who demands punishment in the name of the law. Humanity is found guilty in this legal sense and Christ is then made to suffer the penalty—Christ became a guilty sinner. Second Corinthians 5:21 says, "He made him to be sin who knew no sin." That means he was made to be the one guilty of sin. He was made to be the one who carried actual guilt and the punishment for the guilt. God as prosecutor is not satisfied until the sentence has been pronounced and discharged. Then God, the prosecutor/judge, is satisfied because the punishment has been discharged. So it is appropriate that Reformation documents like the Augsburg Confession of Lutheranism and The Thirty-Nine Articles of Anglicanism, say that the death of Christ reconciled the Father to us rather than agreeing with 2 Corinthians 5:19 that God was in Christ reconciling us or the world "to himself." No, God was the one who needed to be reconciled. It is the prosecutor who has the unmet demand. It is the judge who pronounces the sentence that then Christ suffers on our behalf.
- The third subpattern within the general satisfaction approach is called "governmental." Here God is seen not as either the judge or the plaintiff but as the ruler or legislator. Why does the legislator say there must be compensation or punishment? Not because of

anger. The legislator is patient with the weaknesses of citizens. Not because he or she is personally mad. Not because there is a particular law, because he or she makes the law. But why then is there a law that calls for punishment? Because public order requires it. Education requires it. The moral upbringing of people requires rules. The morale of society requires that everybody know there are rules. The seriousness of sin must be demonstrated, and to demonstrate the seriousness of sin there must be penalty attached to infractions.

- One more family of views of the atonement is worthy of recognition beyond what is usually given in historical texts on the subject. It might be called the *"dynamistic."* It arises independently in more than one context.

The central concept here is that evil represents a power or force field that, once it has been set loose, reproduces itself autonomously. It cannot be boiled down to personalities or social customs. It is more than the guilt of the person who committed a sin; an evil force has been let loose in the world and it keeps on multiplying, bearing evil fruit. The only cure is for this evil force to spend itself against some barrier, or to be absorbed by some kind of receiver, or buffer, or to be deprived of the medium in which it grows.

One place where this view is found is the conception of sacrifice much contemporary scholarship believes was held by ancient Near Eastern civilizations. An evil deed or word was thought of as loosing a chain of destructiveness in the world, but the blood of a sacrifice could stop it. This evil was not conceived of as located in the mind of God, as the one who is angry, or a judge demanding penalty. Rather it was a *dunamis* that would continue to cause havoc until neutralized by a sacrifice.

Interpreters of the Old Testament differ as to whether the ancient Hebrews held this "dynamic" view of sacrifice. One line of interpretation of these matters assumes that the Hebrews shared such concepts with their neighbors with very little differentiation. Others look at the same data and say that when the same sacrificial uses were incorporated into the life of the Hebrew community, they were immediately changed by coming into relationship with the personal conception of YHWH and holiness of the LORD.

The other context for very similar thought is Friedrich Schleiermacher. Here the "dynamic" is less a disincarnate spiritual force field than a phenomenon in the series of evil effects. Until its evil impact has been absorbed or counteracted, evil effects continue the cause-effect chain of evil reproducing itself. The power that evil has to reproduce itself is built into the causal network by definition. Thus there can be no salvation from it except as the causal network is interrupted. This is what happens when someone absorbs evil rather than passing it on. The effect of evil is buffered instead of transferred. Or to change the image, evil is deprived of the reaction of hate that it needs as a medium in which to grow. Christians are called to do this; Christ did it supremely, thereby enabling the Christian to do it in his wake. The supremacy of the sacrifice of Christ is not that it is of another nature than the cross of the Christian, but that it is prior in point of time and is the source of our motivation.

This dynamistic view is similar to the "classical" theme of conflict and victory with the powers, but differs slightly in that the enmity of the powers is allowed to spend itself against the victim rather than being broken by the superior *exousia* (authority, power) of Christ as Lord. It is also similar to the more "objective" satisfaction views, in that the power of sin is not limited to the individual personalities that are its bearers, but it differs from them in that the objective power of sin is not best defined in terms of a legislator or a court but in cosmic terms.

In its favor, this scheme of interpretation affirms the meaningfulness of our suffering as part of the same combat as Christ's. It also seems to fit with the biblical expressions of Christ as the victim of "wrath" or as "made sin for us," which do not really fit the penal understanding as aptly as has often been assumed. It fits fruitfully with some current thought about nonviolent social action as "breaking the vicious cycle" or depriving hostility of its ammunition. It is something like the "psychiatric" view, without limiting the workings of evil to the inside of the estranged person.

The difficulties with considering this view as an adequate modern key to the problem center upon the limited adequacy of the image of "evil as a force" that splashes around like liquid until bottled up, corrodes things like acid until neutralized, or shakes things like a shock wave until buffered. The images of fluid, pressure, and force field seem inadequate to render the personal and political dimensions of the death of Christ. They fit the "Andromeda strain" mythology more than Hebrew history.

The idea of a simple cause and effect chain of consequences that propagates evil, subject to interference and reversal by another cause introduced into the system, is a somewhat mythical rather than really modern understanding of causalty. Nonetheless there is something worthy of respect and attention in this striking concordance of a very old and a relatively new view. It thus will be quite worthy of more attention than is given it by the typical summary surveys on the question. It seems at least to merit inclusion in the list of those images that we hope an adequate contemporary reformulation of the doctrine of the atonement would not exclude as incompatible or illegitimate.

These are the options. Since the Middle Ages there have been no more new systems. Protestantism has generally not only reaffirmed the satisfaction position, but made it more dominant and more nearly a test of faith than had been the case in the Middle Ages. This was true for both established and free church Protestants, both Calvinists and Arminians, for centuries. More recently, the "subjective" line of explanation again became popular in the context of theological liberalism.

Our concern here, however, is not so much to pursue historical development as to evaluate the relative strengths and weaknesses of the satisfaction view. The theory on first view has a number of considerations in its favor. The primary one is that it appears to answer the question. It explains why the death of Christ was absolutely necessary, why nothing else could save us. With the logic of judicial form, with which our culture deals with moral matters, it demonstrates beyond denial that the blameless death of Christ was an absolute necessity. This was the only way God's holiness and love could be reconciled. It takes sin seriously, which could not be said to the same degree of the more "subjective" theories. It appears also at first sight to be parallel to the language of sacrifice through the shedding of blood and to "redemption," payment for liberation.

Recent exegetes like James Stewart and Vincent Taylor much illumined the situation by their exposition of particular concepts and texts. They have, however, not successfully put their gains together in such a way as to answer the question. When Taylor says that the death of Christ was "vicarious, representative, and sacrificial, but not substitutionary," he perhaps knows what he means, but such a formulation neither clarifies the problem nor supplies the answer. We, however, owe a great debt to such exegetes, for they have provided the material the doctrine we seek must put together.

The argument about the atonement is at present at a standstill. On one hand, the exegetes, without having an adequate substitute, are sure of one thing, namely that the Anselmic view is not biblical. We shall see their reasons in detail later. On the other hand, the theologians (apart from the fundamentalists who never left him) are swinging back to Anselm from the humanistic views of a generation ago, blithely paying no attention to the exegetes. Some exegetes and theologians therefore attempt to get along without clear answers, fleeing into sacramentalism, mysticism, or existentialism. This is possible for preachers and monks, but not for theologians or ethicists.

Anselm's judicial imagery envisions God's holiness as akin to a Roman court's judgment of guilt. Humanity's sin offends this holiness, which then demands satisfaction, that is, punishment in the form of death. Since the penalty as such is what God demands, someone else could conceivably pay it. Since, however, everyone is guilty of sin, each person's death only pays his or her own penalty, and there can be no salvation hoped for without divine intervention. The only solution is for a sinless person to die; his or her death could then, since it was not earned, be applied to other's debts. Anselm's question, *Cur Deus homo?* (Why did God become man?), thus receives a clear answer: God became human in order to live a blameless life so that there could be an unmerited death to reckon to other people's credit. Christ literally dies in our stead and God's holiness is satisfied by that death. This satisfaction is valid for whoever believes.

This theory has a number of arguments in its favor, principally in that it answers the question; it makes Christ's blameless death an absolute juridical necessity, the only way to reconcile God's holiness and love. At the same time this answer takes sin seriously, which could not be said of the humanistic theories, and it is also capable of integrating the various imageries in which the Bible speaks of the work of Christ, especially those of sacrifice (and blood) and of redemption.

There are, however, a number of damaging criticisms to which this view is subject, first of all from an exegetical point of view.

- The most basic of these is that, in seeing God's offended holiness as the definition of perdition, the satisfaction view abandons the New Testament affirmation that God is the agent, not the object, of reconciliation (see, e.g., 2 Cor. 5:18–20). The Christian gospel is different from paganism precisely in that paganism sees God as angry and requiring appeasement, whereas the gospel reveals God taking the initiative for our redemption, and *humanity* as needing to be reconciled.[4]
- On a more precise point, exegetes challenge the idea of substitution as not supported in the New Testament. Christ died for us, on our behalf, and in some sense as our representative, but not as our substitute.[5]
- The major criticism of Anselm's view from an exegetical standpoint is however still deeper and consists in the denial that the guilt of sin (past sin) is the real problem of atonement. The New

4. Cf., James S. Stewart, *A Man in Christ: The Vital Elements of St. Paul's Religion* (London: Hodder and Stoughton, 1935), 209ff., 221ff.; Vincent Taylor, *The Atonement in the New Testament Teaching* (London: Epworth, 1958), 171ff.

5. Taylor, 176.

Testament has two other foci of interest that define the lost condition: separation from God and incapacity to do the good. Thus salvation is not primarily the remission of guilt or the cancellation of punishment; it is reconciliation (reestablishment of communion) and obedience, that is, discipleship.

Evidence that God's purpose with humanity is reconciliation and obedience rather than cancellation of guilt is already found in the Old Testament sacrificial system. It is often forgotten—especially when the imagery of sacrifice is applied to the doctrine of the atonement—that Old Testament sacrifice in general was not concerned with the problem of guilt. Most sacrifices dealt with *ritual* uncleanness or required acts of praise. The "sin-offering" was valid only for unwitting sins, the "guilt-offering" only for sins where full reparation could be made. Other sins were dealt with by retributive civil justice ("eye for eye") or not at all. Forgiveness, in the Old Testament as in the New, is a gift of God's grace, not something that can be earned by sacrifice.

- One last exegetical critique has to do with another part of the meaning of the sacrificial system. In various mosaic sacrifices, blood is shed. How does the shedding of blood relate to the problem about which we are talking? Hebrews 9:22 reads, "Without the shedding of blood there is no forgiveness of sins." What does the blood mean? Leviticus 17:11 is part of a longer passage explaining why a Jew should not consume the blood of a sacrificial animal, but should let it flow onto the altar and into the ground: "For the life of the flesh is in the blood; and I have given it for you upon the altar to make atonement for your souls; for it is the blood that makes atonement, by reason of the life."

  It is usually assumed in discussions of the doctrine of atonement that sacrificial language and symbolism are especially compatible with Anselmian theory. Anselmian theory calls for a death, and in the sacrificial system animals were killed. Yet by concentrating on the meaning of death, we misunderstand the meaning of sacrifice. The blood is the life of the animal that is given to God. The life does not need to be destroyed, nor does it need to be taken so that the animal is not there anymore, but in its place are loss and suffering. The meaning of the sacrifice is that the livingness, or vitality, of the animal is put up before God to represent the vitality and the livingness of the offering. To give is to be alive to God. The animal did not die in the place of a human. It goes to God in the place of the human. Precisely the life of the animal, the blood of the animal, goes to God, representing the life of the person who will henceforth live for God. There is only one case in the Old Testament language where the sin is placed on the animal.

> That is the so-called "scapegoat," which is not sacrificed. The goat is chased off into the desert as a bearer of human sin. But when the believer comes to the temple with a flawless lamb, a sheep with nothing wrong with its body, and lays his or her hand on that sheep, it is not to put guilt on the sheep and then have it executed in his or her place. It is to identify with the purity of this gift and then give himself or herself in the purity of this gift to God as an offering.[6]

Every strand of New Testament literature makes clear that God's purpose with humanity is to establish obedience in communion, not only to expiate juridical guilt. Already the prophets gave obedience precedence in their Messianic hope (e.g., Jer. 31). We find the same view in the Synoptics' description of the Kingdom (Matt. 5–7, 19; Lk. 14); in 1 Peter (2:2–4); in Paul (Rom. 8:4; Eph. 2:10; Gal. 1:4; Titus 2:11–14; Phil. 2:12–15), in the Johannine writings (Jn. 15:9–10, 16-17; 1 Jn. 3:5–10, Rev. 19:8); and in Hebrews (9:13–14). Forgiveness, in the sense removing an obstacle to communion with God, is evidently part of God's purpose, but we do not find God preoccupied without guilt, in the sense of our deserving punishment. Guilt in this sense seems rather to be an anthropopathism carried over by Anselm from human concepts of just retribution.

A striking example of the way habitual ways of thinking may prevent seizing the real meaning of biblical truth is the general consensus of opinion, already mentioned, that the New Testament use of the idea of redemption fits especially well with the Anselmic view. This is not the case. "Redemption" in New Testament usage is not purchase out of hock or out of jail, but out of slavery to sin. From being servants of sin we become servants of God. Redemption is a change of masters, and the New Testament use of this term is one of the strongest statements of the truth that the concern of God in atonement is our obedience, not our guilt (see e.g., 1 Cor. 6:20, 7:23; Rom. 6:17–22).

Other criticisms that originate in systematic theology reinforce the exegetical criticisms of the Anselmic view. Systematic theology in this sense does not mean the intrusion of philosophy into the affairs of revelation, but rather the consensus of careful thought about how the content of revelation hangs together.

6. Let it be noted that a far more refined analysis of ancient Hebrew ritual is needed. "Sacrifice" was not one ritual with one meaning but many. Why did it please God? Has it any expiatory function? Vindicative? Civil? All that is clear is that the easy juxtaposition of civil punishment with bloody sacrifice, which makes the Anselmian synthesis so powerful to convince, will not find support in the sources.

- First and worst: Anselm's view forces us to a tritheistic doctrine of God. The idea of a Trinity composed of three "persons" in the modern sense of that word (three personalities, three centers of consciousness or will), is neither biblical nor Nicene (even if the Nicene Creed were binding for us). Nicea emphasized the oneness of the Trinity (the deity of Christ and the Spirit), not the threeness. The idea that Father and Son have separate wills and identities to the point of having transactions with one another has no grounds in the orthodox doctrine of the Trinity, and still less in the New Testament.
- Again, there is the danger of an *opus operatum* view of Christ's work. If the question was, as Anselm stated it, how to have a "valid" death, then that death, having met the requirements (innocence of the victim), tends to have a universal validity whether people want it or not. Thus the Anselmic view can lead to universalism (cf. Württenberg Pietism, Barth).
- Third, Anselm's view grew out of the penitential practice of the medieval church. Penitence is a human work seeking to earn good standing with God and Anselm began his logical edifice by asking, "What human work can have saving merit?" He answered of course, "Only a work of God Incarnate," but Christ's death remains a human initiative directed Godward. This is, as already said, the reverse of the biblical teaching.
- Fourth, Anselm thinks as a lawyer and succeeds in working pardon into the legal system of just rewards. The triumph of the doctrine of the atonement as satisfaction is that the legal structure remains intact. Christian doctrine, however, seems little concerned for legal systems (note Jesus' choice between the pharisees and publicans) and God's grace flexes the law rather than applying it rigidly and destructively.

We are also justified in mentioning a third set of objections: those coming from the direction of discipleship. It is significant that proponents of the Anselmic view, which was formulated in a state-church context where the sacraments mattered more than ethics, have always experienced difficulty in relating sanctification to justification once the two terms have been separated by definitions. Some make sanctification a second Christian experience, others simultaneous but logically subsequent (and dispensable), and others impose a new legalism. No doctrine has adequately resolved the problem, and justification has always applied to the sinner, not the saint. This is not unconnected with certain orthodox and neoorthodox emphases, which deny that there is any difference at all between sinner and saint.

The concept of discipleship is most clearly taught in those New Testament texts that speak of the Christian's sufferings (or "cross") as parallel to Christ's (Matt. 10:38; Mk. 8:34ff., 10:38ff.; Lk. 14:27; Jn. 15:20; 2 Cor. 1:5, 4:10; Phil. 1:29, 2:5–8, 3:10; Col. 1:24ff.; Heb. 12:1–4; 1 Pet. 2:21ff.; Rev. 12:11). Under the satisfaction theory these passages make no sense at all. The Christian's "cross" neither placates an offended holiness nor is the Christians suffering a transaction with the Father. Unless the work of Christ has an ethical sense this whole strand of New Testament thought has no place to fit in. This explains why in preaching about the Christian life many proponents of the Anselmic view abandon it in practice if not in theory.

At the point of the lack of linkage with the issue of obedience, the Anabaptists contributed an original critique. The thought of Anabaptists concerning atonement has not been deeply studied. Much of what they said, preached, and sang in their hymns would fit well within the satisfaction framework, yet there is one point at which we do find documents dealing with the issue and projecting one quite specific criticism.

Among the works attributed to Michael Sattler is a brief tract, "On the Satisfaction of Christ," which, if it is from the pen of Sattler, would have to have been written by February 1527. It is not proven that he wrote it, but since it appears in a collection of tracts related to him, it in any case expresses the stance of the movement he helped found. We have as well a set of theses proposed for debate in Worms by Jacob Kautz just before Pentecost, 1527. There is some reason to consider them to express the thought not only of Kautz but also of Hans Denck, who was in Worms at the time. Both of these texts used the technical term "satisfaction" and state one serious objection to the way Protestantism was interpreting the work of Christ.

The objection does not take the form of an alternative explanation of why Christ had to die. Both documents do, however, insist that the *benefit* of the death of Christ applies only to the person whose acceptance of it includes discipleship, the inward appropriation of the broken will and the outward following in his steps. As the Anabaptists understood it, the other churches, both Catholic and Protestant, offered a cheap forgiveness unrelated to the conditions stated by the Lord himself.

One side of the lack of linkage with the reality of obedience is thus the possibility that atonement, as understood in the satisfaction framework, can be accomplished on behalf of people who neither need to do anything to receive it nor even choose to accept it. The other end of the same shortcoming is that the description of how atonement is brought about has no necessary relationship to the history of Jesus as a man. How the cross happened, the social reality of Palestine, the promises that Jesus proclaimed, and the actions that offended the authorities and led to their killing him are all irrelevant to this view. The only obedience that is required from him is that he committed no sin, but "blamelessness" is certainly a very thin kind of description of the way in which the life of Jesus can be called obedience.

One other element of critical awareness is needed, especially since modern fundamentalism has led many to take the Anselmic theory to be identical with the Bible and the very central test of Christian faithfulness. They need some sense of the history of dogma. The Anselmic theory is the youngest theory of the atonement, coming from the twelfth century. By the time it made its way into the creeds, it was the sixteenth and seventeenth centuries. Of all the theories we talked about (ransom, struggle, incarnation, mystical, moral influence), it is the youngest. It is the one tied most precisely to a particular model of thought, namely the courtroom. It is called in technical terms a "forensic model," referring simply to its analogy to the courtroom. It assumes the forum, the judge, the plaintiff, and the defendant. If you do not think in courtroom terms, the whole thing makes no sense. All the other doctrines, the older doctrines, are much less tied to a particular model of thought—although each has its own particular model—and are less narrow and less culturally limited. If you lived in a society that did not have courtrooms working this way, if you lived in a society that dealt with tensions in society with some other institutional forms, then you could not understand Anselm's theory.

There are other criticisms of the satisfaction view, coming largely from humanistic presuppositions. Taylor, for instance, insists that the idea of punishing the innocent is immoral, and that the idea of imputed righteousness is nonsense. These arguments tell us more about Taylor's prejudices than about the problem at hand. God can punish the innocent and impute righteousness if God wants to; the question is whether that is God's intention or what God did in Christ. Such criticisms do not demand further attention here.

We now have two clear findings. We have seen that the satisfaction theories are the most serious answers found in the history of Christian theology in the sense that they answer the question of piety. They make sense in prayer. They call forth praise, gratitude, and commitment. Therefore they are deeply rooted in the life of the common believer. We need to recognize and respect the theory because of that moral strength.

But we have also seen that it is a biblically unsatisfactory theory. It makes systematic assumptions counter to the meaning of the doctrine of the Trinity. If consistently applied in its own logic it would be ahistorical and universalist in its implications. It gives us a vision of God as a judge rather than as a reconciling and loving Father. It does not fit with the entire biblical stance.

Now what are we to do in the light of these weaknesses and these strengths? One answer is to say, "It is the best we have; it is inadequate, but it is still the best we have. We will use it anyway, when people ask why there had to be a cross." How can you preach about the cross? What can you preach about the cross? How can you make the work of Christ meaningful for man? How can you "paint Christ crucified," the way Paul wrote to one of his churches that he had done before them? How can you do those things, how can you make the cross make sense? The answer the satisfaction models require is that we still have to use the language of guilt. Christ pays by his death the price of our guilt. This is what most people do. Barth, Brunner, and Niebuhr, for example, still use something of this language of paying the price for our guilt as the most appropriate model, in the full awareness of its limits. But is that not to abandon theological responsibility?

Another solution is the antitheological reflex. Why do you need a theory at all? Why can you not just say that Christ died for our sins without explaining why? Without developing all these arguments pro and con? We need not explain why it had to be this way. Can we not get along without this way of reflection, especially if we tried it and it did not work? Especially if for ages we have debated away at this and have not come up with a satisfactory answer? Maybe we should not have asked the question, but this antitheological reflex will not work either. If the theologian does not make an explanation, the preacher will anyway. The preacher will, sometime, somehow, have to make meaningful the work of Christ. He or she will sometime have to say it was necessary (or not), meaningful (or not), and tragic (or not). If the preacher preaches about Jesus, he or she will have to make why things happened they did and how the cross was "for us" bear some meaning for us now. Thus the response to the antitheological reflex boils down to the one we have given before. If we do not develop how the work of Christ saves us, then we will simply permit hymnology, the tracts people read, and nontheological literature with its unstated assumptions to make the decision for us.

It then seems that the only choice left is to look in some other direction for a fuller, more adequately biblical view that is not one of the major streams of traditions. Let us remember the questions we put to those streams and the standards that would need to be met by this doctrinal statement.

An adequate understanding of Christ's work needs to take sin and lostness as seriously as did Anselm. It needs to be consonant with the Bible. It should not be tied to only one symbolic image, like the image of the courtroom. It should not distort the biblical imagery, as the

Anselmic view does when it distorts "sacrifice" and "redemption" into the purging of guilt, despite the fact that each had a different meaning.

Part of what we want to ask of a doctrine is that it be consonant with the other major themes of the Bible. What were some of those other themes we found missing in the Anselmic view? One was the concept of union with Christ. Paul calls it "being in Christ," and John's Gospel calls it "abiding in him and he in us." We observed this "logic of solidarity" at certain points in the development of each New Testament theologian. It is there in John, Paul, and Hebrews as a key concept—never quite proven, never quite given a label, but always present. To be in Christ is to have one's identity derived from a relationship to Christ. The nearest approximation to this concept in traditional theology is the orthodox Reformed concept of "federal headship." "Federal" comes from the Latin for an oath or a covenant, *foedus.* Federal headship means that because God made a covenant to that effect, therefore another person represents humanity by a representative. In the covenant God makes with Adam, Adam represents us all. If Adam obeys, we participate in his obedience. When Adam falls, we are taken with him in his fall. Then again, in the covenant with Christ, he is our head, so that what he does is done in our behalf. This "logic of solidarity," or "federal headship," might be one of the resources to use more extensively and better than the Anselmic tradition uses the idea of incarnation.

But there are other resources that have not been tapped in the old theories of the atonement that also belong in our inventory. We are aware of history as a process. This awareness is characteristic of our age as it was not of earlier ages. We are learning to discern a more Hebraic view of things, which differs from the Hellenistic and later Greco-Roman worldviews. We think of the church as a concrete group of people and not first as an institution, organization or body of doctrine. We think reality goes on in the group awareness of people. History is the only reality we know; we do not think about essences anymore, about substances and *hypostases,* about realities "out there" having being in themselves. We think of reality as happening in personal relationships, in institutional relationships, and in the passage of time. So if we took historicism as a philosophical stance congruent with the Bible, then in reading the Bible we might have a new resource for developing an understanding of the need for the work of Christ.

It fits into this to think more than the other doctrines ever did about Jesus as a man, social figure, teacher, and moral figure—Jesus as acting within the political and the cultural situation of Palestine. We seek some relationship between atonement and his discussions of the kingdom, his forgiving people, his teaching people, his making of people a church—a body of disciples—and his sending people into mission. We see his getting crucified, his raising people from the dead, and his being raised from the dead as a social process. This is a resource for the doctrine of the atonement that has not been tapped by the other views.

The unity of humanity's obedience with Christ's obedience is another element, whose customary absence we just referred to. The cross of Christ demands and enables the cross of the Christian. We might try to affirm the unity of obedience, sanctification with justification, instead of distinguishing between being made righteous and being made good, the way traditional theology separates justification from sanctification as a separate process which comes later and makes us do good. The unity of these two in biblical thought links the unity of our obedience with God's work in Christ, his cross with our cross, his death with our dying with him. This double unity is completely missing in Anselm but is present in the Bible.[7]

Finally, we suggested along the way that the Anselmic theory does not need the faith of the believer and that it does not need the resurrection. An interpretation of the atonement that needs the resurrection and a doctrine that needs the faith of the believer would probably be a better one.

So we want a view of the atonement that is not tied to an archaic worldview (like the descending into hell and the ransom theory). We want a view that must be appropriated (it isn't enough that it happened out there). We want a view that is in history and not just in the mind of God or in some hypothetical heavenly courtroom. We want one that needs Jesus as the fulfillment of promise, that needs Jesus as teacher, needs the resurrection, needs the incarnation, and needs all the language of the New Testament. Now, how shall we put together, how will you preach, and how will you phrase an understanding of the meaning of Christ's death that does all of that? A big order to be sure, but we still ought to know what the order is before we set about stating, preaching, or testing a doctrine of the atonement.

An Alternative Attempt

For the purposes of this collection of introductory materials, it is inappropriate to conclude the introduction to the classical shape of a problem by proposing one "right answer." Yet it is also fitting to demonstrate the usefulness of new hypotheses that seek to free the logjam of an old debate. In that hypothetical spirit the following text, mostly from 1954, is inserted.[8] The student may wish to compare it to Gordon

7. See John Howard Yoder, "The Disciple of Christ and the Way of Jesus," ch. 7 in *The Politics of Jesus: Vicit Agnus Noster* (Grand Rapids: Eerdmans, 1972).

8. Idem, "A Study in the Doctrine of the Work of Christ." Text presented to a study group at Domburg, The Netherlands, 1954.

Kaufman's response.[9] Here I shall attempt to outline as concisely as possible a theological explanation of the work of Christ that will:

1. Answer the questions stated: "What is perdition and how did the death of Jesus remedy that?"
2. Integrate the results of exegesis with the concerns of systematics and of discipleship,
3. Take sin as seriously as does Anselm, and
4. Integrate as well as Anselm the various imageries and terminologies used by the New Testament (we have already seen that neither the idea of redemption nor that of sacrifice supports Anselm's theory as well as had been thought).

Three presuppositions underlie the following argument. They have been exposed elsewhere, proven to the writer's satisfaction, and may thus be taken for granted here. Any disagreement with the following presuppositions should be kept separate from criticism of their use in the present argument.

1. *The notion of faith-union* expressed by the Pauline term "in Christ" and the Johannine "abide in me." In faith, a real identification/communion with God in Christ that may be described but not explained takes place. Here this concept is taken for granted.
2. *The belief that nonresistance is part of the essential nature of* "agape," of God's way of dealing with evil. This has been sufficiently dealt with in pacifist literature and in word studies to need no further elaboration here.
3. *The contention, less directly relevant, that all Christian truth is distorted when the difference between church and world is not clearly kept in mind.* This does not support the doctrine advocated here so much as it explains how the Anselmic doctrine, although ethically weak, could be accepted so generally and so long. Theologians have wanted an answer to humanity's need; they have not in general sought an understanding of discipleship. They could not, since their definition of the Christian had to include every citizen of the Christian West.

The Bible sees being human as being always in a context of choice. Even though many aspects of human situations are causally determined without consent, we are nevertheless always faced by God's "Thou shalt" and "Thou shalt not." Unless these commands of God are

9. Editorial note: The text to which Yoder is referring is unclear.

nonsense (which some existentialism affirms), they mean that humans are really placed before a decision, free to choose to obey or disobey. That we shall afterwards be able to analyze our decisions as having been "caused" makes no difference; at the time of choice, when facing God's command obeying or disobeying, we know ourselves free.

The use of the term "freedom" is philosophical. When the Bible says freedom it means something different, namely, redemption and freedom from sin (and *not*—as some strands in the thought of Luther, Barth, and the neo-orthodox claim—freedom from ethical norms). The term is nonetheless clear, and the only one available, and we shall continue to use it, conscious of its shortcomings. Humanity's freedom as we speak of it here means that in the context of choice before God, which is our condition, both obedience and disobedience are real possibilities.

This real freedom is at the root of all the world's troubles, and of most of theology's troubles as well. So it is that most theologies try to deny it, as do most social strategies. Only God, in fact, really respects this freedom.

The clearest example of theology's denial of freedom is universalism, which amounts to saying that when people think they are in a context of choice, they are not. We think ourselves free to turn away from God, but if we try it we find ourselves roped in after all. The appearance of freedom is thus but a farce, and both human history and God's command a mockery. This is not God's way; it is a human attempt to solve a problem by defining it out of the way.

The problem of evil can be traced no further back than this: the possibility of disobedience is the sole condition for the reality of human freedom and personality. Why then did God take the risk when it would have been so easy, so much simpler, not to create the problem? God could have run people through their paces and never needed to atone for them. Stated this way, the question is clearly out of order, if not sacrilegious. The only answer is that God is *agape* and agape *respects the freedom of the beloved.*

This last statement is the one solid point where no exceptions may be made. It is the starting point of theology, of history, of ethics, of church order, and of every realm where *agape* matters. *Agape* respects the freedom of the beloved even to lose himself or herself. The first revelation of *agape* was thus the creation of human freedom, and no theology or ethics that denies this freedom can be true. Universalism denies humanity's freedom to turn away from God; Constantinianism denies the freedom not to be a Christian; Monism denies humanity's real existence; and totalitarianism or utopianism denies the freedom of choice (and/or sin) in society. Each such system denies the problem it sets out to solve.

God takes the risk of leaving people free; this is the definition of *agape* that lies at the bottom of all meaningful thought. That this lets the problem of evil in by the back door is too bad, but there was no other way and God took that risk, precisely because of *agape*.

The tragic fact is that people disobey, thus proving, in spite of the universalists, the reality of human freedom (that is, the reality of God's respect for human freedom). As long as people persist in disobedience, God's respect for that freedom leads to perdition (whereas annulling perdition by fiat would mean God's abandoning *agape*). The first step is rupture of communion with God, with the resulting inability to do the good and love the neighbor, since the good is possible only in faith-union with God. Within the context of freedom, our evil is met by vengeance from our neighbors, which system of evil for evil, channeled in the State, has a restraining effect on sin. Thus providence, God's care of creation, continues to operate, but in the context of respect for humanity's freedom to sin. The final result of freedom thus abused is death and hell, the consummation of God's respect for our choice to turn away from God.

This order of things thus has, in virtue of God's respect for it, a certain degree of autonomy in the face of God's redemptive will. This is the truth in the ransom theory of the atonement, which says that Satan has certain rights over or claims upon humanity. The same truth is expressed in his name, "prince of this world." Satan is the personification of evil's autonomy in the face of God, but this autonomy must be recognized to be limited, as indicated in the prologue to Job, by the fact that it is an autonomy *granted* by God's creation of history's freedom.

Thus, finding the essential character of the human predicament to be simply the involution of God-given freedom does not mean that the need for atonement is all in our minds, for part of the freedom granted to humanity is the power to influence reality and express ourselves in history.

We can now state the problem atonement must solve. That is, we can now define the state of lostness. Humanity, created for free communion with God and obedience in communion, has turned freedom, this gift of God's love, inside out so that God's love lets us go as we choose. The question is now how God can bring humanity back to communion and obedience, that is, how can God save (as an expression of *agape*) and at the same time leave humanity free (also an expression of *agape*), which must include respecting the hold of human sinfulness? How, in short, to reveal love to us without forcing it upon us, which forcing would contradict love?

The work of Christ is, at its center, obedience (see Philippians 2). Christ was exactly what God meant humans to be: in free communion with God, obeying God and loving others—even his enemies—with God's love. The Nicene Creed seeks to safeguard this truth. This man Christ Jesus was really God working, was a man in *perfect* communion with God. Nicea affirms the reality of God's working in Christ's obedience.

But this perfect love in obedience had to be lived in the world of sinners, respecting the liberty of sinners to be unloving. Thus *agape* comes to mean nonresistance, bearing the other's sinfulness, bearing, literally, his or her sins. If Christ had done anything in the face of humanity's sinfulness other than to be nonresistant, respecting the freedom to sin against him, his work would have been less than perfect *agape.* His temptations center precisely on this point. Laying before him the possibility of shortcuts that would violate human freedom to reject him, the tempter hoped to lead Jesus to take back the freedom that God had given humanity in the first place, rather than go the whole way to save us *within* our freedom. The temptation to use political methods or violent self-defense was one aspect of this possibility.

"The whole way" meant the cross. For, since murder is the worst sin—as it takes away freedom most utterly—so the utmost in *agape* is the utmost in non-self-defense, namely, to undergo murder, respecting the other's freedom to commit the worst sin out of love for the sinner-murderer (1 Jn. 3: 11–12; 3:16). This is what Jesus did.

The imagery of sacrifice is particularly relevant here. For the ultimate sacrifice, the sacrifice of self, is precisely giving oneself utterly to communion-obedience with God. This is what Jesus did in letting God express *agape* through his "obedience unto death, the death of the cross." Thus sacrifice, communion, and obedience are identical. Blood as the symbol of life given is the most striking way of saying this. The sinlessness of Christ is thus not (as for Anselm) a purely legal formality or, as some understand the Old Testament sacrifices, a matter merely of ritual cleanness. Christ's sinlessness is rather the whole point of his life and his obedience-offering. His sinlessness, his obedience, is what he offered to God, and that sinlessness, utter faithfulness to love, cost his life in a world of sinners.[10]

The place of the resurrection in the work of Christ is much less difficult to explain in any theory than the death, but it fits in better here than with Anselm. Ontologically, it is a simple necessity: "Death could not hold him down" (see Acts 2:24). Psychologically, the resurrection is fundamental for discipleship, in that it vindicates the rightness, the possibility, and the effectiveness of the way of the cross.

10. One more note on Old Testament sacrifice. It may be legitimately argued that the point of sacrifice was not to identify one's sins with the lamb by laying one's hands on it and killing it to get rid of the sin—that was done with the scapegoat but then it was not killed. The point is rather that of identifying oneself with the lamb's purity and then offering that pure self to God as a "sweet fragrance," which makes much better sense.

But our present concern is the place of the resurrection in the dialectic of God's love, which sought to save us by respecting our freedom to sin so far as to die at our hands. The resurrection proves that, even when humanity does its worst, turns the farthest from God's communion, so far as to kill God, we cannot destroy that love. Humanity has done its worst, and the love of God is still stronger; it withstands the assault of sin *without* canceling the sinner's freedom, and still comes out on top. This triumph of communion-sacrifice-obedience-*agape* over human rebellion at its worst now stands before humanity as an object of faith, (faith-union, not merely faith-assent). We can identify ourselves with the obedience that swallowed up our rebellion in victory.

Appropriation of Christ's work is by *repentance* and *faith,* but neither of these terms is to be understood as orthodoxy understood them. Repentance means ethics, not only remorse or sorrow for sin; it is the turning-around of the will that is the condition of obedience. The orthodox Lutheran and Catholic idea of repentance (penitence or sorrow for sin) as the condition of pardon is misfocused because pardon is unconditional, a gift of grace.

Faith, likewise, must be understood biblically and de-Anselmized. It is not the mere acceptance of the proclamation that Jesus died because of our guilt. It is rather commitment to the faith-union of obedience made available to us through the perfect and triumphant obedience of Christ. In Pauline usage, faith is identification with Christ's offering of himself in obedience to God; in Hebrews, faith means believing enough to obey when it looks hopeless (this is the meaning of Hebrews 11); in both uses faith means discipleship. The truth of the Nicene-Constantinopolitan doctrine of the Spirit is its affirmation of the true deity of God's working through our obedience.

Forgiveness can then be understood not as the annulment of the sentence pronounced against us by God but as removing the hindrance to communion; the obstacle is our own sinfulness and God's respect for our right to erect that barrier.[11]

The view of salvation as restored communion and consequently restored capacity to obedience fits, better than Anselm's view, *all* the New Testament figures for atonement. It allows us to use the notions, for example, of illumination (the favorite Anabaptist concept), union with Christ, the new Adam, death of the old person and resurrection of the new, healing, and adoption to Sonship, as well as those of sacrifice-blood and ransom-redemption with which we already dealt.

There is thus no gap between justification and sanctification, between forensic justification and real righteousness. There is a gap in the

11. See Vincent Taylor, Forgiveness and Reconciliation: A Study in New Testament Theology (London: Macmillan, 1941).

Christian's life, but it is at the place where God puts it, where we use or abuse our freedom, for we are still in a context of choice. The gap is between our intention (what we are "in faith" when we are in faith) and our achievement (which includes the times we fall into unfaith-alienation-disobedience). Sin for the Christian is thus a contradiction in terms, a paradox. On the other hand, for the sinner, secure in turning-away from God, sin is normal. There is thus a real difference between the sinner's sin and the saint's; this is maintained by 1 Corinthians 11:31–32 and 1 John 1:6–8, 5:15, as versus Anselm, Luther, Barth, and Niebuhr.

Obviously, the terms in which this proposed view is expressed are not biblical but speculative. The definition of love as respect for freedom of the other is entirely conceptual, whereas biblical thinking is concrete and personal. This is, however, not an argument against this doctrine, any more than it is against Anselm's, which is just as unbiblical in form. The test of a doctrine is not the Hebraic flavor of its vocabulary, but its adequacy in interrelating and synthesizing the exegetical material into an intellectually graspable whole. That a doctrine should be intellectually graspable does not mean it is rationally provable. The theology is the handmaiden to biblical revelation, not its substructure.

Accessory Themes

Beyond the narrow task we have been pursuing, grappling with the meaning of atonement demands attention to three subordinate themes:

a. Universalism and/or hell;
b. The "descent into hell" as part of the creed; and
c. The continuing usefulness of the subjective perspective.

The Logic of Universalism.

The term "universalism" is sometimes used in another sense, but in the present connection it means affirming that God's saving intention for all humanity will be successful for all. All people will somehow, sometime, be saved. We have not yet looked directly at this topic. We should survey the case made for it, with some understanding of its origin. More than one stream of theology can arrive at this conclusion. The two categories I have decided to use here are insufficiently discriminating. There might well need to be more than two, but at least there are real differences between these two.

The Omnipotence of Grace.

This theme is found predominantly in the pietistic stream of church history. One gets the impression from certain modern evangelical polemic writing that universalism is characteristic of theological liberalism because it thinks that humanity is so good it cannot possibly be really lost. There is such a position. It is possible, although it is not very logical. The theological liberal is more likely not to know what to do with the word "lost," rather than to say that nobody is in that category. Universalism as a stream of church history really comes from pietism. It is an affirmation of the goodness and the power of God. God is first of all gracious, purposing to save all humanity. God is secondly omnipotent. God can do what God wants or wills. We do not know how and we cannot say when, but all resistances to God must somehow be broken down. Presumably, this must happen beyond the history in which we are living. This position may arise in a strong form, which can bluntly affirm that God will ultimately save everyone. It brought into being the Universalist denomination in American experience. It also brought about (I think this is correct) the only division within Mennonitism that ever had a doctrinal basis. A preacher named Joseph Yoder wrote, about 1870, a poem by the name of *Fröhliche Botschaft* (Joyful Message). The message was that God is love and that the love of God is omnipotent and irresistible. Largely precipitating around the issue this raised, there came into being the group of Mennonites of Amish background who were then called the "Stucky Amish," later the "Central Conference," and ultimately became part of the General Conference Mennonites. It was a movement primarily located in Indiana and Illinois.

A more modest form of this position does not say that all will be saved, but says that we do not have any grounds for saying who will be lost. If God is whom Jesus said, and if God is God, then we cannot fix the limit of the power of God's grace. We cannot negate the possibility of salvation for anyone. We cannot affirm it for everyone, but neither can we negate it as simply as some other theologies have. This is probably a fair statement of Karl Barth's position, again on the grounds of the logic of omnipotence coupled with the meaning of grace.

The Universality of Truth or the Impartiality of God.

Because God is by definition universal, impartial, fair, and undiscriminating, what God asks of humans must be universalizable. God must ask the same thing of all people. It would be unfair to people who have never heard the Christian message or the Hebrew prophets' message to condemn them because they had not accepted it. There must then be another basis on which God is fair to those who have not heard this message. This fits with the Catholic tradition of natural theology, which affirms that many things can be known about God through other paths than the special revelation of the prophets or Jesus.

There must be some other way in which the issue of faith is put to a person who has not had it in the biblical form. People must be able somehow to receive that. There must be some possible way for them to perceive the universe as grace. They learn to perceive the framework in which they live, in which they have the same nature sustaining them, the same mother's love, and the same accepting community that we have. There must be some way for all to perceive the universe as a work of a loving God and to respond to that grace in gratitude and praise—a functional equivalent of Christian faith. Something must be accessible to everyone that is like believing through Christ, otherwise God would be unfair. Again, this view exists in several degrees. The strongest form affirms simply that all people will ultimately be saved even though many of them will not even know about it until the end. The more moderate form says that there is no one who cannot be saved. The message comes to everyone. The universe that offers itself to all is a sign of God's grace. It is a universal sacrament. Of course some people will turn it down. A still more moderate position simply says there can be some people, and may very well be people, who truly trust God for their salvation. These people truly believe that creation is the work of a loving God and call others to receive it in grace. They trust the grace of God for their righteousness, obey and pray, all without knowing the name of Jesus. Karl Rahner speaks here of "anonymous Christians."

What shall we do with universalism on each of these levels? There are several possible responses. One, of course, is biblical in the narrowest sense. Texts in the Bible talk clearly about people being turned away, refused, rejected, and even punished. On the basis of the text, we have to say that element cannot be simply forgotten, wiped over, or dealt with as not serious. If one makes any of these arguments, one must deal seriously with the texts. Doing so would not insure that no universalistic positions could be taken, but it probably would at least rule out the strongest position in each category.

We also need to recognize that a very strong strand of Scriptural affirmation does seem to support the omnipotence of grace. The Bible seems to give room for thinking of punishment and rejection as finally overcome, and as ultimately unable to stand up against the omnipotence of God's goodness, so a simple recourse to text against text is insufficient. There are proof texts on both sides. It is, moreover, not a textual but rather a systematic matter when you put texts on both sides of a question to know which have the broadest, deepest, or highest authority, which swallow up the others within themselves. The statement made in many ways and places that God does not desire the death of any, as well as the statements to the effect that God grace is omnipotent and that what God wants will happen, are just as clear as the others. Now when you put these two traditions or strands together, is either of such authority or such clarity that the other is somehow one chapter within it? If you say, "Yes, God wants to save everyone and God does everything God wants, but cannot quite do this because some reject God," you imply a systematic or a general hermeneutical question and not a question of whether you believe the text.

Another level of argument, which is not unimportant or untheological, is pragmatic. Some think the belief that God will ultimately save everyone will certainly undercut the missionary imperative. Why should you bother to go to another part of the world, bother people, run risks, cause social conflict, and sacrifice time and comfort if it will all come out well in the end anyway? This argument seems at first to have some psychological and logical strength, but it does not really follow as clearly as it seems. There have been powerful missionary people who still held universalistic doctrine. Perhaps we can illustrate this with an analogy from another realm. Strict Calvinism is characterized by the affirmation that everything is predestined. Arminians say, "This ought to mean that you do not care about life and will not try, because God does everything. What will happen, God has already decided." But it is not the case that Calvinists are lazy. Calvinists have been some of the most energetic people in Western civilization in recent centuries. That God had determined something would happen was the reason they had to get on board and be on God's side when it happened. They did not just sit back and watch God do it. So it is also with missionary concern. If the reason you affirm universalism is really rooted in your understanding of God's goodness and power, then you will be with God in the process of saving the world rather than staying at home and letting God do it alone.

A logical consideration in the other direction is not as self-evident but may be just as strong. Preoccupation with human lostness and constant assumptions that there are two categories of people, and that if you do not immediately accept the message you are destined to perdition, can have a negative effect on the capacity of person to be a Christian proclaimer and missionary. It can make persons compulsive, judgmental, and fearful. Most people responded in faith when Jonathan Edwards told them that if they did not respond in faith, they were already sliding into hell. But they responded to Edwards in that way because in his home culture most people accepted him as a preacher. In a post-Christian society, if you tell people what Edwards told them, somehow it does not have the same effect. Your statement of their lost condition does not communicate grace. It is not the background against which you can proclaim your own confidence. So it has often been that the Christian preoccupation with preaching hell—although very meaningful within the church in revival preaching—has had minimum or negative effect in the effort to communicate beyond the Christian civilization.

I suggest another level of response to the logic of universalism is more helpful. That level takes seriously the particularity of biblical faith. Both of the positions of which we have been speaking reach their conclusions because of a concern to generalize. God must be omnipotent, therefore God is good, therefore God will not be unfair to people, etc. One of the peculiarities of biblical faith against some contemporary philosophies and other religions is its particularity. It starts with Abraham and the Jews. The particularity of Israel and the church is characteristic of the way the Bible works and of the way the God of the Bible always works. We would even have to say if we went through some of the patristic debates that YHWH, the God of the Bible, is not the same as the god of natural theology, or the god everybody finds when they look at the stars. The identification was made in the later history of theology, so we still have to work with it. But one should not assume that when the Bible talks about the LORD God, YHWH, it is at all the same person as the God idea, God as pure mind, or God the prime mover of pagan philosophy. If Israel is particular, then God chose only the Jews for that period. If the church is particular—the new meaning of Israel—then being outside this particular history is also meaningful. If it was God who chose to be particular, then we honor neither God's gracious intent nor omnipotence by arguing strongly that God is not particular after all.

Not only Israel and the church are particular. My history is also particular. What I am as a person is what I have become. I do not become *everything* through what I learn and do not learn, the decisions I make, the places I move, the people with whom I become acquainted, and the things that happen to me. I become only one thing. What I have become is all that I am, the only self I have. And it is characteristic of God's purposes for humanity that God made us that way, that God enables *this* autonomy of the creature.

If I have settled on independence, even on open rebellion, or on self-centeredness, then God will respect that. That is what creation means. Now God's power of God can let creatures be autonomous and can still, without crushing that autonomy, open the door for reconciliation. We call that atonement. But the love of God will not drag you in or force the door open if you are trying to hold it closed. So, if we reckon with the biblical faith's particularity regarding both its high view of human responsibility and its peculiar vision of calling, then the saving intent of God for all is that all should be saved through the witness, service, and growth of the church. It is not that apart from this witness God has another track that works just as well, and in fact, carries more traffic. That would be to deny in principle the particularity of biblical faith.

This leads us to a subpoint of the concern for universalism, which is, so to speak, the other side of it. We did not deal at any length with the themes of wrath and hell, although we did touch the matters in eschatology.[12]

The concept of "wrath" in the Bible is anthropopathic. It speaks of God in terms of human feelings. Yet already the Old Testament moves visibly away from a purely personalistic understanding of YHWH's anger. More and more, wrath is seen as a process, a power, something less personal, more autonomous, and independent of God. Just as in the Proverbs, wisdom, *sophia,* was close to sharing the nature of God and yet independent. So it is with wrath. Wrath takes on a character of its own, and is not simply a trait of God's personality. In fact, it is not personal at all. It is more mechanical, like a process. The New Testament clarifies this even further, and Anthony Hanson spells it out carefully at great length. Here, I attempt only to summarize in unbiblical language.

Wrath and hell are the biblical words for the bindingness of our historicity, to put it in contemporary speculative language. The historicity of human nature is that people are what they become. The decisions I make *make* me what I am. I am not anything other than what I have made myself become. What I have decided is decisive. That is quite different from some other anthropologies—contemporary or ancient. I am neither just one sample of an essence nor an arbitrary and meaningless movement on the face of history. I am what I have been doing and what I have become, how I have grown and what I have decided. If by my decisions I have made myself a selfish person, ultimately committed myself to myself, then I do not fight God; I just do not notice or want God. When God lets me be selfish, leaves me with myself (which is another word for hell), God is not being nasty, judgmental, or vindictive. God is being loving because by respecting the freedom God gave me to bottle myself up, the freedom God lovingly gave creatures. God respects that freedom by not tearing open the shell I have built around myself. The respect God has for the freedom of given creatures gives the creature in its rebellion a degree of autonomy over against God.

We saw that this is the value of the ransom theory of the atonement. Some other things are wrong with it, as we noticed on the way through the atonement discussion, but the one thing not wrong with it offended the philosophical theologians of the Middle Ages. It gave some rights to Satan. The medieval theologians said it would not be respectable for

12. Our treatment here partially summarizes three useful texts: C. S. Lewis's allegory, *The Great Divorce* (New York: Macmillan, 1946); Rachel King's *God's Boycott of Sin: A Consideration of Hell and Pacifism* (New York: Fellowship Publications, 1946) is a debating piece combining discussions of hell and pacifism in a surprising but quite convincing way; and Anthony Tyrrell Hanson's study, *The Wrath of the Lamb* (London: SPCK, 1957), which is exegetical and follows the theme of wrath through the Old Testament and then the New.

God to grant Satan any rights—which the ransom theory did—such that he must be paid in exchange for freedom. But Satan does have rights. They are given him by the loving respect God has for creaturely autonomy—for the capacity of God's creature talk back, rebel, walk away, and get away with it. "Wrath" is the word for this process already at work in human experience and "hell" is the word for its finality.

Perhaps we can already surmise from Hanson's conclusions that wrath is not an attitude of God, the way personalities have attitudes. Nor is it an attribute of God in the classical sense. God is not angry and does not need to be propitiated, vengeful, or vindictive. The wrath of God is not a means of education. It is simply the outworking of the process that ensues when we turn against God. It is part of God's respect for the created process, in which good has good results and evil has evil results. If humanity is in rebellion, we call the suffering that results from the effects of rebellion the curse or law. In faith, this suffering still happens. That is, the way sin bears its fruit also affects people who have come back to faith, but then their suffering is part of the process of redemption. So it is that suffering crosses over to the cross of the Christian. The process, if we suffer it in love, *is* redemption, *is* cross, and that same process, if we suffer it in rebellion, *is* the curse.

The next paragraphs encapsulate Hanson's reading of Revelation. The great difference between the two symbolic animals that dominate the book of Revelation—the lamb and the beast—is that the lamb conquers through suffering while the beast conquers through coercion. An empire that abandons itself to the pursuit of power for its own sake is bound to destroy itself in the end. This self-destructive tendency must have been unmistakably obvious to those who lived through the years of the emperors from Nero's suicide on. John uses the symbol of "wrath" not to vent personal hatred against his persecutors but to express the undoubted truth that power for its own sake brings about its own destruction. I said this earlier regarding personal selfishness. John says it in the form of social selfishness, which amounts to the same thing.

This truth needs to be emphasized today. According to John, God's power is manifest in a second way in the world. Inside the Roman Empire the church suffers persecution. Here also the powers of God's victory are seen. The suffering of the cross is perfected in history by the suffering of the Christian church. The lamb is the symbol of this second manifestation of the power of God, but this power also brought judgment. People were not merely handed over to the power of their sins, enduring the consequences of their own and other's misdeeds to the end. The act of salvation itself brought judgment as well as redemption. The cross made manifest not only the love but also the wrath of God. God was not angry at humanity for crucifying the Son, but those who rejected the love of God manifest in the life, death, and resurrection of Jesus Christ, thereby abandoned themselves to utter self-destruction. God spoke finally in Christ, so those who rejected Christ also rejected God. Wrath is therefore God's seriousness with our negative response to God's offer of love. It begins to work itself out in history as: "If you live hatefully, your life will fall apart." It is more of the same when the bindingness of my life—that I have only one life and when it is finished I will not change—ultimately becomes permanent, and I am stuck with what I have made of myself.

Universalism sees love and grace as God correcting or overruling history after it has happened. A "biblical realist" position sees God as enabling, living, and suffering history. This is another way of saying what we said when we began discussing atonement. The cross is necessary if the doctrine of the atonement is to answer the questions with which it is supposed to help. Whatever the reasons Jesus had to do what he did, they must begin with an understanding of human lostness. Although we have dealt with it already, this may throw light back on the general statement of atonement.

Some views of the atonement see God as annulling history. We were lost, but God stepped in and wiped it off the record, blotted it out. Other views of the atonement that see God as suffering, accepting, enabling and healing history seem to be more biblical.

"He Descended into Hell."

The second general footnote to the atonement theme is a phrase we did not pick up when we went through the Apostles' Creed. Between the cross and the resurrection, in its classical form the creed affirms, "He descended into hell." What does that mean? Remember that we backed up to talk about the virgin birth after we came to the creed, because it was the first time we could deal with it. Here as well, after having talked about atonement, a footnote properly goes back to one of the phrases in the creed we had no basis for dealing with then.

The creed, we saw, grew out of the Roman baptismal formula. In that earlier form, "He descended into hell," was not included. The earliest statement of this idea comes from the second century church in Syria and Persia. It is found in expressions of the faith of individuals—personal creeds we could say—but not in any formal document. The first formal document it is in is the Confession of Sirmium, from 359, between Nicea and Constantinople. During this period Athanasius and Arius still fought back and forth. Many different efforts were made to reconcile, mediate, or in some other way decide the controversy between the Nicenes and the Arians. The Confession of Sirmium somehow bridged the debate. The writer of the Creed of Sirmium was Syrian. He brought the text with him from a church in which the concept was current. It did not really have anything to do with the Nicene debate; that is to say "I believe in Jesus Christ who descended into hell" is neither Trinitarian nor Arian. It was simply a strong statement on which both sides could agree. But what does it mean?

In 359 the phrase read, "And he descended into the underworld." "Underworld" was literally "under earth," *ta katachthonia.* And he "took care of things there." The verb is *oikonomesanta,* or "economize." He put things in order there. It is the same verb the creed used for his earthly ministry. In modern English we would call that "doing his thing." It does not say what he did, but only that he did the appropriate thing. "He descended into the underworld and took care of things there. He whom the gate keepers of Hades saw and shuddered." Now what does it mean?

The answer to this question is not self-evident. We shall detail a number of meanings. The answer you choose depends on the authority of the creed. Those who must believe the creed because they are committed to it as a part of their faith are not free to give a text like this any old meaning. They must give it a meaning they can accept. Therefore, they are not really free to ask what it meant then. Here we are asking what it meant then, independently of what we might mean by it now or whether we want to say it now. Incidentally, this phrase is probably the first rejected by people who do not like the creed anyway. That is interesting, because it really does not seem central to Christology.

- One meaning, probably the earliest, is simply, "He died." The abode of the dead, *sheol,* or "the pit," the empty place down there, is characterized as neither good nor evil. It is simply where the dead are. In Acts 2:27, Peter quotes a Psalm: "But thou didst not leave his soul in *Sheol.*" That just means he did not stay dead. He rose. Death could not kill him. He broke out of the place of the dead, *Sheol.* When it is translated as Hades, it is similarly not morally prejudiced. It is not a bad place to be; it is not a good place to be. It is simply where you are when you are dead. So saying that he descended into Hades after he was crucified meant that he really died. Therefore, when he rose, he rose from the dead. That is all it means. He was really human, and when he died he really went where dead people go, just like everyone. So, "He descended into hell" affirms his humanity and the reality of his death.
- The next meaning to which we turn makes the descent the beginning of his saving work. A current idea was that this was part of Christ's preaching. He preached on earth, then went where the spirits of the dead were and also preached to them. First Peter 3:18–20 seems to say this:

> For Christ also died for sins once for all, the righteous for the unrighteous, that he might bring us to God, being put to death in the flesh but made alive in the spirit; in which he went and preached to the spirits in prison, who formerly did not obey, when God's patience waited in the days of Noah, during the building of the ark, in which a few, that is, eight persons, were saved through water.

Verse 18 is an ancient creed. We do not know whether verse 19, which begins to touch on our subject, is part of that ancient creed or not, but it might be. Did Christ preach to the imprisoned spirits "in the flesh" or "in the spirit"? We cannot tell. The same thought picks up in 4:5–6: "They will give account to him who is ready to judge the living and the dead. For this is why the gospel was preached even to the dead, that though judged in the flesh like men, they might live in the spirit like God." Those dead are sometimes understood to be the Old Testament saints in general. When Lazarus died, he went to the bosom of Abraham. That means Abraham and all the fathers of Israel were there, waiting for Jesus to come and preach the same thing he preached to the living. That is a little hard to fit into 1 Peter. Abraham was a believer. These are people who "did not obey when God's patience waited in the days of Noah." So it seems more narrowly that this passage—which is not necessarily identical with the descent into hell, but is the closest to it in the New Testament—means specifically people from before Noah, from before the covenant, from the very ancient days. Why are these specific people captive and why must Jesus preach specifically to them? You will have to imagine, or use some kind of theological reasoning not in the text.

- A slightly different emphasis is reconcilable with the same text. Instead of simply preaching to these captive spirits, Christ liberated them. First Peter 3:19 says the spirits were in prison. Perhaps the place of the dead is a prison from which he freed them. Ephesians 4:8–10 quotes Psalm 68:18: "When he ascended on high he led a host of captives, and he gave gifts to men."(In saying, "He ascended," what does it mean but that he had also descended into the lower parts of the earth? He who descended is he who also ascended far above all the heavens, that he might fill all things.)

  "Descended into the lower parts of the earth" can mean two things. "Lower parts of the earth" might be a genitive of place. If the earth has higher and lower parts, then the "lower parts of the earth" are under the earth. Then the passage refers to what we are talking about, the descent into hell. However, that is not the only possible meaning. "Of the earth" could be a genitive of apposition. Then he descended into what was low, namely the earth.

The earth was lower than heaven. From there he ascends into heaven, that he might fill all things and give, through the spirit, gifts to humanity. So it is unclear whether Paul is talking about a descent into the underworld or the descent from heaven to earth. In the latter case the host of captives would not be the people from the underworld, it would be us—perhaps raptured. It is also unclear from the passage whether the captives he takes with him are captives whom he liberated or enemies who are now his captives. If we look at Psalm 68, which Paul quotes, it is more likely the latter.

- Another shade of meaning is also reconcilable with the former two, but affirms more. In descending into hell, Christ attacked the citadel of Satan. Matthew 16 says that the gates of hell cannot prevail against the church. Hell is not attacking the church. In the imagery of Matthew 16, the church attacks hell. "Gates" are defensive. Medieval preachers connected this with Psalm 24:7–10:

> Lift up your heads, O gates!
> and be lifted up, O ancient doors!
> that the King of glory may come in.
> Who is the King of glory?
> The LORD, strong and mighty,
> the LORD, mighty in battle!
> Lift up your heads, O gates!
> and be lifted up, O ancient doors!
> that the King of glory may come in.
> Who is this King of glory?
> The LORD of hosts,
> he is the King of glory!

This does not mean that heaven should lift up its head because the ascending Christ is entering. It means hell must open its doors. Hell has been besieged and conquered, and the prince of hell is being crushed. So the image is consonant with the dramatic view of the atonement. Christ attacks Satan's fortress and Satan is crushed. He does not only lose the battle on earth, but his fortress and home is invaded and broken down. The medieval preachers also read this in connection with Isaiah 45:2–3, which was addressed to Cyrus:

> "I will go before you
> and level the mountains,
> I will break in pieces the doors of bronze
> and cut asunder the bars of iron,

> I will give you the treasures of darkness
> and the hoards in secret places."

Then, that meant Cyrus would take over Babylon and seize the royal treasure, but the medieval preachers related it to Christ breaking into the capital of Satan's kingdom and freeing all the slaves.

- The last three meanings all have to do with the beginning of Christ's victory. It is also possible to move in the other direction and understand Christ's descent into hell as the extreme form of his suffering. It is not the beginning of victory, but the end of humiliation and the extent of condescension. We find this especially in Reformed theology. There is even a special title for it—*exinanition.*[13] It is the depth of Christ's humiliation not only that he suffered but that he suffered the torments of the damned. He was punished with our punishment—to put it in terms of the penal form of the satisfaction school of thought. Usually this penalty is seen as paid at the cross, but then it does not include the descent to hell. In this view, however, the penalty is further suffering beyond the cross. Just as the damned are punished after death, so Christ shared that punishment. He took upon himself not only our earthly suffering but also our eternal suffering.

Since our work is descriptive and historical, we do not need to decide which of these meanings is "right." Mennonites do not use the Apostles' Creed very often in church, nor is it clear which of the meanings we should have in mind if and when we did use it. In the new Mennonite hymnal the phrase is retained with a footnote: "Hades: the place of the dead."[14] In any case, the discussion of Christ's descent into hell fruitfully displays how the church in her history extended her affirmation of Christ's victory. It goes beyond saving me or us, to say that he also saved those who died before, that he saves the universe, and that he crushes the fortress of Satan. This is in line with the strand of biblical tradition that talks about others being saved beyond the bounds of the visible church.

Back to the Subjective

Our last subpoint returns to the case for the Abelardian view. We dealt with it rather briefly and critically in our introductory outline. Now we recognize that even though it does not answer all the ques-

13. Editorial note: Exinanition comes from the Latin *exinanitio,* "to empty" or "exhaust."

14. *The Mennonite Hymnal* (Scottdale, Pa.: Herald Press, 1969).

tions, it has something significant to say and properly continues to be used. Let us review its strengths.

The following is a student's statement from an earlier year's work:

> Why the atonement? Humanity can only turn to God, not through our own efforts or initiative, but through the calling of the Holy Spirit. When we experience forgiveness it permits us to accept reconciliation. Our lives are changed. God's Spirit abides in us and gives us strength. Humanity is then a new creation. Why did God have to become a man to make this known? Well, there was not any other way. It was a necessary risk. Why was the death of Christ necessary? It was a necessary risk God had to take. And in being the truth among sinful people, being perfect amid the imperfection, being love amid hate, and especially calling us to repent and setting himself up with God, he had to take the risk that people would kill him because we could not stand him. Theoretically we might say that Christ could have lived and proclaimed God's way until he was 65 and never been killed, because his death by itself was not what accomplished salvation, but rather God's forgiveness and human response.

Jesus had to run the risk of getting killed and it was a serious risk. It was greater than a 50 percent risk, and it did happen. Conceivably, the meaning of forgiveness could have been communicated without the death. Thus forgiveness was not dependent upon the death, only the communication of it was. So this is really another, updated, form of the "moral influence" view. We could add a series of positions, which might be called the psychiatric views, with reference to "psychiatry" not as a profession but to a way of seeing humanity that has been illuminated by recent thinking about mental health. If what is wrong with people is that their souls are sick—something in us, not our status before God, not our place in history is wrong—then you can rephrase atonement in terms of a mental hygiene and wholeness. In Abelard, the need is subjective but the work is objective. That is, I needed to be turned around so I would hear God. It was my need, but the work was objective—Christ died out there. But it is possible to say that the work is also subjective. What happened is within me. Thus even more clearly, the cross "out there" is not indispensable, but just fitting. The homiletics teachers Lewis Sherrill states this well in his book *Guilt and Redemption.*[15] Guilt is a subjective state. It is the result of unbelief. It also causes unbelief, because if I am guilty I will not trust anymore. Its effects are then hostility and broken community. Then Christ comes to me. Or my neighbor comes to me and says, "Look away from yourself. Look away from justifying yourself. Look away from condemning yourself, and love God instead."

15. Richmond: John Knox Press, 1945.

Loving God is not so much something having to do with a God out there whom I love. It means I stop looking at myself. I forget self-justification and self-condemnation (which is another form of self-justification). But in order to do this I must break through myself—my self-concerns, defensiveness, and preoccupation with my own righteousness. *I* am the one who must do it. It must be my decision. This decision will make me righteous by making me stop thinking about my righteousness. But although I must make it myself, I cannot make it by myself. So I need a therapist or counselor. That person, because of his or her love for and understanding of me, gets in my way and communicates to me. He or she listens and becomes important to me. Then my hostility pours itself out on him or her. Now if my counselor fought back, that would prove to me that I should not have trusted him or her in the first place. I should not have been frank. I should not have spoken. I should have stayed closed. Then my guilt would remain my own. But perhaps my counselor does not respond to my hostility with hostility. Then the momentum that broke out in response to him or her getting in my way and intervening in my life will carry me out of myself to a place where I can be free from myself for acceptance and help.

There are other forms in which this could be done. Paul Pruyser, a psychiatrist from the Menninger Clinic, once presented at AMBS a paper arguing that all three of the major views of the atonement can be rephrased in terms of mental health. The satisfaction view says there is something wrong with your super ego—God is the judge. In the Abelardian view there is something wrong with your ego. When the problem is your id, that resonates with the victory theme, the "dramatic" view. Paul Tournier is another popular interpreter in this area.

The question we must address to all these views is whether the death was necessary. Is God a reality or merely a symbol for a problem I have? Does Jesus matter as a person, or is he a symbol for any person who comes to me on whom I can vent my hostility? Certainly there is no systematic reason to say these approaches are unhelpful, but we still have to ask whether they help us beyond the point of appropriation. "Appropriation" is the "making-one's-own" of what one believes.

The message of reconciliation may include many elements that fit in with the psycho-Abelardian tradition, but that the message *came* from there is less clear. The cross of Jesus was marked by several characteristics that do not correspond to the therapist who comes to me, listens to me, and opens me up by being willing to absorb my hostility. For one thing, the cross of Jesus was a social issue. Jesus was labeled the "king of the Jews" when he was killed. Further, Jesus' suffering—indeed, his entire ministry—is unconcerned for meeting people on the terrain of their problems of appropriation. Jesus does not discuss their problems when they ask, "Can I accept that?" In fact, he seems conscious about not dealing with that. In Matthew 19, Jesus describes the demands of marital faithfulness. The disciples said, "If that is what it calls for, who can be married?" Jesus did not say, "Here's the recipe for a successful marriage." He left the question unanswered.

When the rich young ruler turned away, people said, "If that's what you demand, then who can be saved?" Jesus did not say, "Here, let me make it easier on you." He called people to forsake everything. So on the grounds of the ministry of Jesus, which led him to the cross, it seems that if you follow Christ, you do not solve the problem of appropriation. You do not get an answer to your struggle of how you can accept this. You forsake your problem of appropriation rather than solving it. You are not your own anymore. You belong to someone else. So the preoccupation of the subjective view—with whether and how I accept, with what it costs me to accept, or with what it costs someone else to enable me to accept—already agrees to meet lost humanity on the terrain of selfishness instead of calling us away from selfishness.

To say it another way: Jesus was judgmental, as the psychotherapist is not, or at least theoretically is not supposed to be. Jesus got in people's way and told them they were doing wrong. He told them to stop and turn around. He did not tell them they were accepted as they were. He told them they could be accepted, and that God is an accepting God. He said that to be accepted by God also means right now becoming a different person.

One of the statements of this position—probably most popularly displayed by Paul Tournier—says that grace is part of the nature of things. The world is forgiving and society is accepting. But you must learn to see that reality. God is the way. The death of Christ was not needed. It reflects the fact that God is forgiving. The human situation is one of acceptance. But you have to accept your acceptance, or else it will not work. Acceptance was there before you were. It is reality. Now, is this true? Is the world really forgiving? Jesus does not say so. Jesus says that God's forgiving initiative is the opposite of the way the world is. Thus at the most, we can illustrate the subjective view with contemporary mental health thinking. It sounds wholesome and helpful—and is wholesome and helpful—on the level of apologetics and interpretation, but that does not help us to go back and find for ourselves a definition of the atonement that will answer the traditional questions in a satisfactory way.

13

Christ as Prophet: Revelation

Preparation Guide

1. Note the place in the sequence and the relative space given to the topic of revelation in the various sources.
2. How does each author relate Christology and the doctrine of revelation: Does "Word of God" always mean the Bible or does it also have the meanings of John 1 or of prophetic usage?
3. Do the authors say that Jesus Christ is revelation:
   a. As a teacher whose words are authoritative?
   b. As an example whose humanity reveals what God wants?
   c. As an agent of atonement, thereby revealing judgment and grace?
   d. In that the fact of incarnation reveals something about human nature?
   e. Or is the function of revelation so tied to the Bible (or some other channel) as not to be applied to Jesus?
4. Do the authors distinguish between general and special revelation? What can be known outside of special revelation? What are the canons of truth in that realm?
5. If the author affirms *verbal* inspiration and *inerrancy:*
   How does he or she relate this (equate or differentiate) to "dictation" or "mechanical" views?
   What are the arguments for his or her position?
6. If he or she does *not* make the above affirmations:
   a. In what sense *is* Scripture then authoritative?
   b. How does he or she actually *use* Scripture in argument and exposition (elsewhere in the text)?
   c. What authority does it have in his practice of theology?

7. Should we expect the Bible to provide authoritative information in other realms, e.g., of the natural sciences or secular history? If not, why not? Because it cannot thus speak, or because it does not claim to? Are examples discussed?
8. Does "revelation" mean the communication of ideas or information, as distinct from other things God does, or is it a general description of all divine self-disclosure? If your texts differ on this point, is the difference verbal or substantial?
9. Is "revelation" subject to the canons of logic? Why or why not? Is there a place for paradox? In what sense?
10. Does your author argue a basic inadequacy of linguistic ("propositional") communication? If not, does he or she argue its adequacy? Or does he or she not identify this issue? What other approach does are suggested?
11. Does the author deal with "fallibility" (internal contradictions, historical error, myth, miracle stories)? What are the conclusions? If the Bible is considered fallible, by what norm is it to be interpreted?
12. Are the rules of hermeneutics part of the doctrine of Scripture?
13. What is the Bible's authority related to that of Christ? Which do we accept because of the other? Is the actual argument and exposition on the doctrine of Scripture dependent on who Christ was?
14. Is it in the Bible because it is true (e.g., "Love thy neighbor") or is it true because it is in the Bible?
15. What do the following texts: Acts 17:22ff.; Romans 1:18–32, 2:12–16; and Galatians 4:8–9 suggest that humankind in general knows without special revelation? What is known? How is it knowable? Do all know it?

Possible Supplementary Readings

Baillie, John. *The Idea of Revelation in Recent Thought.* 1956.

Beegle, Dewey M. *The Inspiration of Scripture.* 1963.

Brunner, Emil. *Revelation and Reason: The Christian Doctrine of Faith and Knowledge.* 1947.

Engelder, Theodore Edward William. *Scripture Cannot Be Broken: Six Objections to Verbal Inspiration Examined in the Light of Scripture.* 1944.

Henry, Carl F. H., ed. *Revelation and the Bible: Contemporary Evangelical Thought.* 1958.

Niebuhr, H. Richard. *The Meaning of Revelation.* 1941.

Packer, J. I. *God Speaks to Man: Revelation and the Bible.* 1965.

Reid, J. K. S. *The Authority of Scripture: A Study of the Reformation and Post-Reformation Understanding of the Bible.* 1957.

Scott, Ernest Findlay. *The New Testament Idea of Revelation.* 1935.

Warfield, Benjamin Breckinridge. *The Inspiration and Authority of the Bible.* 1948.
———. *Revelation and Inspiration.* 1927.
Wenger, J. C. *God's Word Written: Essays on the Nature of Biblical Revelation, Inspiration, and Authority.* 1966.

We move to the third of the three "offices." We spoke of Christ as king and as priest. In each of these relationships we then followed one subform of the topic. We shall do the same again when we speak of Christ as prophet.

In the Old Testament the prophet's role is in some ways more fundamental or crucial than those of the king and priest. We should not oversimplify the opposition between the various roles in the Old Testament, but there was a degree of tension.

Popular scholarship overdid this contrast rather seriously in the age of theological liberalism and the early days of biblical criticism. The priest, they said, was a cultic expert. He went through meaningless but prescribed rituals—sacrifices, burning incense, and motions. The prophet on the other hand was the one who called for ethical righteousness. The prophet was the religious genius of Israel. This opposition, popular between thirty and eighty years ago in Protestant talk, was not exegetically correct. It is not a truthful picture of ancient Israel. The prophet and the priest belong together in the normal functioning of Israel's life. They had different functions, but those functions were not contradictory—they were complementary. More careful reading has overcome that polarization. There were good prophets and bad prophets. There were good priests and bad priests. There were also good and bad kings, although the king was more frequently bad. The prophet, the priest, and the king were all forms of religious expression borrowed from other peoples, although in borrowing the types, Israel changed the king and priest figures less than they changed the *nabi,* or prophet.

But, after having said that all of the social functions of Israel had some relationship to the outside world—none was uniquely biblical or uniquely revealed—the prophet still has a crucial character:

- First we can say it sociologically. Israel gathered around events that were commemorated. The prophet interpreted the events. The prophet spoke to what was going on in history and said what it meant. The priest interpreted nature. He spoke to what is always the same and what happens again every year. The priest managed the interpretation of the cycles of the stars, crops, and flocks. He dealt with stability—with routine and recurrence. The prophet interpreted events that happened but once. If the prophet discerned a pattern in the events, it was a meaningful and directional pattern. Speaking culturally, descriptively, and sociologically (whether it be considered as particular revelation or not), scholars agree that Israel gathered around the meaning of certain events and looked in the direction the prophet said those events led.

- We could say it as well theologically. The *word of the LORD* had in Hebrew thought a unique objective quality. The prophet is simply a channel for this word. It is spoken through him or her. Often, it is spoken with the prophet's personal involvement. The prophet says something he or she agrees with, believes, understands, and cares about, but sometimes it is said without personal involvement. There are times when the prophet does not know what he or she is saying, or does not know what it means, or does not like it. The prophet can neither call back the word nor guide it. The word is almost personified. It goes out and does its work. It was the word of YHWH spoken through the prophets that made Israel what it was. Israel could have been Israel without its priests. Israel was Israel without kings, before and after the royal period. But Israel, to be Israel, had to have prophets. This function was prescribed and described along with the others in Deuteronomy 18. The judge is also there. The king is described, as is the priestly/levitical function.

  Deuteronomy 18:15–18 reads:

> The LORD your God will raise up for you a prophet like me [i.e., Moses] from your brethren—him you shall heed—just as you desired of the LORD your God at Horeb on the day of the assembly, when you said, "Let me not hear again the voice of the LORD my God, or see this great fire anymore, lest I die." And the LORD said to me, "They have rightly said all that they have spoken. I will raise up for them a prophet like you from among their brethren; and I will put my words in his mouth."

Although the description of the prophet is stated in parallel with the other functions, it is also unique. The prophet is like Moses. This is said twice, both in verse 15 and again in verse 18. It is the only office tied to Moses as its example. Moses was not a priest. He left the priestly functions to Aaron. Moses was not a king. The kingly functions, which he seemed to exercise, should be understood as having been carried at two other places. YHWH was the king, and seventy elders were named (at the suggestion of Moses' father-in-law Jethro) to take over the governmental functions. Prophecy is not only the only office tied to Moses. It is also the only office with a history and a stated time when it first took place. The cultural historian could find prophet figures in other times and places, but this beginning is reported as unique. Moses was called to be the prophetic mediator between God and Israel at the mountain.

That the people wanted a mediator was not grounds for reproach. God does not scold Israel for being afraid of God's presence. The mediator whom God establishes is not a priest, but a prophet. He was established at Sinai to speak to the people so they could hear mediately what they could not bear to hear directly.

So much for Deuteronomy's normative statement of the office of prophet. If we follow Israel's history we find that some of the very last words of the Old Testament as we now have it collected—that is, the last paragraphs of Malachi—talk about a prophet who was to be expected. Earlier Israel expected a new pure high priest or a new David, but one of the expectations was also for a new prophet. Malachi is not necessarily the end of the Old Testament either chronologically or theologically, but it is last in the canon as we now have it. Its last words include "Behold, I will send you Elijah the prophet" (5:5). John's Gospel discusses whether or not John the Baptist was Elijah. In one sense he was not—he said he was not—and in another sense he was—Jesus said he did the work of Elijah.

Elijah and Moses appeared with Jesus in the transfiguration. It is significant that Jesus appeared on the mountaintop with two prophets from the Old Testament. It is not two kings—David and Josiah. It is not two priests—Aaron and Zadok or Melchizedek. Jesus is seen glorified with the prophets.

In what sense was Jesus a prophet? He was a teacher, he communicated, and he spoke truths about God. He was a rabbi. He could be called a rabbi or a prophet in the strict social sense. The emphasis of orthodox Protestant theology usually lies here. The prophet in the Old Testament is the channel for revelation, speaking God's words for God. Jesus is a prophet in the same way. He speaks the words of God. So as teacher—as the one who speaks in his parables about the kingdom and in his Sermon on the Mount about good behavior—Jesus is prophet. Orthodox Protestant theology means that Jesus is the instructor when it speaks about the prophetic office.

More basic in the New Testament is Jesus' function *in himself* as revealer, *as* revelation. Not simply his words, but his person is fundamental. Remember in the New Testament portion of the course that one of the major points where the "New Testament theologians" moved beyond the Jesus story's simple statement was in thinking about how Jesus is revelation. In the beginning of John's Gospel the concept of *Logos* says basically this: Jesus is himself the incarnate communication—incarnate *Logos* or Word. Throughout, John's Gospel refers to manifestation in Jesus, to making open and revealing. 1 John begins with reference to what our eyes have seen and our hands have touched. "He was made manifest," not only in John but also in Hebrews, which begins with a specially concentrated reference Jesus' communicative character, not only through his words as prophet but in his person. "In many and various ways God spoke of old to our fathers by the prophets; but in these last days he has spoken to us by a Son" (1:1). God did not speak merely by the *words* of a Son, but the being and presence of a Son. Thus, Jesus in his person is a new communication, manifestation, and revelation that goes beyond what words can do.

So much for a brief summary of what we already said about Jesus in the New Testament. How do we relate this to traditional discussions of revelation? Your theology texts include sections on the doctrine of revelation. How do they relate to the prophetic office of Jesus, or to Jesus as revealer/revelation? Confirm it in your texts; the doctrine of revelation is usually separate from any treatment of Jesus. In its structure it is usually not dependent upon Jesus—not only is it in a different part of the book, but it is written apart from discussion of Jesus. In fact, in most of your theology texts you will find that revelation is discussed before anything is said about Jesus. It comes earlier because the texts deal first with things that have to be dealt with first, and somehow the authors think one must deal with revelation before getting around to what the Bible says about Jesus.

For that reason we shall also deal with the theme of revelation for its own sake. We shall deal with it apart from Jesus because we are talking about how theology has operated, how Christians have theologized, and what theologians do. They deal with the doctrine of revelation by itself, but notice before we go on to that terrain that the division is questionable.

Let us restate the question in terms of vocabulary. Hebrew has several words for "word" and "to speak." As with all words in Hebrew, the roots are consonants. Basically, three words, *dabar* ("to speak"), *naum* (to declare), and *amar* (to speak), can be used in the sense of revelation. Sometimes they refer to an ecstatic experience in which the prophet is "spoken through." The prophet may even speak of his or her ecstasy—"The word of the LORD came to me and said." Sometimes prophetic utterance was poetic and came in rhyme or rhythm. There is, for instance, an interesting hypothesis about the book of Jeremiah. Some scholars argue that we can tell the difference between Jeremiah's original prophecies and those destroyed by the king, which had to be redictated (Jer. 36:22–32), on the grounds that the originals rhymed or had poetic meter, while the others were rewritten in prose.

The famous skeptic of the American revolution, Thomas Paine, identified poetic form as defining prophetic utterance in the opening pages of his *Age of Reason*. This explains how Saul could be described as temporarily one of the prophets: he was seized by poetic ecstasy (1 Sam. 10:10).

"Prophecy" first refers to the event or prophetic experience, and only secondarily to the words the prophets speak. In the Old Testament the word "word" hardly ever refers to a written text. The best way to paraphrase "word" is *"speaking,"* as in "the speaking of God." Speaking does not happen without words. Neither are we talking about so-called mystical experience, in which one senses things that cannot be said, nor about existentialism, which downgrades the utility of speech. Speaking always uses words in a context of personal communication—not words written down and filed away but words where one person addresses another. So the Word of God, according to the Old Testament, is not fundamentally a text or document. It is fundamentally an act of speaking, usually through a prophet.

In the New Testament, "word" is most clearly used in the beginning of John's Gospel with a normative meaning. We are told, "This is the way to understand 'word.'" It refers to the incarnation—that is, to Jesus as the one in whom God's meaning is made clear. Similarly in Hebrews 1 the incarnation is contrasted to the utterances of the Old Testament. The utterances of the Old Testament were in words, different kinds of speech, diverse manners, and through the prophets, but now God has spoken in the Son, and the Son is God's Word. So, significantly, when "word" is used in the Bible, it does not refer to the Bible. It refers first of all to the speech of God in the Old Testament, and secondly to Jesus as revealer.

Conservative Protestant practice traditionally uses "the Word of God" to refer specifically to the Bible. Sometimes it refers to the Bible as read, sometimes to the Bible as simply sitting there on the table, and sometimes to the Bible as what the theologian understands and interprets very carefully piece by piece. If we accept this use because we are part of a culture in which it is established, we should at least be clear that it is not biblical. The Bible does not call itself the Word of God. It saves that term for two other uses.

This might be the occasion for a "footnote" on the complexity of theological conversation. In the sixteenth century, the appeal to Scripture as the center of the Reformation message was clear and made a new impact. If the Word of God is proclaimed—and this did not mean only the Bible, it meant preaching out of the Bible—then things will change. The reformers' confidence in the preaching of the Word was so great that they did not take responsibility for changing things. They thought things would change by themselves. Martin Luther, for instance, did not deal with whether or not the church should be separate from the state. He preached the Word and assumed the Word would take care of it. The Old Testament prophets said something similar: "YHWH has spoken and his word will do its work."

But since the seventeenth century, Protestants do not mean this. They do not mean a power that comes into society and changes things. "The Word of God" is now the name of a stable system, namely, Protestant theology. It is a system we have put together and properly interpreted. It is past communication, which will not take off again and break out anew. The orthodox Protestants of the seventeenth century did not even notice that this change in meaning had taken place.

Two examples can be cited. I would like to cite them respectfully, but both exemplify the complexity of theological conversation when words—especially the word "word"—have to be dealt with in several different meanings. First, Protestants, especially conservative Protestants, insist that "the Bible is the Word of God," when the Bible itself does not say that, but rather says something different. This displays the complexity of trying to be faithful. Second, often in contemporary discussion of the preaching office's centrality to the church's ministry, the rationale that "the Word is to be proclaimed" is given. Certainly I have no interest in arguing with the statement that the communication of God's message is crucial and central in creating and sustaining the church, but to draw from that the conclusion that there should be one particular preacher in the church is counter to some of what the New Testament says. At the same time that one says the proclamation of the Word should renew the church, Scripture proclaims both that unique priesthood, the central clergy form of religion, has been abolished, and that the church is now filled with many gifts, which are all the working of grace.

That was a parenthesis. We have been speaking of Christ's prophetic office, and we suggest it is the correct place to deal with revelation. But we now turn to a set of discussions on revelation usually carried on elsewhere. For many they are prolegomenal. They need to be said first. Very often revelation is discussed at the beginning of a theology text. How can you talk about theology before you know whether the book you are reading has authority? So you have to discuss revelation and Scripture first.

It is also possible to talk about revelation at the end of the course. We could wait until the end of the course and then survey our work by asking, "How did we use the Bible? How does the Bible function in the life of the church?"

If we continued the historical outline we used in the early part of the course, revelation would come rather late. The nature of revelation or biblical authority, in the debating forms we know today, were not much discussed until the sixteenth century. Then, in the debate between Protestants and Catholics, the issue was, at least from the Protestant side: Will you or will you not accept the Bible's authority as over against other authorities?

The issue changed shape in both the seventeenth and eighteenth centuries. The onslaught of rationalism characterized the eighteenth especially. Then the discussion of revelation differed from the Protestant discussion with Rome. What does it mean to affirm revelation over against the skepticism of rationalistic humanity?

In the nineteenth century philosophical materialism and natural science developed. From those perspectives, still another set of questions was addressed to the Bible, and another set of answers was developed that had not been there before. Later in the nineteenth century critical historical analysis developed and took the text of the Bible apart, as scholars take any text apart. When and to whom was the Bible written? Is it a literary unity? When archaeologists and historians check what the Bible reports, do they find that it measures up to their standards? These questions, too, demanded another set of answers.

In the twentieth century, we find encounters with linguistic and cultural relativism. Each of these is a different battle. Each time, Christian thinking about the Bible as revelation—the vehicle and bearer of revelation—has to start over. All of which is to say that, if we discussed the doctrine of Scripture along a historical outline, it would have had to come quite late in our treatment.

Scripture as Revelation

Scripture as revelation is one of the classical issues of theological debate. It has been debated for a long time (at least since the sixteenth century) and is still largely unresolved. At least, when certain groups reach resolutions, they divide Christians quite deeply.

We discussed the themes of the Trinity and New Testament thought historically and descriptively. We discussed the theme of atonement argumentatively. Here, as in eschatology, our initial treatment will be descriptive and comparative. We shall report on several different ways of dealing with the problem. We shall name persons who represent particular kinds of logic as we go along, but our concern is not to debate individual theologians. Just as we narrowed ourselves from Christ as priest to the atonement and debated that independently, so we move from Christ as prophet to the problem of revelation.

We begin on the ground floor, with the most sweeping assumptions that made by most people most of the time. We shall move from there to see the challenges addressed to that approach. Revelation, on this ground floor, is taken for granted as linguistic communication, communication with words. This way of perceiving revelation was dictated for the church by the Greek philosophical heritage of the first church fathers who began writing on this theme. According to them, the form of revelation is language, statements, and propositions. That form is appropriate because God is preeminently mind. The way mind communicates is through words and language. God is mind and humanity is mind. People of course are many other things, too, but especially at the point mind are they compatible with God. This is what it means to be created in the "divine image." Therefore, communication passes from the mind of God to human minds through language. Of course, a host of assumptions quite at home in Hellenistic thought were entailed:

- God is more mind than anything else.
- Humanity, too, really is mind more than other things.
- The ideal has priority over the real and ideas have priority over things.
- Language and mind are so congenial that words are obviously the way mind expresses itself.

When we read in the Bible, "In the beginning God created the heavens and the earth," this sentence came from the mind of God who first thought it then put it, as a finished thought, into Moses' mind. Of course Moses was not around when God created, so he had to be given this thought. Then Moses wrote it down, and because we can read it, we receive communication in the form of a piece of information from the mind of God a communication. That is revelation.

Such preoccupation with understanding revelation as language has continued to be the most basic line, and yet it has also developed. It has not stayed simply the same. William Hordern, in *A Layman's Guide to Protestant Theology,* says fundamentalism is old-time religion, orthodoxy. This is not quite correct. We can examine the differences between fundamentalism and orthodox Protestantism, as well as the differences between either of those and the orthodox Catholicism that preceded both. There are real differences, but there is also real continuity. The changes are developmental, not breaks. Thus, today fundamentalism most radically and confidently affirms that revelation is God's word moving from God's mind to our minds through the text of Scripture.

Initially this assumption was just that, an assumption. It did not need to be argued. It was self-evident. Nobody doubted it. It was not a polemic position. Not only did it not need to be argued, neither did it have the precision of meaning it has today. There was great liberty in interpretation. Origen, for instance, explicitly made the point that every text of Scripture has at least three meanings. Obviously this provides a great degree of liberty both in deciding which interpretation matters most and in determining what authority each meaning has. The medieval church likewise was not rigorous about the verbal character of revelation, because the *church* was really the teacher. Scripture was useful, Scripture was revelation, but the church had to be present as the interpreting body. This again meant there was room for variety.

On an issue on which the church had not spoken infallibly, several views were possible. All views accorded with Scripture until the church said they do not, and of course, the church very seldom spoke authoritatively on particular exegesis. The teacher is not simply an interpreter of the text, but also an authority beside the text. The church can add to or give alternative interpretations of some things Scripture says. No one orthodox theological system was identified with the text of the Bible as came later to be the case.

The Reformation arose against the idea that the church teaches. The reformers wanted Scripture to be its own interpreter, and so they underlined the clarity of revelation in Scripture. But the Reformation at the same time brought individualism. It was not able to find any one correct convincing way to read the Bible. Thus Protestantism was divided. Everyone agreed that Scripture was revelation. Everyone agreed that Scripture is perspicuous—indeed, in standard Reformation teaching, Scripture is so clear that you do not need to be a scholar to understand it. You do not need the help of the church, the pope, or the fathers. You just read it and know what it means. Even a layman can do this. This was *the* doctrine of the Reformation. Most Protestants still hold to it. But it was not true—it did not work. Each Protestant read the Bible alone and came out differently from everyone else. So the doctrine of perspicuity, although affirmed against Catholicism, was denied in practice. Other authorities had to be brought in. Three of them mattered.

- We begin to find the use of a *canon within the canon.* Remember that the canon was the total body of Scripture recognized as standing in judgment over the church. But in order to understand the Bible well, you need to be guided by a statement that condenses it all. People said that before, but in the Reformation, Martin Luther, for instance, began saying it very clearly. The key to the meaning of the Bible is the canon within the canon. You do not find the key on the fringes of the canon. If it is, as with Luther, the message of justification by faith that is the authoritative key, then in Galatians and Romans it is very clear, in the Gospels it is a little less clear, and in the Epistle of James you do not find it at all. Therefore, James does not really belong.
- The Reformation also began a rapid expansion of the use of creeds. There had been creeds before, but really only three, the Nicene Creed, before it the Apostles', and after it the Athanasian—not nearly as widely used, but much more complicated and dogmatic in form. Only the Nicene and Apostles' creeds had any real authoritative character, but in the Reformation every church had to have its own. Lutheranism has the Augsburg Confession, and England its Thirty-Nine Articles. Every Reformed province had to

have its own: Heidelberg, Switzerland, France, Belgium, Hungary, and Scotland. Many more creeds came to be used in order to tell people what it is that the Bible really says, thus admitting that perspicuity does not really quite work.

- Then of course, on another level, the state is also an authority replacing the church in the interpretation of Scripture, especially when you have to deal with dissenters like the Anabaptists.

This is the logical point to mention two other possible normative orientations, although in historical terms they do not yet appear in the picture of the growth of theology as a discipline.

- There is the special authority of the expert in literary analysis, who uses the special resources of linguistic science to update his or her dictionary as archaeology brings more ancient texts to light, to refine grammatical and semantic skills as the science of linguistics evolves, and to widen the data base for comparison as specialized publications on antique cultures stretch out on the shelves. This scholar claims increasing accuracy, never perfect yet always improving, in approximating the early writer's intent and the early reader's probable understanding. This discipline should properly be pursued in a library context. It should be free of the pressures of later interpretations or needs, including confessional pressure to harmonize the content of one text in the canon with any other.
- There is also the conviction that a process of interpretation that respects the text but goes beyond it should properly take place in the believing community, in the power of the Holy Spirit. This authority is projected by John 14 and 16 and follows the procedural guides of 1 Corinthians 12 and 14.[1] This is quite different from the "teaching authority of the church" in the Catholic sense, because its safeguard is the due process in the congregation rather than the sacramental authority of the bishops.

Including these models on the scale should clarify the character of those attitudes operative in scholastic theology.

Not until the seventeenth and eighteenth centuries, with the development of Protestant scholasticism, was a new Protestant view of

1. Cf. the Anabaptist reference to "the rule of Christ" in John Howard Yoder, "Binding and Loosing," *Concern: A Pamphlet Series for Questions of Christian Renewal,* no. 14 (Feb. 1967), 2–32 and "The Hermeneutics of the Anabaptists," *The Mennonite Quarterly Review* 41 (Oct. 1967), 291–308.

Scripture, which came to be considered orthodox, spelled out. Protestant scholasticism undergirded and theoretically exposited the linguistic character of the Bible as revelation as had never been done before. This included, for instance, discussion of the origin of the Bible as inspired in a distinct revelatory event. Revelation was also taken to include forming the canon and preserving it. Orthodoxy affirmed special miracles like the Holy Spirit's intervention in history to put the lid on the canon, to close the Bible, and preserve the text from error. Thus, in the texts we have there would be no significant errors that obstruct the Bible's revelation. This applied even to the vowel pointings in the Hebrew texts. There could be no text criticism because it is a sacred text. There could be no linguistic criticism because this is the Holy Spirit's language.

By this time the Renaissance had done its work. Greek and Latin had been dug out and were rather well understood. The Greek of the New Testament was quite visibly not the Greek of the classic Greek writers. The explanation is then that this is special Holy Spirit Greek.[2]

Not only were theories about the biblical text spelled out at great length, but we also find a doctrine of knowledge. Such a theory about what it means to know spells out in greater detail how God is mind and how being human is to have mind. The "image of God" means that we have the kind of mind that can receive words from God. We are like God in that respect. So the church in the seventeenth century fixed on one philosophy of knowledge, and allowed the entire understanding of revelation to be dependent on it. This affected in turn the meaning of "faith." Faith for the New Testament and for Luther is the stance of a person in response to the work of God. Faith for Protestant orthodoxy is accepting true doctrine as it comes to you in the true book. The system of doctrine, the confession, and the systematic text that stands behind the confession and interprets it are practically identical to the Bible because they interpret the Bible correctly. If you believe those things and accept those truths, you have the faith that saves.

In the literature easily accessible to us, this view of faith is assumed and applied most clearly by Franz Pieper, a conservative Lutheran theologian. Pieper details the debate between the Lutheran and the Calvinist understandings of the Lord's Supper at length. The Lutheran understanding of the Lord's Supper as consubstantiation fits with the doc-

2. I refer to the inspiration of vowel points, the rejection of text criticism, and the affirmation that this is a special Holy Spirit language not to ridicule the cultural level on which the church of the time was in its biblical studies. It could not very well have been otherwise. Rather, these references demonstrate how novel and how sweeping this interpretation of revelation as language is—revelation as identified totally with the words and the texts, so that these have to be special words, uniquely the Holy Spirit's words and documents.

trine of incarnation. It fits, in other words, with the center of the gospel. Because of the incarnation, because God takes up human flesh, therefore it is appropriate that also in the Lord's Supper this human flesh is again made present to humanity. If you deny the Lutheran doctrine of consubstantiation, as Calvinists do, you by implication deny the incarnation. If you deny the incarnation, you do not believe the truth. And if you do not believe the truth, you cannot be saved. So how can a Calvinist be saved? That this is a problem for Pieper demonstrates that for him that faith that saves is the acceptance of true doctrine.

Pieper solves the problem by a theory of "happy inconsistency," whereby it is possible for a Calvinist to deny the implication for the Lord's Supper of the incarnation and yet still to believe in incarnation. The Calvinist is inconsistent and because of that we can still let him or her in. But the entire debate would fail to make any sense if Pieper did not presuppose that the Christian faith through which God saves us is the acceptance of correct doctrine. Neither Luther nor anyone before him would ever have said that.

In the age of Protestant orthodoxy there is no longer any live debate. The Catholics are not present. Other Protestant groups are not present. Interpreting revelatory texts in systematic theology involves work only within our family, church, tradition, or sect. We take all the texts in the Epistles, the Gospels, and Acts, and put them together in a logical outline instead of a narrative outline. They remain the same statements, so they have the same value and make our systematic theology practically identical with the Word of God. Thus, if you do not believe the theology, you are disobedient.

Fundamentalism moves several more steps in the direction of modernity and responds to several additional challenges:

- The challenge of rationalism says you need to prove the claims you make. Fundamentalism responds: "No, if it is in the book we do not have to prove it." The discussion of proof had not taken quite that form before.
- The natural sciences raised the issue of statements that seemed to be in the field of science. We shall return to a few of those later on. Evolution is a sample of this debate. The scientific disciplines seemed to claim, or at least seemed to enable some people to claim, that the beginning of the world did not happen the way the Bible seems to say.
- The scientific writing of history might dispute what happened at the time of Jesus and John the Baptist.
- Epistemology, represented by Immanuel Kant, arose as a branch of philosophy. In place of simply lining up arguments against each

> other, Kant asked the fundamental question, "How do you know?" Instead of answering each question affirmatively or negatively, Kant asked the larger question, "How do you know what you are talking about? How do you know what your words mean?" After Kant asked the question that way, after the criticisms of rationalism and empiricism, *then* when the fundamentalists say, "The Bible is infallible, it has no error in it," they say much more than their ancestors a few generations earlier had said.

Other elements of the development of modern Western culture as well put new challenges to the concept of linguistic revelation. Again it must redefine itself more precisely, narrowly, and argumentatively, or else move in a different direction.

We may summarize the impact of all this development under Hordern's heading, "the threat to orthodoxy."[3] There were several kinds of threats. L. Harold DeWolf, in his book on "liberal theology," makes what he calls "the case for fallibility."[4] There are many ways to line up these arguments, but we can speak for now of four basic logics:

- The first kind of fallibility in the Bible, this argument says, exists in the form of internal contradiction. In Mark 6:8 Jesus tells his disciples when they go out to preach to take along a stick. In the parallels in Matthew 10 and Luke 9 he tells them not to take along a stick. Yet the context is such that the reports are very clearly dealing with the same event. This case is superficial and innocent, but that kind of question can be multiplied considerably by people with the right mindset. Sometimes when the New Testament quotes an Old Testament text, it does not agree with the Old Testament meaning. The New Testament often interprets the Old Testament in ways that would have seemed strange had you taken the Old Testament text alone. There are other kinds of internal contradictions, and if the Bible contradicts itself within itself, of course, it cannot be infallible.
- The second argument is that the Bible makes statements counter to truth we reliably know by other means. We reliably know certain truths from the natural sciences. The Bible sometimes contradicts them. Again, a superficial case: The New Testament says the mustard seed is the smallest of all seeds. That is not true. You can find other smaller seeds. The Old Testament food regulations

3. William Hordern, *A Layman's Guide to Protestant Theology* (New York: Macmillan, 1955).

4. L. Harold DeWolf, *The Case for Theology in Liberal Perspective* (Philadelphia: Westminster, 1959).

distinguish between edible animals and those that are unclean on the basis of whether or not they have cloven hooves and chew their cud. One of the animals that chews its cud, it says, is the rabbit, or the coney. It obviously does not mean any modern European or North American rabbit, but the animal it does mean can be identified, can be found hopping around in Arabia to this day, and that animal does not chew its cud. It looks as if it did. It moves its mouth in a way that looks like chewing a cud, but it does not ruminate. These are two examples of erroneous descriptive statements.

Some go deeper than this, and are more philosophical. An instance is the genetics of Genesis. In the Genesis story Jacob tended flock for his father-in-law. First, for a period of time, he waited for the chance to marry Rachel, but he was given Leah instead, so he waited some more. During all this period he was tending flocks. He had different kinds of arrangements with his father-in-law as to how his shepherding was to be rewarded. The arrangement was sometimes that the spotted sheep born would be Jacob's and the unspotted ones would belong to Laban. At other times it was the other way around, but it always depended on the particular arrangement the two made at a given time (Genesis 30). Jacob manipulated the breeding process of these sheep by placing poles or boards around the place where the breeding took place. When he used spotted boards it brought about the birth of more spotted lambs (he did this when he wanted more spotted lambs because they were what he would get). When the agreement was the other way around, that he would get the unspotted lambs, then he put up plain boards or poles, and the majority of lambs that resulted from the breeding in that environment were unspotted. Genesis reports this not simply as a theory or a miracle but as the factual and mechanistic working out of the biological assumption, believed by most of humankind, that the nature of the offspring of an animal depends upon the circumstances in which conception took place. This idea can be documented in many times and places. Now we have other bases for knowing what determines whether a lamb is going to be spotted, and we know that it has nothing to do with the circumstances at the time of breeding. The Genesis text does *not* tell us that God did a miracle so that in spite of the circumstances Jacob always had more of the flock coming his way. No, the text clearly tells us that Jacob was a very shrewd man. He manipulated things. He used the laws of genetics in his favor. The trouble is that these are not the laws of genetics. This is a conflict between the Bible and natural science.

There are also conflicts on the level of history and archeology. One sample is the city of Ai, which archeologists tell us was destroyed a good time before Joshua could possibly have destroyed it (Joshua 8).

- Third, DeWolf says that in the Bible are morally unworthy elements. War is approved, as are polygamy and slavery. Jesus himself recognizes these as unworthy, and corrects some of them. The fact that he corrects them is already sufficient demonstration that where they occurred before, and where the Bible said they were all right, it must not have been infallible.
- Fourth, the Bible reports things that could not have happened: miracles, some of the statements about the origin of species, or the origin of the universe cannot have been that way. They contradict strong scientific hypotheses about the past or strong scientific generalizations about the present. Miracles just do not happen. People do not walk on water.

This will serve to summarize the case for fallibility made by someone who sought to make it as pointedly as possible. We must recognize that each of these points calls for argument on a different level. One could argue point by point, issue by issue, taking critically the definitions of some terms and the logic of some of the others.

Fundamentalism does respond point by point to defend infallibility. Where for instance the scientific worldview says, "miracles do not happen," we can say correctly that such a claim begs the question. That is not really going back and reading whether they *did* happen, but rather making a philosophical assumption about the mechanical uniformity of nature. We do not need to be committed to those philosophical assumptions. When DeWolf says that the New Testament shows the Old to be morally unworthy at certain points we can respond that progress, that movement is itself revelation. When he says there are internal contradictions, we can read much more carefully, and we can say that the two do not necessarily contradict each other. We can in other words "harmonize" (we will come back to the meaning of that term). Nevertheless the total impact of this critique is much greater than the sum of its details, because it goes with the grain of our society. The answers we give case by case, the apologetic responses, and the harmonizations we attempt, themselves constitute a concession. The defense tends to grant the validity of at least some of the stances that the critic applies.

What can we do in this situation? Very clearly, the main stream of historical formulation concentrated on the unique propositional authority of a text. The modern reader, at least certain kinds of modern readers, raise this kind of objection.

- One easy response is to say that the Bible is still right and these other sources of knowledge are wrong, or at least incomplete. The scientist, for instance, who thinks that species originate along some evolutionary path, works with an hypothesis that is understandable in his realm but which presupposes the causal continuity of the universe from the beginning. That presupposition is questionable; it is a philosophical, not a scientific, assumption. It is not something scientists can ever prove. Archeologists, who claim to have information that challenges the biblical report, have not finished their job. The point is not to challenge completely their discipline, but to point out that they have not brought in all the facts yet. This is the nature of science anyway. It never has all the facts. Therefore we need not feel any real challenge arising out of the present contradiction between two different kinds of pretended knowledge. Perhaps the dispensationalist writers are the most clear in taking this kind of position.[5] They simply say that if a scientist disagrees with anything the Bible says, we know he or she is wrong although we still respect the discipline as useful in its place.
- A second, less radical, approach looks very carefully at harmonization, and gives studious systematic attention to working out ways of seeing that the contradiction is perhaps not as clear as assumed. This concedes that the other sources of truth, and the other points of comparison, or at least some of them, especially the natural sciences, have some validity in their own. We find this position in various forms in some of the mainstream Protestant text, especially those of the nineteenth century, like Strong and Hodge.[6]
- Another clear position says that what the Bible means is evident. We have no difficulty understanding it, and it is clearly wrong at certain points. At those points we knowingly, consciously, and responsibly use other sources of information. If this position is taken systematically and thoroughly, with attention to its assumptions, it is the theological position classically known as "modernism," although that term had a slightly different meaning in Catholic and Protestant history. In both cases it means elevating another source of authority beside which the Bible, at least on certain subjects, and thereby generally, is of secondary authority.
- Another possibility redefines the meaning of revelation as not located in the verbal content of sentences and a text. Nothing, therefore, is threatened or challenged when the text is challenged. The

5. See Lewis Sperry Chafer, *Systematic Theology* (Dallas: Dallas Seminary Press, 1947).

6. Augustus Hopkins Strong, *Systematic Theology: A Compendium Designed for the Use of Theological Students,* 3 vols. in 1 (Valley Forge, Pa.: Judson, 1907); and Charles Hodge, *Systematic Theology,* 3 vols. (New York: Scribner, 1871–1872).

genuineness of the authority of revelation is not dependent upon the inerrancy of the text. We shall return to that position as the major effort of the speculators and theologians of our century.

- Another form, perhaps a subform of the harmonizing position, says (disagreeing especially with the modernist) that the Bible does not mean what it seems clearly to say when it makes claims you reject on other grounds (such as that species came into being in one hundred and forty-four hours). It does not really say the things with which you disagree. It is not that kind of literature. When the Bible is properly interpreted it does not say the things to which modernity objects. It does not really say that the universe was created in the year 4,004 B.C. It does not pretend to speak to the truths of natural science or even of ancient prehistory. This harmonizing approach still leaves open the question of where the line runs between what the Bible means to say and what it does not, and there tends to be conflict about where that line runs. If, for instance, the Bible does not mean to say, as it seems to, that Jacob took advantage of the laws of genetics in order to increase the size of his flock, and we know that the laws of genetics are not those which were believed in those days, then what is the point of the passage? How do you know which passages make a point and which do not? What is the point of the reference to the resurrection? To the virgin birth? To the judgment of the prophets on David? The harmonizing approach must always keep asking the question of the rules whereby the two sorts of authority interact because it does not clearly place one above the other.

We now give our most careful attention to the redefinitions of revelation that attempt to rise above this conflict rather than taking sides, or rather than accepting it as the last word.

- Strong's position is that the Bible is *infallible with regard to its purpose*. This means simply that the Bible will not fail to do what it means to do. It pretends neither to be a scientific textbook nor even a textbook in world history or prehistory. Errors are possible on the level of subjects not intrinsically linked with the purpose of the Bible. It contains no errors that could be religiously damaging. Perhaps this another form of harmonization. It takes the shape, however, of redefining the meaning of revelation or infallibility. Scripture will not fail to achieve its purpose, which is to communicate a theological message.
- Critics very often label another more current and contemporary position *neo-orthodox*. It seeks to find some way to place Christ above Scripture. Scripture's authority is located in its testimony

to Christ. We thereby have a criterion of understanding when to take with total obedience what it says and when to be free not to take it seriously. How do you know when what it says is about Christ? How do you use this criterion? I called this a contemporary position because it characterizes writers like Emil Brunner. Some even see it in the early writings of Karl Barth. But it is not really modern. It goes back at least to Martin Luther, who said that he would accept in the New Testament what does the work of Christ—*Was Christum treibt.* That text or the understanding of the text that proclaims the message of Christ—namely the message of justification by faith—is authoritative in the Bible. The rest we may take as any old sacred book. It is helpful but not necessarily binding.

We might use the word *resonance* to label this approach. Resonance is the capacity of a string or tube, like an organ pipe, to sort out from among a great number of frequencies the particular frequency for which it is set, thereby losing the other frequencies of vibration while reinforcing the ones it chooses. The wind across the top of an organ pipe creates sounds of many frequencies, but the pipe resounds only to one wavelength, and therefore produces one tone. So the size and shape of the pipe determines which of the vibratory frequencies will be reinforced and heard and which (all the others) will go away as the windiness of the organ pipe. It is something like that in the heart of the believer. You read through the Bible and some things resonate. Some things echo. Some things provoke regular vibration. That is the message of Christ. There are other things that do not produce a response and are not heard. Those are the elements left aside when we sue the criterion of the proclamation of Christ.

Some of these writers even claim that this "resonance logic" is the same thing as what classical Protestant theology called "the testimony of the Holy Spirit." For some writers, the testimony of the Holy Spirit is precisely the confirmation that comes to certain texts, messages, or communication, and is in the experience of hearing Scripture. It is the criterion for how Scripture is authoritative. If reading this Scripture grips you, then it is the Holy Spirit who made it grip you. The Holy Spirit is Christ's instrument in creating resonance, whereby you find what in Scripture is of Christ. Thereby you know it is revelation. It is God speaking. The meaning of the "testimony of the Holy Spirit" has varied over the centuries. In the sixteenth century, Calvin and Luther meant that whenever you read Scripture, the Holy Spirit drives you to accept it as God's Word. The testimony of the Holy Spirit is the element of subjective certainty or believingness with which you read

Scripture. Whenever you read Scripture, its authority is an article of faith: it is not something you feel or measure. It does not distinguish between one text and another. It is simply that when you read the text of Scripture, God tells you in your heart that this is the Word speaking to you.

In the eighteenth century an elaborate theology of revelation in propositional form developed. Then the testimony of the Holy Spirit did not apply to reading particular texts but was what drove you in the first place to the affirmation that the whole Bible is revelation. Whether you read it or not, whether you pay any attention to it or not right now, the Holy Spirit is the source of your ability to make that affirmation. In the twentieth century, the testimony of the Holy Spirit was used by some of the so-called neo-orthodox as a critical tool. As I read through the text, the Holy Spirit of God makes it speak to me. When it does not speak to me I can give the Holy Spirit credit for not impressing that upon me. The Spirit does the selection, and therefore I have no problem with the claim of revelation.

- Another of the redefinitions is especially spelled out in Karl Barth's early dogmatic writings. Fallibility is part of being human. It is not sinful to be fallible, just as it is not sinful to be finite. Not to know everything is simply one condition of humanity. To think one knows something, which later turns out on the basis of better sources of information not to be true, is also human. So when we find in the Bible statements that are incorrect according to the natural sciences or today's scientific reading of history, it is simply part of the fallibility of the Bible as a human book. Since it pleased God to take on humanity in the incarnation, and also in the humanness of the Bible text, there is nothing to be surprised about or to debate. It is normal. How else would you expect God to come to humanity except in truly human form? How else would you expect God to speak to humanity except in truly human words? If God speaks in the language of a given century, that language will include the scientific and chronological assumptions of that century. The Word of God is precisely the miracle that it is within the truly finite that God speaks. So if the Bible were infallible, it would not really be revelation because it would not really be human. God would not have come into our conditions to speak to us, and our view of the Bible would fit the Docetic view of Jesus, according to which he was not really a man either.
- At this point conservative evangelicalism responds by strengthening its position on the other side. It retorts that to be fallible is not simply to be finite. Error must be compared not with being finite but with being sinful. If we use the parallel between Scripture and

Jesus, we must run the parallel in the other direction. Just as Jesus was fully human but nonetheless sinless, so God, when using human words, will use words that are fully human but *inerrant*. Just as in using the humanity of Jesus God enabled his humanity to be without sin, likewise in using the writers of the book God enabled their humanness to be without error. Thus we have formulated a concept of *inscripturation*. The Bible is the body taken on by the Word of God in some way comparable to the first chapter of John's reference to the incarnation. The revelatory message of God became this writing by a specific spiritual miracle, work of the Spirit, inspiration, or breathing in, analogous to the incarnation. Carl Henry and Kenneth Kantzer, the most competent contemporary spokesmen of the strongly conservative evangelical tradition in North America, use the term "inscripturation." It does not occur with the same clarity in European evangelicalism.

- But another line of thought has been used more than any of the above. Sometimes it overlaps with others, but not in such a way as to be indistinguishable. This positions moves farther in the direction of distinguishing the Bible's theme. I reported before from Strong that "the Bible is infallible with regard to its purpose." Purpose is on a different level than scientific issues. This can be said more thoroughly. Probably its best statement for easy accessibility is H. Richard Niebuhr's *The Meaning of Revelation*.[7] The book is old but still a satisfactory statement of the position. It appears in other forms in Paul Tillich and some recent or contemporary Protestant writers.

  Niebuhr distinguishes two levels of meaning in history. He does not bother with scientific and cosmological questions. They do not really matter. But history can be seen in two ways—from within and from without. When you read history from without you do it objectively. You use the tools that guarantee that your personality does not get in the way, that your prejudices will not warp your reading. When you experience history from within, it has *meaning*. But how do you get from without to within? These two levels or stages do not merge into each other, so that you could gradually slide across, or incrementally grow, from one to the other. There are two different total stances. To get from being outside of history to being inside it, one must leap, turn, or change. The word for that change is *metanoia,* the New Testament word usually translated "repentance." It is a changing of mindset. The way one becomes part of history instead of watching it from outside objectively is that a symbol becomes meaningful, a story

7. H. Richard Niebuhr, *The Meaning of Revelation* (New York: Macmillan, 1941).

grasps one, or an image is found illuminating. When this symbol speaks to one, when the image illuminates things, then one perceives history differently, namely from inside with commitment—and that is faith, a new start, a new kind of knowledge.

Notice that this description is not yet a theological statement. It is a general philosophical theory of knowledge, a meditation on how people know. People know in two different ways, from the inside and from the outside. H. Richard Niebuhr states this not as something proven by any theological argumentation, but as self-evident, or as something that you could learn by watching yourself, your neighbor, or your civilization talk about experience. Then as a second step he applies this general theory to the Bible. The Bible as seen from outside is history in the objective sense. It tells the story of the Israelites leaving Egypt. It tells the story of Jesus' death. It tells the story of Paul's travels and preserves his correspondence. You can read that from the outside without making any supernatural assumptions, without making any judgment about what it means. You can read the story of Paul as you can read the stories of Julius Caesar or George Wallace—honestly, factually, checking on the reliability of the sources and doing everything else you do when you function as a historian. You do not have to *care* at all. But Israel in the Old Testament and the church in the New confess this history from the inside. Israel says of the escape from Egypt, "That's when God made us a people." Christians say of the death of Jesus, "That was to reconcile us with God." This leap of faith into faith, which is brought about by the encounter with God, is our *metanoia*. When we meet God and come to see our history differently because of that encounter, then this story becomes revelation.

How can our encounter with God do this? How could something happen to the Israelites so that instead of simply saying, "We got across the Red Sea, didn't we?" they could say, "This work of YHWH defines our people, our identity, and our mission in the world?" How can an encounter with God do this? God cannot be right there, the argument continues, in the open and outward history, where historians could see God working. God does not work in a way that any historian could say that at such-and-such a date, such-and-such a place, YHWH came down and did such-and-such things. That would not be worthy of an infinite God. God would, by definition, not be God if you could trace God that way. If an objective historian could document God's presence, it would not be *God's* presence. Well then, could it be that God would send us a word from heaven? God might send us a holy book written in heaven like the Koran. Or God could send us a prophetic word, like Moses interpreting the Red Sea experience. No. That will not work either. How could you know which words to accept? The words of prophetic interpretation are also outer history—just someone talking. Why did the Israelites listen to Moses? Why did they accept Moses' interpretation of their history? Another answer is "mysticism," but it is no answer either, because it consists in a renunciation of answers.

In order to recognize God as God, so that they could perceive God's work as something they could respond to in their history, they must have known God before. There must have been some knowledge of God prior to this event. That prior knowledge of the nature and purpose of God illuminated the event, making it possible to be drawn into it from the inside instead of looking at it historically from the outside. That means, to use traditional language, that before special events have revelatory meaning there must be general *revelation.* There must be a background understanding of God, "general intimations of *deity* and *duty,*" if we want to use a slogan. "Deity and duty" mean the concepts of a higher power and of oughtness, or moral obligation. These general intimations are present in any culture, but especially in ancient culture, so people know perfectly well what they are saying when they say of an event that "God did it." They mean it was done by that powerful, purposive, and moral will called God. So they knew about God before the event in question happened. They had to so they could credit God for it. The event itself is not revelation; it is an event in history. Revelation is not new information. Rather, it makes the event personal. It makes us perceive the event as for us. It makes us perceive it as grace. It makes us, for instance, perceive God's work at the Red Sea as something God did for us, not we for God. It makes us see obeying God as praise and gratitude, not as something meritorious. This switching of our attitude toward that whole story, not because we know anything new about God but because we have come to see the event as God's work, is revelation.

The examples I have used from Niebuhr are the biblical examples, but his argument is not uniquely biblical. It is a general philosophical theory of knowledge:

a) The idea that you have general intimations of God is not tied to the Bible or the events it reports.
b) The idea that certain events are seen as the work of the God of whom you have intimations is not necessarily limited to the Bible, although, of course, that is where Christians and Jews put it. This is a general statement about possibilities for everyone, or at least for the kinds of people we know about. It shows how

> people in general experience things. It is not tied to Jesus, the church or the Bible. However, it can explain itself very well by using them as examples.
>
> Niebuhr's little volume is probably the most well done, the clearest and simplest statement of this approach. "Revelation" is the general name Christians use about their faith and indirectly also about their Scriptures, but it would be just as fitting were it used by existentialists or Bahai believers, because it is a general possibility for human knowing. It happens when you come to see things in a unity of which you are committedly a part, as contrasted with being objective. So revelation or conversion happens anytime this happens to someone. There is a kind of click, leap, or reorientation. The person is the same. The events are the same. The notion of God is the same, but all of a sudden "it clicks." All of a sudden you are within it and committed to it.
>
> This could also be illustrated by Eric Routley's writing on conversion.[8] Again, he uses general human experience as an example. Routley returns to his own school days when he simply did not understand mathematics. He could learn the operations and play them back. He could do them when necessary, but he was not at home within mathematics as a discipline. It was drudgery. Then all of the sudden, in the middle of a class session, it dawned on him, "This makes sense! This is a distinct way of reasoning! Mathematics is a special way of reasoning that goes from assumptions to conclusions and is able to measure a proof and manipulate ideas in a rigorous way." From then on he was a mathematician. He was converted. This is a general theory of learning. It has nothing uniquely to do with Christianity or any religion. It is just how the human mental process works. You can either objectively watch things go past, noting them, trying to memorize them, or you can make it your own. To "make it your own," to *appropriate,* is another word for the phenomenon of revelation or conversion.

After all this redefinition, let us assume Niebuhr's stance. Let us go back over the other positions to ask what we could say about the authority of a text. In the "Christ-above-Scripture" position, which selects by resonance; in the fallibility/incarnation position, which assumes it is quite appropriate for there to be error; or in the various positions that distinguish between levels of reality, we could say that the Bible documents the history we find meaningful. We can say that it enlightens or perhaps communicates in some sense. We could say the imagery or

8. Erik Routley, *Conversion* (Philadelphia: Muhlenberg, 1960).

symbolism that helps us enter into our history is especially powerful in the Bible, but there is no strict clarity. It is impossible in any of these systems, as far as I can see, to affirm with any kind of clarity, to say to oneself, to let it be said to oneself, or to say to one's brother, sister, or church, "This is something to which we must listen, that we must accept, be guided by, and live by, because it speaks with authority." Each of these positions spells out various ways for *not* affirming that kind of scriptural authority.

We still can respect them. None is like "modernism" in simply setting the text aside. Each is respectful and many of them are spelled out with great personal piety and respect for the church's historical working with Scripture. They are not simply question begging, in that the reader uses his or her own judgment, saying "If there is anything I can buy I will take it as revelation, and anything I can not, I will not." (This, of course, would mean that for that person there is no such thing as revelation.) But there is at least no clear speech whereby the church could be governed, renewed, reprimanded, and informed in a way that rises above regular human possibilities. Now whether that is tragic or part of the conditions under which we must work is a question we must continue to explore. At least this is the fundamental difference between all of these positions and the various earlier orthodoxies.

We move now to another kind of definition, quite different in mood and also existing in several different forms. The positions we have surveyed so far seek to be logical. They are refined, scholarly, and careful. But there are also antilogical or antirational redefinitions, several of which go under the name of *paradox*. Paradox has numerous meanings:

- The first of these, in the sense that very competent and wise people have used it, argues that paradox is "necessary by definition because the truth is just too big" for our words. Paradox points to something that cannot be consistently accepted. The reason what God says is inconsistent, by our measure of consistency, is our measurements are too small. Therefore it is normal and fitting, for a real God speaking to real people, that logically irreconcilable things should need to be said. Therefore, all orthodox discussion about understanding the text well and especially about using consistency as a tool for proper understanding is wrong. Harmonizing the texts when they seem to differ, comparing this text and that text so that you can put them together and make deductions from them—as for instance Hodge does at great length—is wrong because, by definition, "truth," God's truth in our language, will have to be contradictory.

We have to say that sin is inevitable, and yet we also have to say that when you commit sin you voluntarily do something you did not have to do. We have to say at once that faith is God's work, that only God can bring about faith, *and* that you yourself must choose to believe. We saw at the same time that God is sovereign and that God is vulnerable, doing battle for our loyalty. Point by point we could go through the list of paradoxes made necessary by virtue of the incompatibility of the infinite and the finite.[9]

- Another understanding of paradox is clearest in the existentialistic writings of Søren Kierkegaard. "Paradox is necessary because faith is by definition scandal." It is not a systematic paradox in the sense with which we just dealt, where every truth has two dimensions that cannot be put together consistently. No, Kierkegaard reasons very rationally, with great logical consistency, and with almost mathematical argumentative techniques, up to one point, and again up to the same point from the other side. The two arguments do not meet because the incarnation and faith are scandals. You must stop thinking. He uses reason up to the point of its limits to prove its limits. The necessary paradox of the incarnation, that God became a man, comes at the point where you must stop asking, "Is that possible?" Of course it is not. To be God and to be a man are by definition not reconcilable. But you believe it, and you must be brought to the scandal of that paradox if you will ever believe. So you use logic up to its limits but then you break with and break logic, accepting the Word that comes through where our capacity to receive a word is broken.
- Another meaning of paradox comes from the other end and looks at human experience. Humans as such are confused and ignorant animals. Our tools for knowing are so inadequate that "all human experience is ambiguous." As there is some truth to any statement we make, there is also some falsehood in any statement that we make. Paradox is necessary not because of the nature of God's speech but because of modesty about who we are.

These three meanings of paradox are among the antilogical or antirational redefinitions, but there are others that may be compatible with them but use other language:

- The personalistic emphasis, instead of using a logical label like "paradox," does not talk about logic at all. It talks rather about person-to-person relationships, about "encounter." God does not

9. Aulén says this especially clearly in *The Faith of the Christian Church*, as does D. M. Baillie in *God Was in Christ*, one of the modern classics on Christology.

send us written messages; God meets us. We do not read books to find God. We encounter the presence of God. This is a very current pattern of argumentation, especially in circles where the appearance of piety in personalistic language has a certain air of conviction about it. With living people, obviously, words do not comprise the entirety of communication. Persons who know each other well can share communicate extensively without speaking sentences. There are physical gestures. There are meaningful looks. There may be even telepathic communication, ways of responding the same way without saying so. So words are not all of our communication among persons. How will you relate this to God? Jesus encountered certain people in his full humanity, and therefore meant *to them* something more than the words he spoke to them. How shall *we* meet God except through someone's words? Can you communicate much with no words at all? And how about the things we need to understand that you cannot encounter? You can never encounter the exodus again, except through words. How will anybody encounter the second coming before it happens? And yet, we are supposed to talk about it. So this personalism, although it seems impressive at first sight and is pious—is rooted in pietism—does not really provide a systematic alternative. It does not provide a way of saying there is revelation.

- On the margin of these nonrationalistic redefinitions is the emphasis in some recent biblical theology on the uniqueness of the Hebrew mind as over against the Greek or Latin mind. Each language brings with it a certain set of logical assumptions. You do not notice them if you study only one language. Neither do you notice it if you only study another language in the same language family, where words and grammar are more or less equivalent from one language to the other. If you move from one language family to another, you discover changes not only in the alphabet, phonics, and the grammar, but also in logic, in what it means for a word to be meaningful. That does not mean that the other language does not have logic. It means it has another logic. It has its own way of making sense. The Hebrew mind, these people tell us, does not work like the Western Greek or Latin mind, with deductive logic that makes generalizations, proves them, and deduces from them. The Greek mind concentrates on the *general.* The more general a statement is the truer it is. The Hebrew mind concentrates on the unique and the particular; not on an essence but on an event; not on a sentence but on a happening. Because the Bible is a book in the Hebraic mind set (even the New Testament) we have to understand it within Hebraic logic, which does

> not care for propositions but talks about events.[10] This claims that the Bible is not illogical at all, not even paradoxical, because paradox is a Western logical concept about the limits of logic. The Bible is logically Hebraic. That means that truth and falsehood, meaning and meaninglessness, are found on the level of a total event to which words are tributary and necessary, but you do not reason with words alone. You do not chop up propositions to know what the subject and the predicate are, what can be deduced from them, and what they presuppose. Such emphasis on the uniqueness of the Hebrew mind fits into other cultural streams of our time, for instance into existentialism or a new romanticism found everywhere in our culture.

Now what are the effects of this redefinition, especially these antirationalistic redefinitions, on the problem of the doctrine of revelation? First of all, it undercuts orthodoxy, because by the eighteenth century orthodoxy was very clearly a kind of rationalism. It made sweeping and fundamental assumptions about reason as the locus and vehicle of knowledge; about logic and the principle of contradiction (that two contradictory statements cannot both be true); and that God is mind and humanity is mind, so that the preeminent relationship between God and humanity is that the mind of God speaks words to human minds.

So logic is the criterion of belief. You cannot believe the impossible. You will find, for instance in the preface to Hodge, that logic is not only a criterion of belief but also a tool of theology. You can extend revealed truth if you deduce from it logically. That is, you can put two revelatory statements together and derive from them a third that is not in the Bible at all but has the power of revelation because it was rationally deduced from the other two. Logic is that central to the way God works. So, the antilogical thrust of the several "paradox" and "biblical mind set" schools of our time undercuts orthodoxy.

But it also undercuts liberalism, because liberalism is also a rationalism. It is confident in the capacity of human reason to know the truth, whether it is scientific, historical, or philosophical truth. Liberalism trusts not only in reason's capacity to know but even in its ability to save. Education will save the world, if people can only be taught. If what we know can only be generalized, liberalism said, then society will move forward, because moral education and education for democracy are functions of reason. The more you mobilize reason and control people through education, science, and the scientific way of thinking even about religion, the farther we will get, not only towards knowing

10. Something of this emphasis can be found in G. Ernest Wright, *God Who Acts: Biblical Theology as Recital* (London: SCM Press, 1952).

truth but also towards saving society. For the theological liberal, truth that is known through reason is accessible. It is generalized. It is manageable. That is why it is so easy to measure the Bible by "known truth." You do know other truths. That is why the conflict with other reliable sources of knowledge is so evident in DeWolf's "case for fallibility."

As the antirationalistic views undercut both orthodoxy and liberalism, they also confuse the debate. Antirationalism at least hints at a possibility the old debate had not taken into account. And so we find especially in the writings of the 1930s that the fundamentalists called neo-orthodoxy "a more dangerous modernism" because it opposed reason in addition to being against revelation. It challenged both pillars of orthodoxy. Liberalism likewise called neo-orthodoxy "a more dangerous fundamentalism" because it could not stand up to the test of reason and did not make a merit of coherence. It did not stand up and argue, "This is right, that is wrong, and therefore we can draw a conclusion." It talked instead about encounter, paradox, and event. We cannot manage that kind of thing. It is irresponsible. Fundamentalism thinks it is modernism. Liberalism thinks it is fundamentalism.

The antirationalist view thinks liberalism and fundamentalism are twins. They both look for a body of truths that can be grasped rationally, that will be consistent with each other and capable of being stated in general propositions that are always valid, from which you can draw conclusions, which you can propagate, translate, and preach with confidence. Both parties assume that words are clear, that when you say "truth," "love," "meaning," or "history," you know, your listener knows, and anyone else can know what you are talking about. They differ as to the source of this body of truth. They differ therefore as to the content of this body of truth, but their assumption about what you do is the same.

Now whether any part of the antilogical stream has a valid case, or whether you can even talk about *valid cases* once you have rejected rationalism, are questions we shall have to leave for later discussion. But let us at least note that the descriptive point is largely valid. Liberalism and fundamentalism are in a sense siblings. They are both in the rationalistic family. They make common assumptions about the nature, findability, and reliability of truth that are completely at home in the Western rationalistic assumptions of European and North American culture. They both place confidence in language as an adequate vehicle for dealing with our problems.

This is where the debate stands, and we probably say that none of the extremes is completely acceptable. Extreme orthodoxy that places the Bible above any other kind of knowledge dodges all the problems. Harmonization sometimes helps but it means that you accept the problem. Consistent liberalism, including several of the redefinition strategies, winds up having no revelation, but only uses the word "revelation" for one's own best judgment. Consistent antirationalism has no clear content. We have mostly mixtures of these three extremes, none of which in itself is possible. Does that mean than an even mixture would be about right? Or can we find some other way through the problem?

Allow me to restate the shift from the Reformation to modernity. In the sixteenth century the debate about the authority of the Bible was a debate against other Christians. They worshipped the same God and they agreed to the centrality of the incarnation in the first century. Scholastic Protestantism and Counter-Reformation Roman Catholicism disagreed about the normative claims of Scripture as relative to the total church tradition. Were there or were there not complementary paths to Jesus and thereby to the God revealed normatively in Jesus?

Beginning with the eighteenth century, on the other hand, the debates are with doubt as such and with competitive truth claims that arise in the name of reason or philosophy. Whereas (a) in the sixteenth century the notion of "word" was within a totally Christian culture, or at least was thought to be, (b) in the seventeenth century, to be "logical" pointed to a rationality independent of the church. Then with (c) Enlightenment and (d) the claims of the natural sciences in the nineteenth century, rationality is (e) philosophically opposed to the church and the Bible. There is continuity between scholastic Protestantism in the sixteenth century and the evangelical orthodoxy of Carl F. H. Henry, but there is a shift in adversaries. Because the Enlightenment (c above) and the antireligious rationalism of the nineteenth century (e above) both looked back at the rationalism of the orthodoxy of the seventeenth century (b above) critically, Henry sees modern claims as antirational. He is supported and enabled in this by the nonrational arguments to which we referred above under the headings "existentialism" and/or "neo-orthodoxy." He thereby fails to see he is arguing against a rationalism very similar to his own.

Here we are skirting the edge of a modern dictionary problem, namely, that the word "evangelical" has more than one shade of meaning, and may in particular contexts have meanings precisely contradictory. On the one hand, "evangelical" is the preferred modern equivalent of "Protestant scholastic orthodoxy," with its central focus on the propositional clarity and authority of the biblical text as communicating something roughly equivalent in content to the basic truths of Protestant systematic theology.

On the other hand, "evangelical," from its other histories of use, means a focus on the personal experience of conversion or renewal of commitment through sanctification. There the primary accent is on the experience of the heart. Doctrinal orthodoxy is presupposed but is considered insufficient, and in fact the accent upon its insufficiency is part of the necessary message for renewal. So modern evangelicalism carries in its midst the old orthodox/pietist debate about whether a theologian must be born again. Mennonites, thanks to our lack of acuity, have been drawn into both kinds of evangelicalism without being aware of their differences.

Can we move past the place where the description of the debate left us? On the one hand, consistent orthodoxy brought unchanged up to the present is obscurantist. It cannot afford to face certain questions, or it can try to meet certain questions by harmonizing and reinterpretation. But it thereby accepts the problem, which already undercuts its axioms. The other side of the gamut is consistent liberalism. It says that in this area, as everywhere else, we should use our own best insight. This, of course, means putting general revelation above special revelation, which means no revelation in the strong sense of the term. It means that every person's best insight in the ongoing process is the best help he has. This may be an intelligent human position to take, but it does away with the concept of revelation in any meaningful sense.

In another direction, we identified several forms of antirationalism, or ways to challenge the propriety of the problem. Of course, they do not have any content, or at least give us no reason to make one particular affirmation instead of a different affirmation.

Most of the writers in your reading mix these elements in various proportions. How satisfactory the mixture seems to any particular writer will depend more on his or her cultural setting than on the clarification of axioms.

Changing Questions

Beyond this debate is another that may throw light on the one we have been watching. The twentieth century saw a revolution in philosophy and culture that changes the question we have been trying to answer. In the eighteenth and nineteenth centuries, philosophy (speaking now not simply of an academic discipline talking about complicated things, but also of the entire intellectual interpretation of the culture by its own thinkers) moved from ontology to epistemology. It moved from asking, "What is? What is ultimate, what is real?" to asking, "How do you know what you think is? What are your grounds for thinking what you say is real?" The symbol and important agent of this revolution was Immanuel Kant. He asked with more rigor than ever before, "How do you think you know?" That question created a revolution in the self-understanding of Western thought.

But recently another move has come, this time from epistemology to semantics. Instead of asking, "How do you know what you claim to know?" now the question is, "What do you mean when you say what you think you know?" If you do not know what you mean, there is no point in asking whether it is real. So the analytical questioning process moves each time one step deeper. In philosophy as a professional discipline the move goes beyond empiricism and positivism to logical analysis, which is the extreme form of concentration on the question of meaning. "What is a meaningful sentence? What makes you think a sentence is meaningful?" In the professional philosophical field, these inquiries become so specialized that philosophers never get around to the next questions of how we know it or whether it is true.

Working linguistics is becoming increasingly important from several perspectives in our culture. This arises partly from the communication industries, partly from diplomacy and international business, and partly from Bible translation. A major chunk of working linguistics developed out of Bible translators' concerns. One of the primary figures in the process was Eugene Nida of the American Bible Society. From this work some new understanding of the place of language in human existence has developed.

Until recently, linguistics concerned the genealogy of language. They called it "philology." Philologists were concerned to map a family tree of languages. How did German, Dutch, English, and Scandinavian all descend from some prior cultural Germanic language? How did language evolve from Latin to French, Spanish, Italian, and Romanian? What are the laws of transformation whereby a later language derives from an earlier language? Can you turn these laws backwards, so that you can reason back past medieval Germanic to "original Aryan" and figure out what it has in common with Sanskrit?

Today the concern is morphological; it asks, "What is the *form* of language? How does language structure itself? How are the structures of Hebrew, Chinese, central South American tribal languages, and the European written languages alike, and how are they different?"

The effect of this all has been a new kind of relativism. Affirmatively, linguistic relativism means that *each language is true,* meaningful, proper, and adequate in its society and culture. Negatively, *no language has meaning in itself.* Language is only and always the expression of a certain group of people who use it this way. If another group of people used the same words and structures in other ways, it would be a different language. Negatively again, *no language is correct,* right, better, or perfect when compared to any other. You cannot even say about languages in general that one is "simpler" or "more evolved" than others. It used to be assumed, before people studied them, that the languages of so-called primitive peoples were primitive languages, that is, that they were made up of barely articulated grunts and squeals. As translators reduced the interpretation of those tribal languages to a science, they discovered that many of them are more complex than the languages of Western cultures. Partly this is because the process of writing a language simplifies certain points. That is why English is so simple. It does not mean that it is easy to learn, but it does mean that many refinements in other languages (like gender, case, and more clarity of mood and tense) have been dropped.

What does this have to do with our subject? Most philosophies (again in the wider sense and not simply an academic discipline) work with great confidence in reason and words because they are monolingual. Plato's confidence that the ultimate reality is the idea in the mind of God is only conceivable if you think there is one and only one word for every idea. But if you are a linguistic relativist, then what is in the mind of God? Which language does God speak? So it is understandable that people in other ages who made much of the linguistic concept of truth assumed God had one preferred language. The rabbis thought God really thinks (from all eternity) in Hebrew. Muslims think God thinks in Arabic. Some of the Indian sages made the same assumptions about Sanskrit. You can only think that ideas are ultimate reality, and you can only assume a linguistically centered process of how God deals with humanity, if you place confidence in your own language as the only language in which truth needs to be handled. At least you can only think ideas are ultimate if the translation problems with which you deal are matters of simple equivalence, like moving from Hebrew to Aramaic or from Greek to Latin. In those cases most of the alphabet, syntactical structures, cases, tenses, and even many of the roots are the same. But if you move among different language worlds, the rational/propositional view of how God communicates must be sweepingly changed.

With these questions in mind, let us now return to the propositional understanding of revelation. We want to take it seriously and see what questions arise from it when we view it from the perspective of the relativity of language. Our procedure is thus similar to how we inquired into the satisfaction theory of the atonement. We were aware of its limitations, yet it was still the most serious theory available. Therefore we started with it and then asked what light could be thrown on the problem by recognizing the shortcomings we observed when taking it seriously. We did not simply argue against it as not in tune with the modern mood. What are the problems involved in any linguistic communication, now that we are more conscious of the problems of language than Augustine was?

The Question of Speaker[11]

The identity of the speaker is part of any communication. You have to know who is speaking before you can be sure what the words mean.

11. These questions come in no necessary order, but there are a number of distinct questions we have to put.

This could be demonstrated by problems like listening to the middle of a radio program or beginning a book in its middle. The meaning of a set of words depends on who says them. The identity of the speaker is part of what he or she says. But then, if we talk about God speaking in sentences, we have to know something about God. This is knowledge of who God is before God speaks. So in general revelation or "natural theology," interestingly enough, both conservative and liberal theologians do the same thing, though in different ways. They both assume a prior process of reasoning from "nature" or "reason" to know something about the God who speaks in sentences, so that when God speaks, they can identify the speech as from God rather than someone else. Nature "out there," the created world, or nature "in here," human nature, "reason," or "history" are the various locations of general revelation whereby we can know something about God. Natural theology is usually thought to prove that God exists, is good and powerful, and that we stand toward God in a relationship of obligation and guilt. In some theologies this knowledge is based on the "divine image" that links us to God and permits us to say about God things that we say about ourselves. For example, "I think and I am in God's image, therefore God thinks."

Take note! This prior information about God is not propositional revelation. We had to have it before God spoke. It may be propositional in that we get it from a teacher, or in that somebody else said it before I thought of it, but it cannot be called propositional *revelation*. It is not received through God speaking in sentences. It derives from the human mind looking at physical nature, human nature, or the nature of history. So behind propositional revelation, *even* for the fundamentalist, a nonpropositional assumption is made. The prior knowledge of the God who later in the logical process will talk to us in sentences is not propositional, specifically biblical, or even specifically Christian. It rather comes from the rootage of this whole realm of thought in the theology of nature, which Christians took on when they went into the Greek world. It depends on human influence.

"General revelation" is revelation only in a secondary sense. It is human insight. We claim it is true, and therefore we call it "revelation." That is, we claim that the things from which we infer God's existence were put there by God, and so we call what we learn from them revelation. But we are the ones making the inferences and thus the meaning. When you look at the universe you can say, "It is orderly. There must be a mind behind it. Let us call that mind 'God.'" You can call perceiving an orderly world "revelation," but you call it that, God does not. God has not spoken yet, or at least you have not yet identified God as a speaker. So "general revelation" depends on human inference. Yet according to the biblical witness, human inference is usually wrong. Human minds, taken alone before revelation, are not trustworthy, according to the Bible. The technical phrase often used for this is "the noetic effect of the fall," the effect of sin on knowing. The normal effect of the fall, according to most theologies, is that the human capacity to know truth is warped by sinfulness. If that is the case, how can we infer apart from revelation the identity of the God from whom we shall receive revelation as propositions? Karl Barth and Cornelius van Til both make this point.

There is a further problem in the same area. When we use the label "revelation" for the prophetic words of a Hebrew prophet, or for the texts written by the authors of the Old and New Testaments, we refer to a person speaking or writing thoughts or experiences that usually are his own. What does it mean for a single communication to have two sources? What does it mean to say at the same time, "This is Isaiah writing" *and* "This is God speaking?" To say, "This is Paul writing" *and* "This is God speaking?"

Are both statements meaningful? Verifiable? Falsifiable? Could you do without one? Could you say, "It is not really Paul, or not really Isaiah?" Some people do say that. But can you honestly say it? Does the text tell you to say that? If, on the other hand, it is really Isaiah, then what does it mean to say it is God speaking?

Some react to these considerations by saying, "Don't ask the question about who this God is who speaks. You must start with the reality of revelation. Just make a leap of faith, accept revelation as revelation, and work from there. Recognize it as a leap you can't reason yourself into, but neither can you reason yourself out of it, and you certainly cannot reason without it. So you might as well make that leap and do theology under the assumption that there is revelation."

In recent Protestant theology, Karl Barth represented this position. He did not explain how you become a Christian or why one works in the field of theology. You assume that is the business of the theologian. It is not his or her business to ask what right he or she has to be there. That also is a gift of God. It is the prior context of the believing community that decided that, so you go on doing theology without asking how you got there. If someone from outside asks how you got there, you can invite him or her to make the leap with you. If you were born and find yourself at home in the Christian context, you are not even necessarily aware of having made a great leap yourself, but anybody else is welcome to do so.

The very same debate occurs in the more traditional Protestant form. The conservative Reformed spokesmen of this same problem in recent North American theology are Cornelius van Til and Gordon Clark. Clark argues that we must merge Christian theology and rationalism, demonstrating the reasonableness of belief in God as revelation. Van Til says in a conservative context the same thing Barth says: that the only grounds for accepting Scripture as revelation is that Scripture says it is revelation. You do not ask any other questions. You cannot. They would not have answers. Both of these forms entail a frank admission that the reasoning is circular, and therefore either back away from the question of truth at a certain point or require some kind of subjectivism. "That is true for me, but I can't really tell you whether it is true for you."

This whole problem of asking, "Who is the God who speaks? How will you accredit God?" was a problem neither in the Middle Ages nor in the age of Origen. In those contexts there was no missionary pluralism, no awareness of where the unbelieving world was. Those thinkers had Christianized the world in which they thought. There was no live polytheism. There was no live unbelief. The only non-Christians were the Jews, who had the same God, or the historically remembered philosophers, whose monotheism had been "baptized." So there was no problem for anyone in equating the God of the Bible with the pure ideal divine mind of Platonism. In those contexts the question, "Who is the speaker?" that underlies any linguistic communication, cannot be answered. Now that it is a question, we cannot simply carry over the thought pattern that had been self-evident.

Of course, if we moved beyond the linguistic analysis of text and proposition to other dimensions of the contemporary mind, this problem would become still more complex. Psychology tells us that when we hear sentences and speech, there might not be a speaker. It may be the unconscious, the self, or society. There are many more questions to ask. We shall not delve into them here, but they would complicate matters still further.

The "Dictionary" Question

What does a work mean by way of pointing to something real? Linguistic communication is meaningful only if there is an objective reference common to both parties. The speaker and the listener or the reader and the writer both need to refer to the same thing with the same label, whatever it is. If there are different definitions, then the words communicate misunderstanding.

We have already run into this as an agenda item in theology. What does it mean to say God is holy? Recently, "holiness" has been interpreted in a sense of moral purity, so one can derive all kinds of things from God's moral purity. But that is not what the Hebrew stem קדש *(qdš)* originally meant. It meant separate, distant, set apart.

We saw that the atonement debate is strongly influenced by how one defines God's "justice." What does justice mean? Does it mean the same thing in biblical as in Roman judicial thought? If one assumes so,

Anselm might be right, but we would probably have to say that "justice" in the Bible and in Roman judicial thought do not mean the same thing.

What does it mean that God is "Father?" It depends on what your father was like. Jesus did not say that God *is* Father; he said you could call God *"Abba,"* which is quite different. *Abba* is not the normal word for father; it is the intimate term of a child who trusts his or her father. It is different than the father of Freud or of Oedipus, for instance. What does it mean that Jesus is Messiah? We know something of the trouble that made. Some people thought it meant a certain kind of king. Jesus said, "No, it means another kind of king." We also drew up a chart of the various meanings of words used for Trinity language.

Not only is there the fundamental question of the need for a common dictionary if there is to be true communication. There are also special differences in the missionary concern, which is the church's business, when you take words to places where the objective referent is not. What does it mean in a tropical country to read Isaiah saying, "Though your sins be as scarlet I will make them as white as snow?" How white does a tropical person think snow is? Any translation will have to be more than a translation. You can go into the science of how it is that snow is white, but unless the person from the tropics is in a physics laboratory with a strong refrigerator, that will not be meaningful. What does manna mean?

The Bible's words themselves change even within the Bible at times. If you have a good Hebrew dictionary you will observe that from one stratum of biblical literature to another, as it grew over more than a thousand years, the meanings of words changed considerably, as is the case with any living language.

At this point the advocates of the doctrine of propositional revelation are not at a loss. It is possible to make refinements. It is possible to work out in greater detail how any given word has different meanings in different times and places, while still insisting on the perfect clarity and reliability of the statements made with those words. It must, however, be admitted that such refinement and recognition of complexity makes using the linguistic assumptions of the fundamentalist view much more difficult and much less secure. In regular practice, therefore, theological conservatives are reluctant to recognize the flexibility and development of language. One example of this is the widespread reliance upon the concordance and "word study" approaches to theology, in which one assumes that the way a word is used in one situation will likely throw much light on how it is used somewhere else.

For our present purposes, it is sufficient to have noted firmly that the objective reference of the terms used in the text *cannot* be part of the text and therefore cannot be the *object* of special revelation. The meaning of the text we call revelatory is thus dependent on a "dictionary" that is not revealed.

We have observed along the way that some of the points we need to make are best made when a particular theological development caricatures them. We saw this as we observed Franz Pieper's trouble with whether Calvinists can be saved. At this present point an excellent example is the "law of first usage," an instrument of hermeneutics. According to this "law," since it is obvious that a word always has the same meaning through the Bible, the Holy Spirit has clarified the meaning for us by placing its first usage in a context where the meaning is clear. Therefore you need only start at the top of the list in a concordance to know whether special terms like "blood," "leaven," "righteousness," or "kingdom" have a certain shade of meaning. This special rule had particular currency in some side streams of American evangelicalism, including certain Mennonite Bible teachers.

The "Hermeneutic" Question

After the "speaker" question and the "dictionary" question, we move to the "hermeneutic" question, in the narrow sense of that term. Here we deal with the criteria of literary interpretation. A statement's meaning differs greatly depending on the kind of literature in which it is found. Poetry is interpreted in one way, parable in another, allegory in another, historical narrative still differently. We cannot agree on what a text means until we agree about the style and intent of the author and first readers. So first of all, literary interpretation demands definition of the type of text we are dealing with. How to interpret certain passages of Romans varies depending on how we balance the notion that it is a theological treatise on the one hand with that of a letter to Christians at Rome on the other. How we read the book of Revelation depends on how we believe a description of a vision is meant to be understood: with the precision of history written ahead of time or with the variety and uncertainty characteristic of dreams.

Another element of the hermeneutic question has to do with handling contradictions that arise in the text between the text and other ideas held to be true or with assumptions that underlie our understanding of our world. As we have seen, there are various ways to resolve such contradictions. Now we note that rules about how to handle such issues are partly constitutive of a text's "meaning."

The need for hermeneutic principles applies to all languages. It applies to mathematics, law, and cryptography, as well as literature. But the more open the story we try to interpret, the more and difficult the hermeneutic problem. The hermeneutics you need to do mathematics are those of a closed system. A mathematician says ahead of time what his or her assumptions are. He or she adds new stated assumptions as needed to keep the system coherent. The hermeneutics of cryptography or law are likewise self-enclosed. When we read an epistle from a growing missionary movement or the vision of the prophet on Patmos, we have none of the same clarity. In the absence of common understandings, we all interpret the text clearly, but we all also interpret the text differently. If we are not aware of the fundamental importance of the hermeneutic problem, then we assume, as fundamentalism does, that when the other person sees differently what the text clearly says, he or she does not really believe. Thus the more naive one is about the hermeneutic problem, the more rapidly one moves to accusing other readers who see texts differently of evil purposes.

In this respect the tradition of the sixteenth century does us little good. It was assumed, in a Europe dominated by one cultural language, and in which the popular languages were all in the Aryan family, that there are no deep problems of interpretation. So the only question was whether you believe. The beginnings of the Reformation tended to encourage this idea. Some of the Catholics were willing to say they did not give final authority to the Bible alone because it belonged to the church. Thus both parties in the beginning Reformation seemed to say that the Bible was clear, but they still debated whether to give it absolute authority.

This assumption, however, was completely incapable of dealing with the divisions within the Reformation. Therefore, Luther had ultimately to say that Zwingli and the Anabaptists did not truly believe the Bible, and the same accusation was projected in every other direction as well.

The standard Reformation statement of this issue is technically referred to by the label “perspicuity.” Perspicuity affirms that the text of the Bible is clear to the honest reader without need for expert mediation. This is a faith affirmation to which we may have occasion to return, but its immediate impact divided Protestantism six ways, convincing each party that the others were intentionally disobedient.

Within this hermeneutic question, which we might also refer to as the question of “grammar,” we not only have to ask what kind of literature our text is and how it relates to the situation in which it was written, we also have to ask what the keys to open up its meaning are. A body of literature is not simply a level plateau. It always has some texts and some themes that are more central than others. We must not only ask what every sentence taken by itself means. We must also ask how the argument proceeds, which statements are most basic, and which are derivative. The search for a key has led Eastern Orthodox Christianity to emphasize the vision of the writings of John. It led conservative Protestantism to emphasize the message of Galatians. It led Pentecostals to focus on the concept of gifts and Wesley on holiness. In each case the biblical interpreter claims not only that this emphasis is found in the text but that it is more central than other emphases.

The Question of the Canon

After the speaker, dictionary, and hermeneutic questions, we still have to ask how to determine which the texts have the authority we call revelation. This is a question of history: Who are the apostles and prophets? It is a question of literature: Which are the texts that can be recognized as the writings of said apostles and prophets? Behind these is the critical question: In which forms and versions do we have most nearly the original expression of the intent of the writers? All these questions taken together may be called the question of the "canon." It has to do with the several levels of problem involved in determining what the text in which we say God speaks is. Answering this question is also essential for the entire concept of propositional revelation. Any answer to the question of what constitutes the canon will use a combination of common sense and historical research. We find within the Bible a few cross references in which the New Testament refers to Old Testament books. More rarely a New Testament writer refers to other New Testament texts or writers. But all of these are too rare to permit us to say that revelation tells us what is in the canon. Yet if the canon is to be determined by common sense and historical investigation, we are once more basing revelation on something that is not revelation.

Usually people with a strongly propositional view of revelation assume that the Bible they have in their hands is the authoritative canon, yet Luther excluded the book of James and the Apocrypha, which were bound in the Bibles of his time. The same church that progressively gradually settled upon the present list of authoritative writings also introduced conceptions of the Mass and the authority of the pope that the conservative propositionalist Protestants reject.

The Question of Audience

After the questions of speaker, grammar, dictionary, and the canon, we still must ask, if we believe in trustworthy linguistic communication, to whom the words were directed. A sentence's meaning does not depend only on who said it and when but also on who is being spoken to. Is revelatory language directed to believers, or does it have the same meaning and the same authority for nonbelievers? If the authority lies in the words themselves, could a clear thinking pagan come up with the same interpretation of the text, or must the reader be a believer?

At this point seventeenth-century Protestant scholastic orthodoxy was radically consistent with the linguistic view. It said that to be a competent Christian theologian you did not need to be a believing Christian. The work of the theologian is a purely linguistic job. Over against this position, pietism renewed certain Reformation emphases and said that the proper disposition of the reader's heart is indispensable to interpreting the Scripture.

Recent conservative Protestant theology has worked with this question by careful distinctions of level between authority, inspiration, hermeneutics, and appropriation. Appropriation means making the text one's own, and obviously depends upon the faith of the believer, but the other levels of objective meaning are not jeopardized by whether the revelation is appropriated or not. We could debate further whether this distinction answers the problem or simply relabels it. In what sense is revelation revelation if the reader rejects it or if it fails to reach and touch him or her? This would take us back to H. Richard Niebuhr's theme.

If we added to the picture particular evangelical perspectives, we would need to insist that the congregation is also part of the interpretative process. The one who listens and reads must not be a lonely believer but rather a member of a body in which each participates in the interpretation process. Likewise we would need to emphasize not simply the believer's open mind but also his or her predisposition to obey: "If anyone desires to obey he will know what the teaching is" (John 7:17).[12] The more fully one seeks to bear the insights of evangelical Protestantism, the less one is able to affirm the solidity and the sufficiency of the text "out there" as an adequate bearer of revelatory authority.

Where does this analysis leave us? Previously we observed how confidence in the linguistic vision of revelation had been dissolved from the outside by the attacks of rationalism, empiricism, the scientific worldview, and more recently from romanticism and existentialism. Now, however, we have seen internal grounds for limiting our confidence in the linguistic approach that arise from taking it seriously. If we look back at the high point of scholastic Protestant orthodoxy and its view of Scripture, it was clearly dependent on a very optimistic view of all the questions we have identified. The dictionary was no problem because Protestant orthodoxy grew from a narrow band of cultural history. The canon was no problem because within the realm of their debate there was no alternative view. They had stopped talking with the Catholics who had a larger canon. The problem of hermeneutics was not difficult because they combined the doctrine of perspicuity with a rigid ap-

12. Editorial note: Yoder's paraphrase is rather loose. The RSV of John 7:17 reads, "If any man's will is to do his will, he shall know whether the teaching is from God or whether I am speaking on my own authority." The NIV reads, "If anyone chooses to do God's will, he will find out whether my teaching comes from God or whether I speak on my own." The NRSV reads similarly: "Anyone who resolves to do the will of God will know whether the teaching is from God or whether I am speaking on my own."

proach to the grammar of their own modern languages and of Latin. The question of the speaker's identity was no problem at all since the Middle Ages had already merged the God of the Bible with the god of philosophy, and there were no others around. The nonverbal dimensions of appropriation and obedience were not important because it was not the business of theology to do church discipline.

Thus in the age of Protestant scholasticism, the whole picture in the field of religion was settled. No new material was needed or conceivable. All that needed to be done was further to refine all kinds of details and translate from there. The practical meaning of the doctrine of infallibility was that every believer had absolutely solid footing for his or her life, faith, and witness. The theologian is simply technically equipped to read that basic text honestly and competently, but the awareness of language's relativity that our age cannot avoid questions all of this. Can we move beyond the restatement of the problem to a renewed affirmation?[13]

Contemporary linguistic insight makes it clear that there is no such thing as an adequate dictionary. Language has meaning only in the culture of its origin. This raises one set of problems for a dead language that is difficult to resurrect because no one speaks it anymore. It creates another set of problems for a living and therefore changing language, so that the people who use it today do not use it in the same way it was used earlier. We observed the impact dictionary shifts have on words like "holy" and "just." No one word means exactly the same thing to two people; no two words are exactly equivalent in the same language or in translation. In addition to this, we must recognize that much communication is not equal to the sum of the dictionary meanings of words. People who do not mean to be poetic or allegorical still communicate very clearly in "slang" or colloquial phrasing, in which opposite terms mean the same thing or the same term means various things. The best samples are taken from nontheological mid-American, mid-twentieth century use:

> If a young man says to a young lady, "When I look at you time stands still," this does not mean the same thing as telling her that her face would stop a clock.

> In the colloquial language of a generation ago the phrase, "What's going on?" the phrase "What's coming off?" and the phrase "What's cooking?"

13. In the following remarks I repeat some illustrations and phrasings presented by the linguist Eugene Nida in lectures at AMBS, as well as similar statements written by him in the *Gordon Review* for December 1957. Nida does not add anything radical to what we have already described, but he does pull it together around the missionary's communication commitment.

all had exactly the same meaning. Yet going and coming are opposites, on and off are opposites, and cooking has nothing to do with either.

We could, of course, sober up and reduce all of these phrases to, "What's happening?" We could think we had solved the problem by distinguishing between colloquial or figurative and literal language. But that reduction is too simple, because the people who say, "What's going on?" have reasons for not asking, "What's happening?" The difference between the two is part of the communication. So if you boil down the total meaning of the communication, which includes the choice of nonliteral expressions, to the liberal equivalent, you deny or sacrifice precisely the point of the communication in its context.[14] But if we recognize that the choice of a nonliteral expression is itself meaningful, we have admitted that there is no one right dictionary.

Likewise it should take very little argument to convince us that there is no one correct grammar. This has been demonstrated by the breakdown of the doctrine of perspicuity, the frequency of heresy accusations, and the introduction of the doctrine of appropriation to explain how revelation is dependent upon the stance of the listener.

If the basic assumptions of confidence in language have been swept aside, what can we do next? I suggest that we should stop asking the timeless philosophical question, "How can we have perfect knowledge that would free us from our finitude?" We should rather put the question from the other end and ask how God has chosen to use our human weakness, including the weakness of our linguistic and literary tools, for God's purposes.

If we go back to the discipline of working linguistics, "we find that within the philosophical inadequacy of language as a tool there still remains the historic usefulness and indispensability of language as a tool."[15] Nida says that effective, essential or roughly adequate communication is always possible. When he says that effective or adequate communication is always possible through translation, he is not promising that every shade of meaning and every connotation can be rendered in one simple text in the second language. Rather, he claims only that the basic point made in any statement can adequately be communicated in another language. Yet the way to attain this is not by paying increasingly closer attention to the text alone but by learning to know more and more

14. This is most dramatically visible in the use of language our culture tends to call "profane." The word "profane" is a peculiar adjective for what it describes, since most of the language to which it refers is actually theological. Yet it is theological language used with a nontheological meaning. The very reason it is used, the fact that the person who uses feels it to be useful, lies in the contradiction between its real theological meaning and the impiety of using it.

15. Again quoting from an old lecture of Eugene Nida.

about the communicative contexts in which particular statements function in both languages. This repeats what we observed at other points: language is a function of a culture and community. There is no such thing as language in the mind of God or in a timeless text.

This definition of effective communication could be broken down into several elements. Most basic of them is a community. A language is used by a given group of people among whom it is meaningful. The community exists and its members talk with each other prior to the formation of the community's canonical literature.

Before the formation of literature, that community has common knowledge; all of its members are used to meeting together. They have a fund of memories and convictions in common. Therefore the major function of their literature cannot be to communicate information in the most rudimentary sense of making people aware of things they did not know before. Its function cannot be to reveal what is already known. The function of literature is rather to correct, document, catechize, and record.

Here we have to come to grips with the basic warp in most doctrines of revelation. They approach the problem of textual authority with *tabula rasa* assumptions, as if communication came into a vacuum from a source of truce. This was not the case in the first century when the New Testament was written. Neither was it the case in the sixteenth century when Scripture brought about church renewal. Nor is it the case now. We already have an immeasurable bulk of words about God. We do not need Scripture to give us information, but to correct, clarify, and help us to catechize within what we already know.

If communication is a function of the community, then the interpretation of that communication must also be a communal process. This makes central (in Anabaptist thought, for instance) a fringe concern in magisterial Protestantism. There must be a believing, obeying, and worshipping community if the meaning of a text is to be properly understood.

We already observed that the concept of infallible propositions presupposes an infallible hermeneutic. At this point J. C. Wenger's presentation is strong and nearly unique among systematic theology texts, although he does not underline the fact. Wenger treats hermeneutics as part of the doctrine of Scripture, rightly and logically.

Faithful reading of Scripture will not simply repeat what was said a century ago, but will always involve shifts in meaning. New challenges will come at the church. In responding to them from the base of the canon the church will constantly develop a new inner focus. There is no one correct "canon within the canon," but there is a thread through the text in the face of every specific question to which we seek to let the text speak. Therefore our faithfulness in reading Scripture will have to be measured not by the stability of our interpretation but by its integrity, flexibility, and the ability to speak to every new question from the same documentary base. The integrity of the believing community consists precisely in its historical movement. A faithful church is not a solid social body but a pilgrim people making choices as they move along. The question, "Where are we going?" is a deeper question than, "What did we say?"

The relationship between the Old Testament and the New is a primary specimen of this problem. At this point the Anabaptists took a clear position over against every other authority of their time. They saw the unity of the Bible in the shape of its forward movement from Old Testament to New, from promise to fulfillment, while their adversaries made of the Bible a flat book of which every part was equally final and authoritative.

This is not only a point of Anabaptist originality over against the magisterial Reformation; it is another point where J. C. Wenger is clear and original over against other systematic theology texts. Some biblical theology texts deal with the movement from Old Testament to New, but it is hardly found anywhere in systematic theology. The biblical theology texts deal with it as an issue, but even they do not generally apply it to the question of a doctrine of revelation. The most conservative orthodox Protestants in fact deny in principle that there can have been any movement from Old Testament to New, since the concept of inspired Scripture as they understand it must reject that.

But if there is movement from the Old Testament to the New, it will also be natural that we expect to find smaller movements of the same kind within each of the Testaments and between the New Testament and the present. We test our conformity to Scripture therefore not by asking whether we keep saying the same thing without change, but rather by asking a more difficult question: Is the way we keep moving in conformity with the way God's people were led to move in formative times?

Try Again to Conclude

After having walked along the mainstream of Western debate about the Bible, we might ask whether it would have been possible to construct an alternative approach that never would have stumbled over those conflicts. Or might it very well be that an alternative approach would have met them anyway, if only in another form? At least sketchily we may now try to construct a different way to say that Jesus is the Word.

Looking back over the total legacy of Scripture, we find a literature produced out of a distinctive narrative. From Abraham through Moses through the prophets, through the scribes *(sopherim)*, through Jesus, Pentecost, and mission to the crystallization of the canon, the story came first. There were real events before they were talked about. Then the community reflected in words on an event, which ultimately produced a written text. The ongoing life of the community continued to remember the same events and was led by the Spirit through additional events that also needed to be interpreted and which, once interpreted, were also worthy of remembering. The life of the early communities, we have repeatedly said, was marked by flexibility, pluralism, and even eclecticism. Over against the earlier custom of writing the history of Christian thought as a single track from Jesus to the present, the contemporary literature leans in the other direction, with the accent upon the great diversity.[16]

Is everything in this diversity true? Is everything anyone says acceptable? If so, then Jesus is not the Word after all. The name "Jesus" has simply become a cipher, a code symbol, for the idea that people claim some warrant from beyond themselves to think or believe whatever they please.

One can simply remember Jesus as the cultural hero or religious figure of one's *own* background, but the challenge of having some definition or other is even greater if and when he is proclaimed to others who had not heard about him with the pretension that he is also "good news" and true for them. The challenge is greater when we proclaim that he will be their judge and should be their Lord. The phenomenon of mission makes the challenge of authority qualitatively more complex and demanding.

Similarly the phenomenon of ongoing historical seriousness makes it more demanding. If the Jesus movement were just one more kind of Gnosticism, teaching people secrets about how things really are beneath the surface, it would be much less demanding than when the claims are made that his righteousness is operative in human affairs, that the ongoing struggle for humanization and justice is his concern, that salvation interlocks with ordinary human history, and that all of this will be brought to a triumphal end by God's ratification and culmination of what began in Jesus.

All of these dimensions escalate the complexity of the truth question and make simple tolerant pluralism impossible as an answer. We notice that those particular theological schools most comfortable with an easy pluralism are also those that have abandoned some of the traits just mentioned: mission, social justice, and the hope of ultimate victory.

If you were the Holy Spirit in the second century, what would you have done with this problem? I suggest you might well have done what actually happened. You would have planted in the minds of many Christians the awareness that if Jesus were to continue to be their Word, there must be some discipline of all the ways people appeal to him. Many call him Lord but do not do what he says. Many people talk

16. Note in the bibliography the works of Bauer, Robinson and Koester, and Wilken.

about heaven but will not go there. Beneath the affirmative confessions on the level of language there must be criteria of substance that are of the same nature as what they measure. If we measure faithfulness to the memory of Jesus, then we need a measurement that connects to Jesus and not merely to contemporary conviction, fulfillment, or institutional verification. With all of the joy and certainty related to ongoing revelations, visions, meditative disciplines, and other kinds of fun input, you would think—if you were shepherding the church through the second century—that the most reliable point of orientation is the oldest writings testifying to the first generation of the life of the church. That thought would not be dependent for you (as it is for modern fundamentalists) on the ability to prove that this literature was in some other sense unique or "inspired." It would suffice that it be ancient and validated by authenticity of authorship.

From the second century on, the function of "Scripture" becomes a necessary part of the church's faithfulness. Moving forward will always include a reference backward. We want to be sure that the Christ we look forward to tomorrow is the same as the Christ of yesterday.

That process of going on with Scripture behind us while trusting in the future presence of the Spirit could have gone on forever. In a sense it is still going on. It, however, was radically interfered with and replaced in the medieval period, as far as most Christians were concerned, with a completely different structure. Our present understanding and concern is not to know just how and when that happened. Nor are we concerned to know whether it was an immediate flip into apostasy, a gradual shift to a new orientation, whether the church was more to blame for it than the state, or whether it could have been absolutely avoided. We simply record that we all came out of the Middle Ages with an utterly different way of handling this problem.

After the Middle Ages, the theologian does theology. The theologian is accredited by three kinds of people: another theologian with whom he went to school, a bishop who certifies his relationships to the institution, and a prince who makes the whole thing legal and pays for it. The theologian continues the process of looking both backward and forward, yet he looks back over such an enormous bulk of material as to change the quality of the operation. The theologian has been taught to believe that next to the Bible is all the tradition of the church, which is of roughly the same quality as the Bible and at certain points is indispensable in order to know what the Bible means. Behind tradition are human wisdom and insight, which have been taken in by the church as the necessary presuppositions and clarifications of the biblical message. This is especially the case since Constantine, but already began with Origen and Tertullian. In this large synthesis, Scripture is less and less important. The phenomenon of "establishment," the axiom of the unity of all wisdom, the sociological axiom that all the people in Christendom belong, the institutional assumption that the theologian is preeminently a scholar living with a guild, and the special authority of the bishop as controller make of the total system an enormously reassuring instrument. The Bible stands behind it all ratifying it, but is helpless to resist it or talk back to it.

The Protestant Reformation meant to change all of that, but chose a particular way to do it. It maintained the sociology of establishment and the professional theologian. It retained the unity of Christendom and the validity of secular wisdom with regard to many kinds of truths, but then it claimed the Bible is above all of them instead of at their root. The bishop was relativized, but the theologian was retained. The notion of Scripture as a receptacle of inspired sentences, rather than the witness to a story, was not changed. The Reformation challenged the adequacy of the concept of "reason" as guide to truth when it saw the use Catholicism made of the ancient philosophers, but the Reformation also retained considerable rootage in the philosophical disciplines of the university, as well as considerable confidence in natural reason as a way to know (for instance) how to organize a family, an economy or a government. What would the earlier commitment to Scripture as judge have contributed to that question?

14

Conclusions Concerning the Discipline of Theology

We have narrated how theology actually functioned in the history of the church, now we will summarize and evaluate.

We begin by recognizing that some specific challenges have been addressed to the discipline of theology. This has especially been the case with systematics, the particular form of theology that measures consistency and evaluates coherence and completeness in the construction of systems.

- G. E. Wright argues that the biblical mode of thought itself is unsystematic.[1] It is rather narrative or recitative. We would do better if we spoke the same kind of language and used the same intellectual linguistic forms instead of thinking systematically. Being logical and systematic in that sense does violence to the nature of biblical thought. Traditional Western systematic theology is a product of the Middle Ages and later periods when Christians had compromised with the Hellenistic world, with its concentration on verbal truth, debate, and deductive reasoning. It polarized the personal versus the rigid. That is not how the Bible deals with truth. People who develop systems are defensive, conservative, and closed to movement. We need more flexible ways of speaking.
- Another challenge comes from more contemporary modes of thought and doubt that ask whether the word "God" means anything and answer that at least in modern culture perhaps it does

1. G. Ernest Wright, *God Who Acts: Biblical Theology as Recital.*

not. The "death of God" has been knocked about in recent religious journalism and has several different meanings. One of them is simply that the word "God" does not point to anything. If there is no reality, then of course all theological language, and not simply systematics, is challenged.

- A relativistic argument says the traditional search for "the truth," the one right answer, is itself culturally naive, immature, or representative of a bygone age. Why do you think there must be one right answer? Perhaps there is no right answer. Perhaps every answer is right. Or perhaps each answer is correct, but only in its place.

If we had the time we should look at each of these challenges and try to respond in a fitting way. The short answer for now will have to be inductive. If you examine the convictions of the people who direct these challenges to systematic theology as a discipline, you find that they also think systematically.[2] The theologians of the death of God try to be coherent. They theologize. They ask questions of consistency and completeness. So after having challenged the possibility of the discipline, they continue to do the same thing. Perhaps they do it with different subject matter, conclusions, or axioms, but the process of theologizing cannot be avoided by saying you do not believe in it, unless you cease to communicate responsibly at all. This does not mean that those challenges are not worth examining one by one more closely than we can here.

Two passages from 2 Timothy can express another slogan for the problem with which we are coming to grips:

> Follow the pattern of the sound words which you have heard from me, in the faith and love which are in Christ Jesus; guard the truth that has been entrusted to you by the Holy Spirit who dwells within us [or among us] (1:13–14).

"Guard the truth that has been entrusted to you by the Holy Spirit" is the same as "follow the pattern of sound words which you have heard from me." One chapter later, after having quoted a verse saying about the faithfulness of Christ, the same author writes:

> Remind them of this, and charge them before the Lord to avoid disputing about words, which does no good, but only ruins the hearers (2:14).

2. This with the possible exception of William Hamilton who only thinks one paragraph at a time and says it is wrong to connect that paragraph to the next one or to the one that went before.

In sum: follow the pattern of sound words but avoid disputing about words. That tension in polarity of instruction defines the job about which we are talking.

Any heresy, schism, or disorder in the church imposes a new set of words. It either says that the words normally used must be given new meaning, or else it says that a new set of words is correct, and we should stop using the old ones. These instructions to Timothy say there is a way of being concerned about continuity with sound words and at the same time not disputing about words. How can you test words without disputing about them? That is the problem with which we must continue to struggle.

Earlier in discussing the New Testament we observed one notion of testing words. Words are to be tested by whether they coincide with Christ. In 1 John 4 they are to be tested by whether they fit with the affirmation of the incarnation. In 1 Corinthians 12 they are tested by whether they fit with the affirmation that "Jesus Christ is Lord." Later we watched the canon develop, which means simply that the apostolic writings as a whole became the point of orientation, but continued to measure words by the incarnation and the affirmation of Christ's lordship. The canon is comprised of the original documents the church used to continue to test what is said, as the church moves into a new age, faces new problems, finds new answers, and wants to know which answers are right.

The more the church is missionary, the more frontiers the church crosses. The more time passes, the greater the need for testing the words we use by their relationship to the original confession. This testing is first of all a process. It is not first of all a body of knowledge or set of truths that once stated will sit fallow. It is a procedure that continues to go back to the source and test again when new questions arise and new answers have been proposed.

In the New Testament, teaching and testing were defined functions necessary in the church. The New Testament church did not assume that the truth was all in the teachings of Jesus or in the teachings about Jesus. It is assumed that truth will continue to come and that new revelations, new workings of the Spirit, will continue. They are expected of the prophets in Acts. They are still expected in the prophets of the post-canonical *Didache.* They are expected in 1 Corinthians 14 as a normal function of the church's life, but they must be tested. No one thought the truth was all settled.

As the church continues to meet new challenges, speak new languages, and enter new cultures in the leading of the Holy Spirit, she always makes new statements she claims are true, but then they have to be tested. They are tested by their link to the core message, the Jesus story. Then they are tested by their relationship to the wider body of primitive traditions, like the Gospels. Then they can begin to be tested by the way the New Testament church read the Old Testament, looking behind itself to find its face there. Then we begin to be able to test them by the coherent systematic thought of three great theologians of the New Testament. The church moved on from there, but this process of testing established the canonical body of statements to which we can go back as point of reference.

There is not only a set of statements, there is also an office. The New Testament specifically refers to the office of teacher, the *didaskalos*. This is not the same as the "apostle," "prophet," or "pastor/bishop" in a local congregation, although it is a function that may be carried at the same time as that of "pastor." The narrative portion of Acts 13 refers to this office, as do the lists of offices of the church in 1 Corinthians 12, Ephesians 4, and James 3, which says that we should hope not to have too many in this is one office because it is especially dangerous. Teaching is a definable function. It is the one function in the church the New Testament says is worthy of financial support (1 Tim. 5:17–18). It is worthy of "double honor," although in a broader sense any itinerant ministry like "apostle" and "prophet" is also worthy of support according to Paul's argument. It is the only office called dangerous (James 3:1). It may overlap with the functions of apostles and elders, but it remains distinguishable. The three terms, shepherd, overseer, and elder, seem to be different terms for practically the same function of local congregational leadership. The teaching function is different. We shall not try to relate this to later historical development except to note that occasionally in the Calvinist Reformation and among Anabaptists the distinction between the teaching office and the overseer was again made.

Why was this role needed in the early church, and why is something like it needed anywhere in the church? It is not needed for the church to be able to speak theologically. Anything the church speaks is always theological. The church has liturgy, prayer, praise, hymns, and preaching, which without any kind of reflection or organization is always theology. The church has an order, a way of dealing with baptism and understanding it, a way of dealing with the communion service and other such celebrative functions of the gathered community. It has a way of dealing with right and wrong behavior. Without reflecting, there is already implicit theology in all of the life of the church, but if we are to be able to test this for its faithfulness, then we must reflect upon it.

Two kinds of reflection—or two functions with the process of reflection—are needed:

- One is expressed in the catechetical life of the church: teaching new believers what it is that Christians know. This can be done in many different ways, and not only in the particular kind of document known as a catechism. It began with an effort to know what is sufficient for a Christian to know in order to be baptized. Then it could be expanded in various ways into concern for what is central, necessary, complete, and/or sufficient. How much must the Christian know to be a faithful Christian? How much at another level must the Christian know to be a teacher? So the process of passing on the tradition is first.

- The second process tests the tradition for coherence. There will be heresies. There were already heresies in the New Testament experience. Some of the statements Christians will make will turn out to be inadmissible. Not everything anyone says the Holy Spirit told him or her to say is right. How then shall we test it? There must be a process that tests for coherence and contradiction.

The *didaskalos* in the New Testament church did those two things. He or she was informed of the body of tradition in such a way as to pass it on to the next generation. He or she was also qualified to interpret it for consistency and contradiction, so as to be able to say what has been condemned as wrong and what must be affirmed as right.

With the passage of time, with the developing complexity and memory of the tradition, reflective theology became more complex. The test for coherence, which began as an effort to identify the heretic, went farther. It came to building systems of thought. One comes to the discovery of certain basic assumptions and presuppositions, upon which the rest will follow. But if you make those assumptions poorly, it will be hard to get back in step. Dogma, that is, specific statements on which a large part of the church agrees, also develops, as we saw in the historical part of the course. So the Nicene statement of Trinitarian doctrine or the Calcedonian statement of the hypostatic union becomes *dogma*, a position from which most of the church can reason with a sense of consistency. There are also theories or interpretations of doctrine that are less precise or normative than dogma, such as Anselm's explanation of the cross. Likewise the catechetical concern of the early teacher developed into many subdivisions, such as philosophical encounters with the present ethos, apologetic adaptations that meet people where they stand, and many others to which we shall return.

Because this theological process developed over the passage of time, we should not be startled or feel off base when we deal with changing ideas through time. For some it is a shock to discover that systematic theology does not deal only with Bible verses, but also with thoughts that developed in the fourth or sixteenth century. Some of our ideas are very late, even though uncritical thinking and unreflective theology identify them with the Bible. We had to notice this about all the contemporary atonement theories, the best of which are at least a thousand years younger than the church. We could see it as well in much of the contemporary debate about the Bible. Considering the nature of the Bible's authority debatable, as well as placing revelation in contrast to other sources of truth, are modern positions that could not have been held before the seventeenth or eighteenth century. Neither is it surprising, nor should it be upsetting or startling, to see that theology continues to work through time with the restatement of problems, instead of thinking that we always go back all the way and only to the beginning to be sufficiently guided by the texts we find there.

We need the process because there is movement in time, and this is why it should be done only (as in the New Testament) in the context of the congregation and of charisma. When the New Testament said the *didaskalos* should do the theologizing for the church, it did not mean that anyone or everyone could be a teacher—only those who are called to it. James warned us there should not be many. Teaching should be done in the context of the congregation, thus it is not a profession a person can learn and then exercise alone in his or her office. It is a ministry within the church. This is not always remembered.

Perhaps we can now visualize some of the difference this makes with a view to interpreting the process character of theology. Some see the theological process as boxes along a chain. An Old Testament prophet or historian makes a statement. As you draw the boxes they should grow because the deposit of canonical texts gets bigger as time goes along. Then you have the right theology in the first century, then you have correct theology in the second century, and you go on to the fifteenth. In each period is a package that is the same as the package before with some translation and updating. Once the canon is complete, the packages remain basically the same. We bring these boxes down to the present with minimal change. As far as possible at each of these points one box is equal to the one that went before except for translation.

But it seems more realistic to think not of boxes on a chain but of a stream. Within this historical stream communicators repeatedly surface—a prophet, an Old Testament historian, or then Jesus himself or the New Testament writers. This theological communicator looks back at the stream that went before and funnels it into the present to which he or she speaks, then he or she makes a statement. The statement has a ripple effect that affects the entire stream downcurrent. There will be small communicators and big ones—those who grouped the whole history of the people and those who speak on a smaller scale. Then comes the point where Christ himself makes the difference between two ages, deciding on one view of Jewish history. In the stream as it goes on from him are the apostolic communicators. At a certain point the apostolic age ends, and then there are other communicators down to the present. In each case a writer looks back, receives, focuses, and communicates, and the communication spreads out and has a certain effect on the later stream. In this exercise *we* are watching the whole stream, trying to know where the banks and main channels are, how you can get out of the stream completely, and where the center of the stream runs. It is more difficult to find security on this model than in the "boxes," but it is more representative of the experience of the church.

These mounting levels of complexity and completeness begin with the New Testament teacher who first simply catechizes and tests for heresy. He or she soon develops a body of axioms and dogma. Perhaps we could make a fuller list now of the degrees or levels of complexity and completeness in the theological process that will happen with the passage of time in any community. It happens in the early church and the early generations after the early church. It happens again in Protestantism. It happens again in Mennonitism. It happens again in each major new movement. There is first of all a kernel proclamation. In the New Testament this was the Jesus story. Then there is a kernel catechism—what a new believer needs to know. And some of the New Testament writings permit the scholar to dig out what must have been the minimum teaching a new believer learned in addition to having heard the Jesus story. Then a body of apologetics develops, asking how you speak to the nonbeliever, whether it means accepting his or her starting point, remaining with your own, or using some of both. We observe this in Paul's teaching at Lystra and at Athens. Then polemics developed, speaking to the wrong-believer, the person who claims to be within the community but stands in such a position that he or she cannot be accepted as correct. Then there is the development of dogma, a fixed point.

These are milestones along the history of the church that you can go back to and use as points of reference. Then the effort to select out of the mass of history some of its main affirmations, not thinking of this as a catechism but as a guide to learning develops. In the Middle Ages they called these "sentences," but we can find similar movements in each Christian tradition. Instead of copying and reading all the original writings, the medieval scholar read books of sentences where, for instance, the main things that Augustine thought were pulled out of his writings and collected in a *Reader's Digest* approach to the history of theology. Then the peak of systematic theology, the *summa,* developed ("*summa*" means total). One writer would try to say everything that needed to be said. Every possible question and every possible answer finds its place somewhere in the outline.

"Systematic theology" is an English label. It is not used in French or German. There one tends to speak of "dogmatics," which means more precisely the study of fixed points in the history of the church. But in the broad sense, systematic theology includes catechism, apologetics, polemics, dogma, the selective approach of the sentences, and the comprehensive approach of the *summa*. Protestantism redoes it, the Middle Ages redid, and every group since then tends to do it again, but the dominant picture we have since the eighteenth century is the Protestant *summa*, like many of your collateral texts, especially Hodge or Strong. Protestants produced this kind of thing at the end of the nineteenth century. It is an effort to put together in one all of the major affirmations of Scripture and the creeds. It guarantees that package will be coherent and complete, and notices especially the points at which it touches and rejects heresies. One tends to think that this summary of Christian theological conviction expresses the faith and tests the faith, thus faith is no longer a matter of trusting or accepting, but is a matter of believing these things, of holding these truths.

Disciplines within Theology

Now we shall make an effort to identify some of the subdisciplines within the total discipline of theology. This is again a descriptive approach. We may be able to return later to ask about the relative value of some of these approaches.

Apologetics

Apologetics as a particular kind of theology was traditionally part of systematic theology. In the seventeenth and eighteenth centuries it became an independent discipline, first called "philosophical theology," and more recently "philosophy of religion." The name changes when the church loses control. When the church controlled Western society it was called philosophical theology or apologetics. When the church lost control of the university, it started to be called philosophy of religion, but they still have the same questions. These questions are those of a person either not committed to a particular faith, or who tries to step out of a particular faith to examine it objectively. It deals with such matters as proof of God's existence and the meaning of religious experience, as these can be talked about with someone who is not within a community of faith.

Today there is renewed debate about the place of this discipline. Karl Barth argued that it does not belong at all. Its very existence entails concessions to unbelief. You cannot do that and still be Christian. Paul Tillich argued on the other side that all theology is apologetic, that everything must be tested by relevance or sifted through the sieve of modernity's demands, and anything the modern mind does not understand does not need to be said.

We ought to ask two questions about this apologetic concern where we see it at work (it works in conservative as well as liberal circles because it is often understood as part of evangelism):

- The first question we ask about the apologetic process is whether its point is faithful. Is what the apologist says true? Does the very fact of adjustment to the mind of the unbeliever or the objective listener distort the truth? Is it being done faithfully? When Paul Tillich states the Christian faith as a response to a question that the modern mind asks, is it the Christian faith that he states? That is the internal question of coherence.
- The other question is whether you should do it at all.

In the simplest apologetic cases, one starts with humanity and argues from there. Any person must somehow accept the existence of a supreme being, something like God. Next, one must logically accept that it follows that this God, if we are to know God, must have revealed God's self. Then one moves to identifying the Bible as the way this happened and finds the Bible refers to a story and the place of Jesus in that story. Different apologetic theologians have done this in different ways, but something like this always has to be done. The significant thing is that it begins with unbelieving humanity and concludes where the New Testament church began—with Christ.

What challenges need to be addressed to this? Can they be made more precise than were our comments about Karl Barth?

- Beginning with the addressee as not a believer assumes that the unbeliever can be trusted epistemologically. It assumes the unbelieving mind is capable of responding to the truth and recognizing the difference between truth and falsehood. It assumes that the standards of proof by which the unbeliever will test what he or she is ready to believe are valid standards to which the unbeliever has access. Yet later (in the Bible or with Jesus) one finds real doubt expressed about whether unbelievers can see straight and whether the standards by which they judge are honest. The Bible seems generally to say that people who are not believers cannot observe objectively—cannot measure by the truth.
- A second challenge addressed to apologetics is inductive. Apologetic reasoning is circular. If you start with humanity, then prove God, then prove revelation and then prove the Bible, you will only convince the person who already wants to be convinced. A real unbeliever could challenge it at any point.
- Another inductive challenge asks whether there are really unbelievers like the ones apologetic theology addresses. Paul Tillich, Dietrich Bonhoeffer, and Rudolph Bultmann (each in his own way) have different definitions of what modern people cannot believe and what they can believe.

So the problem of apologetic theology links not only with assumptions it makes about truth, but also with whether it can find the right kind of people out there in order to address them.

Having noticed the doubts about apologetic theology as an independent discipline, some affirmative things need to be said about its possible continuing usefulness as an auxiliary approach, even if we do not think it is adequate, totally convincing, or a necessary part of theology.

- It may be part of evangelism. Apologetics probably cannot prove to an unbeliever that he or she has to believe except in very exceptional circumstances, but it might be possible to explain to the unbeliever that *if* he or she believed, things would make sense. For instance, non-Christians, reading the theology of Karl Barth, who does not care to be apologetic, have seen for the first time that Christian faith is internally coherent and consistent with itself, and people have been convinced by that coherence of the meaningfulness and attractiveness of the Christian faith. So there is another kind of apologetics, not starting with humanity but explaining to people who start with themselves outside the context of faith, that if they were to accept the axioms of faith there would be a coherent position. It would make sense.
- Another part of apologetics is a negative function that looks at the unbeliever's position from the inside and asks whether it is consistent. It asks whether, if you deny certain things, life can still make sense, whether the nihilistic or materialistic positions of liberal modern humanism are coherent. It is a double negative apologetics in which we look at unbelief, take it seriously, analyze it for its consistency, and seek to explore it from the inside.
- Another use of the apologetic approach is to structure a catechetic apologetic. This is a contradiction in terms, but it is possible to try to teach the faith to people committed to it as if they were not. How would you organize such a catechism? You might start with the New Testament church's message about Jesus, but you might also start somewhere else, by asking for instance, "What is the chief end of all flesh?" Many Protestant catechisms begin this way, using the gradual accumulation of affirmation *as if* someone were starting from scratch as a good teaching technique. Instead of giving people a whole mass of affirmations that they must believe all at once, a catechetical apologetic could put them in some logical sequence. What is the first thing they should believe? What is the simplest thing you can say?
- The apologetic approach might also function in missionary thought, not in convincing people in another culture, but in analyzing the sequence in which Christian mission ought to deal with

> issues. It is an apologetic concern to find points of initial conflict or contact as over against the other Christian affirmations that cannot be meaningfully at the outset of a missionary encounter.

So perhaps the apologetic stance makes some sense as a way of organizing theological material even though it is subject to some critique.

Historical Theology

We practiced historical theology through most of these lectures, with the exception of the last lectures on the threefold office of Christ. The history of Christian thinking about the faith is the only place from which we get the material of our theology. You can only systematize the answers to a question when you have first had answers to the question, and the question had to arise in history before there could be any answer to it. Theology always systematizes around a problem that is central at a certain time. For instance, Franz Pieper, the conservative Lutheran theologian, organized everything around justification by faith; Charles Finney organized everything around Christian experience; and Lewis Chafer around the concept of the millennium.[3] Obviously, the center that any given systematic text uses will shift with time and space. In the Nicene controversy it was the issue of the Trinity; later, it was the two natures. In the Middle Ages it was the sacraments. The Reformation period centered on the problem of justification. In the period of pietism it was around Christian experience, and today (1968) it is hermeneutics.

At any one time the total number of things about which you can talk seems to be a closed package. It seems to be possible to speak systematically about everything Christians have talked about and make of it a unified whole. But then comes a new challenge, just as new as the Trinity was in the second and third centuries before it was settled in the fourth. There is struggle around that new challenge, and a new answer is proposed. Perhaps that answer comes to be accepted as dogma, then you teach and test by it, you relate it to the rest, and it becomes the center of a new system. The question to which the new answer spoke had not been clear before. That is why any answer is new. That is why the system has to be written again. That is why the historical treatment of the development of thought is a necessary corrective to the systematic treatment of developed thought. When you treat thought systematically, you act as if it were not changing, and historical theology deals with it as it changes.

3. See Franz Pieper, *Christian Dogmatics*, 4 vols. (St. Louis: Concordia, 1950–57); Charles G. Finney, *Lectures on Systematic Theology: Embracing Lectures on Moral Government, Together with Atonement, Moral and Physical Depravity, Regeneration, Philosophical Theories, and Evidences of Regeneration* (Oberlin: J. M. Finch, 1846); and Lewis Sperry Chafer. *Systematic Theology*, 8 vols. (Dallas: Dallas Seminary Press, 1947).

But again, there are temptations to overdo the historical orientation:

- One of the temptations is to assume there is only one line. We start with the early church, and then the Montanists break off. Then you have the heresies with which the apostolic fathers dealt, and then the Arians go off. Then various people get lost in the Middle Ages, and then the Orthodox break off in 1054. The various medieval sects separate themselves, then the Catholics get lost and Protestants go on, then Lutherans get off and the Mennonites go on, and then the Mennonite Brethren get off. All the way there is only one line. Once each deviant group drops off its history is no longer noticed. As you read a text in historical theology, you will see that monolinear assumption usually being made, and it is never correct. The other branches are all there and are growing. John Wesley continues to be a part of many movements with which he never had anything to do. So, we have to draw a tree or network instead of a main line, and then draw links across from branch to branch as well as follow the ramifying from the original roots. We see more clearly today than people saw before how incomplete the monolinear historical approach is. Historical theology still remains a very useful tool in analysis if we make that kind of corrective.
- In addition to the monolinear temptation there is also the temptation to accent what is novel. Just as the news media show us riots—even though most of the country is not rioting—because the riots are news, so also the recounting of the history of theology tells what has not been said before and gives little attention to what has been said before. If you read a history of nineteenth-century Protestant theology, you will read about Schleiermacher, Feuerbach, and Ritschl. You will not read about the predominant part of the European Protestant population that continued to make orthodox Lutheran and Reformed statements. You will not read about them because they were not news, but theirs was still the stance of most Christians in that area. This temptation not only accentuates movement but also tends to let some people think novelty itself accredits the new position. If it is old, a position is by definition suspect or maybe even wrong. And a position that is up to date or novel is more likely to be true. In the cheap form this becomes faddism, which is rampant in recent Protestant thought, where if a book sells over a hundred thousand copies it is the new theology for three years until another book sells over a hundred thousand copies. But also, on a serious level, this temptation is expressed in the notion many people have that each age settles a theological problem. The Reformation settled the

problem of justification, or the problem of the relation of nature and grace. Other centuries basically solve other problems. Thus you try to tell the story as not only a story, but also as the accumulation of truths. You assume that the predominant position in a given age was progress over the predominant position in the age that preceded it, such that we stand on top of a growing pyramid, and it is all true.

Anyone whose responsibility is to be *didaskalos* and look at the development of history critically, with the canonical origins as its test, has to question the assumption that each century makes progress. It might be that a new start, not backing up through time but looping back over time to read the New Testament afresh, would tell us that the whole eighteenth or nineteenth century was wrong, or that some other particular well established and apparently convincing idea was headed down the wrong road.

Biblical Theology

This brings us to the specific subdiscipline called "biblical theology." There used to be no such thing because all theology was biblical. One branch of it was exegesis, looking at particular texts and being concerned about grammar, dictionary meaning, endings, and construction. The other part was systematic theology, putting these true statements together in a different order. But now, in between systematics, dogmatics and historical theology on the one hand and exegesis on the other, another discipline has developed. It is like systematic theology in that it reorganizes the texts, looks for major themes, coherence and system, but is different in that it seeks to limit itself to the language, concepts, or thought frames of the Bible. It seeks to be more disciplined in being inductive, saying only what rises out of the text when read carefully and looking at patterns of form as a way of understanding what the biblical writers meant to say.

This newly developing theology has its own strengths and temptations as well:

- One of its temptations is to be ahistorical, to act as if you could read the Bible without reference to later generations or to the fact that contemporary vocabulary does not have the same meanings as biblical vocabulary even if we use the same words. As if, for instance, the church could have lived in the Hellenistic world and still use only Hebrew, or as if we could live with biblical concepts and without using the language with which we grew up in our century.
- Biblical theology's process of working inductively and developing major themes runs the danger of "crypto-systematic theology." It

may have a system, dogmas, and main themes that are not simply biblical, without being aware of them.

Within the *discipline* of biblical theology there has arisen a *school* of theology that (following Hendrick Kraemer) calls itself "biblical realism." This is not a discipline but a particular set of convictions. It begins by criticizing unbiblical views such as the Platonic or dualistic views of things, and then it tries to think the way the Bible thinks. It is like biblical theology, but it claims there is one right position to which you must come that will not be Lutheran, Reformed, free church or something else, but is simply biblical. One of the strengths of this position is that it opens one's mind to take seriously the elements that have been forgotten over the centuries, such as the place of the demonic in the biblical view of society. It enables people to be open to the possibilities that the Bible might think with a different logic than we think with and not necessarily be usable for the kinds of proof our apologetics, for instance, use. This school of thought arose by refusing to take sides between modern fundamentalism and liberalism. Paul Minear, Otto Piper, Markus Barth, and a number of other scholars in their train represent it. It is no longer considered a new thing in theology schools, and since people look for new things, it is already a little old.

Ethics

We move next to the place of ethics in theology. First of all this is a structural question. Who teaches ethics in a theological faculty? The same teacher often taught ethics and doctrine in the eighteenth century, but it was never the same course. There was a very clear dichotomy between doctrine, which was dealt with by theology, and action, which is dealt with by ethics. What is the reason for this dichotomy? Is it that doctrine is more spiritual, or is it that in the field of behavior one can be less sure? It is not quite clear where the difference came from, but it was there quite early. Both realms, doctrine and ethics, lost out in the dichotomy because many important subjects were pulled apart. Is forgiveness ethics or doctrine? Is incarnation ethics or doctrine? Is the church a subject for doctrinal or ethical understanding? Is hope or eschatology a matter for one or the other? Obviously, if your ethics is to be biblically oriented, it will have to include all these elements, and yet usually they are left for the doctrine course. Then ethics has only rules about do's and don'ts.

The very concept of a split between belief and action is itself a doctrinal error. The biblical word does not distinguish what you ought to think and what you ought to do, or if it does so, it is in order to accentuate that the two must be related closely. Ethics has not comprised a distinct chapter in this particular course because it is a prefatory course, and we are describing a field in which it is clear that ethics have usually been left out. But if we were to deal systematically with theology in a specifically biblical stance or Anabaptist stance, then there would have to be some way of restoring ethics into every section of it. Few theologians have tried to do this. Karl Barth did, although we could still debate whether he has done it consistently or correctly.

Then another set of fields has developed in recent years—practical theology, missionary theology—which, like ethics, gradually came to be represented by particular teachers, chairs in a faculty, or books written on the subject. The same problems and comments apply as with regard to ethics. These fields belong within the total systematic approach. Without it systematics is poorer, and without systematic orientation practical theology is poorer. There is no separate substance; there are no separate rules of straight thinking to distinguish among doctrine, ethics, and practical theology. There may be a difference in topic that justifies having different people deal with different sections, but it is only a matter of competence and specialization, not a matter of different areas in which a different kind of logic ought to apply.

In our own work with the three offices in Christology, we noticed along the way each time ethical implications were drawn from the fact that Christ is prophet, Christ is priest, or Christ is king. These ethical implications were not highly different. In each of these relationships it is something about the suffering, reconciling work of Christ that we find that his way of being king and his way of being priest are not really distinguishable. It says something more if we say that his *person* is communication, that Christ as prophet communicates the nature of God not only through his words but also through his deeds, and especially through his reconciling deeds at the center of his victory over evil. This we observed.

We noticed that most textbooks do not deal with ethics at all as belonging within the system of theology. Not that they are opposed to ethics, but it is somehow not their subject. If we were to go through other classical themes of theology—creation, anthropology, the meaning of the fall—again each would have ethical dimensions, and again we would find that in most theology texts those ethical dimensions are not spelled out. There are several ways in which we might pursue further the problem of the place of ethics within theology.

- One level, the one we are closest to right now in Christology, is the actual substance of ethics. How is it that Christ teaches us that our ethics is to be derived from who he was? The New Testament is full of statements to the effect that our ethical life is to be derived from Christ's. The Synoptic Gospels say it in the language of discipleship, and discipleship focuses at the cross. "If any man would come after me, let him deny himself and take up his cross and follow me" (Mark 8:34b). That means that the language of atonement applies to the ethics of the follower. Second Corinthians 4:10 says the same kind of thing. Paul is meditating on himself and Timothy, but what he says certainly applies to all Christians in some sense: "[We are] always carrying in the body the death of Jesus, so that the life of Jesus may also be manifested in our bodies."[4] First John 3:1–12 speaks of being children (*tekna*) of God, sharing the Son's nature. Therefore we will not be like Cain who killed his brother, but like Jesus who gave his life for the brother. John 15 talks about the branch and the vine. Hebrews 5:8–9 talks about the "obedience" of Jesus as the word for atonement: "He learned obedience through what he suffered; and being made perfect he became the source of eternal salvation to all who obey him."

So from every aspect of Christology there are links to Christian behavior. If we think of Christ as the communicator, the prophet, he reveals Christian behavior to us in his cross. If we think of him as the priest, the reconciler, it is his self-giving that works reconciliation. If we think of him in the eschatological language of kingship, it is the cross that moves history. In each of these relationships there are obviously implications for how we behave.

- We could ask the question again on the more abstract level of the form of an ethical text. If you were writing a text in ethics, how would you write it? Here we have been talking about it christologically, in relation to Jesus. We have implied that there is no reason to be less related to Jesus when we talk about ethics than when we talk about anything else. Then why do other ethics texts not talk about ethics from Jesus or even from systematic theology in general? The reason is usually that they derive their ethics somewhere else, for instance, from the structures of creation, common sense, or the nature of humanity. At the point of ethics, the issue of natural theology (about which we have not talked

4. Editorial note: Yoder's manuscript reads, "II Corinthians 4 says the same kind of thing, Paul is meditating on his own place, but he certainly says it for all Christians in some sense; 'I carry about in my body the dying of Jesus so that the resurrection, the life of Jesus, might be made visible in my mortal body.'" Where Yoder found such a translation is unclear. Perhaps it came from memory. Virtually every English translation preserves the plural form found in the Greek similarly to the NRSV: "[We are] always carrying [*peripherontes*] in the body the death of Jesus, so that the life of Jesus may also be manifested in our mortal flesh." Our editorial changes reflect the possibility that when Yoder says, "Paul is meditating on his own place," he means on himself and Timothy (see 1:1). This seems to be the sense of the plural references in 4:1–5, although it is not as clear with regard to 4:7 ("We have this treasure in earthen vessels . . ."), at least if the history of interpretation of this passage is any guide.

much but which you will run across in your texts) is the most sharply pointed.

Many theologians would not want to derive other theological doctrines by consulting common sense, reason, or nature, but are still quite willing to get their ethics in those ways. Few of the great systematic texts, as we have said, have any ethics at all. Of those that do deal with ethics, few relate it directly to Christology. They put it somewhere else—under the mandate to support the social order or the responsibility to self and neighbor. Even those who do link it with concepts of revelation or with the work of Christ do not link it to Jesus, that is, to the man who lived and died in a certain way. They do not get their ethics from the humanity of Christ the way Hebrews did.

This ought to be pursued further. Why is it that ethical systems in general, or rather the people who write theological ethics, center it on something other than the person of Jesus? Even if they go to Jesus, they will listen to a few of his teachings or look to Colossians to see that he is the capstone of creation, so that they can then go to look at creation.

- The third level of abstraction, on which we could ask why ethics does not get a better deal, is that of philosophical hermeneutics. How do we go about finding meaning? If language is reality, which is the most timeless? If the subjects you can talk about as unchanging or eternal are most important, then what happens in history is less basic than what happens on the ideal level of pure language. Ethics is then still less basic than history because it is always subject to change, always undecided, always having to be decided again, and always different the next time. So, orthodox theology seeks ways of dealing with how things are in the mind of God—those truths that do not change. But one does not seek, or does not expect to find in theology, the norms or sources of criticism for the way to behave today because they are dictated by something else.

  If, on the other hand, history were more basic than timeless language—if the fact that you have to make a choice is more basic than the fact in general that history is going on (and this would be the Hebraic way of saying things)—then the first meaning of any doctrine is what it means for behavior. If it does not mean something for behavior, perhaps it does not mean anything. You do not test a statement by asking, "What does this mean in the mind of God?" or "What does this mean when the words are properly defined in God's dictionary?" The first meaning of any statement is the difference it makes in how I behave. That is a modern positivist statement, as far as linguistic philosophy is concerned.

Linguistic philosophy is currently overemphasized, but it makes a point. Our age is marked by cultural pluralisms. There are many groups of people, each with their own language. Every department of a university has its own language. Every theological tradition has its own language. These languages overlap in the mass media and in the business world, but there is still an enormous plurality of language. So you can never ask, "Is that a correct statement?" You can only ask, in a given context, "Is this statement verifiable?"

We saw that language is always meaningful only from outside itself. Language does not have its meaning in its words. You have to know who is speaking and what dictionary and grammar are being used. Remember the several dimensions of all language that have to be brought into its meaning from outside. If we were to think of theology as dogmatic formulae that are most correct when they are most able to stand alone—like a phrase from the Nicene Creed—then as languages become more and more difficult, it is more and more difficult to theologize. It becomes more and more difficult to know in the next context where the line beyond which is heresy runs, simply because we have so many more languages. The people who wrote the Nicene Creed had only one language, and they were a culturally narrow enough group that they could get away with thinking that way. When they distinguished between *homoiousios* and *homoousios,* they all knew what difference they were talking about. They comprised such a small slice of history and culture that they could get away with the assumption that they all spoke the same language and therefore knew what they were talking about.

But when we do not speak the same language, how will we draw these lines? To the extent that theology is doctrine, it is harder and harder, and that is why churches in our age are incapable of defining heresy. But if theology relates to ethics, then we do have a common world in which we behave because we behave with each other. We do know what it means when we behave differently and come to opposite ways of acting with regard to what we do with money, sex, the sword, race, the neighbor, or our housing. We are in fact, through our sociological awareness, through our experience in living with each other, and through our communications media, more able than before to know whether we are behaving the same as others. To the extent to which we would think of theology as abstract philosophically burdened thought, it is harder and harder to know how to test ourselves. If we come to the practical end, it may be even easier these days to know whether we agree on behavior—or if it is not easier, then at least it is possible.

But if propositional dogmatics is *less* central than some people traditionally have argued, and if faithfulness in history is *more* central than some people argue, then to make the propositional dogmatic issue central is itself, if not wrong, at least a challengeable shift of emphasis. Then the function of theology includes not only the two basic statements that we have talked about, catechesis and faithfulness—passing it on and testing it—but also vigilance against shifting your attention from faithfulness in life to faithfulness in thought. It must include vigilance against the danger of thinking that if you say the right words your behavior does not matter. This is, in a new form, an old Anabaptist and Pietist concern, so part of the function of theology and part of the critical testing function of theology is to guard the church against the autonomy of theology.

One reason the faithful church must have theologians is that all the other churches do. The function of theology is to be suspicious of theology. We might like to short-circuit that suspicion by claiming to have no theology, but that is of course not a possible solution. The anti-intellectuals and antitheological people have a theology too. They are just not careful about it. Liberals who want to accept all positions also have a theology. The one kind of theology they reject is the one that draws lines like Jesus did. It is interesting that the people who today claim it is now hard to talk about these things are very much on a theological wavelength, especially if they say, "God is dead." That position has a massive dogmatic concern. It always talks about proper language, whether the word "God" means anything, what you mean by *kenosis,* and what you can say if you cannot talk about ethics. If you do not find meaning anymore in the word "God," they say, at least you can find meaning in what a good person Jesus was. But you do not find in the God-is-dead literature what it means to be a good person, whether being like Jesus means that you are nonresistant, or what to do about sex if you want to be faithful. They still talk about the doctrinal, dogmatic, and linguistic concerns as such, rather than finding discipleship a key to the linguistic concern. So the antitheological trends are not antitheological. They are theological but anticritical. They are against being careful, against moral bindingness as a form, against a covenant community as the context of ethics and theology, against servanthood as the substance of ethics and of theology. So, against antitheological trends, when 2 Timothy 1:13–14 tells you to pay attention to the words you were given and not to dispute about words, it is a good description of what needs to be done and not just a paradox.

Our next excursion into the nature of the discipline is to examine the organization of theology, of a text or of a course. Why does it matter how a text is organized? Or doesn't it? For some people it is unimportant. For others it can be very important, and we want to look at that. The method of presenting material is not immaterial, at least not always. So if you look back over all the texts and compare them, you will find a variety of different organizations. That is why you sometimes had preparatory questions like, "How much space does this get and where does it come in the outline?" "What came before?" "What is it a subpoint of?" "What follows it logically?"

In general we can say there are three types of organization. Under each of these three are subtopics. We shall come out with around ten different ways of organizing a text, wanting to learn not simply by lining them up but by contrasting them and their assumptions.

Logical

First are patterns of organization by logical sequence. That is, the material has to be organized in such a way because it dictates its own sequence. The second chapter depends on the first chapter, you could not write the third chapter without the second, and so on down the line. Under this subdivision of logical patterns or organization are at least four subpatterns.

- One of these could be called *apologetic*. The order in which the material must be handled is the order in which you would try to convince someone. You put first the first thing that would have to be said to someone who does not believe, and you put second what you can only prove after you have made the first point. Thomas Aquinas, Schleiermacher, and many theologians of Protestant orthodoxy used this approach. You begin with the problem of knowledge, because you cannot talk about anything else until you have come to an agreement on how you can talk. Within the problem of knowledge, you deal first with the definition of terms, the place of reason, and the place of revelation. After you have dealt with the place of revelation, you develop a concept of revelation itself, and then of the Bible as revelation. Once you have the Bible as revelation you can start talking about God, Jesus, the world and everything else. This is a normal logical movement. But what if, as we suggested earlier when we talked about apologetics, humanity's capacity to face true knowledge is lost in fallenness? How can you then start by assuming that we can face the knowledge problem reliably from scratch? That is one shortcoming of this approach. Another, of course, is one we will observe in many of these cases: the Bible does not start there. The Bible does not ever start by assuming that the reader does not believe.
- Another approach is the one Strong calls *synthetic*. It is the obvious sequence if you are not apologetically concerned. You start at the top with God, and the next thing you deal with must be creation, because you cannot talk about anything else until there is

something else. Then within creation you have humanity in general, and after you have humanity you can talk about the man Christ and the work of salvation. After the work of salvation, you can start with the church. That again is a logical sequence. But how can you start with God before you know anything about God, or how do you know anything about God if you do not start somewhere else? That might throw us back to apologetics after all. This overdoes, it could be argued, the general concept of "theism," proving God first and then waiting a long time to get around to Jesus. That is a particular view of God. It is not necessarily a Christian view of God. There are other theisms than Christian theism. If you start with God and do not get to Jesus until a long time later, you do not have a real perspective from which to test whether you are importing non-Christian elements into your theism. It also assumes, by leaving salvation to the end, some kind of reliable knowledge about unfallen reality, which is not necessarily acceptable.

- A third logical outline is *Trinitarian*. This outline is followed by the Apostles' Creed. We first say something about God the Father, then about God the Son, and then about God the Spirit. Karl Barth also uses this outline in his *Church Dogmatics*. If the very concept of revelation has the shape of threeness, we have a logical breakdown. We noticed when we went through the Apostles' Creed that it had a certain sequence that made sense. But we noticed, too, that the article on the Holy Spirit was a grab bag where everything left over was put—the church, the communion of saints, forgiveness of sins, the resurrection of the dead, and eternal life. It was not quite clear why that all belonged under the Holy Spirit, except that you were at the end of the creed and had to fit it all in before you finished. So it is about some of the Trinitarian outlines. They appeal to good authority, but it is not quite clear that the logic has a real sequence to it.
- Fourth, the *federal* pattern of organization could also be called logical, although it too can be somewhat arbitrary. Federal theology is the name for a tradition in Reformed thought. The word federal comes from *covenant*. God has made several covenants with humanity over history. According to the dispensationalists there are seven covenants; according to other Reformed traditions there are two, three, or four. It is possible to organize theology along the sequence of the covenants. First was a covenant with Adam before the fall, so under it you talk about creation, nature, animal life, and work. Then there is the covenant with fallen Adam, and there are other things to talk about: the nature of sin, work with the sweat of your brow, children, and history. Then there is the Noahic cove-

nant—start over again and then there is the call of Abraham. Each time a different set of things can be said, and you can work a good bit of the material of theology into this kind of an outline.

Objective

Second, there are the objective types. These types claim that reality "out there" dictates how theology ought to be treated. Authors who use this type do not sit down and think about reorganizing the material; they just read it off of reality. This is less frequent in systematic theology texts, but it can be done.

- One objective pattern of organization is *historical.* We deal with topics in the order in which they arose. If you do this carefully enough, you will get around to all the problems. It will not look like a systematic theology text but it will treat all the same things. We started the course that way. It would have been rather complicated to finish it that way, but we did demonstrate that it can be handled that way—material can be treated in the order that the problems arise. You start with the confession of faith in the earliest church and then encounter Judaism, Gnosticism, persecution, the heresies, and the changing of the worlds into which the gospel went. The New Testament itself tells the story this way, as far as it goes. We did at the beginning. We could have stayed on that path and taught all of the material of systematic theology in the form of the history of people thinking that way, but the sequence would be difficult, and of course you always have to decide which place you are going to deal with in any given era. In the eighteenth century, for instance, will you concentrate on Russia or on France? It would get complicated. It would also not bring to the surface the problems of coherence and consistency—the questions of testing for truth—the way the logical systems do, but it is a way in which specific topics can be organized.
- Another effort to be objective and let the structure be dictated by the material is *christological,* which we would find for instance in Oscar Cullmann's *Christology.* He organizes his material as a kind of dictionary according to the words that are used. Theological literature uses a specific language about Christ, and so we can go from word to word. Once we have explained what each of the words means, we are about done.
- One could also approach theology similarly, but concerning salvation instead of Christ. Then the structure is *soteriological.* You start with lost people and how they are saved, and everything else comes in under that outline. There would be other ways like this that ask about particular problems and let them dictate the outline.

There are still other patterns that can only be called *arbitrary*. That is, they do not claim either a certain logic or objectivity, but just say, "Why don't we do it this way?"

- One of these is *circular*. Horton uses it in *Ecumenical Theology*. Anything you can say in theology presupposes other things you have not said yet. There is nothing you can say from scratch. Anything you say, if you push it, presupposes everything else. No statement you can make in theology is true or meaningful unless it presupposes other things you have not yet said. So there must be a circle, with each position logically presupposing other statements that should have gone before. If I make a statement that is right at one point along the line of the truth, it is not really true if I do not presuppose other statements that logically went before it, and it will necessarily imply other statements that come later. You cannot start anywhere and make a statement that does not need a preceding statement, and that statement would need another preceding statement. If that is the case, then you can dive in anywhere. You can start anywhere, because wherever you start you could have started earlier, and yet there is no place to which you can back up that is the normal presuppositionless starting point. This is an open-ended system in that it can start anywhere and be equally ready to go on.

  You could start with the Holy Spirit. You could start with, "How do I get saved?" You could start by asking, "Who was Adam?" It does not matter, because wherever you start the rest is implied and presupposed. The person to whom you are speaking may determine where you start. Any place is equally good. You will test wherever you start. Wherever you start you will be concerned with consistency, and you can start anywhere. This is not a dead orthodoxy. You can start anywhere, while with orthodoxy you always have to start correctly. This is not apologetics because it is a closed circle. You always have to come back to Christ. It is freer and makes more demands on you because you have to be ready to start anywhere.

  The other pattern I have indicated here as arbitrary is something like *allegory*. John Bunyan's *Pilgrim's Progress* is really a work of theology, but it is organized along the line of the story of a person going through a series of experiences trying to get to the heavenly city.[5] By the time he is finished, you have read a lot of

5. John Bunyan, *The Pilgrim's Progress: From This World to That Which Is to Come, Delivered under the Similitude of a Dream, Wherein Is Discovered the Manner of His Setting Out, His Dangerous Journey, and Safe Arrival at the Desired Country* (Philadelphia: Lippincott, 1897).

> things that could have been dealt with in a propositional systematic theology, but Bunyan chose to do it in the form of a story. Of course, it could also have been still another story. *Pilgrim's Progress* is not the only way to write a pilgrim's progress, so it could have been done some other way.

With this attention to the problems of organization, we should look at what we have not done at all in the course. We have not discussed *prolegomena,* the things to be said before. This means, in most of your texts, the discussion of revelation and reason, the problems that are not quite theological but with which you have to work before you can talk about theology. This presupposes one of the approaches under the logical pattern of organization that I referred to as apologetic in character. If you are starting a catechism, then your prolegomena will be personal. You deal with this person and discuss why it is that he or she ought to talk about faith, so you can have subjective prolegomena. Why do you feel guilty? What do you feel bad about? Do you know you are a sinner? This is before you get around to a doctrine of sin. It involves this person in the process of learning.

If, on the other hand, you deal more philosophically the way the great apologetic systems of the Middle Ages did, then you do not get to the Bible or to the listener for some time. You talk about the concepts of revelation or God. If you are talking to modern people, you have to talk about the problem of knowledge: What business do you have making these claims anyway? What are you talking about, and what right do you have to talk about this subject, or to say that modern people ought to listen? So all of the prolegomena usually deal with reason or revelation. In addition, of course, if you are Catholic you will deal with the fact that it is the church that tells you all these things. For Catholic texts, the church belongs in the prolegomena, at least the office of the church to teach. If you are traditional Protestant, the Bible belongs in the prolegomena, because you have to explain why you accept the Bible before you can read it.

Now these are all significant questions and belong somewhere in the treatment of theology. But we did not answer them when we started. Did any of you feel guilty or cheated that we did not answer them when we started? It was not because I did not think of it, but we have demonstrated, in the practice of not answering them at the start, something about the nature of theology in the church. In the church we already read the Bible, not only in the simple sense of opening the book and looking at the print but in the wider sense of gathering around the story that the Bible tells in the expectation that this story makes us who we are.

After we start reading the Bible in the church, then we are, as a community, ready to ask later how we have been using our heads, how reason has been functioning, and how we have been letting ourselves be told—that is, how revelation has been functioning. We can ask ourselves these things after we have been doing them because then we have some subject matter to deal with. We can be inductive about what has gone on in the life of the church for two thousand years. There we can see reason and revelation functioning, but we do not begin with the fiction of starting from scratch with a blank mind that needs to be convinced. There are no blank minds. There are people in the believing community who already have a running start in faith. There are people who are not in this community, and they also have a running start, in unbelief. There is no such thing as a blank mind in history, so we can see revelation operating, and I hope we can also see reason operating in the life of the church because we are in the church.

But if we are concerned about communicating to people not in the church, the thesis follows that the best apologetics or communicative method is not to accept their starting point or axioms so that we can prove our point on their terms. Rather, the best apologetics is to live before them the reality of the church's functioning with its own inner consistency. Because they are unbelievers, if I accept their axioms, then I am an unbeliever too and do not have anything to prove to them. If I let them watch me living out my axioms, and then I watch them living out their axioms, we have a conversation, but it is not based on my acceptance of their assumptions.

There would be much more to say about prolegomena, especially on the issue of reason as a source of truth in the Enlightenment and a particular kind of Western humanism, but it would be a whole new encounter. We would have to study Western humanism and not just the concept of reason itself. We also have not found that we needed for our purposes to set up any particular rules about logic. We just went ahead with the discussion in the community in which we found ourselves.

I referred earlier to the concept of "biblical theology" as different from both systematic theology and exegesis. In an article on biblical theology in the *Interpreter's Bible Dictionary*, Krister Stendahl throws some helpful light on the nature of theology.[6] It has a helpful way of asking questions that I shall try to play back. The study of the Bible down through the centuries was always apologetic or prejudiced. Everyone read the Bible to prove that his or her position was right instead of reading it objectively. It could only become an objective study, and

6. Krister Stendahl, "Biblical Theology, Contemporary," in vol. 1 of *The Interpreter's Dictionary of the Bible: An Illustrated Encyclopedia Identifying and Explaining All Proper Names and Significant Terms and Subjects in the Holy Scriptures, Including the Apocrypha, with Attention to Archaeological Discoveries and Researches into the Life and Faith of Ancient Times* (New York: Abingdon Press, 1962), 418–432.

people could only read the Bible for what it really says, when they were freed from the assumption that they had to agree with it, that is when they were freed from the assumption that they could use it in their partisanship. Remember that when we talked about the descent into hell, one of the phrases in the Apostles' Creed that has several different meanings, we said that some people were committed to one meaning because their interpretation was dictated by the place of the Creed in their tradition. We could ask more freely what it originally meant (when the Creed's phrase arose in the third century) by not being committed to believing whatever it was that it originally meant.

Stendahl says this about all theologians reading the Bible. If we identify the Bible with our own system, whether that is orthodox, liberal, or something else, we cannot be historically critical of what the text really says. Modern biblical theology in the last century or two has made enormous progress at this point because it separates two questions: "What did it mean then?" and "What does it mean now?" "What did it mean then?" becomes a question of straight history. It can be dealt with objectively because is does not imply acceptance of what it means now. What it means now is what we do with it. About that we are, of course, prejudiced. This is to say we can separate a descriptive and a normative task. The descriptive task asks, "What did it mean when Paul wrote it?" As long as you are not committed to buying it, you can be honest about that. The normative task is then, "What should we do together about what Paul said?" That is still complex, but we at least have freed ourselves from that complexity in order to be able to read the text.

The relation between the two then is the hermeneutic problem, and that is the problem for which there is no one right answer. That is the leap of faith. For example, Jews and Christians have the same Bible, what the Christians call the Old Testament. The Christians say, "Our line is the proper interpretation of our Old Testament." The Jews say, "*Our* line is the proper interpretation of our Bible." There is no way to judge between these two on the basis of the text. If they both stop being defensive and apologetic and look at the text, Jews and Christians can agree on just what a given passage in Isaiah means, or just what a passage in Daniel means. But they cannot on the basis of text judge between the way the Jews make this text their own and the way the Christians make it their own. To say, as Christians do, that the Bible—Old and New Testaments—is a unity is a leap of faith. You cannot do that from the text.

Separating the question, "What did it mean?" from the question, "What does it mean now in the church?" does not finish the job because of the very nature of what we find in the text. What we find when we read it objectively is a story that claims to reach into the present. What we say about the present is that there should be no modern framework, no society, no age in which it should not be possible to read the Bible and make the leap of faith to make it alive today. Stendahl just ends with the paradox. You can only read the Bible honestly if you do not assume that what it meant then is the same as what it means now. That is, you can only read the Bible (or any text) honestly if you cannot equate it with the present, yet you can only be honest with the message that you find in it if you affirm that that message relates to the present because that is what the message says. The link between these two irreconcilable obligations is a leap, and the Bible does not help with that leap. What it said then—what is in the text—does not dictate what it means now, and yet what it says is that it must mean something now. Stendahl's article is a very pointed way to raise the question of theological responsibility. There might be some other way to do it, but it might be less exciting.

Our last digression has to do with something we passed by in reporting at the very beginning of the course: the relation of *kerygma* and *didache*. Remember that C. H. Dodd dug out of the New Testament, especially Acts, an outline that some people identify as the *"kerygma."* We said this is not necessarily the original Greek use of the word, but that it has come to be a technical term for the few affirmations about Jesus, centered on cross and resurrection, which the apostles preached first to unbelievers. Dodd's study went on in other brief creative works. He also pulled out of the New Testament, especially out of the epistles, the idea that there was a core catechism or teaching outline that the early church used in very similar ways. It is to be found in Paul, in Peter, and elsewhere. The church must have had more or less in common a certain way of teaching, especially about behavior. Again he labeled it, and again the slogan became current—the *didache,* the teachings. So for a while there was a strong emphasis in popular literature on the polarity of *kerygma* and *didache,* proclamation and teaching. Now there is a strong reaction to this, especially among Protestant religious education writers. That opposition or criticism enables us to sharpen up what is and what is not valid about the way Dodd and people like him have been heard.

The two Greek words, *kerygma* and *didache,* did not function in the language of the apostolic time with these two meanings. That is clear. *Kerygma* means "preaching" and *didache* means "teaching," but Paul would not have known what you meant if you used these slogans as labels for a certain message or a certain body of content, a certain set of words. Nor can we say that there are two styles of discourse: a preaching style, in which you use a pulpit and pound it and raise your voice and use illustrations, and a teaching style, in which you speak in an ordinary way and spell out your words. That you do not find in the New Testament. Nor is there a two-step rhythm like "Gospel and law" or "believe and then obey," or "first you learn the essentials and then you learn the fullness," or "first justification and then sanctification," or "this is how much a layman has to know and this is how much a preacher has to know." Nor are there two styles of communication. Paul Tillich, in talking about the difference between himself and Karl Barth says that he, Tillich, uses an apologetic style and Barth uses a kerygmatic style. Barth just preaches, just lays it out, take it or leave it, while Tillich is concerned for the listener and therefore tries to speak in a way that answers the questions the listener asks. You cannot use "kerygmatic," and be describing something that exists in the New Testament as a specific approach.

You cannot say either that one of these is gospel and the other is not, that *kerygma* proclaims the gospel and the gospel is the Jesus story, and then the *didache* fills in the fine print and tells you how you have to behave, and that is not gospel. In the New Testament, understanding commands are gospel just as much as is the Jesus story. The Sermon on the Mount is gospel. It is not the Jesus story, but it is the communication of the meaning of the Jesus story in terms of how I will behave differently, and that is good news. That you can behave differently is gospel because it is good news, so you cannot distinguish *kerygma* and *didache* in that one is good news and the other is not, that one is saving and the other is not, that one is religious and the other is not, or that one is related to Christ and the other is not. None of that will work.

But the people who argue that "Dodd is dead" still have not refuted the valid points he made in the first place. Dodd's critics do not deal with the fact that he read the text. The analysis of material that he prints does rise out of things you find in the texts when you read them carefully. He did not set out to make a doctrinaire point. He was not trying to impose his own concept of the place of preaching in the church, or the relationship of the preacher and the Sunday School teacher, or anything like that. He was reading the text. The response to him would have to be in terms of literary analysis rather than in the kind of argument that I have been playing back that one finds so often in the religious education literature.

He did demonstrate that there are different audiences and that it makes a difference whether a Christian communicates to an unbeliever or to a Christian. To unbelieving audiences the apostles told the Jesus story. To committed audiences they talked about what it means to be a follower of Jesus. The listener's identity matters. That point is significant for the continuing life of the church. It does not make sense to spell out in detail the implications of faith to someone who has not heard the Jesus story, because it does not make sense without the Jesus story. Nor is it adequate to keep repeating the Jesus story to people who have already said yes to it without spelling out its implications. So the basic point Dodd made is still valid, yet it still is proper for people concerned for education, that is *didache,* to argue that this does not mean a privilege for preaching over against catechism, or for the pulpit over against the Sunday School room, or for mass evangelism over against the seminary. This kind of polarization was not meant by the *kerygma/didache* distinction. There is nothing lost in admitting that the critics have a point when Dodd is interpreted in that value-laden way.

15

The Rest of the Field

Theology is probably the only classical intellectual discipline in which it is still possible to encounter the traditional use of the word "encyclopedia." In this use, "theological encyclopedia" is one subsection of the field of systematic theology. It gives direct attention to the question of how everything that needs to be taught can be included within a cycle. The word roots that compose the term mean "teaching cycle." The idea is not to produce a book or a whole shelf of books but simply to indicate a schematic way that everything fits in somewhere.

In the early days of other intellectual disciplines the term was also used—in medicine, philosophy, or even mathematics. Only since the French Enlightenment has the term been preempted by another use, namely, a publication in which all of a certain body of knowledge is supposed to be set down.

The reason to do the former is to view generally how many different notions fit together and give special attention to cross references and coherence so as to have the presentation grounded and to make sure one does not forget anything. The concern not to forget has a special ecumenical preoccupation: we are especially likely to lose from view the agenda of other ages and other places.

Any encyclopedic outline differs from the outline of the systematic theology text in that the author of the text will seek a certain equilibrium or balance of form. There will be a concern to have all of the chapters more or less the same size and the subheadings symmetrical. That has not been attempted in this outline because the various chunks and lists which have been put together under one roof come from different places and were formulated without attention to each other. There will thus be overlapping asymmetry. Not all the items that appear at the same point in the outline are commensurate, as the author of a single systematic text attempts to make them. In the present context, namely at the end of a "preface," the primary function of this encyclopedic outline is to indicate to the student the scope of issues to which attention has not been given, which would be dealt with in a more traditional study of dogmatics or systematic theology.

- **I. Prolegomena**
  - **A. The Discipline of Theology**
    1. Its mandate
    2. Its methods
    3. Its materials
       - a. Scripture
       - b. creeds
       - c. the stream of tradition
    4. Its agenda
       - a. the theologian
       - b. the teaching office of the bishop
       - c. the council
  - **B. Revelation and Reason**
    1. Historical reason and historical proofs
       - a. miracles
       - b. consensus
       - c. the nature of historical knowledge
    2. Speculative reason, metaphysical knowledge
    3. Self-knowledge
    4. The nature and possibility of religious knowledge
  - **C. General Revelation**
    1. Order
    2. Obligation
    3. Deity: the theistic worldview
       - a. "theistic proofs"
       - b. "experience"
  - **D. Special Revelation**
    1. Theophany
    2. Miracle
    3. Prophecy
    4. Incarnation
    5. Pentecost
    6. Scripture
       - a. its origins: inspiration
       - b. its transmission: canon
       - c. its authority
       - d. its fallibility
       - e. its interpretation: hermeneutics (see I/A3–4 above)
       - f. its historical-progressive character: the Testaments

E. **Key Themes**
   1. Nature/grace
   2. Law/Gospel
   3. church/world
   4. Faith
   5. Mighty deeds of YHWH

II. God

A. **Existence: Evidences**

B. **Trinity**
   1. Threeness in oneness
   2. Father
   3. Son
      a. person (Chalcedon)
         1) deity
         2) humanity
         3) kenosis
      b. work described functionally
         1) prophet
         2) priest
         3) king
      c. work described normatively
         1) virginal conception
         2) baptism, commission
         3) words, deeds
         4) founding church
         5) cross
         6) resurrection
         7) ascension
      d. work described communically
         1) preexistence
         2) creation by Son/Logos/Sophia
         3) Old Testament revelation
         4) kenosis-humiliation
         5) exaltation-lordship
   4. Spirit
      a. General
         1) creation
         2) providence
      b. Special
         1) prophecy
         2) Jesus
      c. church
         1) Pentecost
         2) Jesus
      d. In Christian life—of VII
         1) conviction
         2) regeneration
         3) assurance
         4) guidance
         5) sanctification, enablement

C. Attributes
1. Absolute
    a. eternal
    b. omni-
    c. one
    d. infinite
    e. simple
    f. perfect
    g. holy
2. Relative
    a. personal
    b. loving, nonresistant
    c. righteous
    d. judge
    e. unique
    f. gracious, merciful
    g. transcendent, immanent
    h. temporal
    i. holy
    j. true
    k. wise

D. God and Evil

E. Grace Alone

III. Creation

A. The Divine Decrees
1. Election, reprobation
2. To create
3. To permit the fall
4. To elect some to salvation
    a. before or after the fall?
    b. on grounds of foreknowledge?
5. To sustain by providence
6. To restore by covenant
7. To restore by incarnation
8. To restore by consummation

B. Prior Creation
1. Angels, Spirits, Demons
2. Other worlds?
3. Evil in creation?

C. The Genesis Account
1. Geological origins
2. Origins of species
3. Origins of man

D. Cosmology, Evolution

IV. Man

A. As Creature: "Original Perfection"

1. Divine image
2. Body/soul/spirit (mind-will-affection)
3. "Historicity"
4. Free will
5. Sociality

B. The Fall

1. Interpretation of Genesis 3–11
2. The effects of the fall on human nature
   a. original sin
   b. perdition
      1) penalty
      2) depravity
   c. death

V. Salvation

A. The Divine Decrees of III/A

1. Election

B. Covenants

1. Adam
2. Noah
3. Abraham
4. Moses
5. David
6. Prophets
7. Jesus

C. Atonement

1. Variety of views
2. Objective/subjective?
3. Particular/universal?
4. Relation to our works; faith, obedience

D. Faith

1. Saved status cf. VII
   a. adoption, sonship
   b. union with Christ
   c. eternal life
2. Justification by faith alone
3. See below "Christian life"

E. The People of God (see below)

F. Christian Life (see below)

G. Humanization: History, the World

VI. The People of God

A. The Two Communities: see "Covenants" V/B

1. Israel
   a. Abraham
   b. Moses

        c. David
        d. Jeremiah
    2. Ecclesia
        a. Jesus
        b. Pentecost
        c. mission

B. The Nature of Sacrament/Ordinance

1. Baptism
    a. pedobaptism?
    b. immersion?
    c. prerequisites?
    d. regeneration?
2. Supper/Eucharist
    a. transubstantiation
    b. open or close?
3. Ministry/ordination
    a. meaning of ordination
    b. normative pattern
    c. priesthood of all
    d. universality of charisma
4. Discipline/penance
5. Marriage
6. Unction

C. Polity

1. Hierarchy
2. Episcopacy
3. Synod
4. Congregation
5. Ecumenism

D. Means of Grace

1. Scripture
2. Prayer
3. Praise
4. Preaching

E. Creed/"Symbolics"

F. Worship "Liturgics"

G. Mission/Evangelism/Service

H. Marks (confessional)

1. One
2. Holy
3. Catholic
4. Apostolic

I. Marks (discerning)

1. Preaching
2. Sacraments

3. Order/discipline
4. Suffering
5. Mission
6. Discipleship

VII. Christian Life

A. Nurture

B. Conversion

1. Repentance
2. Faith/trust
3. Justification
4. Regeneration
5. Assurance
6. Sanctification
   a. forensic
   b. instantaneous
   c. gradual
   d. second
   e. perfect
   f. discipleship in the world

C. Catechesis

D. Religious Education

E. Devotion

F. Obedience (see VIII "Ethics")

G. Temptation

H. Admonition, Restoration, Perseverance

I. Prayer

J. Praise

VIII. Ethics

A. The Nature of Value

1. Rule
2. Utility
3. Intuition
4. Community
5. Motivation
6. Merit
7. Virtue

B. The Nature of Decision

1. Casuistry
2. Situation
3. Intuition
4. Motivation
5. Community

C. The Nature of Sin

1. Image and fall
2. The self

D. Duties Toward God and His Cause
1. Praise/gratitude
2. Obedience
3. See VI, "The People of God"

E. Duties Toward Neighbor and Society: Love
1. Life and health
2. Dignity
3. Truth telling
4. Work and sharing: the economy
5. Education and civilization
6. Political responsibility: the state
7. Intermediate structures

F. Duties Toward Covenant Partner
1. Celibacy
2. Monogamy
3. Parenthood

G. Duties Toward Self
1. Self-affirmation
2. Self-sacrifice

H. The Power and Structures of Evil

IX. Last Things (see II/B3b3 "King")

A. The Literary Hermeneutics of Apocalyptic Texts

B. Philosophical Hermeneutics: What Does It Mean to Say "End"?

C. The Meaning of History
1. World history
2. Mission history
3. Tribulation
4. The taming of the powers

D. The End of History
1. Intermediate state: "sleep"
2. Kingdom—*parousia*—millennium
3. Judgment
4. Eternal death
5. Eternal life

Bibliography

Adeney, Walter F. *The Theology of the New Testament.* 3d ed. London: Hodder & Stoughton, 1906.

Aldwinckle, R. F. *More Than Man: A Study in Christology.* Grand Rapids: Eerdmans, 1976.

Allis, Oswald T., et. al. *Basic Christian Doctrines.* Edited by Carl F. H. Henry. New York: Holt, Rinehart & Winston, 1962.

Aulén, Gustaf. *Christus Victor: An Historical Study of the Three Main Types of the Idea of Atonement.* Translated by A. G. Hebert. New York: Macmillan, 1960.

Aulén, Gustaf. *The Faith of the Christian Church.* Translated by Eric H. Wahlstrom. Philadelphia: Muhlenberg, 1960.

Baillie, D. M. *God Was in Christ: An Essay on Incarnation and Atonement.* New York: Scribner, 1948.

Baillie, John. *The Idea of Revelation in Recent Thought.* New York: Columbia Univ. Press, 1956.

Barth, Karl. *Church Dogmatics.* Translated by G. T. Thomson et al. Edited by G. W. Bromiley and T. F. Torrance. Edinburgh: T. & T. Clark, 1950–1961.

Bancroft, Emery H. *Christian Theology, Systematic and Biblical.* Grand Rapids: Zondervan, 1976.

Barclay, William. *Jesus As They Saw Him: New Testament Interpretations of Jesus.* London: SCM Press, 1962.

Bauer, Walter. *Orthodoxy and Heresy in Earliest Christianity.* Edited by Robert A. Kraft and Gerhard Krodel. Philadelphia: Fortress, 1971.

Beare, F. W. "Canon of the New Testament." In *The Interpreter's Dictionary of the Bible: An Illustrated Encyclopedia Identifying and Explaining All Proper Names and Significant Terms and Subjects in the Holy Scriptures, Including the Apocrypha, with Attention to Archaeological Discoveries and Researches into the Life and Faith of Ancient Times,* vol. 1. New York: Abingdon, 1962.

Beegle, Dewey M. *The Inspiration of Scripture.* Philadelphia: Westminster, 1963.

Berkhof, Hendrik. *Christ and the Powers.* Scottdale, Pa.: Herald Press, 1962.

———. *Christian Faith: An Introduction to the Study of the Faith.* Translated by Sierd Woudstra. Grand Rapids: Eerdmans, 1986.

Berkhof, Louis. *Reformed Dogmatics.* 3 vols. Grand Rapids: Eerdmans, 1932.

Berkouwer, G. C. *Studies in Dogmatics* series. Titles include: *Holy Scripture, The Person of Christ, Divine Election,* and *The Providence of God.* Grand Rapids: Eerdmans, 1952.

Beskow, Per. *Rex Gloriae: The Kingship of Christ in the Early Church.* Translated by Eric J. Sharpe. Stockholm: Almquist & Wiksell, 1962.

Bethune-Baker, J. F. *An Introduction to the Early History of Christian Doc-*

trine: To the Time of the Council of Chalcedon. London: Methuen, 1903.

Boettner, Loraine. *The Millennium.* Philadelphia: Presbyterian & Reformed, 1957.

Boff, Leonardo. *Jesus Christ Liberator: A Critical Christology for Our Time.* Translated by Patrick Hughes. Maryknoll, N.Y.: Orbis Books, 1978.

Bonsirven, Joseph. *Theology of the New Testament.* Translated by S. F. L. Dye. Westminster, Md.: Newman, 1963.

Bornkamm, Günther. *Jesus of Nazareth.* Translated by Irene and Fraser McLuskey with James M. Robinson. London: Hodder & Stoughton, 1960.

Brown, Raymond E. *The Virginal Conception and Bodily Resurrection of Jesus.* New York: Paulist Press, 1973.

Bruce, F. F. *The Message of the New Testament.* Grand Rapids: Eerdmans, 1972.

Brunner, Emil. *The Mediator: A Study of the Central Doctrine of the Christian Faith.* Translated by Olive Wyon. London: Lutterworth, 1934.

———. *Our Faith.* London: SCM, 1962.

———. *Revelation and Reason: The Christian Doctrine of Faith and Knowledge.* Translated by Olive Wyon. Philadelphia: Westminster, 1946.

Bultmann, Rudolf. *Theology of the New Testament.* Translated by Kendrick Grobel. New York: Scribner, 1951–55.

Bunyan, John. *The Pilgrim's Progress: From This World to That Which Is to Come, Delivered under the Similitude of a Dream, Wherein Is Discovered the Manner of His Setting Out, His Dangerous Journey, and Safe Arrival at the Desired Country.* Philadelphia: Lippincott, 1897.

Burrows, Millar. *An Outline of Biblical Theology.* Philadelphia: Westminster, 1946.

Buswell, J. Oliver. *A Systematic Theology of the Christian Religion.* 2 vols. in 1. Grand Rapids: Zondervan, 1962.

Campbell, Alexander. *A Compend of Alexander Campbell's Theology: With Commentary in the Form of Critical and Historical Footnotes.* Edited by Royal Humbert. St. Louis: Bethany, 1961.

Cerfaux, Lucien. *Christ in the Theology of St. Paul.* Translated by Geoffrey Webb and Adrian Walker. New York: Herder & Herder, 1959.

Chafer, Lewis Sperry. *Systematic Theology.* 8 vols. Dallas: Dallas Seminary Press, 1947.

Clark, Theodore R. *Saved by His Life: A Study of the New Testament Doctrine of Reconciliation and Salvation.* New York: Macmillan, 1959.

Clarke, William Newton. *An Outline of Christian Theology.* New York: Scribner, 1914.

Clarkson, John F. *The Church Teaches: Documents of the Church in English Translation.* Rockford, Ill.: Tan Books & Pub., 1973.

Conzelmann, Hans. *An Outline of the Theology of the New Testament.* Translated by John Bowden. London: SCM, 1969.

Creed, John Martin. *The Divinity of Jesus Christ: A Study in the History of Christian Doctrine since Kant.* Cambridge: Cambridge University Press, 1938.

Crehan, Joseph. *Early Christian Baptism and the Creed: A Study in Ante-Nicene Theology.* London: Burns, Oates & Washbourne, 1950.

Cullmann, Oscar. *The Christology of the New Testament.* Translated by Shirley C. Guthrie and Charles A. M. Hall. Philadelphia: Westminster, 1959.

———. *The Earliest Christian Confessions.* Translated by J. K. S. Reid. London: Lutterworth, 1949.

Denney, James. *The Death of Christ.* Edited by R. V. G. Tasker. Chicago: InterVarsity Press, 1951.

DeWart, Leslie. *The Future of Belief: Theism in a World Come of Age.* New York: Herder & Herder, 1966.

DeWolf, L. Harold. *The Case for Theology in Liberal Perspective.* Philadelphia: Westminster, 1959.

———. *A Theology of the Living Church.* New York: Harper & Row, 1968.

Dodd, C. H. *The Apostolic Preaching and Its Developments: Three Lectures with an Appendix on Eschatology and History.* London: Hodder & Stoughton, 1936.

———. *The Apostolic Preaching and Its Developments: Three Lectures.* New York: Harper, 1960.

———. "Matthew and Paul." *Expository Times* 58 (1946–47): 293–298.

Dorner, I. A. *History of the Development of the Doctrine of the Person of Christ.* Translated by William Lindsay Alexander and D. W. Simon. Edinburgh: T. & T. Clark, 1861–1863.

Eichrodt, Walther. *Theology of the Old Testament.* 2 vols. Translated by J. A. Baker. Philadelphia: Westminster, 1961–1967.

Engelder, Theodore Edward William. *Scripture Cannot Be Broken: Six Objections to Verbal Inspiration Examined in the Light of Scripture.* St. Louis: Concordia, 1944.

Erb, Paul. *The Alpha and the Omega: A Restatement of the Christian Hope in Christ's Coming.* Scottdale, Pa.: Herald Press, 1955.

Ferré, Nels F. S. *Christ and the Christian.* London: Collins, 1958.

Filson, Floyd V. *Jesus Christ, the Risen Lord.* New York: Abingdon, 1956.

———. *The New Testament Against Its Environment: The Gospel of Christ the Risen Lord.* Chicago: Regnery, 1950.

Finney, Charles G. *Lectures on Systematic Theology: Embracing Lectures on Moral Government, Together with Atonement, Moral and Physical Depravity, Regeneration, Philosophical Theories, and Evidences of Regeneration.* Oberlin: J. M. Finch, 1846.

Forsyth, Peter Taylor. *The Person and Place of Jesus Christ: The Congregational Union Lecture for 1909.* Boston: Pilgrim, 1909.

Fuller, Reginald H. *The Formation of the Resurrection Narratives.* New York: Macmillan, 1971.

———. *The Foundations of New Testament Christology.* London: Lutterworth, 1965.

Glasson, Thomas Francis. *His Appearing and His Kingdom: The Christian Hope in the Light of Its History.* London: Epworth, 1953.

González, Justo L. *A History of Christian Thought.* Nashville: Abingdon, 1970–75.

Grant, Frederick C. *An Introduction to New Testament Thought.* New York: Abingdon Press, 1950.

Grant, Frederick C. *A Historical Introduction to the New Testament.* New York: Harper and Row, 1963.

Grant, Robert M. *Augustus to Constantine: The Thrust of the Christian Movement into the Roman World.* New York: Harper & Row, 1970.

Grillmeier, Alois. *From the Apostolic Age to Chalcedon (451).* Vol. 1 of *Christ in Christian Tradition.* Translated by J. S. Bowden. London: A. R. Mowbray, 1965.

Hahn, Ferdinand. *The Titles of Jesus in Christology: Their History in Early Christianity.* Translated by Harold Knight and George Ogg. New York: World, 1969.

Hall, Francis J. *Theological Outlines.* Revised by Frank Hudson Hallock. New York: Morehouse-Barlow, 1961.

Hanson, Anthony Tyrrell. *The Wrath of the Lamb.* London: SPCK, 1957.

Hanson, R. P. C. *Tradition in the Early Church.* London: SCM, 1962.

Harnack, Adolf von. *Outlines of the History of Dogma.* Translated by Edwin Knox Mitchell. New York: Funk & Wagnalls, 1893.

Harvey, Van Austin. *The Historian and the Believer: The Morality of Historical Knowledge and Christian Belief.* New York: Macmillan, 1969.

Hefele, Karl Joseph von. *History of the Christian Councils—to A.D. 325.* Vol. 1 of *A History of the Councils of the Church: From the Original Documents.* Edinburgh: T. & T. Clark, 1894–1896.

Hengel, Martin. *The Atonement: The Origins of the Doctrine in the New Testament*. Philadelphia: Fortress, 1981.

———. *The Son of God: The Origin of Christology and the History of Jewish-Hellenistic Religion*. Translated by John Bowden. Philadelphia: Fortress, 1976.

Heppe, Heinrich. *Reformed Dogmatics Set Out and Illustrated from the Sources*. Foreword by Karl Barth. Revised and Edited by Ernst Bizer. Translated by G. T. Thomson. London: Allen & Unwin, 1950.

Hodge, Charles. *Systematic Theology*. 3 vols. New York: Scribner, 1871–1872.

Hodgson, Peter C. *Jesus—Word and Presence: An Essay in Christology*. Philadelphia: Fortress, 1971.

Hordern, William. *A Layman's Guide to Protestant Theology*. New York: Macmillan, 1955.

Horton, Walter Marshall. *Christian Theology: An Ecumenical Approach*. New York: Harper, 1958.

Hunter, Archibald M. *Jesus: Lord and Savior*. London: SCM, 1976.

———. *The Message of the New Testament*. Philadelphia: Westminster, 1944.

———. *Paul and His Predecessors*. Philadelphia: Westminster, 1961.

Hunter, Sylvester Joseph. *Outlines of Dogmatic Theology*. 2d ed. 3 vols. New York: Benzinger, 1895.

Jacob, Edmond. *Theology of the Old Testament*. Translated by Arthur W. Haethcote and Philip J. Allcock. New York: Harper & Row, 1958.

Kasper, Walter. *Jesus the Christ*. Translated by V. Green. New York: Paulist Press, 1976.

Kaufman, Edmund G. *Basic Christian Convictions*. North Newton, Kans.: Bethel College, 1972.

Kaufman, Gordon D. *Systematic Theology: A Historicist Perspective*. New York: Scribner, 1968.

Kelly, J. N. D. *Early Christian Creeds*. New York: Longman, 1972.

———. *Early Christian Doctrines*. London: Black, 1960.

King, Rachel H. *God's Boycott of Sin: A Consideration of Hell and Pacifism*. New York: Fellowship, 1946.

Knox, John. *The Death of Christ: The Cross in New Testament History and Faith*. New York: Abingdon, 1958.

———. *Jesus, Lord and Christ: A Trilogy Comprising "The Man Christ Jesus, Christ the Lord, On the Meaning of Christ."* New York: Harper, 1958.

Kümmel, Werner Georg. *Introduction to the New Testament*. Translation of revised 17th edition by Howard Clark Kee. Nashville: Abingdon Press, 1975.

Ladd, George Eldon. *I Believe in the Resurrection of Jesus*. Grand Rapids: Eerdmans, 1975.

Ladd, George Eldon. *A Theology of the New Testament*. Grand Rapids: Eerdmans, 1974.

Lehman, Chester K. *Biblical Theology*. Scottdale, Pa.: Herald Press, 1971–1974.

Lewis, C. S. *The Great Divorce*. New York: Macmillan, 1946.

Lewis, Edwin. *A Manual of Christian Beliefs*. New York: Scribner, 1927.

Lind, Millard C. *Yahweh is a Warrior: The Theology of Warfare in Ancient Israel*. Scottdale, Pa.: Herald Press, 1980.

Lohmeyer, Ernst. *Die Briefe an die Philipper*. Göttingen: Vandenhoeck & Ruprecht, 1929.

———. *Kyrios Jesus; eine Untersuchung zur Phil. 2, 5–11*. Heidelberg: C. Winter, Universitätsverlag, 1961.

Luther, Martin. *A Compend of Luther's Theology*. Edited by Hugh T. Kerr. Philadelphia: Westminster, 1966.

Machen, J. Gresham. *The Virgin Birth of Christ*. New York: Harper, 1932.

Macintosh, Douglas Clyde. *Theology as an Empirical Science*. New York: Macmillan, 1919.

Manek, Jindrik. "Composite Quotations in the New Testament and Their Purpose." *Communio Viatorium* 13 (1970): 181–188.

Marshall, I. Howard. *The Origins of New Testament Christology.* Downers Grove: InterVarsity Press, 1976.

Martin, James Perry. *The Last Judgment: In Protestant Theology from Orthodoxy to Ritschl.* Edinburgh: Oliver & Boyd, 1963.

Martin, Ralph P. *Carmen Christi: Philippians ii. 5–11 in Recent Interpretation and in the Setting of Early Christian Worship.* Carmen Christi: Cambridge, 1967.

Marxsen, Willi. *The Beginnings of Christology: A Study in Its Problems.* Translated by Paul J. Achtemeier. Philadelphia: Fortress, 1969.

The Mennonite Hymnal. Scottdale, Pa.: Herald Press, 1969.

Minear, Paul Sevier. *Eyes of Faith: A Study in the Biblical Point of View.* Philadelphia: Westminister, 1946.

Moltmann, Jürgen. *The Crucified God: The Cross of Christ as the Foundation and Criticism of Christian Theology.* Translated by R. A. Wilson and John Bowden. New York: Harper & Row, 1974.

Morris, Leon. *The Cross in the New Testament.* Grand Rapids: Eerdmans, 1965.

Moule, C. F. D. *The Origin of Christology.* Cambridge: Cambridge University Press, 1977.

———. *The Sacrifice of Christ.* Greenwich: Seabury, 1957.

Moule, Handley C. G. *Outlines of Christian Doctrine.* London: Hodder & Stoughton, 1899.

Mullins, Edgar Young. *The Christian Religion in Its Doctrinal Expression.* Philadelphia: Judson, 1917.

Niebuhr, H. Richard. *The Meaning of Revelation.* New York: Macmillan, 1941.

Niesel, Wilhelm. *The Theology of Calvin.* Translated by Harold Knight. London: Lutterworth, 1956.

Oehler, Gustav Friedrich. *Theology of the Old Testament.* New York: Funk & Wagnalls, 1883.

O'Neill, J. C. *The Theology of Acts in Its Historical Setting.* London: SPCK, 1961.

Packer, J. I. *God Speaks to Man: Revelation and the Bible.* Philadelphia: Westminster, 1965.

Paine, Thomas. *The Age of Reason: Being an Investigation of True and Fabulous Theology.* Philadelphia: Moss, 1875.

Pannenberg, Wolfhart. *Jesus: God and Man.* Translated by Lewis L. Wilkins and Duane A. Priebe. Philadelphia: Westminster, 1968.

Paul, Robert S. *The Atonement and the Sacraments: The Relation of the Atonement to the Sacraments of Baptism and the Lord's Supper.* London: Hodder & Stoughton, 1960.

Payne, J. Barton. *The Theology of the Older Testament.* Grand Rapids: Zondervan, 1962.

Pelikan, Jaroslav. *The Christian Tradition: A History of the Development of Doctrine.* Chicago: University of Chicago Press, 1971–1989.

Perrin, Norman. *The Resurrection According to Matthew, Mark, and Luke.* Philadelphia: Fortress, 1977.

———. "Son of Man" in *The Interpreter's Dictionary of the Bible: An Illustrated Encyclopedia Identifying and Explaining All Proper Names and Significant Terms and Subjects in the Holy Scriptures, Including the Apocrypha, with Attention to Archaeological Discoveries and Researches into the Life and Faith of Ancient Times: Supplementary Volume.* Edited by Keith Crim. Nashville: Abingdon, 1976.

Pieper, Franz. *Christian Dogmatics.* 4 vols. St. Louis: Concordia, 1950–57.

Pope, William Burt. *A Compendium of Christian Theology: Being Analytical Outlines of a Course of Theological Study, Biblical, Dogmatic, Historical.* 3 vols. New York: Phillips & Hunt, 1881.

Rad, Gerhard von. *Old Testament Theology.* Translated by D. M. G. Stalker. Edinburgh: Oliver & Boyd, 1962–65.

Ramsey, Michael. *The Resurrection of Christ: A Study of the Event and Its Meaning for the Christian Faith.* London: Collins, 1961.

Raven, Charles E. *Apollinarianism: An Essay on the Christology of the Early Church.* New York: AMS, 1978.

Rawlinson, A. E. J. *The New Testament Doctrine of the Christ: The Bampton Lectures for 1926.* London: Longmans, Green & Co., 1926.

Reid, J. K. S. *The Authority of Scripture: A Study of the Reformation and Post-Reformation Understanding of the Bible.* London: Methuen & Co., 1957.

Resch, Alfred. *Der Paulinismus und die Logia Jesu in ihrem gegenseitigen Verhältnis.* Leipzig: J. C. Hinrichs, 1904.

Revelation and the Bible: Contemporary Evangelical Thought. Edited by Carl F. H. Henry. Grand Rapids: Baker, 1958.

Richardson, Alan. *An Introduction to the Theology of the New Testament.* New York: Harper, 1958.

Robinson, James M. and Helmut Koester. *Trajectories through Early Christianity.* Philadelphia: Fortress, 1971.

Robinson, John A. T. *The Human Face of God.* Philadelphia: Westminster, 1973.

Routley, Erik. *Conversion.* Philadelphia: Muhlenberg, 1960.

———. *The Man for Others: An Important Contribution to the Discussions Inspired by the Book Honest to God.* New York: Oxford University Press, 1964.

Ryrie, Charles. *The Basis of the Premillennial Faith.* New York: Loizeaux Bros., 1953.

Scheeben, Matthias Joseph. *The Mysteries of Christianity.* Translated by Cyril Vollert. St. Louis: B. Herder, 1947.

Schleiermacher, Friedrich. *The Christian faith.* 2d ed. Edited by H. R. Mackintosh and J. S. Stewart. Edinburgh: T. & T. Clark, 1928.

Schmid, Heinrich. *The Doctrinal Theology of the Evangelical Lutheran Church.* Philadelphia: Lutheran Pub. Society, 1899.

Schoonenberg, Piet. *The Christ: A Study of the God-Man Relationship in the Whole of Creation and in Jesus Christ.* Translated by Della Couling. New York: Seabury, 1971.

Scott, Ernest Findlay. *The New Testament Idea of Revelation.* London: Nicholson & Watson, 1935.

Seeberg, Reinhold. *Text-Book of the History of Doctrines.* Translated by Charles E. Hay. Grand Rapids: Baker, 1977.

Selby, Peter. *Look for the Living: The Corporate Nature of Resurrection Faith.* Philadelphia: Fortress, 1976.

Shedd, William G. T. *Dogmatic Theology.* 3d ed. 3 vols. New York: Scribner, 1891.

Sheldon, Henry C. *System of Christian Doctrine.* New York: Eaton, 1903.

Sherrill, Lewis Joseph. *Guilt and Redemption.* Richmond: John Knox, 1957.

Smith, C. Ryder. *The Bible Doctrine of the Hereafter.* London: Epworth, 1958.

Smith, George D., ed. *The Teaching of the Catholic Church: A Summary of Catholic Doctrine.* 2 vols. in 1. London: Burns Oates & Washbourne, 1952.

Sobrino, Jon. *Christology at the Crossroads: A Latin American Approach.* Translated by John Drury. Maryknoll, N.Y.: Orbis, 1978.

Sölle, Dorothee. *Christ the Representative: An Essay in Theology after the "Death of God."* Translated by David Lewis. London: SCM, 1967.

Stauffer, Ethelbert. "Appendices III and V" in *New Testament Theology.* Translated by John Marsh. New York: Macmillan, 1955.

Stewart, James Stuart. *A Man in Christ: The Vital Elements of St. Paul's Religion.* London: Hodder & Stoughton, 1935.

Strong, Augustus Hopkins. *Systematic Theology: A Compendium Designed for the Use of Theological Students.* 3 vols. in 1. Valley Forge: Judson, 1907.

Sundberg, A. C., Jr. "Canon of the New Testament" in *The Interpreter's Dictionary of the Bible: An Illustrated Encyclopedia Identifying and Explaining All Proper Names and Significant Terms and Subjects in the Holy Scriptures, Including the Apocrypha, with Attention to Archaeological Discoveries and Researches into the Life and Faith of Ancient Times: Supplementary Volume.* Edited by Keith Crim. Nashville: Abingdon, 1976.

Sykes, S. W. and J. P. Clayton, ed. *Christ, Faith and History: Cambridge Studies in Christology.* London: Cambridge University Press, 1972.

Taylor, Vincent. *The Atonement in the New Testament Teaching.* London: Epworth, 1958.

Taylor, Vincent. *Forgiveness and Reconciliation: A Study in New Testament Theology.* London: Macmillan, 1941.

———. *The Names of Jesus.* New York: St. Martin's, 1953.

———. *The Person of Christ in New Testament Teaching.* London: Macmillan, 1958.

Thiessen, Henry Clarence. *Introductory Lectures in Systematic Theology.* Grand Rapids: Eerdmans, 1949.

Thomas, W. H. Griffith. *The Principles of Theology: An Introduction to the Thirty-Nine Articles.* New York: Longmans, Green & Co., 1930.

Tillich, Paul. *Systematic Theology.* 3 vols. Chicago: University of Chicago Press, 1951–63.

Tödt, H. E. *The Son of Man in the Synoptic Tradition.* Translated by Dorothea M. Barton. Philadelphia: Westminster, 1965.

Torrance, Thomas. *The Doctrine of Grace in the Apostolic Fathers.* Edinburgh: Oliver & Boyd, 1948.

Van Buren, Paul. *The Secular Meaning of the Gospel: Based on the Analysis of Its Language.* New York: Macmillan, 1963.

van Oosterzee, J. J. *Christian Dogmatics: A Text-Book for Academical Instruction and Private Study.* Translated by John Watson Watson and Maurice J. Evans. 2 vols. New York: Scribner, Armstrong & Co., 1874.

Vermès, Géza. *Jesus the Jew: A Historian's Reading of the Gospels.* London: Collins, 1973.

———. "The Use of Bar Nash in Jewish Aramaic." Appendix E to *An Aramaic Approach to the Gospels and Acts; with an appendix on The Son of Man by Geza Vermes,* by Matthew Black, 3d ed. Oxford: Clarendon, 1967.

Vos, Geerhardus. *Old and New Testament Biblical Theology.* Toronto: Toronto Baptist Seminary, 1947.

Warfield, Benjamin Breckinridge. *The Inspiration and Authority of the Bible.* Edited by Samuel G. Craig. Philadelphia: Presbyterian and Reformed, 1948.

Warfield, Benjamin Breckinridge. *Revelation and Inspiration.* New York: Oxford University Press, 1927.

Wenger, J. C. *God's Word Written: Essays on the Nature of Biblical Revelation, Inspiration, and Authority.* Scottdale, Pa.: Herald Press, 1966.

———. *Introduction to Theology: An Interpretation of the Doctrinal Content of Scripture, Written to Strengthen a Childlike Faith in Christ.* Scottdale, Pa.: Herald Press, 1954.

Wesley, John. *A Compend of Wesley's Theology.* Edited by Robert W. Burtner and Robert E. Chiles. Nashville: Abingdon, 1954.

Wilckens, Ulrich. *Resurrection: Biblical Testimony to the Resurrection: An Historical Examination and Explanation.* Translated by A. M. Stewart. Atlanta: John Knox, 1977.

Wiley, H. Orton. *Christian Theology.* 3 vols. Kansas City: Beacon Hill, 1969.

Wilken, Robert L. *The Myth of Christian Beginnings: History's Impact on Belief.* Garden City, N.Y.: Doubleday, 1971.

Winklhofer, Alois. *The Coming of His Kingdom: A Theology of the Last Things.* Translated by A. V. Littledale. New York: Herder & Herder, 1963.

Wolf, William J. *No Cross No Crown: A Study of the Atonement*. Garden City, N.Y.: Doubleday, 1957.

Wright, G. Ernest. *God Who Acts: Biblical Theology As Recital.* London: SCM, 1952.

Yoder, John Howard. "The Authority of the Canon" *Essays on Biblical Interpretation: Anabaptist-Mennonite Perspectives.* Edited by Willard M. Swartley. Elkhart, Ind.: Institute of Mennonite Studies, 1984.

———. "Binding and Loosing." *Concern: A Pamphlet Series for Questions of Christian Renewal* 14 (Feb. 1967), 2–32.

———. "The Disciple of Christ and the Way of Jesus" in *The Politics of Jesus: Vicit Agnus Noster.* Grand Rapids: Eerdmans, 1972.

———. "The Hermeneutics of the Anabaptists." *The Mennonite Quarterly Review* 41 (Oct. 1967), 291–308.

———. "A Study in the Doctrine of the Work of Christ." Text presented to a study group at Domburg, The Netherlands, 1954.

Index

Scripture Index

Old Testament

New Testament